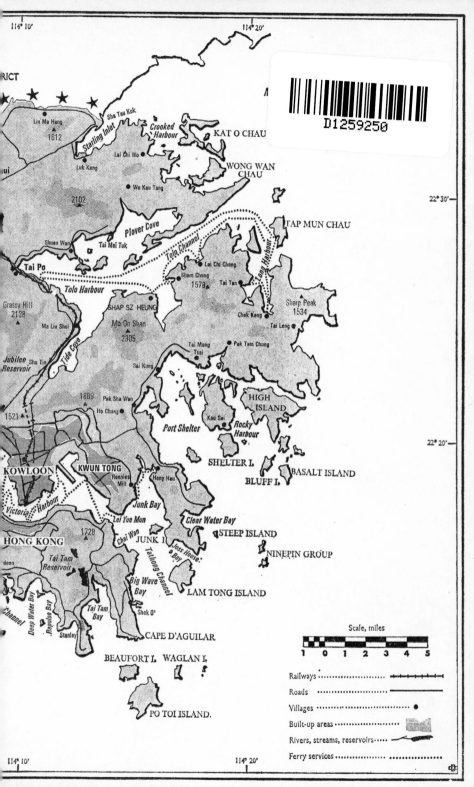

New Territories

HONG KONG:
A SOCIETY IN TRANSITION

Contributors

Joseph Agassi
Judith Agassi
J. S. Cansdale
L. F. Goodstadt
J. W. Hayes
Portia Ho
Ian C. Jarvie
E. Kvan
H. J. Lethbridge
Ronald Ng
J. M. Potter
E. F. Szczepanik
Marjorie Topley
M. G. Whisson

Hong Kong:
A Society in Transition

Edited by
Ian C. Jarvie
and
Joseph Agassi

FREDERICK A. PRAEGER, Publishers
New York · Washington

BOOKS THAT MATTER

Published in the United States of America in 1968
by Frederick A. Praeger, Inc., Publishers
111 Fourth Avenue, New York, N.Y. 10003

© 1968 in London, England, by I. C. Jarvie and Joseph Agassi

Library of Congress Catalog Card Number: 68-19843

Printed in Great Britain

CONTENTS

INTRODUCTION *90/08*

PART ONE

GENERAL SOCIOLOGY OF HONG KONG

I THE STRUCTURE OF RURAL CHINESE SOCIETY IN NEW TERRITORIES   3

Jack M. Potter

II A CHINESE VILLAGE ON HONG KONG ISLAND FIFTY YEARS AGO—TAI TAM TUK, VILLAGE UNDER THE WATER   29

J. W. Hayes

Contents

THE ROLE OF SAVINGS AND WEALTH AMONG HONG KONG CHINESE

Marjorie Topley

PART THREE

SPECIFIC SOCIO-ECONOMIC PROBLEMS
OF HONG KONG

Contents

ILLUSTRATIONS

Illustrations nos. 1, 2, 3, 4, 5, 6, 7, 8, 9, 10, 19, 20, 21, 22, 24 and the endpaper map is reproduced by courtesy of the Hong Kong Government Information Service; nos. 11, 12, 13, 14, 15, 16, 17, and 18 are produced by permission of Lutheran World Service, Hong Kong.

TABLES

INTRODUCTION

I. C. Jarvie

1 Hong Kong as a society

Hong Kong is a British enclave on the China coast at the mouth of the Pearl river. The island from which it takes its name was occupied in 1841 during the first Opium War of 1839–42 between Britain and China and its cession was later ratified in the Treaty of Nanking (1842); further territory was added in 1860 (Kowloon) and 1898 (New Territories—on a 99-year lease) by agreement between Britain and China.[1] It now comprises just under 400 square miles, considerably less than the size of Kent (1,554·7 square miles) or Long Island (1,682 square miles). Much of this land is vertical. A sizable chunk of the mainland area, and most of the 235 islands aside from Hong Kong itself, have very few inhabitants, some none at all. In these islands, and on the mainland among farmers and fisherfolk, the social organization bears some resemblance to what might be called traditional Chinese country life.

The population is largely concentrated in two conurbations on either side of the harbour; on Kowloon peninsula on the mainland side, and in a city called 'Victoria' on the island side. Into this tiny area is packed most of the 3½ to 4 million people in the Colony.[2] Of these, approximately 1·5 per cent are non-Chinese, mainly Europeans—including a local community of Portuguese descent. As far as its general character as a city goes Hong Kong is Chinese, despite being administered under British law by an almost entirely British Higher Civil Service.[3]

[1] On the history of Hong Kong see Morris Collis, *Foreign Mud*, London 1946, and *Wayfoong*, London 1965; George Endacott, *A History of Hong Kong*, London 1958, and *Government and People in Hong Kong*, Hong Kong 1964; J. K. Fairbank, *Trade and Diplomacy on the China Coast*, Cambridge, Mass., 1953, 1964; Edgar Holt, *The Opium Wars*, London 1964. Fairbank's book has a superb bibliography.

[2] All published figures are estimates, only partly based on the Census of 1961; there was a refugee influx in 1962, which, being illegal, was difficult to count accurately.

[3] In 1964 46·3 per cent of the administrative and professional classes of the civil service were filled by locally recruited people (i.e. largely Chinese). (The 1966 figure is 46·1 %.) But this figure is misleading for an estimate of

As a whole the Colony is very rich, and few of the comforts of the affluent society are not available. Most of the population, however, are very poor by western standards (not by Asian standards). But while the gap between rich and poor is very wide, hopeless abject poverty of the kind to be found in India and other parts of S.E. Asia is quite rare.[1] The problems of housing, education, water[2] and public health are daunting; and however critical one may be of the way the government is managing to finance its projects (especially by refusing to increase the minute public debt) and however much one may feel that even more than the very considerable amount already being done could be done, yet it is an impressive sign of richness that the government finances all its projects from current revenue. This will be even more impressive considering that maximum payable tax is pegged at 15 per cent of earnings (and this is the largest single source of revenue, over one quarter of the total). Pessimists predicted that if labour costs began to rise they would destroy the economic prosperity of the Colony for the following reason: the risk of keeping capital in Hong Kong is high, but so are the profits— due to low cost of labour. Change this factor, profits will fall and

[1] This particular difference is a source for endless speculation among the Colony's intellectuals, too many of whom still resort for an explanation to that *omnium gatherum* 'national character'. In so far as there is such a thing, we take it for granted that it is a sociocultural phenomenon: a matter of traditions and institutions, not of race. If Chinese are hard-working and prepared to adapt, that has nothing to do with their descent. But their adaptability is apt to be exaggerated. See further the paper by Professor Agassi and myself. For a study of the poor, see 'Making Ends Meet', *Journal of the Hong Kong Institute of Social Research*, vol. I, Hong Kong 1965.

[2] Three years ago the biggest problem was water. But 1964 saw 5 typhoons and a new reservoir waiting to catch them. And early in 1965 the Chinese Government completed a scheme to pipe enough river water to Hong Kong to supply half of its daily needs, and work was well advanced on a huge new reservoir in the Colony which will triple present storage capacity. Severe drought and the deterioration of relations with China (see chapter 14), led to a recurrence of the problem in 1967. However, in October the Chinese turned on the supply again.

the influence of the 'overseas' (i.e. British) officers. Taking the 46 posts which appear under the heading 'Colonial Secretariat and Heads of Departments' in the 1966 *Staff List, Hong Kong Government*, three are Chinese and two of these are in very minor departments. In the General Establishment list, of the 39 Administrative Officers of staff grades A, B_1, B_2, and C, two are Chinese (in C grade). (See *Hong Kong Annual Reports 1964*, p. 275, *1966*, p. 277 and *Staff List, Hong Kong Government 1966*.)

capital will leave; since it is concentrated in few hands it can and will leave fast. So far this prophecy shows no signs of coming true. The increase in the size and purchasing power of the domestic market resulting from the increasing cost of labour has encouraged capital-formation. Large longer term profits are to be made from products requiring elaborate equipment and skilled and semi-skilled operatives. Thus, both the expansion of the semi-skilled group and the improved wages of the unskilled group have resulted in the beginnings of a rise in the standard of living of lower paid workers. In the light of this, it is difficult to avoid adverse comment on the government's holding down the wages of its lower-paid employees, in the name, it is said, of resistance to wage inflation. On the one hand this aim is not particularly desirable and on the other this technique does not forward it but merely creates large numbers of unfilled vacancies in government service. Despite the government's aim of holding wages down, they rise, as they must if the economy is to grow on a sound basis. The present rate of growth of the economy may well be in the region of 15 per cent, more than double the figure of 7 per cent said to be necessary by Dr Szczepanik—when he wrote the original of the paper republished here—if standards were to go up.

Many people have heard a little about Hong Kong, either from travel books, films or popular novels.[1] Its unique political situation next to mainland China gives it excitement. Hints of crime,

[1] References to the scholarly literature available on Hong Kong will be found in the footnotes to this volume, in the excellent bibliographies in the *Annual Reports* up to 1963 (now replaced by *A Hong Kong Bibliography*, by J. M. Braga, Hong Kong 1965) and in the publications lists of the *Gazette* of the University of Hong Kong. In economics, history and geography quite a lot of material already exists. Sociology and anthropology have hardly begun. But there are one or two popular books which give some idea of the Colony and it may be worth mentioning a few here. Particularly to be recommended are, among general books, F. D. Ommanney's *Fragrant Harbour*, London 1962, Gene Gleason's *Hong Kong*, London 1963, Harold Ingram's *Hong Kong*, London 1952, and Emily Hahn's *Hong Kong Holiday*, New York 1946, and *China To Me*, Philadelphia 1949. Among the available novels, sociologically the most informative is Richard Mason's *The World of Suzie Wong*, London 1957. Leaving aside its demerits as literature, as well as its poor psychology and its portrayal of Suzie and her friends more as maudlin London office girls than Hong Kong prostitutes, it should be said that Mason has packed in quite a lot of true information about the environment, experiences and even some of the behaviour-patterns of his characters. In particular tenement and squatter living conditions, and events leading up to, and life as, a prostitute are accurately enough portrayed. Han Suyin's

smuggling, and large-scale drug-addiction[1] add mystery. And a well-projected image of terrible overcrowding underlines the drama of life here. But naturally this picture is not altogether reliable. The political existence of the Colony is to a very large extent at the beck of Mainland China and, despite Britain's military presence, the present policy of colonial devolution suggests that both sides know it could be had for the asking. Other things being equal (see chapter 14), so long as Hong Kong is more useful than embarrassing to China it can be expected to stay.[2] Serious crime and violence is not excessive; piracy hardly exists; smuggling, gambling, drug-taking and prostitution are the chief large-scale deviations.

Yet the main story to be told about Hong Kong, hardly of interest to the novelists, is how it has changed in the last fifteen

[1] In early February 1965, at a deserted farm in the New Territories, the police uncovered 5,800 lb. of opium and 386 lb. of morphine in supposedly the biggest illegal narcotics haul the world has yet seen. With opium worth HK$500–600 and morphine HK$3,200 per lb. the value of the haul is staggering. (See *South China Morning Post*, 11 February 1965, p. 1.)

[2] No one knows just exactly how useful Hong Kong is to China. Food parcels and the 100 per cent duty paid on them run to millions but are a flea-bite compared to the direct remissions of money through Hong Kong banks to relatives in China by Hong Kong people and overseas Chinese. Furthermore, China has a huge favourable trade balance with Hong Kong (in excess of HK$1,000 million) and she has many investments here which *Pravda* (May 1964) estimated earned her £107m. sterling *p.a.* For the immediate future China needs all the foreign currency she can get and Hong Kong is a major source. See, two articles by E. F. Szczepanik, 'The Embargo Effect on China's Trade with Hong Kong', *Contemporary China*, vol. II, 1956–7, pp. 85–93, and

semi-autobiographical *A Many Splendoured Thing*, London 1952, is hampered by a self-conscious, not to say narcissistic approach; yet she too manages to paint an interesting and often critical picture of her surroundings. Lois Mitchinson's *Gillian Lo*, London 1964, Dennis Wheatley's *Bill for the Use of a Body*, London 1964, W. Somerset Maugham's *The Painted Veil*, London 1925, and more so his play *East of Suez*, London 1931, also contain some useful background. To decide what truth there may be in C. Y. Lee's story of flesh peddling among Aberdeen fishermen on Hong Kong Island would be a study in itself. See his *The Virgin Market*, New York 1964. Much the same goes for titles like *Hong Kong After Dark* and *Hong Kong Madam* which proliferate every year. Other novels like *Ferry to Hong Kong* by Simon Kent, London 1957, *A Coffin From Hong Kong* by James Hadley Chase, London 1962, *The Hong Kong Caper* by Carter Brown, New York 1962, have little of interest. In this *genre* it is perhaps to be regretted that Ian Fleming did not live to write the expected James Bond novel using Hong Kong and Macau locales.

years. Economically things have changed, and these changes, plus the influx of refugees, are bringing about considerable changes in the social structure. This situation virtually makes Hong Kong a laboratory for the social scientist. Its economy, following a period of structural change, is going through a period of extremely rapid growth, virtually unhelped and unhampered by government action. Its social structure is going through nothing short of upheaval in the face of this economic change; plus wave after wave of refugees bringing serious overcrowding and its social effects; plus, not to be forgotten, the ceaseless impact of creeping westernization both in education and in industry. The place is administered, and in a subtle way its atmosphere is dominated, by Europeans who carry an influence wholly out of proportion to their numbers. Let me spell out all this in a little more detail.

Prior to the end of the protracted Chinese civil war in 1949 Hong Kong was a port for the interior of China with a little light industry. Since the early fifties she has become a manufacturing and exporting centre transshipping almost nothing to the mainland.[1] As, so to speak, a case study in economic growth under almost *laissez-faire* conditions Hong Kong is economically fascinating. Equally fascinating are the attempts of Hong Kong Chinese to master western business which involves ideas (including that of maximizing profits) not altogether in accord with received Chinese ideas.[2] Such a profound structural change in the economy has had many social repercussions. It has enabled the economy to grow of its own accord without reference to the China trade. It has meant a rapid increase in the number of regular as opposed to casual workers and in skilled and semi-skilled

[1] The story of this change-over is told (up to 1958) in E. F. Szczepanik, *The Economic Growth of Hong Kong*, London 1958, 1960.

[2] See Dr Topley's paper in this volume, and the paper by Professor Agassi and myself.

'Foreign Trade of Mainland China', *Contemporary China*, vol. III, 1958–9, pp. 64–130. Some further discussion of this question can also be found at several places in E. F. Szczepanik (ed.), *Symposium on Economic and Social Problems of the Far East*, Hong Kong 1962, see especially Dr Szczepanik's own paper 'Balance of Payments in Mainland China', pp. 113 ff. and, further, index references to 'Hong Kong, China, balance of trade with' and 'economic importance to'. It seems clear that more than half of the foreign exchange China earns is earned through Hong Kong. (*Newsweek*, in a cover story, 'Hong Kong: The Running Siege', 31 July 1967, pp. 30–4, estimated China's earnings from Hong Kong at US$700m. *p.a.*)

workers. It has allowed considerable expansion of the white-collar clerical middle class which was previously very small. And this class, educated and sober, are a new market for new kinds of goods—modern comforts. The 'industrial revolution' has also thrown up an entrepreneurial class eager to take a cut of the boom, and to go in for conspicuous consumption. Only with the basis of wealth created by this structural change in the economy has Hong Kong been able to absorb the waves of refugees and huge rate of population increase without significant unemployment.

This diversification of the class structure, plus overcrowding, plus the overall increase in wealth, plus other sociocultural factors has resulted in interesting social changes. Of these, the strong westernizing influences of TV, films, newspapers and magazines, and teenage subculture, are significant—not to mention the western government and the stress on English and a grasp of western ways for success in business and in the government. Family life, in particular, seems to be turning more and more on the western-type significance of the nuclear family and less and less on the Chinese-type significance of the extended family and its strong ties. This is partly because so many families have been broken up by only a part emigrating; partly it is because the younger generation seems less inclined to regard family loyalties as worth preserving in their changed environment, and are free in Hong Kong to exercise this disinclination. Family size among the educated is getting smaller. There is considerable social mobility between the classes. Traditional religion, never a big thing with Chinese,[1] appears to be on the wane, especially in the urban areas, and Christianity is making but little headway.

Life has a certain aimlessness for the local people. Their old values need modification or replacement, and as western values are adopted only in a very selective way these do not provide adequate substitutes. There is little in the way of community or nation-consciousness; Hong Kong Chinese regard themselves as Chinese, period. Indeed the Portuguese are perhaps the only group which regards Hong Kong as its sole home. They are often equally at ease in three or four languages (English, Cantonese, Portuguese and a blend of the latter two known as 'Maccinese' or 'Macau-ese'), and by now their descent is completely Eurasian. The loyalties of most local Chinese lie elsewhere. When China

---

[1] For an extended criticism of this generalization see C. K. Yang, *Religion in Chinese Society*, Berkeley and Los Angeles 1961.

invaded India or exploded her first nuclear device many freely identified with the fatherland and felt proud. This should make it obvious that it is not true that the population is altogether indifferent to politics, yet the myth is widespread amongst the Europeans in the Colony. Chinese politics interest almost everyone;[1] expecting them to be interested in Hong Kong politics is like expecting English people to get interested in parish or Urban District Council politics. There is *less* interest in local Hong Kong politics (except perhaps among settled New Territories inhabitants) than there is in such English local politics because China has no tradition of democratic participation and because the population of Hong Kong, being largely refugee, feels the politics of the homeland to be of overriding importance, dwarfing everything else.

Only half of the local citizens were born here. This means that political fear or economic need brought the other half in and keeps them here. They seem to plod along making a living and occasionally fretting about what the future has in store. Things have changed since they were young, both at home in the fatherland and in Hong Kong. Problems abound and lead to complete confusion. The main problem becomes simply to keep the head above water and hope for the best.[2]

Socially and ideologically, then, Hong Kong is all at sea; neither one thing nor the other. Yet for all its being almost a laboratory for the social scientist where he can watch culture contact between East and West, unimpeded economic growth, rapid changes in the social structure approaching breakdown, a morass of changing standards and values, despite all this, almost no sociological studies on the Colony have been published.

2   The lack of sociological studies of Hong Kong

Hong Kong is well known as a place; but almost unknown as a society. It is much publicized, but almost unstudied. This volume is a pioneer attempt to fill the gap in studies; it is also a collection which only skims off a little of the very rich sociological material to be gathered in Hong Kong. How is it that these abundant

---

[1] The Red Chinese flags flown on 1 October and the Nationalist flags flown ten days later on 10 October (sceptics say sometimes from the same windows!) are indicative of the fact that political divisions are by no means dead.

[2] Cf. P. M. Yap, *Suicide in Hong Kong*, Hong Kong 1958, for a study of those who cannot make it.

riches have until now been virtually ignored by the world of scholarship? First and foremost there is of course the quite overwhelming presence of China proper. This has always overshadowed Hong Kong, and does so still. Hong Kong was traditionally a port of entry into China, like all the Treaty Ports, but hardly a place for scholars to stop for long. Students of China would always prefer to get on into China proper, than to study Hong Kong say, or Shanghai. After the virtual closure of China to serious foreign students by the communist authorities, the value of Hong Kong to scholars lay primarily in the opportunities it provided to study the mainland through the medium of refugees and printed materials. Today this is still a major academic industry in Hong Kong, aided by such organizations as the Universities Service Center, the Union Research Institute, and Hong Kong University's Institute of Modern Asian Studies. Scholars wishing to study Chinese traditional society have tended to go to Taiwan.

But one might still wonder why students of the Commonwealth and Colonies did not take more interest in Hong Kong. Why, for example, none of the Colonial Social Science Research Council grants were made for Hong Kong Studies. At a guess, it would seem that while vast tracts of Malaya, Africa and New Guinea remained unstudied, there seemed little point in singling out minute Hong Kong. Hong Kong was hardly in the forefront of people's consciousness of the Colonies: it wasn't underdeveloped, wasn't poor, was very small, and mainly of political interest.

Yet after the closure of China why did sinologists and anthropologists prefer Taiwan? Size is one answer. Sheer ignorance of Hong Kong's rich sociological material was another. There seems to have been an image of Hong Kong as an island full of refugees. However, closer examination of sinology suggests other answers. Until twenty years ago there were very few sociologists and anthropologists interested in China. Those there were, were nearly all Americans. The traditional British fields of specialization were Africa, Australia and Oceania. One can detect the occasional flavour of anti-colonialism in the way Americans looked at Hong Kong, and thus comprehend their lack of interest in studying a colonial fossil. That there were surviving in Hong Kong quite ancient patterns of social structure didn't filter out to the scholarly world because the American scholars who came here were primarily political experts studying the mainland.

Another reason is that the Hong Kong government did not actively encourage or do research. A number of contributors wish strongly to emphasize that the normal aids to research were not available. The government agencies which in other places systematically gather much of the basic data from which begin many of the sorts of studies found in this book, have in Hong Kong collected (and certainly published) very little. Such collection is now beginning, but there is an almost unfillable gap left behind. To a certain extent this lack of government research stemmed from rather old-fashioned attitudes. More recently the appointment of a Commissioner of Census and Statistical Planning, and the apparent value and relative harmlessness of such research as has been done already, seems to have overcome these attitudes.

Still another reason for the lack of sociological research in Hong Kong has been the dearth of professional social scientists at the academic institutions of the Colony. Until a few years ago Dr Topley was the only sociologist resident, and then in a purely private capacity; then Mr Lethbridge was appointed to the University of Hong Kong. Both were for some time preoccupied with work on other topics. The discovery of Hong Kong as a rich field for sociological research might be dated from 1955 when Professor Freedman of the London School of Economics, a social anthropologist, paid a flying visit to the Colony and perhaps noticed its richness as a field for research.[1] He was not himself able to return to undertake such research until 1963. In a note to a paper written in the same year Dr Topley was able to list in around one hundred words all the anthropological research that had then been done in Hong Kong.[2] The pace has increased since then, especially with the introduction of teaching and research in sociology in the Chinese University of Hong Kong, the founding of the Hong Kong Institute of Social Research, and the establishment of a research organization by the Hong Kong Council of Social Service, which has received $1,000,000 of Government monies for a study of the Chinese family.

Yet the study of Hong Kong itself, for itself, is still not far

[1] See the Preface to his *Lineage Organization in Southeastern China*, London 1958, and p. 140.
[2] See 'Capital, Savings and Credit Among Indigenous Rice Farmers and Immigrant Vegetable Farmers in Hong Kong's New Territories', in *Capital, Saving and Credit in Peasant Societies*, ed. R. Firth and B. Yamey, London 1964, pp. 157–86; the relevant note is at p. 158.

advanced. Most of the scholars who have been to the Colony, and who are presently studying here, are interested in Hong Kong for the extrinsic reason that, in Professor Freedman's words, 'The New Territories . . . have . . . the advantage of offering for study perhaps the best living example (however much affected by British rule and modern changes) of traditional Chinese country life.'[1] The only paper in the present volume which gives much sinological background is Dr Topley's. Most of our contributors have concerned themselves with Hong Kong because its society is intrinsically as well as extrinsically interesting. Of course they do not deny its very great interest to sinologists. We have not felt the need to include sinological papers for the very simple reason that those who have carried out such studies will publish their material in sinological and anthropological journals.[2]

3 The scope and limitations of the present collection

While not unaware of the general sinological interest of Hong Kong society, our aim in putting together this volume has been to piece together a picture of Hong Kong society that draws attention to its intrinsically interesting features and its own special problems. This raises the question of who this volume is intended for, the kind of audience we have in mind. At the risk of trying to serve two masters we have aimed at getting the attention both of scholars in anthropology and sociology, and the intelligent layman who might visit or come to live in Hong Kong, or simply be

[1] See para. 6 of his 'A Report on Social Research in the New Territories', a mimeograph in the Colonial Secretariat Library, Hong Kong.

[2] It might be worth listing those works published or definitely in progress at this time. The authoritative background volume is Professor M. Freedman's *Lineage Organization in South Eastern China*, with its excellent bibliography on the sociology of the region; there is also Professor Potter's book, see p. 18, n. 2, below, and the Royal Asiatic Society (Hong Kong Branch) Symposium, *Aspects of Social Organization in the New Territories*, edited by Dr Topley, Hong Kong 1965, and containing useful papers by Messrs H. Baker, R. Groves, J. Hayes and R. Ng. There are also a few papers in addition to those of Dr Topley (op. cit. previous page and elsewhere in this volume), by Miss J. Pratt, 'Emigration and Unilineal Descent Groups—Study of Marriage', *Eastern Anthropologist*, vol. XIII, 1960, pp. 147–58; Miss B. Ward's 'A Hong Kong Fishing Village', *Journal of Oriental Studies*, vol. I, 1954, pp. 195–214; 'Floating Villages: Chinese Fisherman in Hong Kong', *Man*, vol. LIX, 1959, pp. 44–5; and 'Cash or Credit Crops? An examination of Some Implications of Peasant Commercial Production with

interested in it as a place. Our design was to intersperse a hard core of papers of a high degree of sociological sophistication which both scholars and laymen would find of value, with a selection of less high-powered pieces which recommended themselves either because they had interesting ideas, or because they supplied useful facts and indicated avenues for future research. Such less demanding papers would be more accessible to the layman and would fill in gaps for scholars seeking the overall picture.

We fully realize that this means the reader may find a disquieting disparity of level and of depth of analysis between paper and paper. The best way to deal with this is by forewarning. Therefore I will take it upon myself to discriminate the papers into two groups: what I have called the 'hard core' based upon intensive documentary and sometimes field research, and aiming to be scholarly contributions in their field, and the others which are either aimed much more at the general reader and thus use much secondary material or which have been written by scholars who do not claim expertise in the fields of the social sciences. The hard core is made up of the papers by Professor Potter, Mr Hayes, Mr Lethbridge, Dr Topley, Dr Szczepanik, Mr Goodstadt, Dr Whisson and Mr Kvan. Mr Ng is a geographer interested in sociology. Professor Joseph Agassi, his wife Dr Judith Agassi, and myself make no claim to be sinologists or to have intended our work to do more than make preliminary excursions into the topics we discuss in our several papers. Miss Ho and J. S. Cansdale were both diffident about publishing their observations next to those of trained social scientists. However I am convinced that both explore their topics in a very interesting way and that professional scholars will find that this makes up in part for their lack of sociological training.

The papers have been arranged, however, without reference to the kind of differences of level between papers mentioned above.

Special Reference to the Multiplicity of Traders and Middlemen', *Economic and Cultural Change*, vol. VIII, pp. 148–63; 'Varieties of the Conscious Model: the Fishermen of South China' in *The Relevance of Models for Social Anthropology*, ed. M. Banton, London 1965; and a number of forthcoming papers by Miss Ward. In addition to this published work the following anthropologists have completed or will soon complete studies in rural areas which can expect publication: Professor Cornelius Osgood on Ap Li Chau Island; Messrs H. Baker and R. Groves of the London School of Economics, Mrs Dorothy Bracey of Harvard University in Shatin, Mr E. Anderson in Castle Peak, Mr M. Gregory, and Miss Catherine Beihan in Shek-O.

The arrangement has been designed to progress from a broad view of the rural and thence the urban society, through a study which embraces both the general perspective and particular facets, to a series of studies of selected areas of Hong Kong society. In part one the emphasis is on the general sociological characteristics of Hong Kong; part two surveys attitudes to wealth against the background of traditional China; while in Part III specific social problems are explored critically and in some depth.

Part one begins with three papers on the general social structure in the rural New Territories. Professor Jack Potter presents an overview of the structural features of the New Territories plus some more detailed description of the lineage system and its reaction to change. Mr J. W. Hayes reconstructs the main sociological outlines of a Hakka village as it was 50 years ago, while Mr Ronald Ng gives us a close-up picture of an isolated Hakka village community as it is today. He is concerned mainly with the overall picture, as detailed sociological analysis was not part of his research or competence. Whatever the intrinsic merits of Mr Ng's paper, he manages to depict a remarkable form of rural life where the men are either young and in school, or old and retired, or abroad working. Mr Ng's evaluatory comments on the Hakka people, on *fung shui*, and on other matters, will be of interest to the student of intra-Chinese attitudes. Mr Ng is not himself a Hakka. Next there are three papers on the urban areas of the Colony. Professor Judith Agassi summarizes most of what is known about the general features of the urban social structure and the ways in which it has changed since the war, drawing heavily on the 1961 census, the first for thirty years. She did not carry out any analytical work on the census figures, or compare it with the previous one. There is reason to think the census is already out-of-date and scholars are awaiting the by-census of 1966 with some interest. Mr Henry J. Lethbridge takes a close look at the socio-logical impact of the Japanese occupation—a dramatic episode generally clouded in rather more mystery than would be expected. His aim is to show that the present, perhaps insufficient, measure of rapport between the Hong Kong Government and the business community, as well as the Chinese community, is much of an im-provement over the pre-war period; the improvement, para-doxically, was a result of the Japanese occupation which delivered the death blow to the Colonial Civil Service Mandarinate. Professor Joseph Agassi and I attempt to survey the whole question of how far Hong Kong Chinese have come to terms with the West. Our thesis is: far less than appearances suggest.

Part two is entirely taken up with a paper by Dr Marjorie Topley which spans both urban and rural Hong Kong. I persuaded Dr Topley to allow it to be reprinted because it is a classical and seminal work on the sociology of Hong Kong. In the framework of a careful study of attitudes to wealth and the social roles of wealth in Hong Kong as compared with traditional China and with the West, Dr Topley in fact succeeds in painting an integrated picture of Hong Kong society. The paper was written in 1960 and has been altered by slight cuts.

Part three begins with Dr Edward Szczepanik's paper on the economy and points to the dearth of economic mechanisms and basic factual data which make planning difficult. Many of his ideas, aired publicly several years ago, have yet to be taken up. Next come two closely connected papers on housing. First Dr Judith Agassi looks at what the government and various agencies have provided to relieve the desperate housing situation; she criticizes present efforts on the grounds that they rapidly deteriorate into slums, and are hardly commensurate with the privacy and independence people have a right to expect from public housing. Mr Leo Goodstadt tackles the total housing situation created by population increase, prosperity, and land shortage both from the economic and the sociological viewpoints. His conclusion is that as of 1963 there were no signs that the situation would ever be brought under control.

Overcrowding and poverty throw up two very serious ancillary problems: tuberculosis and drug-addiction. In her paper on TB Miss Portia Ho sets out the facts about its extent and the effectiveness of measures taken to check it. She argues that the disease is so much tied up with social and housing conditions that here as in the west only an attack on those conditions themselves will check it. Dr Michael Whisson turns a practised anthropological eye on the world of the addict and the dope pedlar. He shows how thoroughly integrated the use of heroin is into certain parts of Hong Kong society and how difficult it will be to make any headway against it in isolation.[1]

[1] Since writing this paper in Hong Kong early in 1965 Dr Whisson has completed his research and published it in a book *Under the Rug*, Hong Kong Council of Social Service 1965; see also my review 'Under the Rug', *Hong*

Finally there are two papers which examine in detail problems of westernization as they show themselves in education. Rev. Erik Kvan, setting out to explain the failure of intensively trained and hard-working students to become bilingual, argues that something like a socially induced neurosis may be responsible and that the structure of English teaching as well as methods of teaching may need to be reviewed if it is to be overcome. The final contributor, J. S. Cansdale, takes up the story where Mr Kvan leaves off—when these children come up to the University of Hong Kong. The paper explores the results of a tension between a home background of Chinese language, customs and culture and a University allegiance to western ideas, language and student life. Trying to manage this gap many students suffer a crisis of identity.[1]

4 Value-free versus objective social science

It will be seen from this summary of the papers that some of the contributors have not felt they were obliged to confine themselves to purely descriptive sociology. They have also directed constructive criticism and suggestion where they felt it was appropriate; they have introduced their values. Some might criticize this as not being in the true spirit of scientific enquiry. Such a criticism is based on a rather common confusion between the demand for what is known in the jargon as 'value-free' social science on the one hand, and the requirement that the social scientist pass no value judgements on the other. The question of the objectivity of (social) science is constantly confused with the demand that the (social) scientist be 'objective'. The former is a serious question, the latter demand simply forces the social scientist to conceal his values. The many abstract arguments about whether social science can ever be value free seem to show

---

[1] I am acutely conscious of the fact that a number of obvious topics are not touched on in this volume, especially folk medicine (herbalism, acupuncture, etc.), corruption and prostitution. If and when a companion volume appears these may well be covered.

Kong Tiger Standard, 26 August 1965, p. 8. Early in 1965 another volume on drug-addiction in Hong Kong appeared, Albert G. Hess, *Chasing the Dragon*, The Hague 1965.

convincingly enough that it can.[1] I can see no objection, then, to the social scientist making his own values clear—it need not prejudice the objectivity of his work. An interesting argument for the scientific value of this practical or technological approach has been given by K. R. Popper, my own teacher at the London School of Economics:

> The technological approach is likely to prove fruitful in giving rise to significant problems of a purely theoretical kind. But besides helping us in the fundamental task of selecting problems, the technological approach imposes a discipline on our speculative inclinations (which, especially in the field of sociology proper, are liable to lead us into the region of metaphysics); for it forces us to submit our theories to definite standards, such as standards of clarity and practical testability.[2]

In offering these studies of Hong Kong society to the general public, it is to be hoped that they have passed the tests of clarity and practical testability; and no more can be hoped than that our efforts might lead to a better understanding of what is going on in Hong Kong and thereby perhaps take us a little further along the road towards the solution of some of the more intractable of our problems. If in addition light is shed on parallel social and economic situations, either past periods of rapid economic growth, or present-day cases of the problems of development and change, then we shall have overfulfilled our expectations.

[1] See especially the excellent paper by Kurt Klappholz, 'Value Judgements and Economics', *British Journal for the Philosophy of Science*, **15**, 1964, pp. 97–114.

[2] K. R. Popper, *The Poverty of Historicism*, London 1957, p. 59.

ACKNOWLEDGEMENTS

The idea for this volume arose in discussions between myself and Joseph Agassi, while he was Reader in Philosophy at the University of Hong Kong. The inspiration was a 1963 seminar on economic and social problems of Hong Kong held under the auspices of the Hong Kong Institute of Social Research and chaired by a visiting anthropologist, Dr Maurice Freedman. Agassi organized the seminar and functioned as its first secretary. Before the volume could be got under way, Agassi left the Colony to take up a post in America; responsibility thus fell on me as I was still on the spot. Throughout the compilation and editing I have kept in close consultation with Dr Agassi, and he has gone over the final manuscript of the entire volume. To the various contributors I extend my thanks for making the editing an easy job, and for their comments on the editorial Introduction, to which none of them is necessarily committed. It is a pleasure to thank my research student Miss Portia Ho who, besides contributing, helped me in many ways with the selection and collection of photographs. Judith Agassi's essay on housing originally appeared under the title 'Hong Kong's Housing Problems' in the *Far Eastern Economic Review*, for 7 June 1962; Portia Ho's essay on TB appeared in two issues of the *Far Eastern Economic Review*, 22 and 29 October 1964; Edward Szczepanik's essay appeared in the *South China Morning Post* for 29 and 30 April 1961; Marjorie Topley's paper appeared in the UNESCO symposium *The Role of Wealth in South East Asia and the West*, edited by R. D. Lambert and B. F. Hoselitz, Paris 1963; I wish to thank the respective editors and publishers for permission to reprint.

Hong Kong—Boston—Toronto
1965–7   I. C. J.

PART ONE

GENERAL SOCIOLOGY OF HONG KONG

Jack M. Potter, Ph.D. (Calif.)
Assistant professor of anthropology in the University of California, Berkeley

J. W. Hayes, M.A. (London)
A Senior Administrative Officer of the Hong Kong Government

Ronald Ng, B.A.(HK)
Completing research on a Ph.D. on Rural Land Use in Hong Kong

Judith Agassi, Ph.D. (London)
On the research staff of the Massachusetts Institute of Technology

H. J. Lethbridge, BSc.(Econ.) and BSc.(Soc.) (London)
Senior lecturer in sociology in the University of Hong Kong

Joseph Agassi, Ph.D. (London)
Professor of philosophy in Boston University

I. C. Jarvie, Ph.D. (London)
Associate professor of philosophy in York University, Toronto

I

THE STRUCTURE OF RURAL CHINESE SOCIETY IN NEW TERRITORIES[1]

Jack M. Potter

1 Introduction

Rural Chinese society in the New Territories is of intrinsic interest in its own right as the rural dimension of the Colony of Hong Kong—one of the most distinctive and fascinating societies in the world. The New Territories is also of great interest to students of China because it is one of the few remaining places where traditional Chinese villages and towns still exist in a state approximating their traditional pre-Communist forms.

At present, most social science interest in China is devoted to understanding and interpreting the social revolution that is occurring on the mainland. This is necessary and proper but in our attempts to understand the changes taking place within contemporary rural China we have been handicapped by our appalling ignorance of many important aspects of traditional Chinese rural society. We still know little about kinship and lineage organization in the villages; we know almost nothing about social and economic organization in the market towns and cities; and we have only a vague understanding of the intermediate social, political, and economic networks that bound village to town and towns to the wider society.[2] These are only a few items on a list that could easily be expanded. This unfortunate situation is made even worse by political conditions which at present and for the foreseeable future make first-hand social science research in China impossible.

---

[1] The field research on which this article is based was carried out while resident in Ping Shan, a village of the New Territories, over a period of eighteen months, from August 1961 through January 1963. I would like to express my indebtedness to the Ford Foundation's Foreign Area Training Fellowship Program for the financial support which made fieldwork in Hong Kong possible. However, the conclusions, opinions, and other statements in this article are those of the author and not necessarily those of the Ford Foundation.

[2] For a stimulating discussion of the market town network in China, see G. William Skinner's two articles: 'Marketing and Social Structure in Rural China: Part I' (*Journal of Asian Studies*, vol. XXIV, no. 1, November 1964); and Part II (*Journal of Asian Studies*, vol. XXIV, no. 2, February 1965).

Given these circumstances, it becomes apparent how valuable Hong Kong can be as a laboratory for the study of traditional and modern pre-Communist Chinese society. The great value of the Colony as a social laboratory is that it contains almost all the elements in the traditional society—from lineages, villages, and market towns to urban social and economic organizations of all kinds. Not only is it possible to study each of these social institutions separately, it is also possible in Hong Kong to study their interrelationships as parts of a total on-going social system.

Of course, Chinese society in contemporary Hong Kong is different in many respects from Chinese society on the mainland prior to the Communist Revolution in 1949 and in any case would be representative of only the Cantonese brand of Chinese culture. Nevertheless, if reasonable allowances are made for these limiting and special circumstances, much valuable information can still be obtained in Hong Kong that can not only further our understanding of traditional Chinese society but can also serve as a baseline for studies of Communist China. Since most research on Communist China must rely on documentary sources and refugee interviews, pilot studies on selected aspects of Chinese society in Hong Kong would enable us at least to keep one foot in contact with basic Chinese social and cultural reality—something which is sometimes lacking in contemporary studies of Communist China.

My purpose in this article is to present a brief overview of the major aspects of Chinese social organization in the villages and towns of the New Territories. This discussion must necessarily be limited to a general sketch because of space limitations. The reader must be forewarned that this paper is based mainly upon field work experience on one large and relatively 'progressive' Cantonese lineage near the market town of Yuen Long. Social conditions probably vary a great deal in other areas of the New Territories and among the Hakka and other non-Cantonese ethnic groups. I do believe, however, that the information presented in this paper is generally true of most of the indigenous Cantonese village population in most areas of the mainland section of the New Territories.

2 The new territories

The new Territories comprise the mainland portion of the Colony between the city of Kowloon in the south and the Sham Chun

River in the north. Also included are several hundred islands of various sizes that lie in the waters immediately adjacent to the Colony. In 1961, the New Territories as a whole contained a population of about four hundred thousand and included a land area of approximately three hundred and sixty-five square miles.[1]

By far the largest part of the New Territories, both on the mainland and on the islands, is mountainous and not suitable for agricultural purposes. The eastern half of the mainland section, which includes Tai Po District and the Sai Kung Peninsula, is extremely hilly with village settlements found only on small alluvial plains near the coast and in small inland valleys. The soil in this area is not as deep or as fertile as soil in the northwestern part of the New Territories around the towns of Yuen Long and Sheung Shui where most of the villages are found. The richest agricultural region is in the Yuen Long Valley.

The original inhabitants of the Colony are four in number: Cantonese peasants; Hakka peasants; the Tanka or 'Boat People'; and the Hoklo. The Tanka and the Hoklo are both seafaring fishing people who live most of their lives on the water. One of the major differences between the two groups is that more of the Hoklo have settled ashore. Together they numbered about forty-five thousand in 1961.[2] The Boat People have probably inhabited the South China Coast from time immemorial, long before the settlement of this area by Chinese from the north.

Most of the original inhabitants of the New Territories were Cantonese and Hakka peasants.[3] The Hakka are a Chinese minority group from north and central China who are linguistically and culturally somewhat distinct from the Cantonese but, like the Cantonese, are primarily agriculturalists. The Hakka either entered the New Territories later than the Cantonese or else they lost out in the competition for the best land because they now inhabit the poorer mountain regions of the eastern half of the New Territories. They are in almost exclusive possession of the Sai Kung Peninsula and are the dominant group in the areas surrounding the market towns of Tai Po and Sha Tin. There are

[1] Hong Kong Government, *Hong Kong 1961*, Hong Kong 1962, p. 319.
[2] ibid., p. 38.
[3] For a discussion of the differences between the Hakka and Cantonese in the New Territories, see Marjorie Topley, 'Capital, Saving and Credit among Indigenous Rice Farmers and Immigrant Vegetable Farmers in Hong Kong's New Territories', in *Capital, Saving and Credit in Peasant Societies*, edited by Raymond Firth and B. S. Yamey, London 1964, p. 160.

also Hakka settlements in the eastern part of the Yuen Long Valley around the Tai Mo Shan foothills.[1]

Although Chinese influence had been present in Canton much earlier, Cantonese peasants probably did not begin to settle this southern outpost of China in great numbers until early in the Sung Dynasty. At present, the Cantonese own most of the best agricultural land in the northern and western sections of the New Territories. Over the centuries since Cantonese settlement first began in this area the New Territories has gradually been settled by peasant farmers from elsewhere in Kwangtung Province. The Cantonese have traditionally been the dominant group in the area.

Until its incorporation into the Colony in 1898 the New Territories formed part of *Po On* District of Kwangtung Province and had been an integral part of traditional China.[2] The history of the area from 1898 to 1941 is one of gradual changes resulting from the incorporation of the rural villages and towns into the administrative and economic system of the Colony. Soon after the occupation of the area by the British, an administrative system was established which, although modified several times, has remained basically unchanged up to the present. District Offices were established in the countryside as seats of the new government and police stations were built at strategic locations to maintain law and order. A land survey was undertaken soon after 1900 to establish the ownership of all land in the New Territories for tax purposes and Crown Rent Rolls were drawn up.[3]

In the first decade of this century a rudimentary road network was extended into the New Territories from Kowloon to most of the major market towns. Later the Canton–Kowloon Railroad was built through the eastern part of the New Territories through the towns of Tai Po and Sheung Shui. Better transportation facilities stimulated commerce and trade between the rural areas and the urban sector of the Colony and the market towns of the New Territories began to grow and prosper around this time. In the half-century between 1898 and 1941, the government made some attempt to improve the schools in the New Territories and

[1] Hong Kong Government, op. cit., pp. 35–8.

[2] For a description of life in the New Territories at the time this area was incorporated into the Colony, see James Hayes, 'The Pattern of Life in the New Territories in 1898', in *Journal of the Hong Kong Branch of the Royal Asiatic Society*, vol. 2, 1962, pp. 75–102.

[3] See Topley, op. cit., for a discussion of forms of land ownership in the New Territories.

some progress was also made in improving other social services for the rural population but real progress along these lines was not to occur until after the Second World War.

The Japanese occupation of the Colony during the war, from 1941 through 1945, was a traumatic experience for the villagers of the New Territories and the populaton of the Colony as a whole. During this period the Colony suffered a general economic collapse with severe shortages of food and other goods of all kinds and many business establishments were forced to close their doors.[1] The villagers, according to their own testimony, suffered severe economic hardships during these years and many were close to starvation when the war ended and the British once again regained control of the Colony in 1945.

During the occupation period, the social structure and cultural patterns of the villagers of the New Territories were 'shaken up' to such an extent that they were made susceptible to the rapid and far-reaching changes that were to occur in the post-war years.[2] Although most of the refugees from China were initially absorbed by the urban areas of the Colony, the New Territories has certainly not escaped the impact of post-war developments. Extensive and far-reaching changes have been brought about in the economic and social patterns of the New Territories by the refugee influx from the mainland and the economic development of the Colony in the past fifteen years.

Since 1949, many refugees from the mainland have settled in the New Territories on small plots of land which they rent from the older village inhabitants.[3] These refugee farmers build small wooden shacks on their land and make their living growing vegetables for the expanded urban market. Some of the newcomers have established poultry and pig farms and many of the truck gardeners supplement their agricultural income by raising pigs

[1] Hong Kong Government, op. cit., p. 346. See also the chapter by H. J. Lethbridge in this volume.

[2] I do not mean to imply that the post-war changes would not have occurred in any case. However, it seems that the curtailment of most ceremonial events such as marriages and funerals, or the great simplification of these ceremonies due to lack of finances, made it much easier for the villagers to adopt the simpler urban ceremonial customs after the war. The routine of village life was traumatically disrupted during the occupation, weakening the traditional social and cultural patterns.

[3] For a discussion of refugee vegetable farmers in the New Territories see Topley, op. cit.

and chickens on the side. The refugee farmers have been economically quite successful and at present their wooden houses dot the countryside between the traditional peasant villages.

During the last fifteen years, and especially in the last decade, the excess population from the now overcrowded cities has begun to spill over into the New Territories at an ever-increasing rate. Many lower class Chinese from the city are moving into some of the older villages which are conveniently located near transportation to the cities and near the market towns. Some of these outsiders have found employment in the rural towns but most of them leave their families in the village and continue to work in the city, establishing a suburban pattern of living. Most of the men reside more or less permanently in the city near their place of work and visit their families in the country only on weekends or on the major Chinese holidays, depending on the nature of their employment. The move of urban residents to the countryside has been popular because living conditions in the country are better and more economical than in the overcrowded city and because primary education for the children is much cheaper in the village schools.

Recently, industrial and commercial firms from the city have begun to set up small plants and factories in the rural areas of the Colony to escape the high rent of the cities and this has increased employment opportunities for the rural population. Industry and commerce have stimulated the development of better transportation facilities and this has contributed to the economic development of the rural areas and the expansion of the rural market towns. At present, road networks are being extended into once isolated rural areas and with the road networks eventually go electricity, a piped water supply, and bus service, all of which have led to much improved living conditions for the villagers. Many villages are now connected to the city and towns by frequent and inexpensive bus and taxi service and some of them now even have telephones and street lights. Since the war modern elementary schools have been established in almost all the rural villages and many public and private middle schools have been built near the market towns making education to the middle school level much more common than before the war. Medical facilities, both government and private, have also been greatly improved.

Due to all of these factors—outsiders resident in or near the villages, improved transportation to towns and cities, and improved education and other social services—the New Territories since the war has undergone a process of rapid social, cultural, and economic change which has begun to alter fundamentally the traditional rural social patterns.

3   Market town–Village relations

In addition to the several hundred old-established villages, the scattered homesteads of the refugee vegetable farmers, and the fishing villages along the coast, the New Territories also contains several large market towns and numerous smaller markets. On the south coast not far from Kowloon is the new industrial centre of Tsuen Wan. Although there was some industry in Tsuen Wan before the war, it was mainly an ordinary country market town complete with the usual traditional Chinese business establishments. Since the war Tsuen Wan has been transformed into an important industrial centre and now contains several factories, a large shopping district, and many apartment buildings for the factory workers. With a current population of over sixty thousand, Tsuen Wan has almost become a small city. Other market towns in the New Territories are Yuen Long on the northwest plain which in 1961 had a population of over thirty-three thousand; Tai Po on the east coast with a population of about seventeen thousand;[1] and the adjacent towns of Sheung Shui and Fan Ling in the northeast, each of which has a population of around twenty-six thousand. In addition to these sizeable market towns, there are also lesser marketing centres in some of the larger village clusters scattered throughout the rural areas and ribbon developments of shops along some of the main roads.

The market towns are extremely important in New Territories society because they are the social, economic, political, and recreational centres for their surrounding villages. In most cases, the market town–tributary village area is well defined with most villagers visiting only 'their' town and seldom visiting other more distant towns. The rural social and economic network in the New Territories, as in most of China, has a cellular structure consisting of a market town as the nucleus of a surrounding group of villages. Villages are connected to their central market town like spokes to the hub of a wheel and although there is surprisingly little social interaction between individual villages the interaction

[1] Hong Kong Government, op. cit., p. 38.

between the members of each village and the town is intensive. The towns are extremely important as the transmitting belts for the social, cultural and economic influences from the city to the rural villages. It is not an exaggeration to say that in traditional times, for the majority of Chinese villagers, the market town area for all practical purposes represented the limit of their social universe.[1]

The market town–village units in the New Territories are at present in danger of being 'blotted out' by the tremendous swamping effect of the refugees and the overflow population from the cities but they are still recognizable units in the rural society. In fact, it appears that the relations between villages and town are being intensified with the establishment of better transportation facilities and the rising standard of living. The towns, with their wide variety of shopping facilities and new forms of entertainment, such as motion pictures, are attractive to the villagers in the surrounding countryside. Many of the villagers, especially the young people and the retired elderly men, nowadays spend almost as much time in town as they do in their own village and the town is definitely threatening the village as the centre of rural social life. Now that going to town for many villagers simply means an inexpensive five-minute bus or taxi ride, the villagers go to town for entertainment or to shop almost every day and the old marketing patterns where markets were held periodically on prescribed days throughout the month have given way to permanent daily markets. As Hong Kong's industrial and commercial development continues and as the New Territories' population continues to grow, the larger market towns such as Yuen Long are growing into small cities and the smaller village markets and some of the ribbon developments of commerce along the main roads are in turn becoming small towns.

4   Lineage structure

In traditional times, as at present, the structure of rural society within each market town area was built around the old-established

---

[1] The material included here on the market town–village area as the basic unit in rural Chinese social structure is taken from an unpublished paper entitled, 'The Market Town-Tributary Village Area in Traditional Chinese Society: The Basis for the Commune', which the author read at the Annual Meeting of the American Anthropological Association in San Francisco in Autumn 1963.

lineages (commonly called 'clans' in the literature[1]) such as the Tang lineages of Kam Tin, Ping Shan and Ha Tsuen, and the Man lineage of San Tin. These old and powerful lineages, according to their own traditions, first settled in the New Territories as early as the Sung Dynasty and have unbroken genealogical records that go back for over eight hundred years. As the first groups to settle this area, these lineages very early occupied the best agricultural land in the rich valleys in the north and northwest around Yuen Long and Sheung Shui. These great holdings of lineage land have formed the economic basis for their domination of the New Territories down through the centuries. Later arrivals to the area became dependent satellite villages of these powerful lineages on whose land they first settled so that within each market town area the crucial structural units of rural society are these 'sub-cells', each of which is composed of a dominant landlord lineage and its surrounding dependent tenant villages.

The internal structure of the old established lineages in the New Territories is basically simple:[2] most are composed of from five to ten villages all of which are descended in the male line from a common ancestor who first settled in the area. Over the centuries

[1] According to usual usage, a *lineage* consists of a group of people descended in one line (either through males only or females only) from a common ancestor. A *lineage* differs from a *clan* in that the members of a lineage usually know the genealogical links by which they are related; whereas, in the *clan*, the members may not be able to trace these exact genealogical links. Another difference is that lineages form corporate groups while clans are often less solidary, non-corporate, and more widely spread groups. In the Chinese case, a distinction cannot be made according to the first criteria noted above: all the Tangs in the New Territories can trace their genealogical links from a common ancestor. A distinction, however, can be made according to the second criteria mentioned above—corporate *vs.* non-corporate groups. According to this distinction, I have called groups of localized lineages in the New Territorial *clans*. Even though they are descended from a common ancestor and know the exact genealogical links, they have little unity except in the context of ancestor worship. The local Chinese kinship groups should be properly called *lineages* and not clans. For example, I have termed the Tangs of Ping Shan a *lineage*; whereas, I have used the term *clan* to refer to all the Tangs in the New Territories. The Tang Clan includes a number of localized lineages, e.g. Ping Shan, Ha Tsuen, and Kam Tin.

[2] For a brilliant and pathbreaking analysis of the structure of the Chinese lineage, see Maurice Freedman, *Lineage Organization in Southeastern China*, London 1958. This work has greatly influenced my own thinking on this subject. See also his book, *Chinese Lineage and Society: Fukien and Kwangtung*, London 1966.

as the population of the group increased, men of the lineage moved out from the parent village to found other villages and lineage branches nearby. Each localized patrilineage in the New Territories exhibits a geographical unity in that all the villages form a group which is clearly separated from the other lineages in the countryside. This geographical unity is reinforced by a unity of kinship in that all the male members of the lineage are descended in a direct line from a common ancestor and consider themselves to be 'brothers' (collectively). Each lineage also has unity as a corporate group in that it owns property, is an integral political and legal entity, and has internal machinery for making decisions and regulating its internal affairs. The lineages also exhibit a ritual unity in that all members participate in a common 'church' (in the Durkheimian sense[1]) centred around the lineage ancestral cult. Ideally, the men of each lineage are a co-operative group that protects and supports its own members in conflict with the outside world. The lineage also is (or was in traditional times) a basic unit in the stratification system of rural society that competes as a unit with the other lineages in the surrounding countryside—particularly the other lineages in the same market town area. In traditional times, a man's standing in society depended in large part upon his membership in a particular lineage group.

All of the above unifying elements combined to make the lineage of South China an extremely solidary group in relations with the outside world, whether this be another lineage of approximately equal power or the government. It is for this reason that inter-lineage hostility and feuds plagued the old Chinese administration and still troubles the New Territories Administration down to this day. High internal solidarity in any social group is often matched with extreme out-group hostility.

Internally, however, the solidarity of the lineage was largely a prevailing fiction because the inter-lineage conflict on a higher level was matched by conflict between the sub-branches within each lineage. Intra-lineage conflict was, and still is, endemic because wealth, prestige, and power is not shared equally by the component sub-branches and villages that make up each lineage. Most prominent New Territories lineages contain extremely

[1] Emile Durkheim, *Elementary Forms of the Religious Life*, translated from the French by J. W. Swain, New York, Collier Books Edition, 1961, pp. 59–63.

wealthy men as well as poor tenant farmers, and this has always been the case. Within each lineage, some branches are more powerful and wealthy than the other branches and are able to dominate the entire lineage. If the branches into which a lineage is divided are more or less equal in strength, there is a constant struggle for dominance among them. Each lineage presented a united and solid front to the outside world but, internally, conflict and jealousy between families and lineage branches was the rule.

The powerful lineages of the New Territories, especially the Tang lineages, dominated the entire area for centuries as semi-feudal landowners, and it was from these large and wealthy land-owning lineages that most of the New Territories' officials and gentry members came in traditional times. As scholars and officials, members of the prominent lineages had political power and influence with the government. Political influence and prestige reinforced the economic control of the countryside wielded by these prominent lineages and made their domination of New Territories society unquestioned. It was the leaders of these powerful and influential lineages who formed the political and social *élite* of the New Territories prior to the incorporation of the area into the Colony of Hong Kong, in 1898, and it was the members of this *élite* who organized and armed the peasants in an attempt to prevent the British from occupying the area.

Such examples of co-operation between all or most of the lineages of the New Territories, however, were rare except in crisis situations where they were faced with a common outside threat of such magnitude as to virtually force co-operation. The usual situation was one of extreme rivalry. There appears to have been over the centuries, a constant struggle between lineages for wealth, prestige, and power and this rivalry is still very much in evidence. In traditional times, when the bureaucratic officialdom of China was spread thinly over the country and local areas were left pretty much to their own devices, this rivalry and competition between lineages of the New Territories often broke out into open hostilities. A good example is the 'war' between Ping Shan and Ha Tsuen which is said to have lasted for several decades in the last century with many casualties on both sides. This hostility between the neighbouring lineages of Ping Shan and Ha Tsuen, both of which are surnamed Tang and belong to the same clan, is manifested in the distrust and suspicion between these two groups that still occasionally leads to quarrels and even violence. Almost all the major lineages in the Yuen Long area are reputed to have been involved in quarrels and feuds with all the other important lineages at some time in the past and these feuds are still remembered by some of the older village men.

Rivalry and conflict between the powerful lineages of the New Territories is by no means a thing of the past for even at present the government still has difficulty with inter-village and inter-lineage quarrels and fights in Yuen Long District. The present District Officers, in attempting to mediate between these hostile lineages, are in much the same position as the old Chinese District Magistrates who often lamented the 'barbarism' of the unruly lineages of southern China.

Conflict between the lineages of the New Territories was so prevalent in traditional times that regional political alliances and associations for mutual defence and protection were organized. These political associations in the New Territories often included scores of villages and cut across clan lines so that different lineages, belonging to the same clan, might belong to opposing alliances. In the Yuen Long market town area there has for centuries been a tradition of rivalry between the Tang lineage of Ping Shan and the powerful lineages in Sap Pat Heung. Each of these groups organized a regional alliance of villages for protection against the other faction. The Ping Shan association, known as Ping Shan Kong Saw, includes over thirty villages in the western part of the new Territories reaching out of the market town area as far south as Tsuen Wan. The headquarters of this association is a temple near the village of Ping Shan which is dedicated to the 'heroes' of the association who died in its battles. A similar organization was organized by the villages of Sap Pat Heung to oppose the Ping Shan association: its headquarters is located in a temple near Yuen Long. These old rivalries do not break out into open conflict nowadays because of the presence of the British Government but they are still present.

5   Leadership and politics

The Political structure of the New Territories is just as complex today as it was in traditional times. The complexity arises from the fact that there are two types of leaders present in the rural areas.[1]

---

[1] See Topley, op. cit., for a discussion of village leaders.

On one hand are leaders selected by the lineages solely on the basis of kinship seniority and age, and on the other hand are leaders chosen for their ability and effectiveness.

Each major lineage in the New Territories is headed by a 'lineage elder' who is the oldest man in the most senior generation of the lineage. The lineage head serves as the ritual representative of the lineage in the ancestral sacrifices, chairs important meetings in the central ancestral hall, and oversees the management of the estate of the central ancestral hall. He is given respect and deference by the members of the lineage and is supposed to mediate disputes within the lineage that cannot be settled by the family heads or the elders of the lineage sub-branches.

Just as the lineage head is the oldest man in the most senior generation of the lineage as a whole, each sub-branch of the lineage at various levels has its 'family elder' who is the oldest and most senior man within that sub-branch of the lineage. The duties of the family elders within their branch of the lineage are similar to the duties of the lineage head in the lineage as a whole. Both the lineage head and the family elders are recruited on purely ascriptive criteria and not according to their innate leadership ability.

The other set of lineage and village leaders are selected on the basis of their wealth, status, and their ability to represent the lineage effectively to the outside world. In traditional times, the leaders of the lineages of the New Territories were the wealthy men of prominent lineage branches and those 'gentry' members of the lineages who had passed at least the lowest rank in the Imperial Examinations. These men probably always had more power in the lineage than the lineage elders because recruitment of leaders according to age and kinship seniority alone did not ensure that the men selected would be able leaders. They might simply be uneducated farmers from a weak branch of the lineage who had no real power or prestige at all. The older type of gentry leaders lost power or died soon after the New Territories was incorporated into the Colony in 1898 and a new type of leader arose.

The new leaders of New Territories rural society are a 'gentry' of a new type consisting of wealthy and powerful men (or men with outstanding leadership ability) who come from powerful sub-branches of the dominant lineages. At present, these men are the holders of real power in rural society and they usually control the lineage elders just as the old examination graduates controlled the lineage elders in their day. These leaders are a new type of men able to operate effectively in a new and much changed society.

Since 1898, the political structure of the New Territories has been one of dual character. At the top is the formal administration of the Hong Kong Government and below this the indigenous leaders of the powerful lineages.

In formal terms, the New Territories is under the control of the Commissioner of the New Territories who is responsible, under the Governor of Hong Kong, for administering the entire area. Under the Commissioner are four District Officers who are in charge of the four administrative districts—Tai Po, Yuen Long, Tsuen Wan, and South—into which the New Territories is divided. In the Yuen Long area each district is in turn divided into *heung* (Mandarin *hsiang*), or rural administrative sub-districts, which usually include from ten to thirty villages. Each *heung* has an elected Rural Committee chosen from the village representatives of the *heung* who are in turn elected—one or two from each village. The Rural Committees, each of which is headed by a Chairman and Vice-Chairman, assist the District Officer in matters that concern the villages in their *heung*.[1]

Until recently, the District Officer fulfilled about the same administrative functions as the old Chinese magistrates. He decided minor legal cases, solved all kinds of disputes, and in general *was* the government as far as most of the villagers under his jurisdiction were concerned. Beneath the District Officer and the other top level officials in the District Office (who are usually but not always British career officers) is a staff of Chinese subordinate officers and clerks who handle most of the routine affairs of administration and who have the most direct contact with the general rural population. The subordinate members of the District Office staff are better educated Chinese from the urban areas and they usually look down on ordinary villagers with ill-concealed contempt and disdain. Most of the villagers, many of whom are illiterate, are shy and afraid of all dealings with the government. It is sometimes difficult for an ordinary village farmer alone to have affairs tended to efficiently and speedily at the District Office. This has resulted in a situation where the Administration at the upper level and the villagers at the lower level are separated by mistrust and suspicion.

[1] Hong Kong Government, op. cit., pp. 354–6.

Partly because of this situation, political machines at the village and *heung* level have been organized in the New Territories by local leaders who mediate between the rural population and the government. The political structure of the New Territories is closely connected with the new economic conditions that have existed in the New Territories in the past decade. As the economic development of the urban areas has begun to affect the rural areas and the urban population has expanded into the countryside, land in the New Territories has begun to skyrocket in value. At present the demand for land by urban commercial and industrial firms who wish to expand into the rural areas is especially great and this increasing demand for land, with the accompanying rise in land values, has made possible a lucrative land brokerage business which arranges land sales between urban interests and the local village population. This situation has presented local political leaders with opportunities to make sizable sums of money as brokers since only they have the wide social connections in the city and the prestige in the villages to carry through large land deals.[1] At present, there is considerable competition for political office, not simply for the prestige involved but also for the opportunities that political office gives to make large amounts of money. Well organized political organizations have been formed at the village level to control political offices and to gather the economic fruits of these offices. The increased wealth of the local political leaders, usually the Chairmen of the Rural Committees, has given them the financial resources to maintain their position. Although the election of local leaders is theoretically by democratic methods, actually many elections are decided by bribery or by voting strictly according to kinship lines. The local political leaders are able to use their wealth to buy elections and maintain their power.

The main reason why such local political machines exist in the New Territories is that there is a genuine need for the villagers to have effective leaders with outside connections and power who are able to represent their interests to the government and to the wider society. In many cases these leaders *are* effective in helping their people in dealings with the government, the police, and outside business interests. In return for the opportunity to make money from their offices, the successful local leaders perform this essential function of mediating between the villages and the wider

[1] See Topley, op. cit., pp. 168–9, for a discussion of land brokerage activities in the rural areas.

society. The new leaders perform essentially the same functions for the villagers as did the old educated Confucian gentry who mediated between their lineage and the old governmental bureaucracy. The only difference is that the society has changed a great deal in the past half-century and a new type of gentry is needed.[1]

6 The changing economy

The rural inhabitants of the New Territories are at present a remarkably prosperous group of people by Asian standards. This is evident to even the casual visitor to the market towns of the New Territories where shops are filled with modern electrical appliances from all over the world and fruit stands along the streets are piled high with expensive imported fruit from California. The cinemas and teahouses are nightly packed with people from the surrounding villages who come into town for recreation. Compared with the dreary life of the mainland peasants the villagers of the New Territories, in material respects at least, lead a good life indeed. This is not to say that there are no sections of the New Territories population such as some isolated villages, some fisherfolk, and some refugees who are extremely poor. There are such examples of extreme poverty but they are the exception rather than the rule. Even the refugee vegetable gardeners are able to make an adequate and sometimes even comfortable living from their small plots of land.

The New Territories population is prosperous because they have participated in the 'economic miracle'[2] that has occurred in the Colony in the years since the Second World War. Industrial and commercial development in the urban areas has created new jobs and economic opportunities for the villagers of the New Territories. The villagers are moving rapidly into every sector of the expanding economy from service occupations to work in the

[1] For a more detailed discussion of political behaviour in the New Territories, see Maurice Freedman's article, 'Shifts of Power in the Hong Kong New Territories', *Journal of Asian and African Studies*, vol. 1, 1966, pp. 3–12.

[2] For a more detailed discussion of the effects of economic development on a New Territories village, see the author's book, *Capitalism and the Chinese Peasant: Social and Economic Change in a Hong Kong Village*, Berkeley and Los Angeles 1968. The author expresses his gratitude to the University of California Press for permission to use material from this book in the present chapter. For a general discussion of economic development in Hong Kong, see Edward Szczepanik, *The Economic Growth of Hong Kong*, London 1958.

textile factories. Over the past fifty years there has been a gradual trend for rural men and women to move into non-agricultural occupations and this trend has been greatly accelerated by the tremendous economic growth of the Colony in the post-war years. The participation in new occupations outside the village has led to increased prosperity and higher living standards for the rural population.

Village farmers have also benefited from the Colony's population growth and increased prosperity. After the war, the refugee influx from the mainland greatly expanded the urban market for vegetables, pork, poultry, and other foodstuffs of all kinds. To take advantage of this opportunity, the village farmers have since the war been rapidly switching from the traditional two-crop rice agriculture to an increased reliance upon vegetable growing for the urban market.[1] This change in the agricultural practices of New Territories farmers was aided by two factors. One was the influx of refugee vegetable gardeners into the New Territories who taught the farmers successful vegetable growing techniques. The other factor was the establishment of an efficient Vegetable Marketing Organization after the war by the Hong Kong Government. The new Vegetable Marketing Organization furnished a fleet of trucks to carry the farmer's vegetables to the city market which made it much easier and more convenient for the farmer to market his produce. The new marketing organization also allowed the farmer to keep more of the market price of his crops by eliminating the middleman's excessive costs, which in traditional days amounted to a large percentage of the market price.[2] Farmers were highly motivated to switch from rice agriculture to vegetable growing because they can make more money growing vegetables than they could growing rice and because vegetable growing allows them to have a continuous income throughout the year instead of the twice-yearly income they had from rice agriculture.

At present, most of the farmers have fairly good incomes and

[1] Topley, op. cit., pp. 170–1, asserts that only the immigrant farmers grow vegetables in the New Territories. This may be true in some areas of the New Territories, but in P'ing Shan the indigenous farmers are very rapidly changing over to truck gardening and are ceasing to grow rice. This same process of switching from rice agriculture to truck gardening also appears to be common in other villages of the Yuen Long District.

[2] For a discussion of the traditional marketing procedure in the New Territories and its replacement by the new Government Vegetable Marketing Organization, see Topley, op. cit., pp. 179–82.

are certainly much better off now than they were before the war. A higher income has given them the capital necessary to finance modern farm improvements such as chemical fertilizers, modern insecticides, and gasoline water pumps for irrigation. The adoption of these new farm tools has increased the efficiency of many of the farmers and has led to higher farm yields. At present, only a few of the wealthier farmers have all the new farm equipment but these innovations will probably soon spread to most farmers in the New Territories as vegetable growing continues to spread and as farm income increases. The farmer's income and general standard of living has been so much improved in recent years that it is not uncommon to see a farmer at work in his fields smoking a Camel cigarette and listening to his Japanese-made transistor radio!

Although most New Territories farmers are tenants who rent their land from private landlords or ancestral estates, this high rate of tenancy is at present not really a serious problem. This is because the value of the produce grown on the land has increased much faster than the rise in land rents. Most land rents have remained close to the traditional rate which was based on the assumption that the farmer would grow only two crops of rice on the land every year. Now that most farmers grow vegetables, they achieve a much higher income than they did from rice but continue to pay the old rent. In most instances the tenant farmers have benefited more from the changed agricultural conditions than the landlords and it appears that the relative benefit that the two groups receive from the land has shifted in favour of the farmers in the last few years. Even though a majority of the farmers are tenants, they are still able to make a good living growing vegetables and raising pigs.

Increased prosperity and higher living standards among almost all sectors of the New Territories population has enabled the villagers to eat better, to wear better clothes (many villagers now wear western-style clothing), to have more money available for recreation, and to have money to purchase new goods and services. Village families can afford to give their children a better education and many young people from the villages can now go to middle school. Better education has enabled many of the younger people to move into higher status and better paying occupations with the government or in the commercial firms in the city.

On the whole, living standards of many of the villagers of the New Territories, especially those members of the old-established land-owning lineages, are even higher than living standards among urban workers. Most villagers own their own homes and therefore do not need to pay the high rent that is common in the cities. Also, many of the villagers in the wealthier lineages have shares in ancestral estates that in some instances are worth as much as several million dollars.

Other extra sources of income for many of the villagers are remittances from family members who have gone abroad and rents from houses. Many village men from the New Territories, especially from the Man Lineage at San Tin, have gone to England to work in Chinese restaurants and the money they remit from abroad has substantially increased the income of their families.[1] Another important new source of income in some villages near the main roads is the renting of houses to the outsiders from the city who are moving into the villages at an ever increasing rate. In some of the wealthier villages many people are now selling land to obtain sufficient capital for building houses to rent to the outsiders.[2]

7 Religious patterns

The religious life of the villagers of the New Territories, like most other aspects of their culture, is at present a curious mosaic of traditional and modern Chinese patterns influenced by Western ideas. In traditional times, the villagers had a rich and varied religious tradition and an extraordinarily complex system of magical beliefs and practices. Among the older generation of villagers, especially the women, belief in the traditional religion is still strong, but modern education and contact with urban ideas has increased religious scepticism among some of the younger men and women. Traditional beliefs are, however, by no means absent among the younger generation because in many cases their scepticism is only a thin facade that conceals a deep seated belief in the old traditions, or a lingering fear that the old ideas *might*, after all, be true. The persistence of traditional beliefs in religion and magic is related ultimately to the persistence of the traditional

[1] Hong Kong Government, op. cit., p. 51.

[2] For an excellent discussion of the economic attitudes and practices of Hong Kong Chinese, see Marjorie Topley's paper, below.

world-view of the villagers. The villagers now participate in a society that in many ways is vastly different from the traditional society but their basic goals and values—health, security, and success in this world—have remained largely unchanged. The conditions within which the pursuit of these goals take place are also basically the same as in traditional times. Better education and improved economic conditions have given the villagers greater opportunities to achieve success but the basic fact remains that the valuable things in life are still limited and success can be achieved by only a relatively small number of people. The core beliefs of the traditional system of religion and magic were intimately related to these basic facts of life: only a few could achieve success in a highly competitive society and these few achieved success not only because they were capable and hard working but also, and more importantly, because they were 'lucky'.

If any one idea could be taken as the essential idea in Chinese religious and magical beliefs, it would be the concept of 'luck'. 'Luck' is really not a good translation of the Chinese idea because it does not indicate the overriding importance of this idea in Chinese thought. Perhaps 'fate' or 'destiny' came closer to the traditional Chinese conception, but the best translation for this idea would be 'mana'. As is well known, many peoples around the world, including the Pacific Islanders and the American Indians, have a belief in an impersonal supernatural power, variously called 'mana', *wakan*, etc., which is perceived as the source of all efficacy in the universe. If one perceives the similarity between Chinese beliefs in 'luck' and the belief in mana, this gives the key to understanding traditional Chinese magic and religion. Those people who possess 'luck' succeed in life, while those persons who do not possess 'luck' are failures in their worldly undertakings. The idea of 'luck' is the Chinese *ad hoc* explanation for success and failure. A person succeeds in business because he is 'lucky'; he fails because he is 'unlucky'. The goal in traditional religious and magical activities was, therefore, to gain control of mana or 'luck' and to avoid those practices which led to a decrease in one's control of 'luck'.

An important source of mana (or 'luck') which could aid human action in this world were the beneficent beings that inhabited the Chinese supernatural world. These consisted of the *zan* (Mandarin *hsen*) which included large temple deities of Buddhist or Taoist origin, local tutelary deities, and most importantly, the ancestral spirits. These deities were worshipped mainly to obtain their help in the earthly struggle for success. If one could receive aid from these powerful supernatural beings who were imbued with large amounts of mana, then one would become 'lucky' and be able to ward off the attacks of the *kwai* (malevolent supernatural beings who caused all misfortune and failure in the world). One could also try to capture mana by arranging one's dwelling place and one's ancestral tombs to capture the *fung shui* (Mandarin *feng shoei*) influences that pulsed through the convolutions of the earth's surface. The Chinese conception of *fung shui* is really the same as 'luck' or mana and this idea is intimately connected with all their other religious and magical beliefs. If one can capture good *fung shui*, this will enable individuals, families, or entire lineages, to achieve worldly success.

Traditional values, which were overwhelmingly concerned with success in this world, have not been changed by the new social and economic conditions—if anything they have been intensified —and the dominant motivation of most of the villagers of the New Territories still is to become a wealthy and powerful man. Since the social conditions within which these valued goals must be pursued are similar to those present in the traditional society, the basic system of religion and magic, which functions primarily to aid in the quest for success, has also exhibited a remarkable degree of persistence.

Even some of the most 'modern minded' and 'progressive' men in the New Territories still perform the traditional religious and magical rites designed to ward off the malevolent *kwai* and pro-pitiate the powerful temple and ancestral spirits who might aid them in their drive for success. The ancestor cult, belief in *fung shui*, as well as continued belief in fortune telling and other magical practices, have remained extremely important in the lives of the villagers and have persisted to some extent among the younger and better educated generation. The traditional religious prac-titioners—the Taoist Priest, Spirit Medium, fortune teller, and the Buddhist priests and nuns—continue to perform their roles in the traditional religious system and they still receive a surprising amount of patronage.

Christianity has not made much headway among the villagers, at least in the area near Yuen Long where the author worked. There were many Christian churches and missionary bodies oper-ating in the area but they appear to have converted very few of the indigenous village population. Those villagers who have become Christians have done so mainly because of the economic benefits available from the missionary relief organizations and the educational opportunities available for those who join the Catholic Church. Several of the young people in the villages where I worked occasionally attended church services but this was done as a social affair and regarded mainly as an opportunity to meet potential marriage partners; it was not done out of any deep belief in Christianity. Several of the older members of the village in which I worked definitely resented the Christian churches and missionaries because they tended to look down upon traditional Chinese beliefs. There does appear to be a lessening of belief in some of the older traditional religious and magical beliefs among the younger generation but the traditional attitudes have by no means disappeared and Christianity has offered no really successful substitutes.

8   Family life

Family life in the New Territories has not escaped the changes that have taken place in almost every other aspect of rural society. The New Territories at present exhibits a wide array of forms of marriage and the family, ranging from strictly traditional families based on parental arranged marriage to more modern nuclear families of western type based upon free marital choice. Almost all the stages of change in Chinese family and marriage patterns that have occurred in China over the past fifty years can be found in the contemporary rural society.

As in almost all other areas of life, there is a sharp discontinuity between the older and younger generation of villagers. Most of the families of the older generation are based upon arranged marriages of traditional type and family relations tend to follow more or less closely the traditional Confucian family precepts which emphasize the superiority of males and the importance of age. Most families of the younger generation, especially those young people who have received a good education and who work in the city, are based on free marital choice and the relations between husband and wife tend to approximate western ideals. The participation of young village men and women in the urban economy has been one of the crucial elements leading to change in traditional marriage and family patterns. Most of the young people who go to work in the city have contact with western ideas of romantic love and have an opportunity for courtship that might not be possible in the more conservative rural area.

There is also a great difference in marital and family patterns between different social and economic strata in New Territories rural society. Most farmers still practise the old style marriage customs complete with sedan chair and the ancestral hall banquet and most farmers marry young people from farm families in other rural villages. Almost all of these marriages are arranged by the parents. On the other hand, most non-agricultural families practise the new-style marriage customs and many marriages among this group are made with young people from the towns and cities or with refugees living in the countryside. Most of these marriages are based upon free choice. In this instance, as in most other areas of social custom, the farmers tend to be the most conservative segment of the New Territories population. This is especially the case in the poorer farming villages which are relatively isolated from the main roads and from the market towns.

The change from parental arranged marriage to free marital choice has had a profound effect upon the structure of the village family. The older family was based upon the ties between parents and son and the tie between husband and wife was not emphasized. Marriage in the old days was spoken of as 'taking a daughter-in-law' rather than 'taking a wife' and the parents' control over their children's marriage symbolized the importance of marriage as a family affair rather than a personal affair of two young people. The parents' selection of a bride for their son emphasized quite clearly their authority over the young woman who came into the family for she was chosen by her parents-in-law rather than her husband.

At present, with more and more of the young people from the villages choosing their own marital partners from people in the towns and cities and from the refugee population in the New Territories, the structure of the traditional family has been threatened and the ties between husband and wife are becoming more important than ties between son and parents. This is especially true in cases where the son brings a city girl back into the village to live. These modern-minded young women are sometimes openly disdainful of their old-fashioned mothers-in-law who are in most cases uneducated village women. The village women reciprocate with a very low opinion of the 'city girls' who they say are lazy and worthless. This situation leads to conflict within families over everything from the control of family finances to the proper way to feed and care for infants. Conflict between mother-in-law and daughter-in-law, of course, was a built-in feature of the old family structure but nowadays this conflict tends to have a new content. At present the daughter-in-law is just as likely to dominate her mother-in-law as the other way around and this is quite different from the traditional situation.

Modern marriage ceremonies practised in the rural areas are similar to those practised in the urban areas and are much simpler and much less colourful than the traditional ceremony. In traditional times, and at present in the old-fashioned marriages, during the period of engagement elaborate traditionally defined gifts pass back and forth between the two families. Nowadays, in the more modern-style marriages, the groom usually gives a lump sum of money to the bride's family to take care of the expense of buying the traditional wedding cakes to distribute to the bride's relatives and to help pay for the wife's trousseau. In traditional marriages the boy's family sends a bridal sedan chair to the girl's village to bring the bride back to her husband's village. This was a colourful procession complete with cymbal players, red flags, firecrackers, and the playing of Chinese oboes. In some of the modern marriages held in the villages in recent years, the groom comes to the girl's village in person and takes the bride back to his home in an automobile decorated with a red sash and a doll placed on the hood dressed in a Western-style bridal costume. The traditional marriage costume of the bride and groom are much simplified in the modern marriages. Instead of an elaborate feast and banquet given for the entire village in the ancestral hall of the boy's lineage, nowadays the banquets are held in the restaurants of the market town or city and not nearly as many relatives are invited.

At present, the traditional ceremonies are observed only when one villager marries another villager and the parents arrange the marriage. When a villager marries a refugee or a person from city or town the new-style marriage customs are observed. This adoption of urban patterns of marriage is only another example of how New Territories customs are being modified to conform to the more prestigious urban patterns.

9   The future outlook

It has not been possible to go very deeply into any aspect of New Territories rural society mentioned above but this brief sketch will suffice to give some indication of the general nature of Chinese rural society in the Colony and how rural social patterns are being rapidly transformed by the refugee influx, improved education, and the penetration of economic influences from the urban areas.

It is always hazardous to attempt to predict the future course of events in any society, but it does seem possible to forecast with a reasonable amount of certainty the changes that will occur in the social, economic, and cultural patterns of the villagers of the New Territories over the next few decades.

It appears quite likely that in the next generation most of the social and cultural patterns of the villagers will change to closely approximate the semi-western social patterns of the present urban Chinese population. Marriage will probably be almost entirely based upon free choice and the family will be more like the western nuclear family than the traditional Chinese family. It seems also likely that the position of women in the family and in the wider society will be improved due to the fact that village women are participating more and more in new occupational opportunities and now receive an education almost equal to males. There will still probably be more families in the village that will include a mother or father of the male head than is found in western society because the absence of social security and old age pensions makes it mandatory that sons continue to support their parents in their old age.

There promises to be a continuous growth of industry and commerce in the rural areas as businesses and factories move out from the overcrowded cities. Hopefully this will present many new employment opportunities for the villagers and their standard of living will continue to improve. The occupational structure of the villages will probably continue to change from the traditional reliance on agriculture to an increased reliance on non-agricultural occupations. Within the agricultural sector of the economy, the old pattern of two-crop rice agriculture will soon become a thing of the past and most of the village farmers that remain will be engaged in truck gardening.

As economic development in the New Territories continues and as the population continues to grow, it seems certain that the market towns will grow into small cities, following the pattern of Tsuen Wan, and that they will continue to expand at the expense of surrounding villages and adjacent farmland. Many older villages near market towns such as Yuen Long have already been absorbed by the expanding towns and this process will undoubtedly continue at an accelerated rate in the future. As the market towns are transformed into small cities, it is probable that some of the larger villages which at present contain only several small shops and a few stores will in turn grow into small market towns.

As the overflow population from the cities continues to move into the rural areas, the indigenous population will be soon almost totally 'swamped' by these outsiders. This will undoubtedly speed up the process of acculturation to the urban Chinese patterns. It is also probable that the old villages, as relatively separate communities, will soon cease to exist and that areas near the towns and near the main roads will have a blanket type of settlement. This is already occurring in many areas of the New Territories such as Ping Shan.

It seems almost certain that most of the traditional rural social and cultural patterns that have characterized the villagers of the New Territories for almost one thousand years will be changed beyond recognition in the next decade or two. And with the disappearance of traditional rural culture in the New Territories there will be no remnants of traditional rural China left anywhere, except perhaps on Taiwan.

II

A CHINESE VILLAGE ON HONG KONG ISLAND FIFTY YEARS AGO—TAI TAM TUK, VILLAGE UNDER THE WATER

J. W. Hayes

Tai Tam Tuk[1]—the name means 'the edge of the big water-way' —is a reservoir and boat anchorage on the southern side of Hong Kong island. It is a favourite beauty spot and its bay is still in permanent use as a boat people's anchorage and is well known to week-end yachtsmen. It was a village long before it became a reservoir. The Hong Kong Government's printed reports relating to the construction of the reservoir in the second decade of this century show that a village community of some eighty persons was removed to make way for the scheme, whilst other records reveal that the Tai Tam Tuk families were supposed to be removing a mile or two away to the adjoining rural area of Chai Wan.[2]

In their turn, most of the former inhabitants of Chai Wan were removed into the new resettlement estate which was built there when redevelopment of this hitherto outlying area of Hong Kong island began a few years ago, and the estate office records facilitated contact with the sole surviving member of Tai Tam Tuk village who happened still to be living at Chai Wan at the time of this second removal. She had been born in the neighbouring village of Stanley in 1890 and had come to Tai Tam Tuk to be married in 1905. Together with the rest of the villagers she had moved from the reservoir site in 1914. In good health and with a

[1] All names of persons, things and localities are given in a Cantonese form of romanization. The place names are in accordance with *A Gazetteer of place names in Hong Kong, Kowloon and the New Territories*, published in Hong Kong by the Government Printer in 1960. Where not otherwise stated, the source of my information is the elderly persons mentioned in the opening paragraphs. I am grateful to Mr Ling Tak-lok for help with translation. Notes on p. 47 and on p. 50 try to carry the background back to before 1841.

[2] See the *Hong Kong Hansard: Session 1914*, Hong Kong 1914, pp. 15–16 and 51. The population of Tai Tam Tuk at the 1911 Colony Census was 76. See *Papers laid before the Legislative Council of Hong Kong*, hereafter styled *Sessional Papers*, Hong Kong, in this case for 1911, p. 103 (23).

retentive memory, she was able to give a full description of life in the old village. She was also able to refer me to another old lady (b. 1885), now living in Shau Kei Wan, who had lived in the village from 1900 until her first husband died in 1909 and she remarried one of the labourers working on the reservoir. These two old persons have been of great assistance in creating a picture of Tai Tam Tuk in the last years of its history.[1]

Enquiries among the boat population confirmed that the older fishermen and their fathers had been born at Tai Tam Tuk, which shows that it has been used as a permanent anchorage by a group of Tanka boat people for at least the last eighty years. The mother of one of them is still alive. She was born there in 1884[2] and has been able to supply additional information concerning the relations between the boat people and the villagers. She referred me to a brother several years younger than herself, who has also given much help.

As might be expected, Government's printed records supply a considerable amount of information about the village. This is mainly contained in the 'Blue Books' forwarded to the British Government every year since 1844, three years after the foundation of the Colony, and in the annual reports of various government departments.[3] These records, together with miscellaneous information collected from elsewhere and the recollections of the four old persons mentioned above, make it possible to give a fuller account of this small village during the latter part of its history than might be expected in the light of its extinction fifty years ago. Thereby, the curtain is partly raised on the village side of Hong Kong's history, a subject which has been generally neg-

[1] One may perhaps question the value of information given by village women since in imperial times they were usually illiterate. On the other hand, they undoubtedly saw more of village life through spending most of their time in the village.

[2] I saw her traditional square of red cloth on which, as usual, was written the date and hour-cycle of birth of herself, her husband and all her children.

[3] The *Blue Books* are a kind of annual colony report in which information and statistics are given under various heads. The early annual reports can be found in *Reports on the Past and Present State of Her Majesty's Colonial Possessions*. In the 1840s these were published in London by Clowes and Sons for H.M.S.O. The *Blue Books* were published in Hong Kong in continuous series and there are copies available in libraries here from the early 1870s onwards. The Annual Reports of various government departments were published in the *Sessional Papers* mentioned above, or in other government publications, by the Government Printer, Hong Kong.

lected by western writers.[1] To this extent, a study of Tai Tam
Tuk, otherwise a village of no significance, is of greater interest
than might otherwise be the case.

There is an epic quality about the locality. Its scenery and the
fate of its village are equally compelling. The village was situated
at the head of a large inlet of the sea and was surrounded on three
sides by steep hill slopes which rise in places to a height of well
over a thousand feet. Behind the village the lower reaches of the
hills were thickly wooded in the mid-nineteenth century, probably more so than any other part of Hong Kong island at that
time.[2] The grandeur of its scenery is still impressive today and can
best be appreciated if one stands half-way along the Shek O Road
and looks down towards the reservoir. Equally, it is not difficult
to conjure up the growing and inchoate sense of uneasiness experienced by the villagers in the years after 1883 when construction work for the first of the Tai Tam series of reservoirs began
in an upland valley at some distance from the village, though it
was not until thirty-one years later that the village had to move
for the last and biggest of the three reservoirs that were constructed in this place.[3]

Tai Tam Tak has to be seen in its proper perspective. When it
first came under British rule in 1841 it was a small and remote
village situated on an outlying and sparsely populated island off
the long coastline of Kwangtung.[4] At that time it had a population

[1] Mr G. B. Endacott's two recent histories, *A History of Hong Kong*,
London 1958, and paperback 1964, and his more recent *Government and People
in Hong Kong*, Hong Kong 1964, have gone into the official side of managing
the local Chinese population, but so far as I know no detailed work on the
individual villages of Hong Kong island has apparently been attempted,
at any rate in a western language.

[2] See *Sessional Papers*, 1892, p. 352.

[3] See the article 'Tai Tam Water-works, Hong Kong' by J. Orange in
Minutes of Proceedings of the Institution of Civil Engineers, vol. C, pp. 246–76.
For a description of the later engineering works at Tai Tam Tuk see the
Hong Kong Government's *Administrative Reports for 1917*, Q. 71. As for
the villagers' probable feelings, my remarks are based on my experiences in
removing two villages from another reservoir site in the New Territories in
1957–60.

[4] Hong Kong formerly belonged to the San On district of the Kwong
Chau prefecture which contained 14 districts. The whole San On area was
part of the Tung Kwun district until 1573 when it was established as a
separate administrative entity. See Rev. Krone, 'A Notice of the Sanon
District' in *Transactions of the China Branch of the Royal Asiatic Society, Part VI*,
Hong Kong 1859.

of about fifty persons.[1] This number suggests that the village
was established sometime in the eighteenth century.[2] Its inhabitants were Hakkas,[3] and by the time of its removal in 1914 there
were two clans living in the village. The Chung clan with its ten
families was then in the majority. There were also two families of
the Yau clan, amounting to a dozen persons. A few years before
a third clan had been living in the village. Two Chan brothers,
who like their father had been born in Tai Tam Tuk, had recently
left to live in Stanley. Whether the ancestors of these Yau and
Chan families were living in the village in 1841 is not known for
sure: the Chung clan must certainly have been.[4] The first Chung
to settle there is said to have come direct from the Mui Yuen area
of Ng Wah district, over one hundred miles away, but it is no
longer remembered what brought him to Tai Tam Tuk, and, as
happened in so many cases, the family record[5] was lost during the
Japanese war. The origins of the other families are no longer
remembered.

What did the village look like? A Government Paper of 1887[6]
shows that there were still only twenty houses in the village by
that time. Of these thirteen had been included in the first land
survey presumably made some forty years before. These dwellings
were of one-storey, and small, averaging 400 square feet in size.
My informants tell me that the houses were constructed of mud
brick made, as elsewhere, by the villagers themselves with earth
from their own fields. The foundations and the actual work of

[1] See the brief mention in the useful 'Note on the Island of Hong Kong'
by A. R. Johnston, H.M. Deputy Superintendent of Trade, first published
in the *London Geographical Journal*, vol. XIV and reprinted in the *Hong Kong
Almanack and Directory* for 1846.

[2] Tai Tam Tuk was very likely founded, as were most local villages, by
one arrival with or without his family. His children, grand-children and
great-grand-children might have amounted to fifty persons by 1841.

[3] For a description of the Hakkas see J. Dyer Ball's *Things Chinese*, Hong
Kong and other places, this edition 1903, pp. 323–6.

[4] The family graves indicate their long settlement at Tai Tam Tuk. It
may also be deduced from the land records, which give no names, that the
Chans and Yaus may have been there too in 1841.

[5] Genealogical records are still kept by many clans in most old villages in
Hong Kong and the New Territories, though in many cases they are bare
recitals of family descent and dates of births and deaths.

[6] *Sessional Papers* 1887. This table is taken from one of the appendices to
the *Report from the Hong Kong Land Commission of 1886–87 on the History of the
Sale, Tenure, and Use of the Crown Land of the Colony* published by the Government Printer in 1887. See the Appendices, pp. 40–1.

construction was probably left to masons and carpenters from Shau Kei Wan and Stanley, the two nearest market centres. As is common in the villages of Hong Kong and the New Territories, the door jambs, entrance posts and lintels of the houses were cut from local granite, and the roofs were made of red tiles. The floors were of beaten earth. The Chung family had an ancestral temple among their houses, but the Yau and Chan families, being fewer in numbers, had not. There was a small temple just outside the village dedicated to the goddess Tin Hau.[1] To the rear of the village there was the usual grove of large trees, mainly banyans. The houses stood beside the main stream which provided the villagers with water for drinking and daily use. It was tidal below the village and was crossed by a wooden bridge erected by the village people.

The houses stood in two rows, rather in the manner described by Chadwick in his report on the sanitary condition of Hong Kong in 1882, where he wrote: 'The usual type of village consists of a double row of houses facing a street. The back of one row of houses is at or above high water mark.'[2] Tai Tam Tuk had no surrounding wall. Some of the houses were in a ruinous condition in 1914, which is usually the case in the smaller and poorer villages in South China where frequent typhoons and heavy rains combine to shorten the life of these simply-constructed dwellings. Perhaps in consequence, most families in the village had several houses. For instance, one of my informants, her husband, his parents and his younger unmarried brother shared three houses and one shed, but ate together as one household.

The villagers were farmers and their principal crop was rice which was cultivated on the terraces that stretched up the sides of the valley behind the village. These fields were fertile and are said to have produced a good yield, because the land was well-watered by the perennial flow of water that came rushing down the ravines and joined the mountain stream which flowed into the sea near the village. Indeed, it was the quantity of water available locally which ultimately spelt disaster for the village. An account of harvest time in one of the Hong Kong villages appeared in one of the numbers of the *Illustrated London News* for 1858 and is

[1] See E. T. C. Werner, *A Dictionary of Chinese Mythology*, New York 1961, p. 303 under Tien Fei.
[2] See *Mr Chadwick's Reports on the Sanitary Conditions of Hong Kong*, Eastern No. 38, printed for the use of the Colonial Office in November 1882, p. 43.

worth repeating here, not only because it is possible that Tai Tam Tuk was the village in question,[1] but also since it describes village routine at one of the important seasons of the year.

On the 1st of November (1857) I took a walk with a friend into the interior of Hong Kong and saw the process of rice-harvesting, beneath a bright, hot sun, the entire village population hard at work getting in the second crop of paddy. The principal part of the labourers are women, owing probably to the fact of the men being generally engaged in fishing. The paddy rice grows to a height of about two feet six inches. The fields are little patches of about fifty paces, on account of the unevenness of the ground. The rice is thrashed out of doors: first, in a tub with a screen, by a man, who takes a bunch in his two hands to strike the ears against the edge of the tub and then gives the rice again to be thrashed on a floor made hard with *chunam*, the Chinese asphalt. Ploughing is here done with a very primitive plough and a wonderfully small bullock, as the ground is soft and does not contain a single pebble. . . . After being harrowed, it may receive a crop of sweet potatoes, or ground nuts. The women work with children on their backs. No one appears too young to take a part in the work. In the next fields are sugar-canes.[2]

This extract mentions the cultivation of sugar-cane[3] and ground

[1] From various pieces of information it may be deduced that the village was probably either Pokfulam or Tai Tam Tuk.

[2] *Illustrated London News*, 16 January 1858. This description could apply equally well today. See also Johnston, op. cit., for a general description of the agriculture of the island in 1841–2.

[3] This was seemingly in general cultivation in Hong Kong in the nineteenth century. Miss C. F. Gordon-Cumming in her *Wanderings in China* (London, 2 vols. 1886), vol. 1, p. 23, gives a description of crushing sugar-cane in the nearby village of Little Hong Kong. 'A little farther we paused to watch a most primitive method of crushing sugar-cane between two stone-rollers, which are turned by three bullocks, the juice falling between the rollers into a bucket beside the man who feeds the machine with fresh cane. Another man at the back of the rollers removes the crushed canes.' A slightly fuller description of this process is given in G. N. Orme's 'Report on the New Territories 1899–1912' in *Sessional Papers*, 1912, p. 51. After processing 'the juice is boiled on the farmstead, and the cakes of rough brown sugar, into which the boiling syrup sets, supply the local demand, as well as the raw material to be treated in the European sugar-refineries of Hong Kong'—see T. G. Selby, *Chinamen at Home*, London 1900, p. 59. For peanuts see Selby, op. cit., p. 58.

nuts. These crops were not grown at Tai Tam Tuk during the time my informants lived in the village, though they recalled that they had been cultivated until fairly recently, together with vegetables such as greens, sweet potatoes, garlic, onions and various kinds of yam. The quantities for this produce and of the rice yields for the second half of the nineteenth century are recorded in the annual 'Blue Books' produced by the Hong Kong Government. They supply yearly figures for Tai Tam Tuk and the other Hong Kong villages year by year over a period of some fifty years.[1] One must presume that these figures are reasonably accurate. Since some of the early land records of the British administration are also available,[2] the two together provide some valuable

[1] See, for instance, the *Blue Book* for 1871, p. 145.

[2] Unfortunately it is not too easy to tie in the existing land records with the returns of produce given in the *Blue Books*.

The original (about 1841) registered holdings of the village, *in toto*, are listed in the table at pp. 40–1 in the appendix to the *Report of the Land Commission 1886–1887* mentioned at note 6, p. 32 above. There are also Village Rent Rolls from 1856 onwards whose value is limited by the fact that they give numbers and rents for houses and the corresponding agricultural holdings but provide no names or areas—though they do show that most villagers must have been peasant proprietors living in their own houses and cultivating their own land.

The first registered holdings show that a population known to be around 50 persons relied upon 115,500 sq. ft. of agricultural land (approximately 2·65 acres). By the time of the Land Report (1887) a greatly increased amount of land is said to have been cultivated (equivalent to 16 acres) and it is specifically stated in the table that none of this land was in the occupation of licensed or unlicensed squatters. Yet the agricultural yields for paddy and vegetables are very low by comparison with the returns of adjacent areas. I can only conclude that there was an error in the figures or in not mentioning the squatters who appear, after all, to have been living and farming in the area, according to the reports submitted to the Board set up following the enactment of the Squatter Ordinance in 1890, which are in the Library of the Colonial Secretariat, Hong Kong.

What is probably the last word over the village holdings can be ascertained by deductions based on the compensation figures given in the *Hong Kong Hansard: Session 1914*, p. 51 and at p. 11 of the *Administrative Reports* for 1914; and on the fact that compensation for fields was awarded at one-quarter cent per square foot (personal communication from Mr W. Schofield, a former Hong Kong Cadet Officer 1911–38). These show that in 1914 the villagers were compensated for approximately 6·6 acres.

For purposes of comparison, it is interesting to note that in the early 1950s a Hakka village of 7 families and 47 persons in the mainland portion of the New Territories cultivated 9·58 acres, of which 53% was owned by the villagers and 47% rented. Of this total 7·85 acres were capable of producing

material for the study of the agriculture of a group of Southern Chinese rural villages that could be unique for this period.

In 1914 the Chung households owned about forty fruit trees of various kinds, mostly tangerine and pumelo, but, curiously, no lichee or mango, two trees commonly found in the village orchards of this area. These trees were private property and not, as in some villages, a communal venture where the fruit was collected under common arrangements and either shared, or else sold and the proceeds credited to clan or village funds. The Chan and Yau families had no fruit trees.[1]

The Tai Tam Tuk villagers were accustomed to strip the lower branches of the hill pines as a source of fuel for their stoves, but towards the end of the nineteenth century the government forest guards and sentences of fines or imprisonment imposed on those villagers who were caught deterred them from following this ancient but unsatisfactory practice.[2] These pines were planted by the villagers. Timber and brushwood were a marketable product and it is likely that the village people sold it in Shau Kei Wan as well as using it at home.[3] It has been estimated that the annual

[1] The villagers also kept bees. The house in which Mrs Chung lived had three of the usual cylindrical rattan basket hives hanging under its eaves. Orme, op. cit., speaking of the New Territories says (p. 52) ' . . . the honey is sold almost entirely to the local chemists, by whom it is utilized as medicine'.

[2] See the yearly reports of the Botanical and Forestry Department, 1880–1900. For a typical one see *Sessional Papers*, 1894. Tai Tam Tuk was remote and it is obvious from the small number of forest guards (see *Sessional Papers*, 1894, p. 268) and difficulties in getting them to do their duty (see *Sessional Papers*, 1888, p. 215) that for many years the villagers must have done as they pleased on the hillsides.

[3] Describing a journey in the Amoy region in the 1850s Sir Harry Parkes wrote, 'The road was literally crowded with people, nine-tenths women, bearing to the city the produce of their mountain villages, in the shape of

two crops of paddy and one catch crop per annum. See the article 'An Agricultural Survey of a Village in the Lam Tsuen Valley' in *Food and Flowers, No. 3*, issued by the Agricultural, Fisheries and Forestry Department of the Hong Kong Government, published by the Government Printer in August 1953.

The comparison shows that Tai Tam Tuk was poor, which would account for Lobscheid's description of the place in 1859 as being a village inhabited by persons 'in a state of great poverty' (see 2, p. 44 below). It is unlikely that outsiders owned other land in the valley which could have been rented by the villagers.

output of one acre of forest was approximately eleven piculs (12·16 cwt.).[1]

In the extract from the *Illustrated London News* quoted above, it is mentioned that the village men were generally engaged in fishing. This is a useful reminder that the sea provided a supplementary source of food for the inhabitants of coastal villages which could be exploited at need. At the end of the nineteenth century the villagers of Tai Tam Tuk did not fish from boats—though they may well have done so previously—but, in the main, used throwing nets.[2] These nets were made by the villagers from a kind of hemp, which they were able to buy in the shops of Shau Kei Wan. Such nets were in common use in this region at the time, though they are rarely seen today, having gone out of general use about the period of the Pacific War, 1941–5. I have been told that, fishing in this way, a man standing up to his chest in the shallows could catch fish up to a catty in weight. Such fishing was normally carried out in the first half of the lunar year, but could obviously be resorted to whenever food was scarce or when the villagers fancied a change of diet. The Yau families had a stake net which was operated from one of the headlands during the season.[3] The sea also provided the villagers with seaweed which was washed in fresh water, mixed with tree leaves and rice or its husks and fed to the pigs. It was commonly used in this way in this region and was sometimes dried to keep for later use.

Though to a great extent self-sufficient, as was still usual in the first decade of this century,[4] the villagers visited the nearest

[1] See *Hong Kong Annual Report* 1938, London, H.M.S.O., 1939, p. 59.

[2] My enquiries in Lantao, Saikung and Hong Kong show that the villagers of the seaboard area of Hong Kong and the New Territories seem generally to have had a much closer connection with the sea before the Japanese war, and relied far more upon it for their livelihood then than now. Fishing was carried out by stake net or from various types of small craft operated by one to four men, the boats working singly or in pairs. For throwing nets and a description of the kind then in use in north-east Kwangtung (Swatow) see the *Imperial Maritime Customs Special Catalogue of the Chinese Collection of Exhibits for the International Fisheries Exhibition 1883* (Shanghai, Inspector General of Customs), p. 8. Also Orme, op. cit., p. 55.

[3] See Orme, op. cit., p. 54.

[4] More so in 1841. Johnston, op. cit., says 'A small quantity of flax is grown and prepared for household uses by the (Hong Kong) villagers'.

timber, in thick planks and spars, bamboos, firewood in stacks, rough fuel, branches etc., charcoal, paper, also some good vegetables. . . .' (See S. Lane Poole, *Life of Sir Harry Parkes*, London 1894, p. 155.)

market town fairly regularly to purchase additional necessities of life. In the case of the Tai Tam Tuk people, the nearest market centre was Shau Kei Wan,[1] a fishing port three miles east of the village, which had probably served the villagers as such before 1841, as well as since. Shau Kei Wan also served Tai Tam Tuk's neighbours, including the villagers of Chai Wan and the inhabitants of the more distant villages and hamlets of the Shek O and Stanley peninsulas.[2] Communications were rudimentary up to 1914 when the road from Tai Tam Tuk to Shau Kei Wan was still a mud track.

Around 1910 my informants say that the villagers paid weekly visits to Shau Kei Wan where they bought clothes and other manufactured goods, peanut oil for their lamps, salt fish, preserved vegetables and meat. The villagers could also obtain the services of specialists like blacksmiths, herbal doctors, fortune tellers, coffin-makers and so on, and would generally sell there any surplus produce and livestock to shops which sold such articles. In passing it should be noted that the pigs which were kept by most families were not generally reared for their own use, but were regarded as a source of additional income.[3]

Shau Kei Wan also represented a place where the village men—those of them who remained at home and did not seek employment in Hong Kong or further afield—could seek company and relaxation in the tea houses and other places of entertainment. The Tam Kung temple[4] there was always an attraction to nearby villagers at the celebrations on the god's birthday in the fourth

[1] The land population of Shau Kei Wan district was 1,355, 1,455, 2,561, and the boat population 2,102, 7,133, 4,338 in December 1858, 1859 and 1860 respectively. (See the Census Returns in the Hong Kong Government Gazettes for 5 March 1859, 18 February 1860 and 22 February 1862.) A few years later Shau Kei Wan was credited with 307 houses and shops and 603 boats. (See Mayers, Dennys and King, *The Treaty Ports of China and Japan*, London 1867, p. 49.) In 1871 the land population of the Shau Kei Wan area was 2,360. (See *Blue Book*, 1871, p. 114.) It rose steadily until in 1911 the land population was 11,727 and the boat population was 6,440. (See *Sessional Papers*, 1911, p. 103 (23).)

[2] There were no periodic market days in Shau Kei Wan in the period 1900–14, nor apparently previously either. Every day was a business day, probably because of the presence of a large fishing population.

[3] See Lockhart's 'Report on the New Territory' in *Sessional Papers* 1899, p. 544, and Orme, op. cit., p. 52.

[4] For this god see V. R. Burkhardt, *Chinese Creeds and Customs*, Hong Kong 1958, vol. III, pp. 105–7.

moon when Chinese opera performances were held for the customary four days and five nights. There, too, the Tai Tam Tuk
people could meet villagers from neighbouring places, with
many of whom they would be linked by marriage, either in the
present or past generations.

As was customary with any Chinese rural community, the male
villagers married the women of surrounding settlements to which,
in turn, their sisters and daughters went as wives. For instance,
Mrs Chung and her mother-in-law both came from the Stanley
villages two miles away and her sister-in-law was a Chai Wan
woman. Wives came not only from the Hong Kong villages.
Some of those whose names were given to me came from over
the water, two from Kowloon villages and another from Hang
Hau in the present New Territories. These marriages were all
arranged, and like Mrs Chung, who did not know or see her husband until she had arrived in his village by bridal chair, these
women had no say in the matter. However, widows did remarry
and in the two cases quoted to me had pleased themselves about
a husband.

Though evidence is not complete on this point, it appears that
the small size of the village led the families to look outside for
wives and not to seek for them among the other clans since this
might lead to quarrels and bad feeling between persons whose
lack of numbers, as well as the remoteness of the place, made it
advisable for them all to be on friendly terms. In one case known
to me from a Hong Kong village, this was taken as far as the
erection of a special wall between the two sections of the village
inhabited by different clans in order to lessen disputes caused by
children.[1]

A second point should be made. Tai Tam Tuk was a Hakka
settlement and seems to have remained so during its history. The
marriage links of the old persons to whom I have spoken, and
those of their relatives both in their own and immediately senior
generations, show inter-marriage with Hakka settlers from adjoining villages and not with displaced families from the town,
whether Hakka or Punti.[2] This is what one might expect, because

---

[1] See p. 7 of my typescript article, 'Some Villages in the north-western
part of the Kowloon Peninsula in 1898', submitted to the Conference on
Asian History held in the University of Hong Kong in 1964.

[2] Punti = Cantonese. See Lockhart, op. cit., p. 542, and Orme, op. cit.,
p. 44; also Dyer Ball, op. cit., pp. 206–7 for speech variations.

of the network of contacts resulting from marriages in previous generations—the local villages had a seventeenth or eighteenth-century origin, perhaps earlier in some instances[1]—as well as the obviously greater suitability of village wives for village work. In this direction, then, the proximity of the city had made little or no difference to custom up to 1914.

From marriage I now turn to religion which, in one of its forms, the Confucian, is very much related to family life. First of all, there were the religious ceremonies connected with ancestral worship. In Tai Tam Tuk, where the Chung clan accounted for three-quarters of the villagers, their ancestral duties were centred on their ancestral temple. The members of the Chung family burnt paper and lit joss sticks at the family altar on the 1st and 15th days of every month and also on the main Chinese festivals throughout the lunar year. The new Year and the dates of birth and death of the first male ancestor to settle at Tai Tam Tuk were the occasions for particular celebrations within the clan, and at Ching Ming, or the first grave festival, the families went to the tombs of their forebears. Most of these were situated in a lucky site about two miles from the village. The will to fulfil the ancestral duties was very strong and could involve considerable inconvenience. A man whose mother had remarried when he was a boy had taken him to Tam Kon Shan, one of the Lema group of islands. These lie over ten miles off Hong Kong, separated by seas which can sometimes be very rough. Notwithstanding the difficulties, this man returned regularly to worship at the tombs until increasing age and the Communist occupation of the Lemas put a stop to his visits.

Another form of worship was carried out at the Tin Hau temple not far from the village. This had been established by the early settlers and was the special property of the village. It was used by the villagers and occasionally by passers-by on their way through the valley. Here again, paper and joss sticks were burnt on the 1st and 15th days of each month, but the biggest celebration of the year took place on the 9th day of the 3rd lunar month, which was celebrated locally as Tin Hau's birthday. On this day, every family in the village took it in turns to worship in the temple and the occasion was marked with special feasting.

[1] See E. J. Eitel, *Europe in China*, London, 1895, pp. 127-34. Eitel does not state his sources of information, and such research into village history as is still possible is necessary to establish the facts of the case.

Another object of local worship was a natural feature, being a stone weathered into the shape of a lion. This was worshipped as a kind of local place god[1] all the year round, and at the important festivals during the lunar calendar it came in for its share of offerings of food, whole chickens, pieces of pork etc.

However, these types of worship were not rigidly separated. From what I have gathered, it seems that, despite differences of emphasis, practically every festival day was taken as an occasion to pay some respects to all three objects of veneration, the ancestors, the temple and the shrine.

At this point it is convenient to bring in the boat people, for, as mentioned in the opening paragraphs, the villagers were not the only inhabitants of the area. There were about twenty families of boat people permanently based on the bay at the time the village was removed.[2] This was an entirely separate community from the land people. They lived on boats and not on the shore and spoke a form of Cantonese, whereas the villagers spoke Hakka. About half these boat families were named Cheng, whilst the remainder belonged to four or five other clans.[3] The boat people in the Tai Tam Tuk anchorage had their own family and other celebrations and did not join the village people in the worship at Tin Hau temple. This belonged to the village and had no significance for the fishermen who regarded it only as a nameless small temple or *miu tsai*. Neither did they worship the stone lion that was venerated by the village people. Instead they worshipped at two local shrines to gods styled *tai wong ye*, which were located at different points on the coastline of Tai Tam Bay. Their worship was rather

[1] See Werner, op. cit., pp. 412–15 under She Chi.

[2] It would be more correct to say that they were always at Tai Tam Tuk during the main typhoon season from the fifth to the eighth lunar month of every year, fishing the surrounding waters for the rest of the year.

[3] It was very likely a man from one of these boat families who, under the recorded name Chun-Fat-Che, gave evidence against a mandarin junk charged with piracy in May 1874 during the Chinese so-called blockade of Hong Kong. 'I am a fisherman and have a small fishing boat about 18 feet long. It has one sail and carries myself and wife, my four sons and their two children. My fishing place is at Stanley, Tai Tam and Cape D'Aguilar. I have fished there ever since I was a child and I am 62 years of age, and my father before me. My son generally accompanies me in another boat.' See p. 51 of *The Blockade of the Port and Harbour of Hong Kong by the Hoppo, or Farmer in Canton of Customs Duties Levied upon Chinese Vessels. Proceedings of a Public Meeting held at the City Hall, Hong Kong on 14 September, 1874* (London, probably 1875).

peripatetic depending on where their fishing took them in local waters, though they always went to Aberdeen at New Year and for the celebrations on the birthday of the Hung Shing god at his temple there in the second lunar month.[1]

I have had an opportunity of discussing relationships at Tai Tam Tuk from each side and it is clear from what has been said that in daily routine, as in religion, the two communities went their different ways. The boat people had very little to do with the village people, and vice versa. This is reflected in how little each of my informants knew of the other's daily life in places like Tai Tam Tuk despite long settlement side by side.[2]

There is evidence that in some places the fishermen were exploited by the land people.[3] This was apparently not the case at Tai Tam Tuk in that they were not charged when they attempted to bream their boats on the beaches, which was usually required twice every month, nor were they asked to pay for grass and firewood when they collected them from the hillsides. The only restriction which seems to have been placed upon them was that they were not allowed near the village in their search for fuel; presumably because, on grounds of personal convenience, the villagers wanted the areas round the village for their own use instead of having to go further afield for their supplies. This is understandable and cannot be considered as an oppressive measure.

Besides breaming the shore was also used for dyeing and drying nets. A visitor to Hong Kong in the 1870s writes of a nearby locality:

> In 'Deep Bay' (Deep Water Bay) we found a colony of fishers boiling their nets in an exceedingly tall vat, containing a decoction

[1] The boat people only fished in the surrounding area and generally did not go any distance from their base. Fishing at night with bright lights was common in Hong Kong and Kowloon at this period and before. See J. H. Gray, *China*, London 1878, vol. 2, p. 295, also Orme, op cit., p. 54. The Hung Shing god is described in Burkhardt, op. cit., vol. III, pp. 106–7, and Gray, op. cit., vol. I, pp. 156–8. By 1914 fishermen were apparently using dynamite in local waters. The reports of the Hong Kong Alice Memorial Hospital for 1904 and 1905 mention two cases of injuries to fishermen caused by this dangerous and wasteful expedient.

[2] Even allowing for the advanced age of my informants it is necessary to emphasize this fact. I have come across the same thing in the New Territories where similar communities of farmers and fishermen have lived side by side for several generations.

[3] See my article on Peng Chau Island in the New Territories in the *Journal of the Hong Kong Branch of the Royal Asiatic Society*, 1964.

of mangrove-bark, which produces much the same rich brown colour as our own fishers extract from alderbark. Here, however, it is considered necessary subsequently to steep the nets in pig's blood to fix the colour. Those in common use are made of hemp, but others are made of a very coarse silk, which is spun by wild silk-worms, which feed on mountain-oaks. In order to give these additional strength, they are soaked in wood-oil.

We saw nets of very varied shape and divers-sized mesh hanging up to dry all along the shore, beneath the weird screwpines. I am told that at the beginning of every fishing season they are formally consecrated to the Queen of Heaven, the protectress of fisher-folk, to whom sacrifices and incense are duly offered, while the nets are outspread before her to receive her blessing.[1]

Relations between the two communities were apparently limited to an exchange of basic commodities. The boat people occasionally sold fish to the land people who, in turn, sometimes sold produce to the fishermen, though such economic interdependence as existed was lessened by the villagers' own fishing activities. The land people also sold grass and firewood to the boatmen when the latter preferred to buy them instead of collecting them for themselves. The boat people's main markets for selling fresh fish were the more popular centres of Shau Kei Wan or Stanley, and it is interesting to note that they did not always sail to those places but often walked there over the hills, carrying their fish in two baskets hung at each end of a pole. At this time, however, the bulk of their catch was salted and sold to salt fish dealers in Hong Kong.[2]

The way of life described in the preceding paragraphs was not, of course, unique to Tai Tam Tuk but, with variations, could be found in the other Hong Kong villages and in all the coastal areas and islands of the San On and adjacent districts of the Kwangtung province. It was characterized by self-reliance in most things that concerned their daily life, the extent largely depending upon the remoteness of the district. This was largely the case at Tai Tam Tuk after 1841, despite the proximity of Victoria and its

[1] Gordon-Cumming, op. cit., p. 24.
[2] See Lockhart, p. 43 and Orme, p. 53. See also Johnston, op. cit., for salting fish at Stanley in 1841-2.

trading marts, though there was a general decline of self-sufficiency as the century drew to its close.

My informants state that the villagers of Tai Tam Tuk were accustomed to doctor themselves with herbal remedies when they were indisposed or fell ill. This reliance upon herbal treatment is mentioned in an authoritative report on the adjacent area of the New Territories dated 1912 in which there is a list of efficacious herbs which could be gathered from the local hillsides.[1] These were prepared for medicinal purposes by knowledgeable persons, of whom there were always a few in each village, either persons who showed a special skill in this direction or had inherited it from preceding generations.

Turning from the care of the body to the nurture of the mind, self-reliance usually extended to the field of education. In nineteenth-century China the burden of providing education for village children lay with the elders of the villages acting, no doubt, in conjunction with the parents of children of school age. My enquiries into the villages of the Southern District of the present New Territories lead me to conclude that they took these responsibilities seriously. However, a village as small as Tai Tam Tuk would not usually attract a teacher because of the small number of potential scholars and the ensuing small stipend. Rev. Wilhelm Lobscheid[2] seems to indicate that there was no school at Tai Tam Tuk before the Hong Kong Government established one there in 1857. Writing in 1859 he says 'this romantically situated village is inhabited by Hakkas, all uneducated, and in a state of great poverty'.[3]

The new school got off to a good start with twenty-one scholars but soon dropped to about a dozen due, says Lobscheid, to the fact that 'parents have not yet learned the value of education and are consequently unwilling to make great sacrifices for their children'. He would have recommended closing the school had

[1] Orme, op. cit., Appendix F, p. 63.

[2] Rev. W. Lobscheid, *A Few Notices on the Extent of Chinese Education and the Government Schools of Hong Kong*, which was printed at the China Mail Office, Hong Kong, in 1859. I am grateful to Mr J. M. Braga who made this rare book available to me.

[3] Lobscheid, op. cit., p. 45. Rev. Ph. Winnes, writing in the *Report of the Morrison Education Society for 1863–64*, says: 'Popular education in this (San On) District . . . is, generally speaking, in a deplorable state as regards the Hakkas. We may find small villages in which scarcely *one* person is to be found who can read and write.' He attributed this state of affairs to poverty.

not the village headman solemnly promised a regular attendance of at least ten or twelve pupils. He goes on: 'I have therefore engaged an humble, willing teacher, who is satisfied with a small salary, and who will, I trust, by degrees raise the people from the low ebb of their deplorable ignorance.'[1]

This unpromising start appears to have characterized the school at Tai Tam Tuk for it seems to have a chequered history, and was not regarded highly by the authorities. When the inspector paid his annual visit in 1879 he found the school closed when it ought to have been in session,[2] whilst an earlier Education Report (1868) mentioned that the school was closed because the teacher had been indicted for highway robbery.[3] The Government school there seems to have been closed in the first decade of this century, though my informants tell me that a private school was still being conducted at the time the villagers moved from the valley.

The early records of Hong Kong and the surrounding area show that the local inhabitants had an unenviable reputation as pirates and robbers. There are many unflattering references of the kind which make this point.[4] However, these early reports tend to overlook the fact that, unlike the mass of immigrants to the new city of Victoria and its suburbs, who were largely single men with nothing to lose from occasional riot and unlawful activity, the majority of the inhabitants of the farming villages of Hong Kong island must have been generally indisposed to violence on account of their families, fields and houses and an established way of life.

In fact the village people had a good reputation. A guide to

[1] For this paragraph see Lobscheid, op. cit., p. 45.

[2] See *Supplements to the Annual Report on Government Education in Hong Kong*, III, Prize Distribution . . . 5–7 February 1880 (n.p.).

[3] Endacott, *History*, p. 229. See also his chapters XIII and XX for a general account of education policy in Hong Kong in the nineteenth century.

[4] See, for example, the account of Hong Kong given in Mayers, Dennys and King, op. cit. An example from the adjoining area is given by Rev. C. Gutzlaff in his *Sketch of Chinese History Ancient and Modern* (New York, 2 vols., 1834), vol. 2, p. 219. In October 1833 an old ship about to be broken up was laid on the beach near the Ke-aou island (near Macau). He goes on to say that the inhabitants 'who are generally dreaded as pirates' pilfered several valuable articles belonging to the vessel following which there was trouble between the villagers and the crew. The former turned out 'armed with matchlocks, pitchforks, knives, daggers and spears' and obviously appeared a most unsavoury lot to the ship's company.

navigation on the South China coast published in 1806 quotes a report on Hong Kong and its approaches dated September 1793 which says of the island,

> You will be supplied here with almost every kind of refreshment; especially fish, hogs, beef and poultry. We found the Inhabitants very civil and were daily on shoar at the Villages, and fowling in the interior parts of the Islands [*sic*].[1]

A few years after 1841, the botanist Robert Fortune wrote:

> In all my wanderings on the island, and also on the mainland hereabouts, I found the inhabitants harmless and civil. I have visited their glens and their mountains, their villages and small towns, and from all the intercourse I have had with them I am bound to give them this character.[2]

Another observer, McKenzie, speaking particularly of the Hong Kong villages, stated:

> The inhabitants, from our knowledge of their character, appear to be industrious and obliging. . . . From all accounts they seem in general to have been very peaceably disposed; nor did they exhibit any marked approbation or disapprobation, on their transfer to the British sway.[3]

In this connection, it is also interesting to note that when the Kowloon Peninsula was taken over by the British Government in 1860, the proclamation addressed to the inhabitants of the area was at pains to distinguish between 'the old inhabitants of this site who are indeed orderly people' and newcomers who were suspected of being 'thieves and outlaws'.[4]

From various accounts these people were under the control of their own elders when the island and, in due course, the adjoining

[1] See Dalrymple's *Observations on the Southern Coasts of China and the Island of Hainan*, London 1806, p. 20* (after p. 20 in the text).

[2] Robert Fortune, *Three Years Wanderings in the Northern Provinces of China*, London, Second Edition, 1847, p. 17. He qualifies his remarks slightly but the substance is as stated.

[3] K. S. Mckenzie, *Narrative of the Second Campaign in China*, London 1842, p. 160.

[4] For the Chinese and English versions of the proclamation see Government Notification 41 of 1860 dated 24 March 1860 in the Hong Kong Government *Gazette*.

area passed under British rule. In his *Closing Events of the Campaign in China* Captain Loch writes (again, possibly of Tai Tam Tuk):

> The path now wound round a tongue of land to the left into a small dell, where there were a few houses built in a line. The patriarch and ruler of this community was standing foremost, ready to receive us. This universal custom of acknowledging the superiority of age has been recognized by us throughout the island.[1]

McKenzie also mentions being entertained by a village elder 'during an excursion into the interior' of the island.[2]

---

[1] Captain G. G. Loch, *Closing Events of the Campaign in China*, London 1843, p. 21.

[2] McKenzie, op. cit., p. 163. It may be useful here to sketch the outline of the Chinese government's control of the area before 1841. Together with the other villages of Hong Kong island, Tai Tam Tuk was governed by a sub-district deputy magistrate from his *yamen* in the Kowloon Walled City. This officer was a subordinate of the district magistrate of the San On district whose *yamen* was inside the walled city of Nam Tau, outside the present Colony boundary, and was responsible for the administration of the whole district. It is unlikely that the villagers of Tai Tam Tuk ever saw either of these officers in person, unless one of their number had committed a serious crime beyond the jurisdiction of the elders. There was also a military officer at Kowloon and the villagers might have seen the patrolling vessels and their crews, representing a kind of marine constabulary, which came under his charge. His soldiers also manned the small posts located at various places in the surrounding area. (For background information from a later period see Krone's article mentioned above and Lockhart, op. cit., pp. 545–7, 551–2 and 563.) The subordinate government personnel were probably a nuisance to the people of the surrounding district in that their discipline was probably slack and they were demoralized by bribes and squeezes levied on opium and other smugglers using the anchorages between Hong Kong island and Lin-tin. See G. R. Sayer, *Hong Kong, Birth, Adolescence and Coming of Age*, London 1937, p. 33.

There does not seem to have been any civil or military establishment on Hong Kong island before 1841. Johnston, op. cit., wrote in 1843 'no public buildings were found on any part of the Island of Hongkong when it was first occupied by the English, except a small tumble-down Chinese house at Chek-choo (now Stanley) and another at Shek-pie-wan (now Aberdeen) where the petty mandarins stopped occasionally. . . .' These officers were probably engaged on police and tax collection duties. It is fairly certain that the villagers would have paid the imperial land tax. This was collected by officers who appear to have come from the district city. There are reports of the district magistrate's officers still attempting to collect land taxes at Stanley as late as 1844. (See Endacott, *History*, p. 57.) The boat people of Tai Tam Tuk may have been subject to the usual annual charge of 400 cash

The Hong Kong authorities were at first happy to adopt this method of government in the villages and elsewhere and gave these men official recognition as *tepos* or village constables.[1] In 1858 they instituted a salary for these men in order to brace them to their duties.[2] These sums appear in the yearly *Colonial Estimates* of the time. Because of the small size of the village, the *tepo* for Tai Tam Tuk received a salary of £12 10*s.* per annum which was one of the lowest salaries for these officers. However, this system was discontinued only a few years later when the Governor of the time introduced a cadet scheme for European officers whereby, it was considered, direct control could be exercised over local people.[3]

Notwithstanding the abandonment of the *tepo* system, there is evidence to show that the elders of the villages continued to exercise their authority as they had done long before 1841.[4] In a report on the land system of the Colony presented in 1887,[5] the Commissioners remarked that this was the case though they noted, with regret, that the people were more prone to take their problems for settlement to the triad elements in the local community rather than to the Government. At Tai Tam Tuk just before the village was removed for the reservoir, the oldest man in the Chung clan was regarded as the head of the community. He looked after the ancestral hall and took charge of the village weighing scales, though the negotiations with the Government seem to have been handled by Mrs Chung's father-in-law who was younger and more active. Generally, however, there were few problems of organization in the village because of its small size,

[1] See Endacott's *History*, pp. 26-7.

[2] See Ordnance No. 8 of 1858 in the Hong Kong Government *Gazette*.

[3] See Endacott's *History*, pp. 108 and 114.

[4] Eitel, op. cit., p. 166, writes in 1895, 'Yet although this (the *tepo*) system is now officially not recognized and has been replaced by the Registrar General's Office the Chinese secretly adhere to their own system faithfully. The Chinese people in town are at the present day under the sway of their own headmen (the Tungwa Hospital Committee) and the people in the villages are ruled by their elders, as much as ever.'

[5] See note 6, p. 32 above; also *Sessional Papers* 1887, Report, p. xxvi.

said to be levied on the 150 boats privileged to fish in local waters which, again, the San On magistrate was still trying to collect in 1844. (See Eitel, op. cit., p. 215.) However, after representations by the Hong Kong Government, the provincial treasurer of the Canton province indicated that any claims to the land tax would now be relinquished. (See Mayers, Dennys and King, op. cit., p. 59.)

and except in a crisis the villagers went about their own business individually, even in matters of ancestor worship.

By way of comment on the foregoing, the value of historical reconstructions of village life in Hong Kong fifty years ago and more is perhaps open to question on the grounds, some might say, that they cannot be considered typical of the pattern of life in Chinese villages outside British territory. On the other hand, the detail of life in the Hong Kong villages is given in the local Government's printed records, where information as to their population, land tenure, agriculture, health, education etc. are available in considerable detail for a continuous period of sixty years that begins soon after the occupation of Hong Kong in 1841. This is not the case with villages in nineteenth-century mainland China—nor even with those in the New Territories after the lease of the territory to Great Britain in 1898.[1]

But whilst this information is undeniably valuable for students of history and sociology, it is necessary to decide the extent to which it loses its intrinsic value because the island was under British rule. To answer this question one must establish the extent to which, if any, British rule and its effects removed any similarity in daily life and background between the Hong Kong villages and similar villages on the mainland. Whilst the final answer requires a detailed study of the Hong Kong villages of a kind that, so far as I know, has not yet been attempted, certain differences are obvious.

It is certain that greater security resulted from British rule because it was direct and close at hand: this is attested by many reports for the early years of the Colony which show the gradual diminution in crimes of violence and of the unwelcome attentions of gangs of hill robbers or pirate bands.[2] Though remote, Tai Tam Tuk must have benefited from the police station which was situated at Stanley from 1845 onwards,[3] and from the considerable number of troops that were stationed there in the

---

[1] The section of the *Blue Books* dealing with the agriculture of the New Territories gives useful figures for produce in respect of areas between 1905–8, but thereafter only gives total figures. Moreover, the files of the District Administration, New Territories for the period up to 1941 were destroyed during the Japanese War.

[2] See, for instance, Mayers, Dennys and King, op. cit., and Government publications for the period.

[3] See the *Blue Book* for 1846 published in *Reports on the Past and Present State of Her Majesty's Colony Possessions 1846* (London, Clowes & Sons for H.M.S.O.), p. 235.

nineteenth century.[1] Equally, piracy in local waters, planned and executed from British territory, seems to have become less common after 1866 due to the measures then taken by Governor McDonnell.[2] Of course, the Hong Kong villagers themselves were probably not entirely blameless beings. Though basically settled, with much to lose from unrest and actual disturbance, they were probably not above taking opportunities for gain and resorting to violence if the need arose or was thrust gratuitously upon them. But as was the case with violence imposed from outside, villagers' own opportunities for unlawful gain and riotous conduct diminished considerably with the imposition of settled British rule.

Certain other important characteristics of Chinese rule were also removed. In the matter of land administration the British Government seems to have put a stop to the general 'overlordship' of absentee landlords and their practice, apparently without proper justification, of levying charges on a greater area of land than was actually registered in their name—though this seems to have been tolerated by the Chinese authorities. Such levies were apparently a feature of land tenure on Hong Kong island before 1841 and something which villagers had perforce to accept whatever the rights or wrongs of the situation. They continued to be made in many of the present New Territories' villages until this considerable area was added to the Colony in 1898, after which the British Government put a stop to it there also.[3]

[1] See, for instance, p. 5 of a *Report on the Sanitary Condition of Hong Kong and Kowloon for 1864* prescribed to both Houses of Parliament by Command of His Majesty in 1865 (Military).

[2] See the Harbour Master's Report for 1887 in *Sessional Papers*, September 1887–December 1888, p. 258.

[3] This subject is not well-documented nor, apparently, is very much known of it at the present time. The Tang family, a rich and powerful Cantonese clan whose main estate lay in the present New Territories, were apparently the registered owners of most of the cultivated areas of Hong Kong island before 1841 (see Sung Hok-pang 'Legends and Stories of the New Territories', Part III, Kam Tin, in *The Hong Kong Naturalist*, vol. VI, 1935, pp. 212–18, especially p. 212, and vol. VIII, 1937–8, pp. 201–7, especially p. 205; also Mayers, Dennys and King, op. cit., pp. 2–3). Lobscheid, op. cit., p. 36 was told by the headman of a Hong Kong village near Aberdeen in the 1850s that his first ancestor to arrive there *circa* 1668 took a lease from Tang 'the acknowledged owner of the soil'. To what extent the Tangs levied legitimate rent charges, or exacted rent for greater areas than they were in fact the proper owners, is not known but they were seemingly guilty of the

The significance of these charges and the fact that they were stopped in Hong Kong after 1841, and in the New Territories after 1898, is that, in this and other ways, the villagers were rid of the, for them, close and frequently harmful connection between the land-owning scholar gentry and the local authorities that was an established feature of Chinese district rule. To this extent, therefore, it must be accepted that the background of 'interest' and influence which so frequently dictated events in Chinese villages was different in Hong Kong after 1841.

However, it also appears that the daily life and internal affairs of the villagers were otherwise little affected by the change-over. This enhances the value of the returns relating to the Hong Kong villages, and since the main differences are obvious enough, accounts of these communities may still be presumed to have some value for historians and sociologists.

---

latter elsewhere, albeit these charges were inconsiderable. See pp. 10–11 and notes 44–5 of my article on the Kowloon Villages in 1898 quoted above and note 12 to my article on Cheung Chau 1850–98, *Journal of the Hong Kong Branch of the Royal Asiatic Society*, 1963. I quote from the former, p. 11:

> These rent charges are mentioned in the various reports of the New Territories Land Court which determined the possession of land after 1898. It is not certain on what basis the Tang clan made its charges for the So Uk area, but reliable information in respect of other places makes it clear that they were almost certainly the recognized owners of at least part of the land for which they took payment. For instance, when in 1862 the southern part of the Kowloon peninsula passed into British hands, 169 'red deeds' (i.e. registered documents bearing the official red chop) were produced to the Anglo-Chinese Land Commission on demand, of which 78 were held by the Tang (Teng) clan . . . in respect of 276 acres, out of a total of 452 acres of land in private hands.

The Tangs' ownership of land in Hong Kong island seems to have gone back before the establishment of the San On district in 1573 as in his article quoted above Sung states that the entries were in the land registers of the Tung Kwun district, which before that date embraced the whole of the later San On district.

For a recent interesting review of certain aspects of Southeastern Chinese society during the last hundred and fifty years, from the viewpoint of a social anthropologist, see Maurice Freedman's *Lineage Organization in Southeastern China* (London 1958) which relates to Fukien and Kwangtung. A paperback edition was published in 1965. Professor Freedman has followed up this earlier work with his *Chinese Lineage and Society: Fukien and Kwangtung* (London 1966) which makes use of newer literature, older writings that he had not previously used and his own field work in Hong Kong in 1963.

III

CULTURE AND SOCIETY OF A
HAKKA COMMUNITY ON
LANTAU ISLAND, HONG KONG
Ronald Ng

Within the last hundred years, there have been great changes in
every corner of these four hundred square miles of the South
China coast. In 1923 Dr Sun Yat Sen was able to remark that
there had been more modification in less than a century here in
Hong Kong than had been seen in China with a history of four
thousand years. Even though the changes have been rapid and
significant, they have not occurred with the same degree of intensity in all parts of the Colony. In some of the more remote
areas glimpses of the past can still be traced. The community of
Tung Chung is one of many amongst this type but it is certainly
the largest of them all both in terms of area and of population.

Remoteness from the developed centres of population in the
Colony has allowed the Tung Chung Valley community to retain
its traditional way of life with all its grandeurs as well as its
shortcomings. Though there are several much-frequented over-
land routes to other relatively densely populated parts on Lantau,
contact with the city is provided only by the daily ferry service
which plies between the island and Hong Kong at inconvenient
hours—inconvenient at least for the city dwellers who would
generally find it difficult to make a daily excursion to Tung Chung
on most days of the week. The comparatively high fare charged
is another hindrance to a merger of city and rural life. Cheung
Chau at equal distance from Victoria is what it is today, a suburban residential township, largely because of its more frequent and
efficient ferry link with the city enabling people to live on that
island and work in town and at the same time enjoy the lower cost
of living.

The fourteen villages in the Tung Chung community have a
sizeable fishing settlement attached to them. The land and sea
communities are interdependent in more than one way and should
be considered an integral entity. The harvest of the sea is daily ex-
changed with the produce from the land. Money is used in all transactions but it has only a very short journey to take. The proceeds

from the sales of fish go almost immediately to the shops which in turn pay it to the farmers for the grain purchased. The requirements of the people are low and their wants few. Food is their chief concern and its carbohydrate and protein composition is kept in a nice balance by this mutual exchange. They constitute an interesting case of 'symbiosis' in which the subsistence economy of both groups is rendered complete by this crude system of division of labour, not between various members of any particular village but rather between two entirely different ethnic groups each specializing in its own trade. Hakkas in many areas have to participate in coastal fishing and trapping in order to supply their own source of protein, but in Tung Chung this job is trusted to a people which these land-owning Hakkas considered inferior.

Tung Chung is one of the few communities in the New Territories which can boast of a large number of emigrants. However, there are hardly any emigrants as such—they are mainly 'expatriates' if the term is extended to include all those who work outside the valley and send back regular remittances to support their families at home. The native village is their home base and they all make occasional visits: the younger ones to contract a marriage suit, the older ones to spend a festival or vacation with their families and eventually to retire to the village, wealthy and leisured. Though the community has sent generations of young men to work in the city or places abroad, it has not lost a single family to them. One of the things the average villager fears most is to be rootless and adrift in the world. When the ancestral home has to be abandoned, sometimes for as trivial a reason as the suspicion of the luck of the village having run out, the whole village will act as a single unit under the direction of a body of elders.

On the other hand, not many recent immigrants have been encouraged to settle in a community like that of Tung Chung. This might be the result of a lack of economic incentive to go to these remoter areas. Refugees are constantly searching for a better livelihood; that is one of the reasons why they left their native land in the first place. Economically disadvantageous effects of distance on agriculture can be offset against lower rents and this in the past attracted a number of refugees to Tung Chung. Many of these settlers found that their patience ran out and they left the valley but others adapted themselves to such an extent that it is almost impossible to differentiate them from the local populace—apart from the accent which they can hardly alter, and the sites of their dwellings which are specified in such a way as not to impede the 'fung shui' or the 'natural harmony' of the villages.

1 The Hakka background

Little do the Hakka remember that *their* ancestors were once, like these refugees, driven south by political and economic circumstances. The original home of this migratory people[1] was somewhere on the Shantung peninsula of North China. After several waves of barbaric invasions and successive periods of crop failure and famine the Hakka were forced to leave their home in search of new land. The process started in the fourth century A.D. and by the time of the establishment of the Ching Dynasty in the seventeenth century, the migratory wave had reached the south China coast. Twentieth-century migration of the Hakka has been mainly directed overseas. These Hakka Chinese have been of particular importance in the economic development of most South-East Asian countries.

It was probably in the few years after 1669 that the first Hakkas began to settle in Tung Chung. Long before the arrival of these immigrants, Lantau had been an important trading post on the Chinese coast. Contacts with the outer world had already been established by the first century of the Christian era.[2] The next few centuries saw rapid replacement of the primitive tribes by migrating Han Chinese. By 1278, Tung Chung was important enough to have attracted the wandering court of the last Sung Emperors to stay in the valley for several months. Under Mongolian rule, Lantau and Hong Kong became a haunt of pirates, but with another change of dynasty the area was once again peopled by peaceful and industrious settlers from the neighbouring districts.[3] When the Hakkas reached the Hong Kong vicinity, they found that all the best land was already under cultivation by the Punti, as the locals are still called. But fortunately, for the Hakkas at

[1] The Hakka has even been described as of a different race from the Chinese!

[2] Lo Hsiang Lin, *Hong Kong and its External Communications Before 1842*, Hong Kong 1963, p. 2.

[3] E. J. Eitel, *Europe in China*, London and Hong Kong 1895, p. 127.

least, the Manchu emperor ordered an evacuation of the coast for fear of the remnants of the defeated Chinese dynasty staging a comeback. This royal edict was repealed on the recommendation of a local Mandarin who reported the desolation of the coastal areas which immediately fell into the hands of the pirates, as well as the hardships suffered by masses of dying evacuees who had swelled the ranks of beggars and thieves in Canton city. When the survivors were allowed to go home after a sojourn of seven years, they found the Hakkas following closely in their wake. These hardworking and land-hungry immigrants occupied all the land left vacant and immediately set to work on developing new fields by clearing the forest and terracing the slopes. The Hakkas are known for their remarkable dexterity in shaping and using stone for building purposes, so in a very short time the cultivated acreage was almost doubled. But the removal of the forest cover, which disturbed the ecological balance, initiated violent outbreaks of malaria. It seems that these vigorous migrant Hakkas stood up to the challenging situation much better than the Puntis. More-over, continuous immigration permitted a rapid increase of the Hakka population in spite of recurrent heavy losses to malaria.

Apart from their acquired ability to survive, the Hakkas have several other distinguishing characteristics. Many writers who have been associated with, or studied, them seem to have become admirers. For example, Eitel considers them the cream of the Chinese race[1] and Victor Purcell thinks them the most deter-minedly independent.[2] On the whole, the average Hakka strikes the casual visitor as an individual who is hard-working, con-scientious, physically as well as mentally determined, neat and tidy.

The Hakka is often praised for his love of work. But this would not be apparent from a glimpse at the rural scene in a Hakka community. In every village, one finds women hard at work in both house and field while the men sip tea in the village cafe. Most of the children go to school and do not participate in farm work to the same degree as those in Punti (or Cantonese) com-munities. This has been explained by some as a manifestation of the great obedience and respect owed to the men, but in reality, it is the result of cultural and economic factors. As late-comers to already highly developed agricultural areas, the Hakka seldom

---

[1] E. J. Eitel, *Ethnological Sketches of Hakkachinese: an outline History*.
[2] Victor Purcell, *The Chinese in Malaya*, London 1948.

found enough land for their subsistence and even if land was available, it was of such an inferior quality that it was difficult to make ends meet by agricultural resources alone. They were thus worse off than other Chinese when faced with rising population. Emigration was the only possible outlet and it has become part of the culture that the able-bodied must leave the village to seek work in a new land, braving the future to better the fortune of the family. The responsibility for the family, including the farm, is left entirely in the hands of the eldest in the family, in lineage if not also in age. The males in the village are therefore either too young to go out to work or too old to labour under the hot sun. Thus one part of them chant loudly the lessons taught by the school master, the other retell stories of Sandakan, Ipoh, Djakarta or even London and Liverpool.

2   The daily routine

Village activity is concentrated between dawn and dusk. The twelve to fourteen hours in-between see a lot of work done. A brief meal is served in the morning to mark the beginning of the working day. If the cattle are on the plain, they are led to the slopes to graze on the coarse grass. This task is performed by children not attending school or by the elderly women. The younger females go round the rice fields and do whatever there is to be done and come home to prepare the noonday meal. Afterwards, more farm work is done until the whole family returns to take the fullest meal of the day. The rest of the daylight hours are spent in the courtyard chatting and doing odd things around the house.

There is a marked difference between the rhythm of farm work in the various seasons of the year. The cycle of activities is governed by rice cultivation, and labour requirements are most unevenly distributed. In the three peak periods, each lasting for about a fortnight, planting or harvesting occupy most of the day and the meals are prepared in the morning and brought to the field in bamboo baskets. Those who have a few children to run around can have a constant supply of hot green tea, others have to do with cold tea, for not a moment can be spared and the fields may be a considerable distance away from the homestead. Very often, the baby is carried on the back while the mother does the back-breaking job of transplanting rice. When the crops are in the field, there is relatively little work to be done. In bygone days the women engaged in some weaving, joss-stick making, and tea-preparing work. With the introduction of manufactured items and the falling off of prices of native products, these industries have since gone out of production. After planting a crop of sweet potatoes in the harvested part of the rice fields, the villagers spend much of the winter season collecting firewood from the hillsides.

The usual working team consists of the mother and wife of an emigrant. Males only stay in the village until they are sixteen or so and then leave for the city or places abroad. They have so little training and experience in farm work that few of those who have returned and retired can participate in the field processes. In fact, if they have to work this reflects the unreliability of the junior members of the family.

3 Village organization

The chief role played by those who have returned to the village after a lifetime of experience abroad, is to act as leaders of the village community. The village headman, now instituted as the Village Representative sitting on the Rural Committee, is the key figure in Hakka village organization. To him is owed the respect and obedience of all members in the village. This may be seen as the inevitable result of the long years of migration into a hostile land in which the newcomers had to group around a leader for protection. The Representative is supposed to be elected once every five years, but it is apparent who is to be chosen beforehand. This leader is usually the most senior in the lineage of the clan. If the village is multi-clan, he belongs to the dominant clan.[1] Power vested in him is never specific but he forms an invaluable liason between the villagers and the Government District Office and the Police. He also arbitrates in village and family disputes. When a decision is reached, sometimes after consultation with other elders in the clan or the village, his words become law. Rural development is particularly easy when the Representative is knowledgeable and possesses a high degree of integrity. Affairs concerning several villages are brought forward in the Rural Committee, presided over by a Chairman elected from among

[1] On lineages and clans see Professor Potter's paper, especially note 1, p. 11.

the representatives. In a Hakka community there does not seem to be a decrease in the intensity of loyalty from family to clan, clan to village, or village to community as is experienced in other parts of the New Territories. This may largely account for the stability of Hakka Society.

A possible defect of the system may appear to be the lack of participation by young people, and power being vested in persons with a lower educational attainment than many others in the village. These elderly leaders may be less inclined to rapid progress and may not be well-versed in affairs of the modern world at large; yet they would certainly do better than the younger generation in commanding the respect of all ranks. Their experience, though often out of date, is a tremendous asset. They are responsible for the smooth functioning of the village organization by solving on the spot disputes concerning land, or water rights with very little more to rely upon than their own memory of what has been done before on a similar occasion. A younger person would find these problems difficult to solve as there are practically no written records for private arrangements honoured as precedents for all to observe. There is, for example, no document of any sort to indicate how the irrigation water from a particular co-operatively constructed weir should run and how long a certain field should be irrigated, or in time of drought which plots should have priority with the irrigation water.

Besides, the aspiration of today's educated young man is not to stay on the farm or even to become a village leader. The constantly expanding economy of the Colony and the rapid increase in industrial employment opportunities in the urban areas, offers great prospects to an educated farm youth, even though his education is only to primary level. The number of young men working away from Tung Chung is remarkable. It is a rare thing to find a young man behind a plough in the valley today. Dissatisfaction with the life of the village and inability to make use of the education obtained there are compelling reasons for these youths to leave the rural home to seek a better life in the city. On the other hand, as the village cost of living is lower than that of the urban areas, complete emigration of entire families from the village is still unusual because the wage offered is often not sufficient to maintain a family in the town. On the contrary, there are evacuated tenants from the cities settling in the less remote market towns to enjoy this benefit. The traditional

concept of having one's roots in the land and the more practical
consideration of having something to fall back on in times of
difficulty, are other factors preventing a complete withdrawal
from the village.

4 Ritual and belief

Many aspects of Hakka life are governed by superstitious observations, and the village Representatives are very often the sole
spokesmen in such matters. The Hakka have been exploiting
'*fung shui*' beliefs so much that a few of the better educated amongst
them have violently attacked those who adhere strictly to these
geomantic principles to the extent that they become detrimental
to traditionally Chinese concepts of high aspirations in life. It
must be noted that *fung shui* is not a religion of any kind. At best
it is but a 'pseudo-science' as a Cambridge scholar calls it.[1] It is
argued that the growth of population, honour and fortune of a
family, a clan, and a whole village hinge around the arrangement
of the elements of wind and water. This is taken to mean the
environmental setting, both immediate and distant, of the house,
the graves and the village. Then the whole environs, including
the vegetation cover around the village settlement, and even a
particular tree around the settlement are taken into account.
Fung shui has hindered the development of the rural areas. Proposed development projects have often been determinedly objected to on grounds of this superstition. There have been cases
like the demand for a guarantee against future loss of life if some
particular trees were removed in the course of building a road
linking the village with a nearby market town.

One of the finest expressions of Chinese culture is the tremendous influence of filial piety—which is carried over into the life
hereafter in the form of ancestor worship. Burials are often elaborate and there are several festivals commemorating the ancestors.
However, Hakka customs of burial are so much influenced by *fung
shui* beliefs that there are serious deviations from this general
code of behaviour. Coffins are buried roughly on the hillside
without raising even a tombstone. Worse still, they are exhumed
and transferred into urns placed in a shady spot on the lower
slopes, waiting for the geomancer to locate a spot with good *fung
shui* elements to ensure good fortune for the descendants. Some-

[1] J. Needham, *Science and Civilization of China*, vol. II, Cambridge 1963.

times a hundred years may lapse before a satisfactory site can be found and in this period of time many pieces of bone may be scattered and thus lost when the urns are broken by the cows grazing on the hills. Indeed, the number of burial sites found around each village is small in proportion to the population of the settlement.

It is believed that these urn-burials are the result of long years of migration through China. Because of filial piety, the bones of the ancestors were carried on the back as the family moved south. The idea was to find a suitable burial place in the new land so that the descendants could still worship the ancestors in their new home.

However, *fung shui* beliefs are not without practical advantages. The villagers consider what they call a *fung shui* grove around the village an abode of the mountain spirits who watch over the village fortune. It is also believed that living trees have the power to prevent evil spirits from penetrating the settlement. The maintenance of a grove of trees provides shade for humans and animals alike. Especially during the summer when the crops are in the field and there is little farm work to be done, the villagers spend much time out of doors chatting with neighbours or doing odd jobs. In earlier times pigs and chickens roamed the groves in search of food and were protected there from the tremendous heat of the tropical sun. Another indirect use is the protection afforded by the trees in helping to reduce the force of the typhoon gales and by forming a line of defence against bandit attacks. The dense foliage cools the breeze blowing through the village by evapo-transpiration and the leaves halt the dust and dirt carried by the wind, making the village a nicer place than it would otherwise be. Furthermore, the dead branches are collected for fuel. But the most important function of these trees seems to be that they afford protection against soil erosion and rolling boulders. Their existence ensures a high water table so that the village wells will be full even in the dry season. Though some of these advantages are no longer of great significance to the villagers, the presence of the *fung shui* grove will always be advantageous to the village.

It is quite often erroneously thought that the rural peasants are a highly religious people on account of the huge quantities of joss-sticks burnt. When the villagers are asked of their religious beliefs, their usual reply is either 'believing in god' or 'worshipping god'. This 'god' is not Buddha, as is so frequently assumed. The term embraces a whole range of spirits of one form or another including trees and stones of odd shapes. In reality, this 'religious belief' is but a manifestation of superstition. The essence of folk beliefs comes in the form of a bargaining with nature for ensuring longevity, continuation of the lineage, fortune of the person and the family or a good crop. Though Hakka is not the only group of Chinese who does this, it is certainly more influenced by superstitions than the others. This is not difficult to understand as the Hakkas were a migrating group settling in areas almost totally different from their home in north China. When these pioneers were living close to nature with very little power to ameliorate the natural environment to suit their life and requirements, they might be expected to turn to a form of nature-worship in almost a state of hopelessness. Malaria, for example, was prevalent in Tung Chung for centuries and the only 'medicine' used was the ash of a piece of yellow paper with a specific inscription supposed to have the charm of warding off the evil spirit who had been causing the trouble. The same applied to cattle diseases and infections where the cure was the hanging of a piece of red paper folded in the shape of a triangle, blessed at the village temple, around the neck of the affected animal. Even today, such methods are still resorted to until the case becomes urgent and only then a doctor or a veterinary officer is consulted.

The village temple has a great significance in the 'religious' life of the peasants. The idol worshipped by the villagers is a legendary hero of the Sung Dynasty who gave up his life in the service of his emperor when he was pursued by the invading Mongols. The deeds of this warrior have great appeal to these Hakka peasants who honour bravery and loyalty. The temple was erected in the first days of the settlement of Tung Chung valley by these immigrants from the north who naturally had great affection for a hero who had braved tremendous hardships like those experienced by these people. Ever since his deification, miraculous deeds have been attributed to this god. It is believed by the residents of Tung Chung that he has the power of giving advice of all types and can predict all fortunes. Therefore, the birthday of this god, almost observed as a thanksgiving ceremony, is treated with such reverence that large sums are spent every year on the sacrifices and feasting. The most important of all the implications is that this festival which is observed almost exclusively on Lantau, punctuates the life of the rural folk by giving them a much-needed term of holidays. The success of a Rural Committee session is measured by the grandeur of the celebrations at this particular festival where crowds of people are attracted from all the nearby districts. There is so much importance attached to this great festival that different dates have to be chosen for neighbouring districts so that they do not clash with each other.

In as many ways as one can imagine, this Hakka Community of Tung Chung represents one that belongs to bygone days. Indeed, the community can be said to have a 'fossil' form of life: so basic is its outlook and so superstitious are its beliefs. Tucked in a remote corner of the Colony, more than two hours away by a ferry that runs but once daily, Tung Chung retains much of its original characteristics, its charm and its peacefulness. But one cannot refrain from wondering whether the educated youngsters will put up with the lack of material progress and opportunities for self-advancement.[1]

[1] In addition to the books already mentioned, the following were consulted: E. J. Eitel, *An Outline History of Hakkas*, Hong Kong (n.d. 1895?), Kuo Shau Wah, *History and Culture of the Hakka People*, Taipeh 1963 (in Chinese), Lo Hsiang Lin, *An Introduction to the study of the Hakkas in its Ethnic, Historical, and Cultural Aspects*, Hsingning, Kwangtung, China, 1933 (in Chinese, with an English Abstract), Ta Chen, *Emigrant Communities in South China*, Shanghai 1939, J. W. Hayes, 'The Pattern of Life in the New Territories in 1898', *Journal of the Hong Kong Branch of the Royal Asiatic Society*, vol. 2, 1962, pp. 75–102, R. H. Tawney, *Land and Labour in China*, London 1932, Martin C. Yang, *A Chinese Village*, London 1947.

IV

SOCIAL STRUCTURE AND SOCIAL STRATIFICATION IN HONG KONG[1]

Judith Agassi

Up to 1949 and the establishment of the present Communist régime in China, the movement of population between Hong Kong and the neighbouring Kwangtung Province was rather free, and many of the urban Chinese inhabitants of Hong Kong were only temporary residents and maintained their ties with their ancestral homes in China. Each new major disturbance in Southern China would bring with it a wave of immigrants; some joined the ranks of the Overseas Chinese mainly in the countries of south-east Asia, some would return home as soon as conditions had become more favourable, and only a few became permanent residents and British citizens. There grew up, however, a community of Hong-Kong-based Chinese merchant and banking families—some of them extremely prosperous, and they became the traditional spokesmen of the Hong Kong Chinese population.

Up to World War II Hong Kong's population was small. According to the 1931 Census there was then a population of 849,751 people living in Hong Kong, 96·85 per cent of the population were Chinese, and those born anywhere outside China constituted 3·15 per cent of the population. Britons manned most of the middle and upper grades of the Government apparatus, the police, and the British forces stationed here. Some of the British residents and most of the other non-Chinese belonged to the international commercial community of Hong Kong.

The urban population lived in the two cities of Victoria and Kowloon. The urban economy centred round Hong Kong harbour's role in the entrepôt trade with China: trading, banking, shipping, ship chandling, compradores, and shipbuilding and breaking. Though there were quite a number of artisans practising the traditional Chinese handicrafts there was hardly any industry.

---

[1] An unpublished paper prepared as a trends report for an International Symposium on 'A Cross National Research on Social Stratification and Social Mobility in Asian Countries', organized by the Centre for East Asian Cultural Studies in Tokyo in April 1963, Chairman Professor K. Odaka.

With the Japanese invasion of China in 1941 a wave of immigrants reached the Colony. The Japanese after occupying Hong Kong interned the 'enemy aliens' who had not been evacuated. The recently swollen Chinese population declined rapidly, as many left looking for better conditions on the mainland. At the end of the Pacific War the entire population was only about half a million. The re-establishment of British sovereignty started the return to pre-war normalcy and also the return of many of the pre-war residents. Constitutional reforms gradually introducing internal self-government (in line with what was done in other British Colonies) were planned. But in 1949 the victory of the Communist armies in China brought about great changes: Britain speedily recognized the Peking régime; Peking, though officially claiming sovereignty over Hong Kong, in fact refrained from any action aimed at ousting the British authorities. Nevertheless the mere continued existence of Hong Kong as a separate political entity became from this date onwards dependent on external, near-imponderable factors.

1   The post-war industrial revolution

At the same time a growing stream of refugees poured into the tiny Colony. The majority were villagers and townspeople from Kwangtung Province and from the city of Canton. But there arrived also considerable numbers of refugees from other parts of China: industrialists and businessmen, especially from Shanghai, bringing with them capital, know-how and international business connections; professional people and academics from all over China; Nationalist government functionaries and army officers who did not want to settle in Taiwan.

The traditional China trade which had been already disrupted by war, Civil War and Revolution, came to a standstill with the western embargo which followed the outbreak of the Korean war in 1950. Immigration continued to remain high for several years and then levelled off to an estimated 60,000 a year; the population was found to be 3,133,131 in the 1961 Census. 1962 brought another wave of 'illegal' immigrants and the population is now estimated at $3\frac{1}{2}$–4 millions. Fortunately the economic situation was saved by an astonishingly quick industrial revolution using the availability in Hong Kong at the same time of capital, know-how and business-connections as well as a near-unlimited supply of cheap labour; additional favourable circumstances for investment in industry were the relatively high adaptability and diligence of this labour force, the weak trade-union organization, the lack of legislation fixing minimum wages and limiting working hours and the extremely low taxation on business profits.

2 Occupational groups

The following picture of the relative importance of the various branches of the economy—as far as employment goes—emerges from the tables of the 1961 Census: 40 per cent of the labour force is now employed by industry. The main industry is textiles, which employs over 16 per cent of the labour force; other branches are food, paper and printing, metal, plastics, leather, rubber, chemicals, and lately also electronics. Some are fairly large and modern but there exist also a great number of very small, family-type undertakings that possess only very simple industrial equipment, are financially rather weak, and are completely dependent on favourable market conditions.

Trade union activity has continued to be rather weak and is split between Communist and Nationalist organizations and only the working hours of women and young persons have been restricted by law. Nevertheless wages, especially of several kinds of skilled workers, where a shortage has been felt, have been rising steadily. There is little prolonged unemployment, but very little security of employment; there still exists no unemployment insurance or benefits and not even a public labour-exchange.

Side by side with modern industry the traditional trades—such as ivory- jade- and wood-carving and embroidery—continue to be practised—often with the help of some machinery. These oriental arts and crafts as well as custom-tailoring find a market among the ever-growing stream of visiting tourists.[1]

A great deal of construction work is being done; office blocks and luxury hotels are going up at a quick rate; as a result of the mass immigration there exists an acute housing shortage, especially for lower-priced housing. The building industry is booming and extremely lucrative. Investment in building sites and the construction of tenements, flats, and offices seems to be the current Hong Kong recipe for accumulating wealth rapidly.

---

[1] Figures for 1966 are 505,733 (estimate: *Hong Kong Annual Report* 1966, p. 166), and this figure excludes servicemen.

Though shipping and commerce no longer occupy first place in the economy, Hong Kong still serves as an important port of transit, with more than 12,000 movements of ocean-going ships in and out of the harbour each year.

There is some shipbuilding—especially of small pleasure craft —ship-repairing, and shipbreaking is of importance.

Over 14 per cent of the labour force are employed in all forms of commerce. Of these a disproportionately large number seem to be occupied in the retail trade. Over 100,000 persons try to make a living as hawkers and newsboys.

In spite of the rapid industrialization, domestic service still is a numerous occupation; in fact the 'amahs' form the largest single occupational group (18·78 per cent) among women in the labour force. As far as income and standard of living goes, domestic servants who have free accommodation and utilities in addition to their money wages are better off than most unskilled and semi-skilled women workers in other employment, and their wages have been rising steadily.

5·08 per cent of the working population are classified as 'professional', 3·32 per cent as 'managerial', and 6·49 per cent as 'office and clerical workers'. The government services and the urban services are progressively being manned by Chinese—though the top administrative positions are still predominantly occupied by British Colonial Servants. While in 1958 only 34·80 per cent of the posts in Class I and II, the professional and administrative classes in the public service, were held by Chinese, the current (1964) figure is 46·3 per cent.[1]

It is interesting that only 3·96 per cent of the working population obtain their living from farming and forestry, and 3·40 per cent from fishing. As rural families in Hong Kong are not appreciably larger than urban families, this means that the population of the Colony of Hong Kong is now overwhelmingly urban and dependent on industry and commerce for their living. Only 29·66 per cent of the heads of farming households give as their principal crop the traditional wet-rice growing, whereas 35·9 per cent grow mainly vegetables. Many of these vegetable farmers do not belong to the indigenous Hong Kong farming population but are recent immigrant farmers who rent their plots from the indigenous villagers. Other sizable agricultural groups are the

[1] See footnote 3, p. xiii of the Introduction to this volume for further discussion.

14·22 per cent of farmers who are principally pig keepers and the 11·28 per cent who are principally poultry keepers.

The growing importance of vegetable growing, pig and poultry raising as compared to rice growing is due to the large, ever-growing, and easily accessible urban market for these products. It is interesting to note that only the families of the conservative rice-growers are on the average larger than those of the population at large.

3   Rate of economic participation

Out of a population of 3,133,131 in 1961, 1,211,999 were 'economically active', and of these 864,795 were men and 347,204 were women. The rate of males aged 15 and over who are 'economically active' is as high as 90·5 per cent—compared with 85 per cent in Japan. Most of the 'economically inactive' women are to be found among the 472,949 housewives (however 2,043 of the 'housewives' are men!).

But the bulk of the 'economically inactive', 51·92 per cent were to be found among the 1,277,035 children of 14 years and under who formed 40·8 per cent of the population. A number of children, 24,452, mainly between the ages of 10–14 who are not attending school, are at work and no doubt more act as unpaid family workers; the employment of children under 14 is illegal but the law is not observed very strictly and it is not likely to be kept as long as primary schooling is not made compulsory and free.

14·05 per cent of the population—a very high percentage—were infants four years old and under, who, as they need constant attention naturally also restrict their mothers' capacity for 'economic activity'.

There are relatively many young persons aged 15 and over, 91,232 of whom are students. The age group 14–24 was found by the Census to be abnormally small, only 367,838 or 11·75 per cent (there were especially few 18- and 19-year-olds), obviously as a result of the severe conditions of life in South China from 1938 to 1945 and in Hong Kong from 1941 to 1945. Consequently the 91,232 students who overwhelmingly belong to this age group constitute nearly one quarter of it. There is also a much smaller group of vocational trainees and learners—only 11,172.

On the other hand the group at the other end of the age scale, those 65 and over, are relatively very few, only 87,918 or 2·99 per cent of the population and they account for only 5·26 per cent of the economically inactive. There are 21,175 persons classified as retired and pensioners. Therefore, while the young are a serious burden on the working population of Hong Kong, the old apparently are not.

In addition to the housewives, infants, students, and the old retired and pensioners, there are 56,426 persons classified as economically 'independent', not being employed, employers or working on their own account. This, in Hong Kong, does not mean that all these people are 'rentiers', i.e. living on the interest from a tidy sum of invested capital. In fact many of them are 'landlords' in a very small way, the majority not owning the flat or tenement they let, but being its chief tenant or even its sub-tenant; nevertheless they are able to live on the profit made by subletting parts of it. This abnormal situation is of course one of the results of the housing shortage.

4 Employment status

The 1961 Census registered the entire economically active population according to their 'employment status'. Though it gives no clear indication as to the income, standard of living or social status of those belonging to the different groups it is of some significance to the subject of this survey: nearly 1 million out of the nearly $1\frac{1}{4}$ million economically active are employees, 57,400 are employers and 123,861 work on their own account. The employers of course include the wealthy employer of hundreds as well as the many employers of one or two; those who work on their own account include some free-lancing professional people as well as the many hawkers and street-artisans. Among the employees, by far the largest group, 64 per cent, are classified as 'in-workers, permanent, paid at a monthly rate'. This group includes nearly all the salaried professional, managerial, administrative, clerical employees as well as many of the sales workers. It is therefore not clear what percentage of Hong Kong's manual workers has already achieved this usually more favourable and more secure status; nevertheless this group seems to be growing.

Nearly 10 per cent of the employees are permanent in-workers who are paid at a daily rate; over 5 per cent are casual in-workers and paid by piece-rate; slightly more are unpaid family workers (who work for their bed and board); and nearly 2 per cent are out-workers, nearly all of them women.

5 Income

No specific research into income, family budget and standard of living of Hong Kong's population has ever been undertaken and there exist no reliable and up-to-date statistics. The 1961 Census did not ask any questions pertaining to money income or expenditure.

However two unpublished surveys which were made in 1957 by research workers on the staff of the University of Hong Kong provide some useful information: The 'Resettlement Survey'[1] gives a picture of the incomes and family budgets of a sample from a selected group of people; all the families were housed in 'resettlement blocks', their squatter shacks having been demolished by the Government. The second survey, the 'Housing Survey',[2] chose a representative sample of the population with the exception of the squatters, a large and mostly low-income group; though chiefly interested in housing and rents, the survey also enquired into the total monthly money income of households. The result was that 55·6 per cent of those questioned living in regular accommodation had a monthly money income of HK$300 or less, and 87·4 per cent of those questioned among the resettled squatters were in this group.

Wages have risen somewhat since 1957. According to the *Annual Report* 1964 (p. 22) the usual daily wage-rates in 1964 in industry were the following:[3]

skilled	HK$8·60 — $26·00
semi-skilled	HK$5·30 — $14·50
unskilled	HK$4·80 — $9·50

According to these figures families which have only one breadwinner can only have a monthly income of over $300 if they are

[1] C. S. Hui, W. F. Maunder and J. Tsao, *Hong Kong's Resettled Squatters. The Final Report on the 1957 Sample Survey of Resettlement Estates*, typescript, available in the library of the University of Hong Kong.

[2] W. F. Maunder and E. F. Szczepanik, *University of Hong Kong, Hong Kong Housing Survey*, 1957, mimeo, available in the library of the University of Hong Kong.

[3] These figures showed a slight rise in 1965, only to fall again, in 1966, to the levels of 1964.

relatively well-paid skilled industrial workers. A great many sales workers and the lower grades of clerical workers are also still paid less than $300 per month. The number of those having salaries large enough to pay salaries' tax might be culled from the annual reports of the Inland Revenue Department.

6   Standard of living

There are in Hong Kong no signs of wide-spread hunger or any cases of starvation. However, medical examination of school-children in the poorer areas has discovered a high percentage of undernourishment. No reliable figures fixing a 'poverty-line' exist. It is clear that many unskilled workers are still paid a wage which is insufficient for the support of a family, and that only the high participation rate in work of the young, the old and of the women of the lowest income groups can keep those families going without resorting to charity. A good deal of assistance in money and in kind is given by the Government Welfare Department and numerous charitable organizations. Several of the latter also give free medical treatment, do vocational training and re-training, and give money-loans and equipment to make families self-supporting.

The greatest causes of acute poverty are chronic tuberculosis[1] or drug-addiction of the breadwinner[2]—and both are very considerable problems in Hong Kong. Otherwise there is little continued unemployment among the able-bodied.

The general impression is that standards of food are relatively high—few eat an absolutely monotonous and deficient diet—and that standards of clothing are relatively high and are rising. However the standards of housing of the mass of the population are depressingly low. A large part of the working-class—though working and able-bodied—cannot on the free market obtain any accommodation which is up to the minimum standards of living space and hygiene accepted in the west.

The cost of housing also constitutes the chief depressing factor on the standard of living of the 'lower middle classes'. They either have to live in overcrowded premises and without a minimum of privacy or to spend a disproportionately large part of their income on housing.

It has not been established if the relatively low cost of primary

---

[1] See Miss Ho's paper, below.
[2] See Dr Whisson's paper, below.

schooling constitutes a real burden on low-income families. It is, however, clear that the high cost of secondary education constitutes quite a burden on the 'lower middle classes', i.e. on the lower and middle grades of clerical workers, small shopkeepers, etc.

A rather prosperous, mainly commercial, and partly professional upper middle class seems to be growing. There is a constant demand for modern, well-appointed, and very expensive flats, and the number of private cars on the roads is constantly rising.

Hong Kong has since early times had a number of extremely rich businessmen. They are still in evidence and not shy of exhibiting their wealth.

7 Ranking of occupations

No reliable information exists on this subject. My superficial impression is that occupations are pretty well ranked according to the income they bring. An exception might be the desire of persons with an adequate degree of schooling to enter non-manual, white-collar occupations even if the job they can find brings in a salary which is lower than available manual jobs. There certainly exists a surplus of applicants for lower range clerical jobs while there is a scarcity of certain kinds of skilled construction workers and of sailors.[1]

The great majority of students, or their parents, seem to rank subjects of study according to the expected money return they will bring. There is little esteem for study and for the scholar as such.

8 Social mobility

Here again no specific research has yet been done. Hong Kong's society is overwhelmingly an immigrant society in the process of industrialization. It has a disproportionately large number of children and a small number of old people. However it is becoming more settled. The number of men is no longer so much in excess of that of women. The percentage of the Hong Kong born in the population is rising.

Most of the adults in the population have in the recent past broken their ties with their birthplace and former way of life.

---

[1] One certainly still frequently meets contempt for the 'coolies', for the men and women doing the heaviest kind of physical work.

Some obviously were forced to leave behind their possessions and positions and this meant a lowering of their social position. Immigrant professional people were faced with difficult examinations. For them the knowledge of English, and better still of English and Cantonese, is essential for success.

But for the great mass of immigrants Hong Kong meant either no lowering of standards of living or only a temporary one. Recent waves of immigrants left behind constant scarcity and malnutrition, and had lost most of the private property they had ever possessed.

Of course many came from rural surroundings and had to adjust to different occupations.

Kinship, also in the wider sense of common origin from the same 'clan'-village, is a great help in the absorption of immigrants; relatives provide temporary shelter and food and help to find jobs.

Though his wider family seems often to contribute to the expenses of study of a promising youngster, especially in the middle classes family ties and obligations seem to restrict the young in their attempts at making individual careers for themselves.

9   Education

Nevertheless the greatest factor for social mobility in Hong Kong is no doubt education. The rate of literacy has been rising considerably. In 1931 only 51 per cent of the population aged 10 and upward could read, 74 per cent of the men and only 19 per cent of the women. According to the 1961 Census 75 per cent of the population over 10 are now literate, 91 per cent of the men and 58 per cent of the women.

The great majority of children now receive primary schooling but many leave before completing it. School attendance is somewhat lower in rural areas and there are veritable pockets of illiteracy and very low school attendance among the boat-dwellers and among the Hoklo speaking communities.

While the lower income groups still send fewer of their daughters than of their sons to primary school, among the middle classes girls equally with boys are given secondary education. A considerable number of children of skilled workers and of the lower middle classes are sent to secondary schools at great sacrifice. There exists enormous pressure for success in the many examinations, as school certificates and diplomas are the recognized means for social betterment.

10 Language

93·25 per cent of the population were born either in Hong Kong or somewhere in Kwangtung Province. Cantonese is the language of the great majority. Indeed 86·2 per cent of the population usually speak Cantonese. Some indigenous farming and fishing communities speak Hakka, but most of their children and many of their adults also understand Cantonese. Only among the Hoklo speaking rural communities does there exist a real language barrier. There is also a group of middle-aged and elderly immigrants from the coastal provinces and Northern China who do not speak Cantonese.

The knowledge of English is a great economic advantage in Hong Kong. In spite of many years of teaching English only 8·73 per cent of the population speak both Cantonese and English, but this percentage certainly should be rising. The most-seriously handicapped are the 4·07 per cent who speak neither.

V

HONG KONG UNDER JAPANESE OCCUPATION: CHANGES IN SOCIAL STRUCTURE

Henry J. Lethbridge

1 *Avant le déluge*

The Japanese attack on the Crown Colony of Hong Kong was launched on 8 December 1941. After four days of fighting, the British garrison, composed of British, Canadian, and Indian troops, was forced to evacuate the New Territories and Kowloon peninsula and withdraw to Hong Kong Island for a last-ditch stand. The Japanese landed on the northern tip of the Island on 18 December and the Colony fell finally on Christmas Day, 1941, when Sir Mark Young, Governor and Commander-in-Chief, formally surrendered the Colony.[1] The Japanese remained in control of what they called the 'conquered territory of Hong Kong' until the issue of the Imperial rescript, accepting the Potsdam declaration, on 14 August 1945. On 16 August, the Colonial Secretary, Mr F. C. Gimson, interned in 1941, emerged from Stanley camp to re-establish authority and set up an emergency administration. When the task force despatched by the British Pacific Fleet entered Hong Kong harbour on 30 August 1945, he was there to greet Admiral Harcourt and to demonstrate that the colonial régime was back in business.[2]

During the occupation, which lasted a little over three-and-a-half years, the Japanese authorities attempted to eradicate all signs of previous British rule and western influence. The purpose of this paper is to examine some of the changes introduced or inspired by the Japanese and to assess their effects upon present Sino-British relations within Hong Kong. My thesis is that the

[1] See S. Woodburn Kirby, *The War Against Japan*, London 1957, vol. I, and *Despatch by Major-General C. W. Maltby on operations in Hong Kong from 8th to 25th December 1941* (Supplement to the *London Gazette* of 27 January 1948, No. 38216).

[2] An account of the re-establishment of civil government is given n F. S. V. Donnison, *British Military Administration in the Far East, 1943–1946*, London 1956, chs. VIII and XI. The Hong Kong Government *Annual Reports* for the years 1947–9 also contain much interesting material.

occupation worked ultimately to the benefit of the leaders of the Chinese community, for although never wanting a Chinese government in Hong Kong they had always worked to make the Government of Hong Kong 'their' Government. I also wish to show how, as a result of the occupation, the European business-men entered afterward into relationships with the post-war Hong Kong Government different from those which obtained before—relationships far less antagonistic.

The Japanese, although they failed in the long run to establish a Japanese New Order in Asia, succeeded in establishing the foundations of a New Order in Hong Kong, the structure of which has since become clear. This New Order may be roughly summed up in Carlyle's words on *laissez-faire* as 'anarchy plus the constable': the post-war Hong Kong Government moved far closer to business interests, whether Chinese or European, than in pre-war days. The blowing up in 1946 of the Japanese war memorial overlooking Wanchai gap, a huge pyramidal edifice, with a samurai sword concealed ritualistically in its foundations,[1] symbolized the end of Japanese military control but not, as I hope to demonstrate, a return to the rigidly stratified, Victorian-colonial society of 1941, dominated by the Peak (1,800 feet above the City of Victoria) and the 'Peak' mentality. The British Mandarinate collapsed in 1941: it has never been replaced.

In 1940 Hong Kong was a commercial, though not yet an important manufacturing, centre. It was principally a centre of international trade, an *entrepôt* highly sensitive to political and economic changes on the Chinese mainland; and an important military and naval base. The population then numbered approx-imately 1,846,000 of whom about 750,000 were refugees from the Sino-Japanese conflict.[2] In that year there were only some 800

[1] A considerable proportion of the money donated came from Chinese residents and associations. For example, the *Hong Kong News* of 12 December 1942, reported that Y. 2,500 had been donated by the Kowloon Rice-Sellers Syndicate. Most members of the Chinese Representative and Chinese Cooperative Councils felt obliged to donate; often these donations were a form of danegeld, sent to placate the predatory Japanese authorities.

[2] *1940 Blue Book* (Annual Blue Book of Statistics). The total population in the census year 1931 was given as 849,751 (the Chinese numbered 821,429, or 96·67 per cent of the population). The results of the 1931 census were published in an official report written by W. J. Carrie: see *Hong Kong Sessional Papers*, No. 5, of 1931. Some of the difficulties encountered by census takers in Hong Kong are discussed in the 1962 *Annual Report*, ch. 1, and in the three-volume *Report on the 1961 Census* by K. M. A. Barnett.

factories, employing about 30,000 workers.[1] Some index of Hong Kong's low level of economic activity compared with post-war growth is given by statistics for transport for that year: 4,400 private motor-cars, 360 motor-cycles, 385 public cars and taxis, 1,200 commercial motor lorries, and 109 tram-cars.[2] Compared with the present, Hong Kong was provincial (culturally it is still so), dowdy and quiet. Shanghai in the pre-war years was the natural habitat of that now almost extinct species, the Old China Hand, and the nerve-centre of western enterprise in the Far East. In Hong Kong, status was given, at least for the European, by position or rank,[3] in Shanghai by money; but Shanghai in the 1930s was a self-governing commercial community, like one of the cities of the medieval Hanseatic League—Hong Kong a Crown Colony administered by a caste of officials, mostly educated at public schools and finished at Oxbridge. The social differences between these two western-controlled enclaves on the China coast may be likened to that existing in nineteenth-century England between Birmingham, the home of the *parvenu* business-man, and London, the home of the genteel banker and broker.

Hong Kong's population in 1941 was split into two main groups, Europeans and Asians, poised against each other. Each contained a number of important sub-groups. At the top of the European pyramid were the colonial officials who had entered the colonial service as cadets straight out from England. If of superior rank, they lived mostly in the Peak District,[4] a desirable rural area then barred to Chinese residence, which they shared

[1] E. F. Szczepanik, *The Economic Growth of Hong Kong*, London 1958, p. 135.

[2] Figures given to Sir Shouson Chow by the Traffic Department of the Hong Kong Government. See *Hong Kong Commemorative Talks*, Hong Kong 1941, p. 70. The figures refer to the year 1939, but few cars were imported into Hong Kong after that date because of the war.

[3] Kitty, the heroine of Somerset Maugham's *The Painted Veil*, on arrival in the Colony soon became aware of status differences: 'Kitty, coming to Hong Kong on her marriage, had found it hard to reconcile herself to the fact that her social position was determined by her husband's position . . . she had understood quickly that as the wife of the Government bacteriologist she was of no particular consequence.' See *The Painted Veil*, London 1925, 1952, p. 18.

[4] The Peak District Reservation ordinance, No. 4 of 1904, states: ' "Peak District" means all that area of the Island of Hong Kong situated above the 788 feet contour . . . it includes Mount Cameron, Mount Gough, Mount Kellett and Victoria Peak.'

with the richer Taipans (bosses) and businessmen. Although Taipans were rich, higher colonial officials had, or at least thought they had, the social edge over them, and social and professional relationships between officials and businessmen were often uneasy, at times turbulent. The constitutional history of Hong Kong before the war, from the European point of view, was a battle between the commercial and business community to make Government move with the times in the interests of commerce and trade, and the attempt of Government to curb the hard-faced businessman, often of Scots ancestry, who refused to be soft-soaped by what he usually regarded as a supine administration too much in the pocket of the traditional Chinese. For example, the Kowloon Residents' Association formed in January 1921 (its members were Europeans), in a policy statement, criticized Government officials and the unofficial members of the Legislative Council on the grounds that their 'knowledge of local conditions was gleaned from a panoramic view of the peninsula from an elevation of 1,200 feet'.[1]

The clash between Government and business may be illustrated by the example of the 1894 petition for representative government organized by T. H. Whitehead of the Chartered Bank of India, Australia and China, supported by Thomas Jackson of the Hong Kong and Shanghai Banking Corporation, Paul Chater, a rich broker, and Dr Ho Kai, an influential spokesman of the Chinese. This petition, widely signed by the Hong Kong ratepayers, was despatched to Lord Ripon, the Secretary of State. Lord Ripon rejected most of the petitioners' arguments; but the following year the Governor saw fit to increase by two the number of unofficial members of the Legislative Council.[2] The 1894 petition was a high point in the conflict, but antagonisms remained until the fall of Hong Kong, and lingered on in Stanley camp for civilian internees. At Stanley the interned elected businessmen rather than officials to look after the camp and the interests of the inmates (although, of course, in high-level discussions with the Japanese, the Colonial Secretary took the lead).[3]

[1] See G. B. Endacott, *Government and People in Hong Kong, 1841-1962*, Hong Kong 1964, p. 144.

[2] See Endacott, op. cit., ch. 7, and the same author's *A History of Hong Kong*, London 1958, p. 244 ff.

[3] See John Stericker, *A Tear for the Dragon*, London 1958, pp. 160-1: 'What was left of the Europeans in this, a captive colony, elected their own new government to rule their small restricted world, and half the people

The Government of Hong Kong before 1941 was, therefore, in an invidious position. It was faced by two, at times truculent, opponents: a concentrated community of people from the British Isles and a 'native' population with strong emotional, although not always patriotic, ties towards the homeland, China, a resurgent nation of 500 million. Each of these groups wanted to influence the Government to promote either Chinese or European interests. Each wanted to make Government 'their' Government.

The 1931 census showed that few Chinese regarded Hong Kong as their home. Only 33 *per cent* stated that they had been born in Hong Kong. However, even this statement cannot be taken to mean that such persons thought of it as their permanent home. On the other hand, the establishment of the permanent Chinese cemetery at Aberdeen was important: 'it was a significant proof of the existence of what one might call the Hong Kong Chinese'.[1] No census was taken in 1941, but it seems safe to claim that the population of 'Hong Kong Chinese' had increased substantially by the date; so that there were in 1941 numbers of Chinese with a stake in Hong Kong keenly interested, not so much in throwing out the British, as in manipulating and using the Administration. These 'Hong Kong Chinese' would include those born in Hong Kong and those who had been settled in Hong Kong for a long time.

The Chinese community in 1941 was represented by three unofficial members of the Legislative Council and one unofficial member of the Executive Council. These were respectively: Lo Man-kam, Dr Li Shu-fan,[2] William Ngartsee Thomas Tam and

[1] Lennox A. Mills, *British Rule in Eastern Asia*, London 1942, p. 390.

[2] The Hong Kong Government *Gazette*, 20 June 1941, announced that the Hon. Mr Li Tse-fong had been appointed 'an unofficial member of the Legislative Council in succession to Dr Li Shu-fan'. There was also an unofficial member representing the Portuguese community: Mr Leo D'Almada e Castro, first appointed in 1937 in succession to Jose Pedro Braga.

who voted for this new government were government servants themselves. Of a great number of candidates, including several senior members of Government, after a fair election only the Commissioner of Police was elected to represent Government and he was elected by the Police Force, his sole parishioners. The internees, as a whole, willed their future to the heads of big companies. These included the giant combines such as Imperial Chemical Industries, Shell Oil, the British-American Tobacco Company, and the shipping firms of Jardine, Matheson and Butterfield and Swire . . . (but) we never denied that negotiations with the Japanese . . . were the duty of the Colonial Secretary.'

Sir Robert Hormus Kotewall. These Chinese non-officials were expected to advise the Government, particularly with regard to Chinese affairs. Naturally the British expected them to be Establishment front men, but they were seldom afraid to press vigorously their own points of view and that of the Chinese community as a whole. Robert S. Ward claims 'they were in fact little more than instruments of the British colonial government, and, whether as the result of deliberate selection or *faute de mieux*, they were rarely highly regarded by the Chinese themselves, and often they were not actually Chinese'.[1] But they were more than the 'instruments of the British colonial government' that Ward claims them to be: they were concerned to see that justice was done to themselves *as Chinese*, as non-Europeans. The British were forced to choose Chinese representatives from a restricted list of eligibles; candidates had to be British subjects because of the need to take an oath of allegiance, and men of substance, free to leave business concerns and attend weekly meetings and a variety of official functions. Nevertheless, they were chosen only *after* they had worked themselves up through a Chinese system of influence and power, understood and accepted by the Government itself. Even before a Chinese reached the Legislative or Executive Council, he was vetted by his own community.

In brief, a Chinese on the way up had several possible moves to make. One much trodden road was to be made an unofficial Justice of the Peace and to seek to become a member of the District Watch Committee[2] or the Urban Council or a director of

[1] Robert S. Ward, *Asia for the Asiatics*, Chicago 1945, p. 14.

[2] In 1946 it was decided that the District Watch system was out of date. The force now consists of fifty District Watchmen who are paid by Government to perform certain duties for the Chinese Secretariat, which would otherwise fall on the regular police. In 1941 the District Watch Committee had the following members: The Secretary for Chinese Affairs (chairman), Sir Shouson Chow, Sir Robert Kotewall, Li Po-kwai, Ts'o See-wan, Chau Tsun-nin, Lo Man-kam, Wong Ping-sun, Tam Woon-tong, Dr Li Shu-fan, William Ngartsee Thomas Tam, Li Jowson, Li Tse-fong, Samuel Macomber Churn, Ngau Shing-kwan. The Tung Wah Hospital Advisory Board then comprised: The Secretary for Chinese Affairs, Sir Robert Kotewall, Lo Man-kam, Dr Li Shu-fan, Sir Robert Ho Tung, Ts'o Seen-wan, Li Po-kwai, Chau Tsun-nin, Wong Ping-sun, Tang Shiu-kin, Chau Shiu-ng, Lo Min-nung, and Yeung Wing-hong. The Po Leung Kuk (Society for the Protection of Virtue, i.e. for the protection of women and girls) Permanent Board of Directors was another key Chinese association. In 1941 the directors were: The Secretary for Chinese Affairs (President), Sir Robert Kotewall, Lo

the Tung Wah Hospital or some other similar association. The District Watch Committee was a body of some 120 Chinese constables and detectives, maintained by private subscription and controlled by a committee of fifteen Chinese, which met under the chairmanship of the Secretary for Chinese Affairs. The duty of the District Watch was to patrol certain Chinese districts, but its committee developed into an informal advisory council on Chinese affairs. The Tung Wah, a charitable association founded in 1870, with prominent Chinese as its directors, was mainly engaged in tending the sick; but the Tung Wah's committee also developed an advisory role and was consulted by Government. The Urban Council evolved from the Sanitary Board set up in 1883; with the introduction of election in 1887 the Board became a type of municipal council concerned primarily with the maintenance of public health. In 1936 the Sanitary Board was replaced by the Urban Council, with eight unofficial members, three of them Chinese nominated by the Governor. A rich Chinese whose income did not derive from the practice of one of the professions or who lacked inherited or landed wealth would normally seek to be admitted to one or all of these and other associations and so, together with a display of public munificence, enhance his status.

The banker Li Tse-fong[1] (later to play an important role in the Chinese Representative Council established by the Japanese) became an unofficial Justice of the Peace in 1931, a member of the District Watch in 1940, and unofficial member of the Legislative Council in 1941. He was also a member of the Board of Review, the Board of Education, the Auditors Advisory Committee (For Accounts in Chinese), a member of the Court of the University of Hong Kong and was appointed by the Governor in 1940 to the

---

[1] The *Business Directory of Hong Kong, Canton and Macau*, Hong Kong, Far Eastern Corporation, 1939, lists Li Tse-Fong as Managing Director, and Sir Shouson Chow as the Chairman, of the Bank of East Asia, Ltd. See also *Hong Kong Directory, 1953*, p. 1281.

Man-kam, Dr Li Shu-fan, William Ngartsee Thomas Tam, Li Po-kwai, Au Lim-chuen, Tam Woon-tong, Ts'o Seen-wan, Sir Robert Ho Tung, Chau Tsun-nin, Tang Shiu-kin. The Chinese members of the Urban Council in 1941 were: Dr Chau Sik-nin, Tang Shiu-kin and Li Tse-fong. Dr Chau was an elected and the others appointed members. See *Hong Kong Civil Service List for 1941*, Hong Kong 1941.

Urban Council. The businessman, Sir Robert Kotewall[1] (later, under the name of Lo Kuk-wo, chairman of the Chinese Representative Council) was made a Justice of the Peace in 1916, an unofficial member of the Legislative Council in 1923, and an unofficial member of the Executive Council in 1936. Membership of the last meant that Sir Robert had finally arrived at the top. In between these important translations Sir Robert, among other things, became a member of the Court and Council of Hong Kong University and a member of the Executive Committee of the Chinese Chamber of Commerce.

To achieve high status, usually a function of wealth for the Chinese in Hong Kong, for the higher reaches of the civil service were closed and there was no native gentry class, a Chinese had to 'buy' himself into various social positions by displays of munificence and as noted above, by participation in a wide range of charitable and welfare organizations known to the Chinese community. To achieve high status a Chinese had, therefore, to prove himself by public works.[2] Broadly speaking, the leaders of the urban

[1] Sir Robert Hormus Kotewall (1880–1949): Kt., cr. 1938; C.M.G., 1927; Ll.D. (Hon.), 1926. Son of Hormusjee Rustomjee Kotewall, yarn merchant. Educated at Queen's College and Diocesan Boys' School. Entered the Hong Kong Civil Service in 1896 as a Fourth Clerk in the Police Headquarters, after a competitive examination in which he came first of the candidates. Promoted to be First Clerk in the Magistrate's Court, Victoria, in 1913. In 1916 he was appointed Chief Clerk in the Colonial Secretariat and in the same year was made a Justice of the Peace. Resigned from the Civil Service the same year and was invited by Lau Chu-pak and Ho Fook (both former unofficial members of the Legislative Council) to become a business associate. In 1923 he was invited by the Governor, Sir Edward Stubbs, to act as an unofficial member of the Legislative Council during the absence on leave of Ng Hon-sze; upon Ng's death some months later, Sir Robert was nominated by the Governor to fill the substantive post, serving in all over three terms of four years each, which was then an unprecedented occurrence, requiring the special assent of the Imperial Government. In 1936 he was nominated to succeed Sir Shouson Chow in the Executive Council, from which he resigned upon the liberation of the Colony in 1945. (It is claimed by Robert S. Ward, op. cit., p. 7, that financial difficulties of Sir Shouson Chow 'are supposed to have had a part in his displacement by Sir Robert Kotewall, to whom he never willingly yielded primacy'.) Sir Robert was the principal, R. H. Kotewall and Co., director, Chinese Estates, Ltd, etc.; and prominent on the committees of many Hong Kong charitable and other associations, too numerous to list. Details about Sir Robert Kotewall are given in Professor Woo's book. See also: 'Appreciation by K. K. Li', *South China Morning Post*, Hong Kong, 25 May 1949, and *Who Was Who*, 1941–50.

[2] For example, Sir Robert Ho Tung (1862–1956), a millionaire before he

Chinese community in 1941 were *parvenu* businessmen, whose wealth and status was newly acquired; it is not surprising that some of these businessmen were prepared to work with the Japanese, at least during the early years of the occupation so as to maintain positions that had been recently won by the use of ruse, acumen, diligence and a measure of luck. They attempted to operate under a Japanese colonial régime as they had under the British. For the British Government had provided an umbrella under which Chinese social organization continued to exist.

It follows that prominent Chinese in Hong Kong were prominent firstly because they were rich; but that with wealth a number of prestigeful positions became available. The rules of the game were well known to socially mobile Chinese and the system was not, as Ward seems to infer, one imposed by aliens: it was rather a Chinese adaptation to the peculiarities of a colonial régime. This system of upward mobility had its roots in the old China, though it should be noted that the acquisition of wealth was more important in Hong Kong than in China proper, for Hong Kong has never been a mere microcosm of the homeland. There are some differences in social organization between the two.

Professor Woo Sing Lim's book *The Prominent Chinese in Hong Kong*[1] (1939), an example of the type of hagiographic writing some Chinese scholars indulge in, lists in order (it is safe to say in order of precedence) the following Chinese: Sir Robert Ho Tung, Sir Shouson Chow, Sir Robert Kotewall, Dr Ts'o Seen-wan,

[1] Professor Woo's book is written in Chinese, with summaries in English. Published by Five Continents Book Company, Hong Kong, 1939. He says: '(the order in which they are placed) is merely what I believe to be the most satisfactory manner of arranging them, and was done with no intention of being partial to anyone.'

---

was thirty, in 1925 gave HK$50,000 toward the cost of the teaching staff at the University of Hong Kong and at the same time another HK$50,000 toward the University Endowment Fund; in 1931, the year of his Golden Wedding, HK$200,000 toward the cost of an Industrial School for boys at Aberdeen; in 1936 an aeroplane costing HK$50,000 to mark the fiftieth birthday of the Generalissimo Chiang Kai Shek; and post-war a gift of HK$1,000,000 to the University of Hong Kong. These were only a few of his numerous benefactions. But Sir Robert, for reasons difficult to determine, was never nominated to either the Legislative or Executive Councils. See his obituary in the *Far Eastern Economic Review*, 3 May 1956, and references in B. Harrison (ed.), *University of Hong Kong: The First Fifty Years, 1911–61*, Hong Kong 1962. There is also a sketch of his life in Professor Woo's *The Prominent Chinese in Hong Kong*.

Chau Tsun-nin, Lo Man-kam, Dr Li Shu-fan, Ho Kom-tong and Li Yau-Tsun. It would seem that precedence was given to Sir Robert Ho Tung because of Sir Robert's position as one of the richest men in the colony and because of his numerous benefactions; and Sir Shouson was placed second, in this table of precedence, by reason of his great age (he was born in 1861) and his distinguished official career in Imperial China; he was also rich and held numerous directorships. Sir Robert Kotewall on the other hand was placed third it would seem, not primarily because of his prominence as a rich businessman and his position as the only Chinese member of the Executive Council, but because of his successful career in the Government of Hong Kong: in 1916, at the age of 36, he was appointed chief clerk in the Colonial Secretariat, at the time one of the highest positions held by a non-European in Government. Thus although wealth was a primary determinant of status in Hong Kong, extra-economic factors must also be taken into account. Professor Woo's book, however subjective, is probably a fair reflection of how Chinese notables in Hong Kong saw things.

It is extremely difficult to determine how far prominent and influential Chinese were satisfied with the state of pre-war affairs in Hong Kong—with their status and the colonial régime in general. They were subject to various currents of thought: to winds of change blowing in from China (though I do not think this should be too exaggerated), to the complexities of local politics being played out in neighbouring Kwangtung Province, and to the general threat of Japanese expansion. They must have noticed also the rising tide of agrarian radicalism, canalized by the Communists, which was unleashed by events of the 1920s. And they must have been aware that Europeans, especially the Americans, were increasingly challenging the moral basis of colonialism. Nearly all the journalists covering Chinese affairs in the 1930s had a left-wing bias—one only has to list such influential writers as James Bertram, Edgar Snow, Freda Utley, Agnes Smedley, Emily Hahn, among others.[1] But what seems clear is that when a clash occurred between their economic and political (or patriotic) interests the former often won. The 1925 general strike and boycott, inspired by the Kuomintang at Canton, attracted little support from prominent Hong Kong Chinese. Sir Shouson Chow,

[1] I am not suggesting prominent Chinese read these books: I merely claim that such books reflected a climate of opinion.

for example, speaking in support of an Ordinance introduced to make illegal political, but not economic, strikes, said (apropos Kuomintang agitators):

> It is this class of mischief makers . . . that this Bill is designed to deal with. Hong Kong is no place for them. We do not want Bolshevism or Communism. We cannot afford to have the economic and financial structure of the Colony periodically shaken or undermined. What we want are peace and good order, and the right to follow our callings without let or hindrance.[1]

Sir Robert Kotewall also supported the Government on this issue and was instrumental in obtaining a special loan in London for assisting foreign merchants of the Colony until normal trading was resumed.

Lennox Mills, an American political scientist, writing in 1941 after a period of research spent in the Colony, says:

> The racial bitterness which has caused so much trouble in India is not found in Hong Kong . . . Patriotic loyalty in the sense in which it is found in Great Britain does not exist save in a few instances. The vast majority are loyal because their self-interest dictates it.[2]

G. B. Endacott, in an attempt to explain the political serenity of the Hong Kong Chinese, writes:

> The conspicuous absence of political agitation in Hong Kong in contrast to an emergent Asia cannot be explained away; in fact many administrative and constitutional agencies have been created over the years by which the system of Crown Colony rule is modified to enable the Government's actions to be discussed and broadly supported with little electoral machinery.[3]

All the prominent Chinese who made public speeches in 1941 in celebration of Hong Kong's centenary as a British Colony praised the fruits of Sino-British co-operation. Sir Shouson Chow in a wireless broadcast said: 'Hong Kong's development and growth may be attributed in a large measure to her sound and just administration and to the peace and security which she offers to

[1] See *Hong Kong Hansard*, 1926, pp. 36–9, and pp. 44–5.
[2] op. cit., p. 410.
[3] *Government and People in Hong Kong*, p. vi.

trade, investment and industry.'[1] Sir Robert Kotewall was even more explicit than Sir Shouson about the benefits of British rule:

No less productive of good has been the relationship between Government and people. In this matter, one all important factor has been the principle of giving the Chinese community a voice in government through representation on the Executive and Legislative Councils. In 1925 the Executive Council was enlarged to include a member, representative of the Chinese community;[2] while, on the Legislative Council, there are three Chinese members. In the urban Council, adequate representation for the Chinese has been provided. These provisions in the Colony's constitution are important; but still more important is the practice followed of consulting responsible Chinese opinion before a decision is made.[3]

We may conclude that prominent Hong Kong Chinese engaged in trade and commerce, although aware of currents of change, clearly realized Hong Kong's unique position and value as a place to which funk money could be conveniently sent from China. They realized it was an area with a reasonably honest administration[4] compared with the homeland and that it was a political haven from the see-sawing political strife in China. But being Chinese, more fundamentally racialist than even Anglo-Saxons, being Chinese still harbouring resentment at the west's monopoly (at that period) of technological know-how and other skills, their attitudes to the British were sometimes equivocal or ambivalent or paranoic or even revengeful—as became clear during the halcyon early days of the Japanese occupation when bottled-up racialist hates were allowed to burst forth. There was tension between public and private faces. But the Chinese had, of course, a number of real grievances about which presumably they were less reticent in private than the public speeches of Sir Shouson Chow and Sir Robert Kotewall show. A few of these grievances will be outlined

[1] 'An Octogenarian Remembers Hong Kong's Progress and Prosperity', *Hong Kong Centenary Commemorative Talks, 1841–1941*, Hong Kong 1941, p. 69.

[2] Sir Shouson Chow, who served two terms of office, 1926–36.

[3] 'Anglo-Chinese Co-operation—Past, Present and Future', ibid., p. 47.

[4] Hong Kong has suffered its quota of scandals, some of seismic proportions. Just before the Japanese invasion, there was a series of public hearings on allegations that some Government officials had other than purely professional relations with contractors building air-raid shelters on the Island.

in the following paragraphs; but I have no space to detail the grievances of other non-European groups: Indians, Portuguese, Eurasians (the latter had a special problem: they suffered from an identity neurosis, usually absent from the Chinese).[1]

One disability the Chinese suffered from in 1941 was residential: no Chinese, unless a servant, was permitted by law to live on the Peak. As a guide book of the 1920s puts it:

> The Peak District, which has its own church, club and un-official civic body, is reserved for Europeans. Here it is that the Colony's higher officials live, the Governor in the wet season forsaking his official residence in Upper Albert Road for Mountain Lodge, his summer residence situated on a com-manding site. . . .[2]

The Peak also had its own hospital—the Matilda opened in 1906—built for the benefit of people of European or American birth; and the front row of seats of the Peak tram, which linked the higher and lower levels of the Island, were reserved for the Governor and his staff.[3]

This segregationist policy was a direct consequence of the Peak District Reservation Ordinance of 1904, section 3 of which read:

> It shall not be lawful (save in accordance with the previous provisions of this Ordinance) for any owner, lessee, tenant,

---

[1] '(In the 1931 Census) only 837 persons declared themselves to be Eurasians, the remainder of the presumed number of Eurasians calling themselves Chinese, and many of the other descriptions claimed cannot be identified with any actual ethnic division or nationality.' K. M. A. Barnett, *Report on the 1961 Census*, vol. 2, p. xlviii. Some Eurasians thought of themselves as, or identified themselves with, the Chinese; they were probably less subject to psychological stresses and strains than Eurasians who claimed equal status, or identified themselves, with Europeans. But some who speak Cantonese as a home language still describe themselves as Eurasian. Emily Hahn, a sharp observer of the pre-war Hong Kong scene, lived with two Eurasian girls during the early part of the Japanese occupation, and describes their attitudes: ' "We're Eurasians," said Irene. "That's why they never tried to send us away when the evacuation took place last year, you know. Only *pure* Englishwomen were sent away." . . . "And now," said Phyllis, "only *pure* Englishwomen are being interned." ' *Hong Kong Holiday*, New York 1946, p. 101. (The Japanese did allow Eurasian women married to Europeans to enter Stanley camp: it was optional for them.)

[2] *Hong Kong: A Brief History and Guide of the Hong Kong and the New Territories*, Hong Kong 1924, p. 100.

[3] Li Shu-fan, *Hong Kong Surgeon*, New York 1964, pp. 17–18.

or occupier of any land or building within the Peak District to let such land or building or any part thereof for the purpose of residence by any but non-Chinese, or to permit any but non-Chinese to reside on or in such land or building.[1]

This ordinance, revised in 1930 and 1937, was repealed finally on 26 July 1946.

The reason usually given by Europeans for the necessity of the 1904 Ordinance is that it was a measure introduced to prevent breeding of the malarial mosquito in European residential areas. The legislators, under pressure from European ratepayers, argued in 1904 that Chinese were as yet unaware of the virtues of environmental sanitation and that to allow them to live cheek by jowl with Europeans would invite hazards to health. Joseph Chamberlain, at that time British Colonial Secretary, 'agreed with the principle of reservation "where people of clean habits will be safe from malaria" but he objected to excluding Chinese of good standing . . .'[2] Section 4 of the Ordinance read consequently: 'It shall be lawful for the Governor-in-Council to exempt any Chinese from the operation of this Ordinance on such terms as the Governor-in-Council, shall think fit.' But few Chinese resided on the Peak before 1946. The one exception, so far as I have been able to establish, was Sir Robert Ho Tung.

Whatever the merits were of this Ordinance and the cogency of the arguments advanced in its favour, Chinese took it to be an example of racial discrimination and the residential separation practised in other parts of the British Empire, notably India. This is the view expressed by Lo Man-kam,[3] an unofficial member of

---

[1] See also No. 8 of 1918, and No. 25 of 1937.

[2] Endacott, *History of Hong Kong*, p. 284.

[3] Sir Man Kam Lo or Sir Lo Man-kam (1893–1959). Kt, cr. 1948; C.B.E., 1941; LL.D. (Hon.), 1951. Senior partner Lo and Lo, Solicitors and Notaries Public, Hong Kong. Educated in England. In 1915 passed the Solicitors' Final Examination, taking the first place in the First Class Honours. Served on many commissions and public committees, notably the Salaries Commission of 1947. Unofficial Member of the Legislative Council 1935 to 1949. Unofficial Member of the Executive Council from 1946 to his death in 1959. Lo was also a keen amateur sportsman and did much to encourage Chinese to play Western-type games. See his radio talk: 'Progress in Sport among Chinese in Hong Kong', printed in *Hong Kong Centenary Commemorative Talks*. In 1918 he married a daughter of Sir Robert Ho Tung. For further details see: *Who Was Who*, 1951–60.

the Legislative Council, after the second reading of the 1946 bill repealing the ordinance. Lo claimed that:

> after the enactment there was very strong and bitter opposition to this measure on the part of the Chinese community, and in this opposition the Chinese General Chamber of Commerce took the leading part . . . the Chinese then had no particular desire to live on the Peak. Their opposition was based solely on grounds of racial discrimination. . . . This Ordinance has been a source of resentment to the Chinese ever since its enactment and I feel sure the repeal of this Ordinance will give universal satisfaction to the Chinese.[1]

Lo's comments are supported by the statement made by the Colonial Secretary in introducing the bill: 'It is considered that the repeal of the Ordinance might tend to encourage building and reconstruction in the Peak District and that it would be out of harmony with the spirit of the times to retain the Ordinance.'[2] The Colonial Secretary's occult reference to 'the spirit of the times' may be taken to read that the Government understood that things had changed not only in the world outside but in Hong Kong, so that a more careful handling of racial frictions was necessary than in the past. The Japanese propaganda campaign waged in Hong Kong against colonialism (western-type) and colour prejudice, together with over three-and-a-half years of diligent indoctrination of the population, had left behind a legacy in 1946. The Colonial Secretary was right in sensing that things had changed: there could be no complete return to the *status quo ante*.

In July 1940 the Government, because of the Japanese threat to the Colony, evacuated a number of British nationals. The majority, of pure European descent, were sent to Australia, but on the way the ship disembarked a number of Eurasians at Manila, on the excuse, presumably, that they would feel more at ease among brown- or yellow-skinned people. The evacuation raised a storm of protest within Hong Kong—it was attacked both as a gross example of racial discrimination and as unfair because senior Government officials were able to keep wives and families with them, whereas others were persuaded to send them away. Leo d'Almada e Castro, the representative of the Portuguese in the Legislative Council, and Lo Man-kam, senior Chinese unofficial

---

[1] *Hong Kong Hansard: Session 1946.*   [2] ibid.

member, led the protestors and pressed home the attack upon Government with great vigour and good sense.

On 25 July Leo d'Almada e Castro asked in the Legislative Council the following questions: 'Did Government draw the attention of the Home Government to the following: (*a*) that there is in the Colony a large number of British women and children who are not of pure European descent? (*b*) the consequent discrimination involved in the said order?'[1] H. E. The Officer Administering the Government (N. L. Smith) felt obliged to make a lengthy statement defending and excusing the evacuation scheme, part of which ran:

> As regards the allegation of racial discrimination in the War Cabinet's explicit instruction, it has always been held, in the original 1939 evacuation scheme, that special treatment would be necessary for persons with no real domicile in Asia and it had been hoped that India, Macau, Indo-China and China itself would be the natural destination for all others.[2]

Later the same day, at a meeting of the Finance Committee, the issue of discrimination was again raised by Lo Man-kam, who argued:

> the position, as it appears to us, is that the tax-payers of this Colony are being made to pay for the evacuation of a very small and selected section of the community and, whenever necessary, for their maintenance and support during an indefinite period, leaving some 99·9 percent of the population uncared for and unprotected when an emergency does come.[3]

Lo Man-kam's strictures were supported by Leo d'Almada e Castro:

> In this matter of discrimination, and generally on the question of evacuation. . . . Government, I think has forfeited to a very great extent the respect and confidence of the community. That, of course, is Government's business. But that is not all. Government has also placed an appreciable strain on the loyalty of a large section of the community, and I am not going to be an accessory after the fact to any measure which has brought it about.[4]

[1] *Hong Kong Hansard: Session 1940*, p. 100.
[2] ibid., p. 103.　　[3] ibid., p. 112.　　[4] ibid., p. 113.

Lo Man-kam then returned to the lists and brought up the question of the Eurasian evacuees in Manila:

I have indirect complaints of disgraceful discrimination meted out to some of the evacuees in Manila . . . my information is that people were weeded out deliberately by Government officials on the advice of two ladies and sent to places which were not fit places to accommodate anyone.[1]

The two ladies who sorted the sheep from the goats were, it appeared, European. There is no need to give further document-ation on this issue: I bring it forward as an example of how Chinese and Eurasians reacted to the covert, though occasionally open, racialism of the European ruling class. Other issues raised at this time (*circa* 1939) make this clear.

The Compulsory Service Bill of 1939, designed to mobilize British nationals in Hong Kong, gave concern to Lo Man-kam. At a meeting of the Legislative Council Lo Man-kam addressed the Colonial Secretary in these words:

I understand, Sir, that there has been rumour as to the pos-sibility of racial discrimination being made in regard to pay on mobilisation . . . (my point) arises from a deep conviction that volunteers working for a common cause should receive equal treatment, and from a just resentment that any racial dis-crimination should exist in any matter whatsoever.[2]

Yet the introduction of the Immigration Control Bill, 1940,[3] the first of its kind in Hong Kong's history (previously free ingress and egress had been permitted to Chinese) obtained the support of Lo Man-kam, Dr Li Shu-fan and William Ngartsee Thomas Tam, the three Chinese unofficial members. All gave their assent at the second reading of the Bill in the Legislative Council; but Lo Man-kam, the watch-dog of Chinese interests, always quick to spot signs of racial discrimination, added a note of warning in his peroration: 'My colleagues and I intend to maintain a close in-terest in the operation of this measure, and we shall have no

[1] ibid., pp. 115–16.

[2] *Hong Kong Hansard: Session 1939*, p. 97.

[3] See *Hong Kong Hansard: Session 1940*, pp. 161–6. This was a bill 'to regulate the entry and departure of persons into or out of the Colony, to prohibit the entry of undesirable immigrants and to confer various powers in con-nexion therewith'.

hesitation in making to Government any representation which we may consider it our duty so to do.'[1]

Prominent Chinese gave little trouble about this revolutionary piece of legislation, which is surprising since they knew the Japanese were steadily penetrating into south China and driving before them flocks of panicky refugees, all terrified by stories or personal knowledge of the famous sack, or rape, of Nanking. But the prominent Chinese, the Hong Kong notables, realized the economic consequences of permitting unrestricted immigration into an already overcrowded Colony and the effects this would have on trade and commerce, on law and order. The Bill went through without opposition. Before it did, though, the Chinese unofficial members examined it from all angles to see whether it contained any affronts to Chinese racial pride. Clearly it did not.

Socially the Chinese in pre-war days were discriminated against in a number of ways. The larger, more snob and chic hotels, like the caravanserais of globe-trotting Englishmen in Cairo or Bombay or Singapore, either excluded, or did not make available all their amenities to, the 99·9 per cent of the population mentioned by Lo Man-kam. In some hotels, such as the now-demolished Hong Kong Hotel, some only of the public rooms were open to Chinese guests; in others, Chinese could not stay overnight, that is, they could not slip under the sheets. Clubs, such as the Hong Kong Club,[2] the Taipan's frosted window on the world, were then restricted; and the Hong Kong Jockey Club was controlled by an all European committee of stewards, mostly bankers and Taipans.[3] The closed-shop principle exercised in those days by European stewards and clubland heroes was attacked with great gusto by Lieutenant General Rensuke Isogai, first Japanese Governor of Hong Kong. He was reported as saying in 1942: 'In the past, the British Government used wrong methods and means to conduct horse racing here. The British way lacked justice and gave enjoyment to only a special class of people to satisfy their own selfishness and for their own benefit. This is against the true principles of racing.'[4] But racing remained the sport of kings even

[1] *Hong Kong Hansard: Session 1940*, p. 163.

[2] This is not so now.

[3] The stewards in 1930 were: C. Gordon Mackie, R. M. Dyer, V. M. Grayburn, Sir Joseph Kemp, J. J. Paterson, T. E. Pearce, W. E. L. Shenton, F. Sutton, and P. Tester. Today (1965) there is one Chinese steward: The Hon. Sir Sik-nin Chau.

[4] *Hong Kong News*, 26 April 1942.

under the Japanese, for the Lieutenant-General's new Jockey Club committee in 1942 had Ho Kam-tong, a rich Chinese, as Chairman, and Li Tse-forng, managing director of the Bank of East Asia, as one of the stewards.

There is no need to give further examples: prominent Chinese, in particular, in pre-war Hong Kong were obviously aware of racial discrimination, of slights and hurts that damaged their self-respect and dignity as Chinese. Each reacted to it in his own way. The bland picture presented by colonial officials and the military that all was quiet on the Eastern front in Hong Kong was belied by the events of the Japanese occupation. It seems to me, then, that the underlying antagonisms that existed between Chinese and British were more racialist in origin (consequently more difficult to exorcize) than economic or political, although these three factors must be, to some degree, inter-related. The Chinese wanted more influence to swing things their own way, more represent-ation of their interests (interests as seen by the notables), more influence over Government and the removal of particular grievances: the rich wanted to feel that they were really sitting on the top of the heap; and the poor, it can be surmised, wanted to be left free to gain a livelihood without too much interference from officialdom. Since a large proportion of this last group did not regard Hong Kong as their permanent home, it can be inferred that they were little interested in the question of political change.

So far I have discussed only three groups of people—the pro-minent Chinese, the colonial officials and the Taipans.[1] I have done so because I believe that alterations in their relationships were more important for post-war Hong Kong than changes in the attitudes of other groups, though the latter cannot of course be summarily dismissed. Unlike most British colonies and ex-colonies, there were in Hong Kong, as Dr Marjorie Topley notes,[2] two social classes of Westerners: Taipans and those in uniformed supervisory jobs, who were often born in Hong Kong and usually able to speak good colloquial Chinese. And the Chinese population was divisible into, or consisted of, a number of groups of interest to sociologists, such as dialect groups—Cantonese, Hakka, Tiuchew, etc. These groups and sub-groups could be dealt with in a longer, more detailed study, but in this short paper I must

[1] Not all Taipans remained rich; fluctuating economic conditions in the 1920s and 1930s eliminated some Taipans.

[2] See below, pp. 191-3.

neglect them. In the following section I shall discuss mainly the activities of a small sample of prominent Chinese—those who were members of the Chinese Representative Council, the Chinese Co-operative Council or one of the District Bureaux.

2 *Le déluge*

The Japanese occupation fell into several phases.[1] First there was a short period of military occupation. This ended on 22 February 1942, when Lieutenant-General Rensuke Isogai became the first Japanese 'Governor of the Conquered Territory of Hong Kong'. During the first year of his rule conditions were reasonably good —as good as they could be in wartime and given Hong Kong's peculiar and vulnerable dependence on imports. This was a period when many local businessmen thought that trade would sooner or later pick up, when cheerfulness kept breaking in. But after February 1943 conditions steadily deteriorated; the slow strangulation of Japan's seaborne trade and the destruction of her merchant marine meant that the import and export of goods into Hong Kong became exceedingly hazardous. Finally, 1944 witnessed the plummeting downward of living conditions, acute food shortages leading to the virtual starvation of the population and the almost complete atrophy of the economy. This last phase continued until the Japanese surrender of 16 August 1945. I shall concentrate mainly on the events of the second phase: the first year of the Governor's rule.

The Japanese never succeeded in setting up a unified administration in Hong Kong; several administrative structures existed at one and the same time; there were a number of competing authorities, never a proper centralization of authority, such as existed under the British. The armed forces, the civil administration, the gendarmerie—each clung to its autonomy. The first Governor, Rensuke Isogai did, however, make clear what Japa-

[1] Kathleen J. Heasman distinguishes three periods, connected with financial and political events: from the capitulation to June 1943, a period distinguished by confidence in the currency; from June 1943 to June 1944, a period of upward movement in prices connected with the banning of the Hong Kong dollar; and from June 1944 to the surrender, marked by mounting inflation and starvation of the population. See Kathleen J. Heasman, 'Japanese Financial and Economic Measures in Hong Kong', *Journal of the Economics Society*, Hong Kong University Economics Society 1957, p. 65.

nese intentions were. As he saw it, his first task was to enlist the support of the influential Chinese for the Japanese war effort and to convince them that a Co-prosperity Sphere, in which Hong Kong would have a place, would be to their advantage. He made clear, at the same time, that the issues involved in the war were clearly racialist: a war of the coloured races against the whites, a war of emancipation like a slave revolt, a holy war against the materialism of the west.

Although Asians are often whiter in pigmentation than many Europeans so that a white-coloured dichotomy is somewhat ambiguous, the ideas behind the Governor's racialism were clear: the westerner's insolent superiority had to be destroyed, and the easterner must acquire a new status in the world. But the Governor had a number of practical matters to cope with: he had to make Hong Kong a habitable and hospitable place to live in for those Chinese allowed to remain domiciled within its borders. The Governor knew that the business of Hong Kong was business, and this view had the full support of prominent Chinese.

Yet despite the return of various foreign concessions to the Chinese (to the puppet Nanking régime of Wang Ching-wei) the Japanese never seriously considered returning Hong Kong to any type of Chinese régime or group. Hong Kong was always referred to as a 'conquered territory'; and it became clear, as the war progressed, that the Japanese intended to preserve Hong Kong as a part of the Japanese Empire, like Taiwan or Korea, and as a naval base like Kwangchow Bay.[1] Japanese propagandists were presented, in consequence, with a dilemma, one which they never successfully solved. They ranted about the past evils of colonialism, of discriminatory treatment suffered by Asians under the British Raj, but they remained *in situ* as colonialists themselves. Their claim to be superior colonialists was based on the dubious premise that since they were racially akin to Chinese they were automatically closer to their charges than the British had been.

As soon as Sir Mark Young surrendered the Colony and British troops and officials were moved into internment camps, a feeling of 'school is out' swept over a number of non-Europeans, a feeling that the tables had been turned at last. The sarcastic editor of

---

[1] Kwangchow Bay, one of the best harbours in South China, was leased by the Chinese to the French in 1898. It was occupied by the Japanese on 21 February 1943.

the *Hong Kong News* wrote: 'They were about a thousand in all, including a number of women, mostly wearing slacks, who provided a sight seldom seen in the Colony by carrying large bundles behind their backs, though several put up a bold front by arriving in chairs.'[1]

A number of confessional letters and articles on the theme of racialism appeared in the press. A prize-winning essay on 'How to achieve an ideal East Asia' contained these sentiments:

> Those of us who have lived in the seaports and big cities of Asia have noted this differentiation between the Occidental and Oriental, not only in the political and economic fields, but also in social walks and life. While the clubs and homes of the Oriental are open to all races without any barrier of colour or race, the opposite is the case with European clubs and homes. This strong propensity of the Westerner to classify his social acquaintances strictly on a racial basis and with particular reference to colour, is the very antithesis of the Oriental who judges men and receives them in his house or club according to character, with no thought of colour or nationality.[2]

Great attempts were also made to discredit the former colonial administration, and it was attacked as racialist in conception. The *Hong Kong News* claimed, on 3 January 1942, that British civil servants in Hong Kong 'represented the bottom of the Civil Service examination list, since Hong Kong being the most easterly had to take those left over after all the other successful candidates had chosen more interesting posts in London, India and elsewhere'.[3] A further editorial of 20 February 1942, suggested that 'callow British youths just out from school and half-witted Englishmen were often placed in charge of departments over the heads of Asiatics who, perhaps, had spent nearly half their lives in these very same departments and who, therefore, knew their

[1] *Hong Kong News*, 5 January 1942. This newspaper first appeared as an English weekly in 1939. It ceased publication on the outbreak of hostilities but resumed publication on 26 December 1941 in the former Morning Post Building. The Managing Director was Toshihiko Eto, who published two other newspapers from the same office: the *Hong Kong Nippo* (in Japanese) and the *Hong Kong Yat Po* (in Chinese). The former was first published in 1909 and the latter in 1932. Before the war their circulation must have been very small in Hong Kong. *The Newspaper Directory of China (including Hong Kong)*, Shanghai 1939, published by Carl Crow, makes no mention of them.

[2] ibid., 1 January 1942.   [3] ibid., 31 January 1942.

work inside out'.[1] The *Hong Kong News* argued that Japan would change all this:

> Japan has come forward to establish a New Order for East Asia, and it is time that equality should be restored to the Asiatics. It was not uncommon for a Chinese or Indian, who had long service in the Government, to have to obey the orders of a young upstart, newly arrived from 'home', who knew practically next to nothing, and who nevertheless received several times more pay. The local staff were forced to work for a small sum while their 'masters' enjoyed a typically comfortable colonial existence.[2]

The same newspaper printed soon after an article on 'The Question of Colour: British Snobbery that Destroyed an Empire' by one Peter M. Wong. Wong praised the Japanese and cited the following case:

> Already the Japanese have set a fine example by appointing an Indian as Commissioner of Police at Kuala Lumpur. Never before has an Asiatic risen above the rank of Inspector in the Malayan Police Force. . . . The question of colour, creed or class will never again rise in the social or economic structure of East Asia. Thanks to Japan, we are now a free people and the shapers of our own destiny. The question of colour is *dead*.[3]

I give these quotations to show how the Japanese were able to exploit feelings about past injustices so as to swing the Hong Kong population to its side, or at least to keep it neutral, in the war against the west. But the Japanese never succeeded in winning over the Chinese totally to their ideas. They did so many foolish, impolitic things to offend a proud and prickly Chinese population, seemingly liberated from colonialism, that by the end of 1942 most Chinese, apart from a few die-hard, bitter-ender collaborationists, had acquired an antipathy toward 'new-order' colonialism. By that date it became clear that in many ways Japanese colonialism was far more despotic, bureaucratic and corrupt, and less rational and efficient, than the British variety. The Japanese had attempted to change Chinese attitudes and establish a structure of control by methods far more brutal, coercive and stupid than those used formerly by the British. The

[1] ibid., 20 February 1942.   [2] ibid., 9 January 1942.
[3] ibid., 17 February 1942.

typical British official, it should be noted, was a university man, nurtured on the humanities, and often of a scholarly turn of mind; like his colleagues in India, he rarely remained unaffected by his contacts with an ancient civilization—and in Hong Kong, for example, the young cadet was expected to learn Cantonese. Such officials often behaved like Mandarins but, on the whole, like tolerant and civilized Mandarins. On the other hand, the evidence shows that many Japanese officials, usually seconded from the armed forces, behaved like feudal overlords—like bibulous, lecherous, loot-loving crusaders, who had forgotten what their crusade was about.

But it is important to note that disillusionment with the Japanese was not necessarily followed by a newly-found loyalty to the former colonial régime, which in any case had been far too remote a presence for most Chinese. As Ward notes: 'Chinese reaching Chungking from Hong Kong as late as the fall of 1944 corroborated earlier reports from the "Conquered Territory" to the effect that there had been and was then very little underground activity directed at hampering Japanese control.'[1] The sudden collapse of British power in the East was too difficult to explain away; the humiliation of the British in Hong Kong too visible. British prestige could not be re-built in so short a time. An editorial of 14 January 1941 in the *Hong Kong News* gave powerful expression to this mood of disillusionment:

> Today the British and Americans have a much greater respect for the Oriental soldier—for in Hong Kong, Malaya, and the Philippines the outcome has been the same: the vaunted super-men of the white races have melted like butter. . . . In eighteen days of conflict it was all over—a horrible muddle of in-efficiency and helplessness which has bequeathed a miserable aftermath.

The drawing together of the Chinese and British communities—as I hope to show—came *after*, not during, the war. What the Japanese did during the occupation was to alienate the population stage by stage; first the masses, who lacked food and work,

---

[1] Ward, op. cit., p. 77. Ward was under-estimating Chinese opposition to the Japanese in Hong Kong. Guerrillas were active in the New Territories and one of their most successful exploits was the blowing up of the railway bridge over Waterloo Road in Kowloon. See also: Sir Lindsay Ride's chapter 'The Test of War' in B. Harrison (ed.), op. cit.

and then the middle classes who found they could make little money.[1] But this alienation was not followed during the occupation by a 'love the British' phase.

Still, by the end of 1942 the Japanese did have some achievements to their credit. All transport services were speedily rehabilitated. The Kowloon–Canton Railway was cleared and re-opened; tram and ferry services running with a daily steamship service to Canton and Macau. Gas, electricity and water services were also in operation. Food supplies were maintained, though at a low level, and distribution through rationing effected—rice in January 1942, sugar in June, oil and firewood in July, salt in August and matches in September.[2] Confidence in the currency was maintained. But these creditable achievements, together with the attempts made by the Governor to revive economic life, were overshadowed by the events of the early occupation days, by the puritanical killjoy obsessions of the Japanese authorities, and by the Japanization policy pursued.

Chinese, particularly middle-class Chinese, were appalled by the orgy of rape that spread over the Island in the period of chaos following the surrender. Exaggerated stories were probably told about the numbers of rape victims, but the feeling of horror that such stories engendered, whether true or false, tarnished the reputation of the Japanese occupiers. It is not known how many women were violated—Dr Li Shu-fan, an eye-witness of the fall of Hong Kong, suggests the figure was over 10,000. In his words: 'The actual number of women raped will always remain a question; but it was large—10,000 would be an under-estimation—and the methods were appallingly brutal. At my hospital we treated rape victims ranging from the early teens to the sixties.'[3] Moreover, the Japanese seemed unable, in the eyes of Chinese, to distinguish between 'good' girls (family girls) and prostitutes. One of the first statements issued by the Executive Committee of the Chinese Chamber of Commerce, 13 January 1942, demanded, therefore, 'protection for family women through the re-opening of

[1] Some local people made money out of the war, especially those who acted as buyers or agents for the Japanese forces.

[2] Kathleen Heasman, op. cit., gives a detailed account of economic conditions during the occupation. Miss Heasman, a lecturer in Economics at the University of Hong Kong, was interned at Stanley. Her main source of information about economic conditions came from the *Hong Kong News*, which was supplied to the camp until June 1945.

[3] Li Shu-fan, op. cit., p. 111.

brothels'.[1] Soon after the Japanese complied and established special red-light districts: one was set up at West Point for Chinese and another at Wanchai for Japanese. Segregated areas —euphemistically named 'pleasure resorts'—were also established in Kowloon and the same apartheid principles applied. And on 16 November 1942, Chan Lim-pak of the Chinese Representative Council let it be known that the Japanese were considering allowing a business syndicate to run such a centre in Shamshuipo (Kowloon). There is of course money in vice, and the motives of some members of the two Chinese councils in agitating for the re-opening of the brothels were not entirely moralistic.[2] But the outbreak of rape, looting and lawlessness—from the Japanese point of view—had an important effect: it made prominent Chinese desperately anxious to collaborate with the Japanese so as to obtain concessions for the Chinese population and limit excesses. The price the Chinese had to pay for a measure of stability and law and order was—collaboration.[3] Understandably, many did collaborate, as in those countries occupied by the Germans.

It is not possible in such a short article to list all those Japanese actions and policies that irritated and alienated the Chinese, and the following examples certainly do not pretend to be comprehensive. But perhaps two things above all destroyed Japanese chances of 'Taiwanizing' the Hong Kong Chinese. First the Japanese administration revealed itself to be corrupt, cruel and irrational in its working—money talked: there was little social equality. Secondly blatant attempts to turn Chinese into Japanese, and Hong Kong into a little Yokohama, were bitterly resented.

Residents who stayed in Hong Kong during the occupation all agree that in order to obtain anything from the civil administration money or gifts had to be passed over to officials.[4] And since

[1] *Hong Kong News*, 13 January 1942. This refers to the petition presented to the Japanese military on 10 January.

[2] The Japanese also attempted to control the sale of opium. Twelve authorized retail depots were established by them, and all opium addicts had to register with the civil administration.

[3] It is difficult to define the term 'collaboration'. In a sense nearly everyone in occupied France 'collaborated' with the Germans at one time or the other. But it is possible to draw a distinction between quislings or intellectual collaborators (those spiritually committed to an occupation authority) and opportunists.

[4] Emily Hahn's *China to Me*, New York 1944, and *Hong Kong Holiday*,

the Japanese relied often on Chinese underlings—most of the police were Chinese or Indian—the habit of 'squeeze' reached extraordinary proportions. The rice rationing stations, set up by the Japanese but run by Chinese-staffed district bureau offices, may be cited as an example. At these stations, poor Chinese were usually offered poor quality, or under-weight, rations of rice unless they paid extra—i.e. over the official price.[1] Corruption was rife, far worse than under the British. And many members of the Hong Kong underworld and triads were recruited by the Japanese as petty officials or informers. Naturally the code of conduct followed by such people left much to be desired.

The Japanese civil administration, as I have mentioned, was also much more tough-minded and paternalistic than the British and the penalties it imposed heavier. A mass of petty regulations descended on the heads of the population. For example, dogs taken out into the streets had to be muzzled or chained;[2] mahjong and dancing were prohibited in public places;[3] the excess population was 'encouraged' to leave, but little attempt was made to see that it arrived at its destination alive;[4] residents had to indulge in an annual house-cleansing campaign, supervised by the authorities;[5] a curfew was imposed and difficulties were made about cross-harbour journeys—complaints were made that at the ferries Chinese women were stripped and searched by Japanese or Indian police; Chinese and other nationals were expected to bow before Japanese sentries[6] (who were thought to represent the

---

[1] One of the main problems confronting the Chinese Representative Council was rice distribution and rationing—an equitable rationing system was never set up.

[2] *Hong Kong News*, 5 September 1942.

[3] ibid., 22 July 1942.

[4] At the end of August 1945 the population of Hong Kong was estimated at less than 600,000 inhabitants—500,000 according to some estimates.

[5] *Hong Kong News*, 20 March 1942. The period 17–25 March was fixed for this campaign. It was a thorough one: 'even holes on walls and other places through which mice or insects may crawl must be covered up, and measures for catching mice should be taken'.

[6] In a statement to the press, Lo Kuk-wo 'addressed his compatriots to observe the general rule of bowing to Nipponese sentries. He said people should be grateful to the sentries for the excellent services they are rendering in protecting the territory and preserving peace.' *Hong Kong News*, 26 July 1942.

---

op. cit., both contain much information about civilian life in Hong Kong under the occupation. Emily Hahn because she claimed to be married to a Chinese national was permitted to live outside Stanley Camp.

Emperor); cholera inoculations became compulsory,[1] etc., etc. Obviously, many Chinese were unaware of, or consciously evaded, these regulations: but the regulations remained and could be used as an excuse to trounce any Chinese if a Japanese felt so inclined. But such regulations and laws appeared in most cases either illogical or irrational or offensive to the mass of Chinese.

The Japanization of Hong Kong began almost immediately after its fall. The first stage was the eradication of things British —such as the removal of shop signs in English[2] and the re-naming of streets, districts and public buildings in Japanese.[3] Statue Square—cluttered with effigies of Victorian and Edwardian governors and other prominent English notabilities—received rapid attention: one of the first statues to be dismantled was that of Sir Thomas Jackson, first Chief Manager of the Hong Kong and Shanghai Banking Corporation from 1876 to 1902. This statue, in Japanese eyes, represented British enterprise and commerce in the Far East, and its removal had a symbolic importance. At the same time, the disappearance of most Englishmen from the streets,[4] together with the taking over by the Japanese or their agents of the European-owned department stores, shops, businesses and hotels,[5] gave the central business district a pseudo-Oriental look. The eradication of the visible signs of the previous British occupation went hand in hand with a conscious policy of indoctrinating the Chinese population into Japanese values and ideas.

Most Japanese festivals and ceremonies were observed in Hong Kong and the local population was expected to take part in them. The following festivals, among others, were celebrated:

[1] Under the British, cholera inoculations were never compulsory. During the occupation some Chinese, in order to sell certificates to those who funked being inoculated, suffered innumerable jabs. Emily Hahn mentions one Chinese who died as a result of nineteen needle jabs in one day.

[2] *Hong Kong News*, 21 February 1942: 'A four-day campaign was launched on 15 February, with members of the various district bureau aiding in the work.'

[3] Some examples would be Katorido-dori (Nathan Road), Higashishowa-dori (Des Vœux Road Central), Taisho Koyen (Botanical Gardens), Mido-riga Hama (Repulse Bay).

[4] A few Europeans, for various reasons, were permitted to live outside the civilian internment camp: such as Dr P. S. Selwyn-Clarke, former Director of Medical Services, and a Colonial official who claimed Irish nationality.

[5] The Kowloon Hotel was re-named the Yokohama, the Gloucester the Matsubara, the Peninsula the Toa.

the October Kanname-sai Festival—the first harvest festival; the November Niname-sai Festival—harvest thanksgiving day; Tenchosetsu—the Emperor's birthday; the Yasukuni Shrine Festival —a festival commemorating Japanese war heroes; Meiji Setsu— the anniversary of the Emperor Meiji. These festivals became public holidays; government offices closed, and the local population was expected to display Japanese flags and appropriately solemn facial expressions. The Yasukuni Shrine Festival was especially revered and local Chinese, wherever they happened to be, were expected to stand up and observe one minute's silence as a mark of respect to those dead Japanese who had been engaged, at the time of their death, in liberating Asians from Western influence. Even specific historical episodes, of interest to patriotic Japanese, were celebrated in Hong Kong, such as the anniversary of the Mukden affair—the Manchukuo anniversary as it was called—for 'the Mukden Affair can be said to be the starting point of Nipponese-Chinese Co-prosperity'.[1] But why the local Chinese should show any tenderness toward or interest in such alien ceremonies and festivals was never convincingly explained.

It followed that a knowledge of the Japanese language was after 1941 an important economic and social asset for a Hong Kong Chinese. Not only were businessmen and others expected to use Japanese when addressing mail to Shonan (the new name for Singapore) or other parts of the Japanese Empire, but the Japanese calendar was given official status. On all documents Chinese were expected to use the Japanese system of dating from reign titles—Meiji, Taisho or Showa; thus in 1942 a Chinese seventeen-year-old was legally obliged to give his year of birth as Showa One. All Government officials of course had to know Japanese; for example, candidates for the Taxation Bureau of the Finance Department needed at least 'a middle school education and knowledge of the Nipponese language'.

Since Japanese in 1941 superseded English as the official language, all schools had to introduce Japanese into their curricula; in primary and middle schools four to five hours per week were normally devoted to it. By February 1943 there were thirty-nine schools, apart from private ones, specializing in the teaching of the Japanese language.[2] But throughout the occupation the

[1] *Hong Kong News*, 18 September 1942: a joint declaration issued by the Chinese Representative and Co-operative Councils.
[2] *Hong Kong News*, 15 February 1943.

number of young people receiving any type of education was always below the figure for 1940. For example, the head of the Wanchai District Bureau complained to the Governor in October 1942, that there was only one school in his district compared with thirty before the war.[1] Education became a luxury; as a pupil of Queen's College (Hong Kong) wrote after the war:

A very serious problem that troubled every householder was that there was no chance for boys and girls to go to school. The cost of living was so high that every member of the family had to do his or her part to help find more and more money merely to exist. How could a bread-winner afford the luxury of education?[2]

The Annual Report 1946 goes so far as to claim that 'so far as can be ascertained the largest numbers of pupils receiving education at any time during the Japanese occupation was less than one-tenth of the 1941 total of 120,000, and the number had shrunk by August 1945, to as little as 3,000'.[3]

The Japanese attempted to turn out a corps of young Chinese, able to handle the Japanese language, for employment in Japanese-controlled offices and agencies. They established a Teachers' Training College in the former premises of St Stephens Girls College. At this institute two courses were offered: the first to train 'middle-class clerks' and the second to train teachers. The curriculum included 'Japanese language, public citizenship, the teaching of the true Oriental spirit, and Japanese morality, customs and social habits'.[4] Later, in 1943, a scheme was introduced to encourage Chinese students to carry on higher studies in Japan. On 18 February 1943, the *Hong Kong News* reported that the Head of the Civil Affairs Department had entertained three Chinese students, about to depart to Japan, at a tiffin party. But few Chinese took advantage of the scheme; moreover, few Chinese in 1943 thought that Japan would win the war— a Japanese education was becoming too great a risk by that date.

The policy of Japanization was not successful; it was bitterly

---

[1] *Hong Kong News*, 28 October 1942.
[2] Gwenneth Stokes, *Queen's College, 1862–1962*, Hong Kong 1962, p. 157.
[3] *Annual Report 1946*, p. 46.
[4] *Hong Kong News*, 5 March 1943.

resented, and informants claim that Chinese school children took little interest in learning the Japanese language. Japanese propaganda was inept and unconvincing: few could believe after a year's occupation that a 'New Order' had been established in Hong Kong. The *Hong Kong News* on 26 November 1942, advertised the sale of a book by one Chen Mei-fun entitled *An Israel Inspiration*, 'a spirited analysis of the origin and progress of Jewish intrigue in international politics, revealing a Democratic-Jewish plot to carve up China, which was forestalled by Nippon'.[1] This is a typical example of the absurdities of Japanese propaganda in Hong Kong. By the end of 1942 the mood of 'school is out' was over: the Japanese had proved themselves to be more discriminatory, racialist and arrogant than the British.

I have sketched in this picture of wartime Hong Kong so as to provide a backcloth against which the activities of some prominent Chinese may be viewed. For these people had to adapt to a new, more dangerous and chancy environment than the prewar. They were caught in cross-currents and subject to a great number of pressures. To begin with, their business activities were circumscribed and limited because of war conditions; they suffered much badgering from, and had to kowtow to, the Japanese authorities in ways more humiliating than in the past; they were forced to repudiate the Nationalist régime based on Chungking and its western allies, and expected to praise publicly the puppet government set up by Wang Ching-wei at Nanking; and they had to support, of necessity, a policy of Japanization in Hong Kong and all that it entailed. Yet, at the same time, being Chinese themselves, most of them felt morally obliged to protect, in so far as they were able, the Chinese population and the Chinese way of life. Clearly, their position was difficult, uncomfortable and tense.

The first Chinese to emerge and make a public appearance was Tung Chung-wei, the treasurer of the Chinese General Chamber of Commerce, an influential body first set up in 1887. Tung, together with other committee members, drafted a long petition which was sent to the Japanese authorities on 10 January 1942. The petition dealt with such matters as: food, fuel, water, electricity, telephones, public safety, currency, communications and, as noted, prostitution. The petition argued for a return to normal conditions in Hong Kong and gave its opinion as to how this could be achieved. Then, on 12 January, the Chamber's Executive

[1] ibid., 26 November 1942.

Committee, under the chairmanship of Tung, held a special meeting at which a 'Rehabilitation Committee' (later changed to 'Rehabilitation Advisory Committee') was organized. This committee comprised nine, all leading, members of the Chinese business community at that date, and its chairman was Lo (or Law) Kuk-wo (that is, Sir Robert Kotewall), and vice-chairman, Chow Shou-son (Sir Shouson Chow).[1] (The Japanese did not recognize British titles or honours, so both Sir Robert Kotewall and Sir Shouson Chow had been forced to revert to plain 'mister'.) The Rehabilitation Committee was given Japanese blessing and on 13 January 1942, its members were received at the Peninsula Hotel (then the seat of the Japanese military authorities) and its credentials publicly assured. On 6 February 1942, three new members were added to the original nine.[2]

The Rehabilitation Committee had little power, but it did carry out some humdrum activities for the Japanese, such as selling Japanese flags—priced HK$3 and HK$5 each—for display at celebrations marking the end of the first month of the Japanese occupation. It also helped to organize a welcome, on behalf of the Chinese population, for the incoming Japanese Governor, Rensuke Isogai, and saw to it that most of the former Justices of the Peace, rich merchants, prominent businessmen and other Chinese notables were present on that occasion. Much of the Committee's time seems to have been spent in trotting off to Japanese celebrations and making polite, deferential remarks about the virtues of the new régime. For example, on 11 February 1942, the Committee members paid a formal visit to the East Asia Board and offered felicitations to Colonel Okada and other high-ranking Japanese officials on the occasion of Japan's Empire Day. But the Rehabilitation Committee, because of its composition, did have strong links with business, did in fact represent business interests, and one of its most successful pieces of lobbying was to get the Japanese to despatch rice merchants to Annem in April 1942, for the purpose of buying rice to feed a hungry Hong Kong population and re-establishing the rice trade.

The Rehabilitation Committee—after holding fifty-nine meetings—was superseded, on 30 March 1942, by two councils; the 'Chinese Representative Council' and the 'Chinese Co-operative

[1] The other members were: Lo Man-kam, Li Tse-fong, Li Koon-chun, Tam Nga-shi, Li Chung-po, Tung Ching-wei and Wong Tak-kwong.
[2] Dr Wong Tung-ming, Kong Tai-tung and Cheng Tit-sing.

Council'. Both of these organs owed their existence to a decree of the Japanese Governor, who was anxious to speedily set up an administration, a system of local government and a structure of control. The Chinese Representative Council had at first three members—Lo Kuk-wo, Lau Tit-shing and Li Tse-fong—but on 18 April 1942, a fourth member, Chan Lim-pak, was added. The Chinese Co-operative Council's chairman was Chow Shou-son, and its vice-chairman Li Koon-chung. It is said that Sir Robert Kotewall and Sir Shouson Chow were placed on separate Councils because of previous antagonisms between the two men.[1]

The Japanese put great pressure on prominent Chinese to join these councils and it follows that, in most cases, membership in one or the other of them meant morally or politically practically nothing.[2] In any case, most prominent Chinese would accept it as quite natural that they should be once again playing leading roles in their community, holding public positions and acting as guardians and custodians for the Hong Kong Chinese. At the same time, they were again in a position, as under the British, to defend their entrenched positions and interests. Hence it is not easy to sort the sheep from the goats, nor have I that intention. As a prominent and distinguished Chinese has written: 'These two bodies were a weird mixture of quislings, honest men and bitter enemies of the Japanese. They were given no power whatsoever. At most they made "recommendations" and the Japanese palmed off onto them the blame for obnoxious decrees and laws.'[3] It would be safe to say that participation in the activities of these councils was a form of insurance, or an escape-hatch which allowed survival in the midst of so much misery.

Sir Robert Kotewall and Li Tse-fong have already been referred to, but it should be noted that Sir Robert claimed, and no one has contradicted him, that 'he was advised by three of the leading and senior members of the Hong Kong British Government, Mr R. A. C. North, Mr (later Sir) Grenville Alabaster, K.C. and the late J. A. Fraser, M.C., to co-operate with the Japanese to the extent that the interests of the Colony's Chinese might be

[1] Ward, op. cit., p. 64.

[2] Two former foreign ministers in the Chinese government—Dr W. W. Yen and Eugene Ch'en (Ch'en Yu-jen)—were caught by the Japanese in Hong Kong, but although much pressure was put on them neither one collaborated with the Japanese. Some prominent Chinese escaped to Free China, among them Dr Li Shu-fan.

[3] Li Shu-fan, op. cit., p. 154.

safeguarded . . . it was not until he was assured by the three officials mentioned that his action would not be misconstrued by the British Government and would not be considered or regarded as an act of betrayal of trust that Sir Robert Kotewall was finally prevailed upon to agree to helping the Chinese community in formulating plans for the protection of their interests'.[1] But Chan Lim-pak (1884–1944), a notorious reactionary, was given no such assurance—during the siege of Hong Kong he was under arrest as a suspected fifth-columnist.

Chan (his name is sometimes romanized as Ch'en Lien-po) was born at Namhoi, Kwangtung Province, in 1884. He became a rich Canton merchant early in life and had a large number of business interests—he was, among other things, a director of the Nanyang Brothers' Tobacco Company and Canton comprador (Chinese manager) for the Hong Kong and Shanghai Banking Corporation. In 1924 he organized the Merchants' Volunteers, 'an armed organization supplied and financed by the British and by the wealthy compradores of Hong Kong and Canton',[2] which attempted to oust the Kuomintang from Canton, but he was unsuccessful; the putsch failed and his levies dispersed by a mixed force of Whampoa cadets, workers and peasants. He then fled to Hong Kong and returned to business activities, having on one occasion to leave the Colony and skip bail rather than answer charges alleging embezzlement of funds of the Nanyang Brothers' Tobacco Company. Chan's reactionary and anti-Nationalist background appealed strongly to the Japanese. And the Fook Hing Oil Refinery Company, of which he was Managing Director, was one of the first Chinese firms granted permission by the Governor's Office to engage in manufacturing. In November 1942, the *Hong Kong News* announced that the firm was manufacturing washing soap—an item in very short supply at that time —to meet local requirements.[3] Chan never survived the war: he was killed in an American bombing raid on the *Reinan Maru* on 24 December 1944, whilst on the way to Japan.

Lau Tit-shing (1889–1945) was 'a successful but relatively obscure Chinese merchant of the older type under British rule in Hong Kong'.[4] He was little known to the public before 1941

---

[1] 'Appreciation' by K. K. Li, *South China Morning Post*, 25 May 1949.

[2] Harold R. Isaacs, *The Tragedy of the Chinese Revolution*, Stanford 1961, p. 68.

[3] See also *Hong Kong News*, 24 May 1962.   [4] Ward, op. cit., p. 65.

and is not mentioned in Professor Woo's book. He appears to have been thoroughly brainwashed by his early education in Japan, from which he returned pro-Japanese and anti-western. On his return to Hong Kong—after graduation from Kyoto Imperial University—he became president of the Chinese–Japanese Returned Students' Association. And during the occupation he was especially active in educational affairs in Hong Kong, taking a keen interest in the Japanese-controlled Teachers' Training College. At one of its graduation ceremonies, held in April 1942, Lau asserted that 'the British relied on their material resources whereas the Japanese relied on their spirit. The result of the recent hostilities demonstrated which was better.'[1] He appears to have been quite sincere in his opinions—he believed in a 'White Peril'—and was totally committed to the Japanese side. A good example of what he felt, and of his identification with the Japanese, is given in one of his statements to the *Hong Kong News*:

> The fall of Singapore will be of great benefit to overseas Chinese. . . . Britain has encouraged Japan and China to slaughter each other, hoping that she could profit by their wounds to swallow them both up at once. . . . We must fight there (in Burma) with the ferocity of animals. . . . Our method must be to add the totality of our Chinese forces to the Japanese Army and fight together.[2]

Lau, who had been in ill-health for some time, died on 9 April 1945, and the Japanese sent a special letter of commendation for services rendered to his family. The letter was delivered by a Staff Officer representing the Governor and, according to the *Hong Kong News*, 'this is the first time since the occupation of Hong Kong by the Imperial forces that such an honour has been bestowed upon any person, and is a token of the appreciation of the Authorities for the meritorious services given by the late Mr Lau'.[3]

Lo Kuk-wo, Chan Lim-pak, Li Tse-fong, Lau Tit-shing and Chow Shou-son were the key figures in, and spokesmen for, the two councils; but as the war progressed, Chan Lim-pak and Lau Tit-shing rapidly came to the fore and the others dropped more into the background. Like their fellow collaborationists in Wang

[1] *Hong Kong News*, 3 April 1942.   [2] Ward, op. cit., p. 65.
[3] *Hong Kong News*, 13 April 1945.

Ching-wei's puppet government—such as Chou Fu-hai and Ch'en Kung-po[1]—retreat from their position was scarcely possible. They had made too many foolish and intemperate statements and had backed the Japanese horse too heavily. Moreover, they had maintained close connections with Wang and his friends at Canton. In June 1942 both Lo Kuk-wo—who probably could not avoid going—and Lau Tit-shing paid an official visit to 'President' Wang at Canton. Both Chan and Lau made fiery statements in support of Wang's declaration of war—10 January 1943—against the United States and Great Britain. But even Lo Kuk-wo on this occasion was inspired to demand that 'all Chinese must try their best to support China and Japan to work for the early victory of the sacred war and for the establishment of the East Asia Co-prosperity Sphere'.[2] Yet in a message sent to the *China Mail* in early 1941 he asked the Hong Kong population 'whether we have done enough to relieve or minimize the sufferings of our compatriots in China and of our friends in England, who daily, and every hour of the day, are facing unprecedented perils with such heroic fortitude'.[3] However, many of the public speeches and declarations made by members of the councils should not be taken seriously nor analysed or scrutinized in detail. They were words demanded by the etiquette of a colonial relationship, responses evoked by a colonial social order. We may surmise that behind the public face and the public speech often lurked dislike and anger—for flattery can be more insulting than truth.

The two councils had few points in common with the former Executive and Legislative Councils. The Representative Council was expected to gather suggestions and petitions from individuals and groups and to refer these to the Co-operative Council, a larger body, for more detailed discussion and comment. Recommendations were then to be passed back to the Representative Council for conveyance, together with suggestions as to what action should be taken, to the Governor's Office. In fact both Councils gathered suggestions and petitions from the public, and

[1] Chou Fu-hai was former Minister of Finance and Mayor of Shanghai in the Wang Ching-wei government. He was exonerated of treason by the Kuomintang, but he died in a Chinese prison in 1948. Ch'en Kung-po, who succeeded to the Presidency on Wang's death, was executed for treason in June 1946.

[2] *Hong Kong News*, 11 January 1941.

[3] *Hong Kong Centenary Commemorative Talks*, 1941.

there seems to have been no clear division of function between the two bodies; nor were any express powers delegated to them. They were both advisory and non-executive bodies: they had little influence on Government policy.[1] The Japanese regarded them as listening posts in the population, as institutes of public opinion, as gatherers of rumour. But they did serve other purposes: in them were corralled many prominent and influential Chinese, now administrative captives of the 'New Order'. The Councils also provided a façade of respectability; seemingly the Chinese were now governing themselves under the eyes of a benevolent Japanese occupying force.

The composition of the Councils did not undergo much change throughout the period of Japanese occupation. Chan Lim-pak and Lau Tit-shing both died before the end of the war; and in March 1945 Kwok Chan, a member of the Co-operative Council, and Ling Fu-cho were made members of the Representative Council; at the same time, membership of the former was increased to twenty-five. It appears that the Representative Council met daily, certainly during the first year of its existence; and the Co-operative Council twice weekly, on Mondays and Thursdays. Since full records of the Councils' deliberations do not appear to have survived the war—no *Hong Kong Hansard* was published during the occupation—historians must now rely for details of their activities mainly on reports, much toned down, given in the *Hong Kong News*. It is difficult therefore to write accurately about what they did, or about the faction fights which presumably took place at some of their meetings.

A few weeks after the establishment of these twin councils, the Governor divided Hong Kong into three areas—Hong Kong Island, Kowloon, and the New Territories—over each of which he set an 'Area Bureau', controlled by a Japanese with a Chinese staff. These 'Area Bureaux' must not be confused with the 'District Affairs Bureaux', a parallel organization and structure of control. Hong Kong was divided into twelve, and Kowloon into six, administrative districts—each under a district affairs bureaux headed by a Chinese 'official in charge'. The chief of the Civil

---

[1] Some of the difficulties faced by Council members in their dealings with the Japanese were given by Lo Kuk-wo at the trial of Colonel Noma, the Japanese Gendarmerie Chief. See Douglas M. Kendrick, *Price Control and its Practice in Hong Kong*, 1954, appendix 6, pp. 95–7, and *South China Morning Post*, 14 January 1947.

Affairs Department of the Government explained that the district affairs bureaux were the

> same as those in towns and villages in Nippon; they cannot be regarded as autonomous bodies as they are being supported by the Governor's Office . . . apart from the distribution of rice, the bureaux will henceforth look after the distribution of other essential commodities of the populace and look after public health and other welfare work.[1]

In time, the district affairs bureaux developed a large number of functions: such as taking censuses, repatriation of residents, supervision of house cleansing campaigns, changing of street names, recruitment of street guards, issuing of certificates and forms, and so on. Ichiki, chief of the Civil Affairs Department, pointed out that the district bureaux had three main functions: to act 'as a first-line administrative body of the Government; as an autonomous organ administered by representatives of each district; and as a supplement to the Chinese Representative Council'.[2] But Tomari, chief of the General Affairs Department, said at a later date that the 'main duty of the district bureaux . . . is to make all the people co-operate fully with the authorities',[3] and this is probably what the Japanese authorities wanted them to do. In August 1942 a District Bureau Advisory Council, composed of well-known merchants, was formed to act as a link between the twin councils and the bureaux; but, once again, the relationship between the councils and the bureaux was never precisely defined.

Soon after the setting up of the system of district bureaux, a further administrative sub-division took place: Hong Kong and Kowloon were divided into wards, each with an elected ward leader, and in September 1942 the Hong Kong Bureau appointed seven hundred and seventy-seven 'responsible' citizens to look after conditions in the streets in which they lived. Thus stage by stage the Japanese involved more and more Chinese in their administrative machine and developed a structure of control that reached right down to the street-level. It meant, as with the Nationalist Chinese revival of the old *Pao-chia* system,[4] that every-

[1] *Hong Kong News*, 20 July 1942.
[2] ibid., 19 August 1942.   [3] ibid., 6 October 1942.
[4] This was a mutual responsibility system in local government. Ideally, one hundred families formed a *chia* and ten *chia* formed a *pao*.

one had to watch everyone else and feel responsibility for the actions of his neighbours.

Thus the Japanese were able to draw into the administration and local government of Hong Kong many more Chinese than the British had ever used. First there were the twin councils— the four-man Representative Council, the leading organ, and the twenty-two-man (later twenty-five-man) Co-operative Council, each under the chairmanship of a well-known and influential Chinese citizen; then the eighteen district advisory bureaux, each with a chief, a deputy chief, and Chinese staff; and finally the several thousand ward and street leaders. Moreover, the Japanese employed many Chinese in their various government agencies. Clearly, many more Chinese than before were being given official status and position, and a public role to perform. Despite the fact that many of these committees and bodies were ineffectual, lacked power and were Japanese front organizations—instruments of control used by a totalitarian state—they did at least make many Chinese feel involved with the government and administration of Hong Kong. More people were publicly recognized by the Japanese. And being Chinese, such people were able to look after the interests of the public and at the same time advance those of their families; and public position meant access to scarce items —food, clothing and other wants. In certain ways, this situation must have appeared more satisfactory than that under the British Mandarinate, when very few Chinese were admitted, as it were, to Government's high table. Of course this point must not be pushed too far—Chinese were plagued with many humiliations and by the aberrations of an erratic Japanese soldiery and gendarmerie.

3   *Après le déluge*

When Admiral Harcourt's task force entered Hong Kong harbour at 11 a.m. on 30 August 1945, 'on every junk and on nearly every house there flew the flag of China'.[1] It seemed to spectators as though, after some three-and-half years of the Japanese presence, the ordinary Chinese had forgotten about the British; or that if he remembered, thought the Nationalists would soon be administering the Colony as a constituent part of Kwangtung Province.

[1] F. S. V. Donnison, *British Military Administration in the Far East*, London 1956, p. 202.

The Chinese appeared to the British to be cheering for the wrong team; but Admiral Harcourt gave immediate recognition and support to the provisional administration set up by Mr F. C. Gimson; and then on 1 September proclaimed the establishment of a Military Administration which governed Hong Kong until 1 May 1946, on which date the Administration handed over to the civil government, with Sir Mark Young back in Government House after an interrupted governorship.

One would have expected, in line with events in Europe in the years 1944–6, that a starved, angry and aroused Chinese population would have wreaked vengeance on those people who had worked prominently for the Japanese or had spoken publicly in their favour. In France, according to Robert Aron,[1] some thirty to forty thousand collaborators were executed, often summarily or at the hands of the mob. In Hong Kong a few Japanese—notably the Japanese executioner at Stanley Prison—and some Chinese underlings, informers and torturers were lynched or manhandled; but after a few weeks things simmered down, and the *Annual Report of the Hong Kong Police Force 1946–7* lists only one murder in which the motive was suspected to be collaboration with the enemy. Those who were prime targets of mob revenge in other occupied countries—such as the public servants of the Vichy régime—went scot free in Hong Kong; although for a short time there were 'bewildering cross-currents of recrimination and denunciation'.[2]

Several reasons may be brought forward to explain the immunity of many prominent Chinese after the war—some of whom were felt to be traitors both to the British and Chinese governments. To begin with, they had in fact acted as a shield between the people and the Japanese; they had attempted to represent the needs of the Chinese population. Thus at a meeting of the Chinese Co-operative Council on 16 August 1943, Li Koon-chun raised the motion that in order to prevent hardship to unemployed Chinese about to be forcibly evacuated to China, the General Charity Society, in conjunction with the Repatriation Office, should be allowed to devise means of evacuating such people 'to

---

[1] Robert Aron, *Histoire de Vichy*, Paris 1959, p. 651. The right-wing claims there were 105,000 victims: see *Le Livre noir de l'épuration*, Paris, Lectures françaises 1964, p. 8.

[2] *The British Military Administration: August, 1945, to April, 1946*, Hong Kong 1946, p. 2.

their home, village or places nearby so that they will not be left stranded and unable to find any food'. The twin councils and the district bureaux had shown public spirit and an earnest desire to alleviate hardship—these associations were not just mutual-aid societies for the prominent, or centres of corruption. And the British when they returned in a chastened mood—felt no strong desire to prosecute any one, apart from notorious war criminals who were dealt with by special War Crime Courts. The English-language newspapers supported this policy; and though some ex-Stanleyites in the first few months of liberation wrote bitter letters to the press, the editors soon muted the collaboration issue. Like Government they saw the need for rehabilitation, the need to get the economy started again and the businessmen, whether Chinese or European, back in their offices.[1] Any hunting down of members of the business community or other notables—very much an 'in group'—was a moral luxury Hong Kong felt it could not afford at that time.

Again, it may be surmised that Government was worried by events over the border, in a xenophobic China ardent to reclaim China's lost territories. In 1945 Hong Kong remained the sole survivor of the old 'unequal treaty' system, and an anti-colonial United States did not—at that date—favour British retention of Hong Kong. At one time there were no fewer than fifteen quasi-official Chinese missions in Hong Kong seeking to install themselves on various pretexts. The local branch of the Kuomintang and the missions were prominent in smelling out collaborators and traitors—at times using accusations of collaboration as a means to extort blackmail. In these circumstances, the British needed Hong Kong Chinese, Chinese loyal to the concept of a separate status for Hong Kong, even if some among this group had worked seemingly for the establishment of a Japanese 'New Order' in Hong Kong. Moreover, in 1945 the Hong Kong Government was under pressure to surrender Chinese collaborators to the Chinese; so that in 1946 it was forced to introduce a Chinese Collaborators (Surrender) Bill 'to make arrangements to provide for the surrender of persons of Chinese nationality other than British subjects, who, during the period 7 July 1937,

---

[1] This statement needs qualification: it had been planned that the Administration should monopolize the import and export trade for the first six months, but under strong pressure from the community the colony was reopened to private trade on 23 November 1945.

and 16 August 1945, collaborated with the Japanese'. Three such collaborators were arrested and subsequently deported under the Deportation of Aliens Ordinance, 1935, and two other arrests were made but as the evidence available appeared insufficient they were released. But the rights of such people were protected by law. The 1946 Ordinance thus protected Chinese against the arbitrary inquisitions, often inspired by malice, of the Kuomintang. British justice must have appeared extraordinarily humane compared with the Japanese or Nationalist varieties.

As for the Chinese notables as a whole, they soon closed their ranks and demanded that there be no witch-hunt, no prosecution or persecution of their fellows. British refusal to take action against those who had profited from, or been implicated in, the Japanese occupation, had a curious result; as Dr Marjorie Topley notes: 'Some people made money during the Japanese occupation —trade with Japan was highly disapproved of before the war. It is said that public disapproval of such individuals was weakened because the government took no action against them.'[1] A report of the British Military Administration admits that: 'No new figures emerged as the leaders of Chinese opinion, and the Administration relied upon the Government's prewar Chinese advisers; such disapproval as there was from certain sections of the public was at no time strong enough to produce alternative candidates.'[2] But given the system (discussed above) by which Chinese acquired status and position—both functions or corollaries of wealth and munificence—it is difficult to see how Government could have uncovered new leaders, Hong Kong 'Hampdens', ready to step into the shoes of pre-war advisers. But another fact should also be taken into account in explaining the way the collaboration issue was handled: in 1945 there were only some six hundred thousand people in the Colony—the rest had died or been forcibly evacuated. Those who returned after the war had little first-hand knowledge of events under the Japanese occupation and were unlikely to be feeling too bitter about the former leaders of the Chinese community.

Sir Robert Kotewall—no longer known as Lo kuk-wo—was in poor health after the war and resigned from the Executive Council, to which he had been re-appointed in 1941 and of which he was still technically a member in 1945, just after the liberation. But,

---

[1] Marjorie Topley, op. cit., p. 205.
[2] *The British Military Administration*, op. cit., p. 4.

as K. K. Li wrote in his appreciation of Sir Robert on the latter's death:

> in spite of certain unkind rumours to the contrary Sir Mark Young as well as Admiral Sir Cecil Harcourt both wrote to Sir Robert assuring him of their high regard for him, and fully recognizing the extremely difficult position in which he was placed at the time of the surrender.[1]

This statement would seem to be confirmed by the fact that at Sir Robert's funeral in 1949 the Governor sent his A.D.C. as his representative, and that the Acting Secretary for Chinese Affairs was also present. Li Tse-fong, appointed to the Legislative Council in January 1941 (the normal term of office is four years) was not re-appointed to that body in 1946; but he continued to be represented on the committees of several charitable and other associations. Sir Shouson Chow—the ageing leader of the Chinese community: 84 in 1945—did not return completely to public life; but on his death in 1959 his family received a message of sympathy from H.R.H. the Duke of Edinburgh. The new members of the Legislative Council appointed in May 1946 were Chau Tsun-nin, Lo Man-kam and Dr Chau Sik-nin; the Chinese unofficial members of the Executive Council were Chau Tsun-nin and Lo Man-kam. All these immediate post-war appointees had been prominent in welfare work during the war and had done their best to lessen the severities of the Japanese occupation.

Chinese informants tell me there was little resentment during the occupation against the members of the twin councils; that Chinese understood that such people had to bow before the Japanese Governor and occasionally shout 'Banzai!' But those who bowed lower than others and with greater alacrity, or shouted too vociferously, were noted. What we can now say about most of the members of the councils is that they accepted nomination either to protect their families and interests or to mollify the severities of the occupation. Few were proper quislings, few allowed themselves to be brainwashed by the Japanese; they remained implacably Chinese and racialist. When asked what they did during the occupation they could use Sieyes' answer, about his life during the French Revolution—like him, they had survived.

In the New Territories, although the people there had suffered less during the occupation, the return to normal conditions was

[1] See 'Appreciation' by K. K. Li, op. cit.

longer and more difficult to achieve than in the urban areas of the Colony. The rural areas of the New Territories had been penetrated by Communist guerrillas—members of the East River Striking Force and the Kwangtung Anti-Japanese Guerrilla Forces—and by Nationalist and British agents. The Japanese never effectively controlled the whole area, although district bureaux had been set up, together with an Area Bureaux at Taipo. The New Territories had had a long history of lawlessness, faction fights and clan feuds. The 1900 *Report on the New Territory at Hong Kong* mentions that:

> clan fights have been a common practice in the San On District for centuries and it has been not unusual for groups of villages to combine together for purposes of offence and defence. . . . Some of these (New Territories) villages are walled . . . to afford the inhabitants greater security if attacked by robbers and to place them in a stronger position for purposes of defence in case of clan feuds.[1]

The war intensified in some cases the existing feuds and in others widened the gap between village elders and villagers. Referring to the latter problem, the *Annual Report 1946* notes:

> During the Japanese occupation some of the elders died and though many declined to have dealings with the invaders some were prepared to collaborate with the Japanese in order to obtain privileges and monopolies. With the return of British administration, it was discovered that one of the results of war had been to create a schism between the older men and the younger men. . . . The only method of choosing a council of elders who could be regarded as representative and on whose authority Government could rely, was by popular election in each district.[2]

Elections were first held in some districts in 1946; after that date, a system of rural committees, with representatives from the twenty-eight sub-districts of the New Territories, was established.

Even in the New Territories there was no real purge, although rancorous enmities continued to fester for a number of years. By

[1] *Report on the New Territory of Hong Kong*, 1900, Cmd. 403, H.M.S.O., London, p. 5. See also Maurice Freedman, *Lineage Organisation in Southeastern China*, London 1958, p. 105 ff.

[2] *Annual Report 1946*, p. 7. For an account of guerrilla activities on Lantau Island see the *South China Morning Post*, 27 March to 26 April 1946.

the time Sir Alexander Grantham arrived in July 1947 to succeed Sir Mark Young as Governor the collaboration issue was practically dead in the Colony. The two War Crimes Courts, which had been established by Royal Warrant with authority to try Japanese war criminals in respect of any war crime committed in the Far East Command, closed down the following year; one in February 1948, after dealing with seventeen cases in Hong Kong involving fifty-two accused, and the other in April 1948, after having tried five accused on charges of ill treatment of civilians in the New Territories. Lieutenant General Rensuke Isogai (Governor General of Hong Kong from February 1942 to December 1944) was tried at Nanking by a Chinese War Crimes Court on evidence prepared by the Hong Kong War Crimes Investigation Team for causing the wholesale arrest and deportation of Chinese civilians from Hong Kong. Of the approximately nineteen thousand Japanese P.O.W.s and civilian internees in the Colony in 1945 nearly all had been repatriated by the end of 1947.[1] Yet despite the fact that it was estimated the Japanese or their minions executed over ten thousand Chinese during the occupation,[2] only twenty-nine defendants (mostly of Chinese race) other than war criminals came before Court for high treason or breach of the Defence Regulations. Of these only three were convicted and sentenced.[3]

The British Government's decision to prosecute as few Chinese (and other non-Europeans) as possible was a sensible one in the circumstances, and a similar decision was taken in respect of the large number of Indians who worked in one capacity or other for the Japanese. In 1941, there were between four to five thousand Indians in Hong Kong. Apart from those in the armed forces, a number were serving in the Hong Kong Police[4] and as watchmen for Government buildings and private firms; another group was engaged in business. During the war the affairs of the Indian community were managed by the Japanese sponsored India Independence League in Hong Kong, a branch of the organization set

---

[1] *Figures given in British Military Administration,* op. cit.; up to April 1946, 17,998 Japanese P.O.W.s, and internees, 2,619 Formosans and 289 Koreans had been repatriated. Left in the Colony—at that date—were 1,288 P.O.W.s and internees and 282 war criminals.

[2] Harold Ingrams, *Hong Kong,* London 1952, p. 242.

[3] See: *Report of the Hong Kong and Kowloon Magistracies for the period 1st May 1946 to 31st March, 1947.*

[4] About 800 in 1941.

up in Tokyo by Rash Behari Bose, Subhas Chandra Bose and other Indian emigres.[1] The League's officers gave support to the Indian National Army, raised in 1942 from Indian P.O.W.s in Japanese hands and Indian civilians in Japanese-occupied territories.[2] On liberation those Indians who had been extremely active in the League's affairs in Hong Kong were mostly left alone. The Japanese had set up front organizations for other national or racial communities, such as the Filipino Association whose president was a certain Dr Atienza; Portuguese were allowed to register with this association. Even the Eurasians were encouraged to form a Eurasian Mutual Aid Society. But the political activities of these groups compared with the Indian Independence League were quite negligible.

It is now time to come to some conclusions about the collaboration problem. The Japanese occupation of Hong Kong and South-East Asia demonstrated that Asians could govern themselves, that this was not a special attribute of the European. Collaboration was mainly a form of insurance taken out by non-Europeans against the risk that the former colonial powers would fail to return after the war. When it became clear that Japan would be ultimately defeated many Chinese assumed—in line with declarations made by some Allied leaders—that Hong Kong's status would be changed ultimately and some sort of Chinese administration installed. Asians had 'collaborated' with European colonialists before the war and continued this habit by collaborating with new colonialists—the Japanese. It was wisdom to do so. Moreover, there was confusion about which group in China represented the Chinese nation—most Chinese before the Communist takeover felt a diffuse loyalty either to something called 'China' or 'Chineseness', or to a village or region.[3] Hence when Europeans used the term 'collaborator' to denote Asians who had

---

[1] Subhas Chandra Bose (1897–1945) arrived in Berlin in March 1941 and, after a journey by submarine, in Toyko in 1943 to take over the India Independence League, first founded by Rash Behari Bose in Japan as far back as 1916. Chandra Bose was flying back to Japan when his plane crashed in Taiwan.

[2] A number of these soldiers were tried in India after the war.

[3] The Cantonese term *Heung Ha* is used to describe 'the province, district and village from which each person derives his ancestry, usually in the direct male line and usually for many generations, even if neither he nor his father has ever set eyes on that village or knows the way there'. *Hong Kong: Report on the 1961 Census*, vol. 2, p. xlviii.

been too friendly with the Japanese occupiers they were using the term disingenuously. No comparison can be made, then, between occupied Hong Kong and occupied France. In France collaborators were citizens of what had been an independent country: in Hong Kong this was not the case. To whom and to what did the Hong Kong Chinese properly owe allegiance? The post-war British Administration appears to have understood this problem, which was basically a conflict of loyalties caused by the anomalous position of the Hong Kong Chinese. These people felt loyalties and ties to their families and kin, to some association smaller than the Chinese nation, to some group contained in Chinese society, but not to the concept of a nation-state.

In May 1945 an exploratory meeting was held in London between representatives of the China Association, the Hong Kong planners and the Colonial Office to examine ways and means by which a larger measure of self-government could be introduced into a liberated Hong Kong. The meeting concluded that this could be partially achieved by converting the pre-war Urban Council into a genuine Municipal Council, to which certain functions of government might be delegated. It was felt, however, that detailed planning should be deferred until the civil government had been re-established. When Sir Mark Young returned he referred to this matter in his first public statement; and at the first meeting of the resuscitated Legislative Council the point was taken up by Lo Man-kam. 'Your return, Sir,' he said, 'signifies the birth of a new Hong Kong, which, in surviving the ordeal of the war years, has learned to appreciate the inestimable boon of law and order, *the sense of responsibility in a greater measure of self-government foreshadowed by Your Excellency*, and the need to strive for and attain an even higher standard of life and living through unity of purpose and effort . . . imbued with this spirit, thankfully rejoicing in deliverance from an intolerable yoke, *resolved to advance the interests of the Colony as a whole and not those of any particular section of the community*, we cordially welcome Your Excellency's resumption of the Presidency of this Council and assure you, Sir, of our wholehearted co-operation and support'[1] (author's italics).

Although the Urban Council has not been converted as yet into a fully elected Municipal Council on the British model,[2] the

---

[1] *Hong Kong Hansard: Session 1946*, p. 18.

[2] The Urban Council (Amendment) Bill of 1956 increased the number of

Administration's interest in extending democratic procedures in Hong Kong signified that in 1946 a mild reformism was in the air and that the older type of benevolent despotism practised before the war was under review; for the Administration was now, or felt itself to be, on probation—facing both a Chinese population that had been separated from its control by the Japanese inter-regnum and an increasingly nationalistic China. Under these changed conditions, it found it expedient to adopt a more placatory and less racialist attitude. Few Officials now possessed a whole-hearted faith in the white man's mission to rule—many had lost faith in imperialist ideals. They had returned to Hong Kong on sufferance, as trustees looking after the assets of a defunct colonial system, in which only a few Europeans now believed.

The repeal of the Peak Residence Ordinance,[1] together with the Governor's 1946 statement that the people's views on constitutional reform would be sought, were indications, among many, of this change of heart and of Government's earnest desire to win over the population. The Administration succeeded in achieving the latter, less by promoting political reforms—for few have emerged since 1945—than by its successful attempts to rehabilitate the economy and by getting people back into gainful employment. It successfully wooed, and entered into wedlock with, the influential business community—a fruitful alliance for both parties.

On 23 November 1945, the Colony was thrown open to trade and in the following month the first commercial ship arrived in harbour. During this early period of rehabilitation over 23,000 free meals were provided daily to feed the destitute, a system of rationing and price control established, the basic coolie wage raised from twenty-five cents to one dollar, and the Hong Kong dollar successfully re-introduced. At the same time as the poor

[1] Proclamation No. 14, issued by the Military Administration in 1945, made provisions for repatriation (or cash in lieu) for former members of the Hong Kong Volunteer Defence Corps. Since these provisions discriminated in favour of Europeans, they provoked considerable public resentment and discussion. These provisions were later modified to include a greater degree of equality of treatment for all concerned. I mention this example to show that the 'racialist' issue was very much to the fore in those post-liberation days.

elected members from four to eight and likewise the number of nominated members. Ordinary members have a clear majority over the six official members.

were being helped, the businessmen were given specially favourable treatment. For example, the public utility companies were supposed to function under the general supervision of Government. In fact, their boards of directors were allowed to run things by themselves and Government control was only nominal; their shareholders were safeguarded by the Government's agreement to meet any losses and pay a fair rent for the use of the companies' property and plant. Government found itself in such a position in 1945 that it was forced to prop up the business community and ensure its group survival. Many of the Hong Kong notables benefited from this policy—and no doubt felt gratitude, or at least less antagonism, toward the Administration, one that now saw eye to eye with them on many things and was prepared to guarantee, or provide conditions, for their continued existence as a status group. The prominent Chinese had come into their own and had found their credentials endorsed by a Government that desperately needed them, that sought their loyalty. This, then, was the start of a process that drew Government and business more closely together than had been the case pre-war.

In Stanley internment camp, European businessmen, *pong-paan*[1] and Government officials lived cheek by jowl for over three-and-a-half years. They shared in common the cruel experiences and boredoms of prison life, and developed from this enforced propinquity more neighbourly feelings than before the war. When these people were liberated in 1945 they had acquired an *esprit de corps*, the feeling of belonging to an exclusive club—a club of 'ex-Stanleyites'. These feelings, informants tell me, were carried over into peacetime and led to a *rapprochement* after the war between some European businessmen and Government Officials. Many had been 'in the bag together'—there was more informality than before. Although we can only speculate about this, it would seem plausible to argue that, as a result of these common experiences and trials, relationships between the members of these two influential groups—between Government Officials and European businessmen—became less uneasy and more man to man. The status barriers had disappeared.

Sir Alexander Grantham, Sir Mark Young's successor at Government House, outlining his policy to the members of the

---

[1] This term, given here in its Cantonese romanization, refers to Europeans in uniformed supervisory jobs, such as the police, and so distinguishes them from Taipans.

Legislative Council in July 1947, declared: 'It is readily assumed that because there is a majority of officials the slightest wish of Government is "steam-rollered" through this council. I am sure that no one knows better than the Unofficial Members that this is not so. The opinions of the Unofficial Members carry a great deal of weight; as they should, and it is rarely except in the matters of highest importance that the Official Majority is used.'[1] These remarks throw some light on the important role then being played by the Unofficial Members—nearly all of whom were businessmen or had business interests—and on the very close liaison that had already developed between Government and the business community. The Government's advisers were selected from and represented the business community and the small group of Hong Kong notables. They or their allies were also represented on a number of other important committees which had developed advisory functions *vis-à-vis* Government. It follows that this system of representation operated like a Freudian super-ego or censorship mechanism between Government and the mass of the population; Government could only glean a partial account of the felt needs of the community, a biassed account because of the assumptions accepted by their representatives.

Later events, such as the Communist takeover of China in 1949, followed by the flood of refugees, including entrepreneurs from Shanghai, merely fortified this tendency—of making the leaders of the business community the most important and powerful pressure group in the Colony and the unofficial formulators of Government policy. The refugees imposed an enormous financial burden and social problem on the Colony, one that could only be partially reduced by drawing them into jobs provided by businessmen, for Hong Kong has never known a Keynesian Financial Secretary nor an Administration prepared to prime the pump. To this day, the public utilities are privately owned. The *laisser faire* philosophy of the businessman has become, in a modified form, that of Government—there is no tradition of 'municipal socialism'. Hong Kong continues to prosper, as *The Economist* notes, 'on a governmental philosophy of *laisser faire* that one had not expected to meet this side of the nineteenth century'.[2] Yet Government has often been more progressive in its views than the leaders of the community; but, since it may at times lack

[1] *Hong Kong Hansard: Session 1947*, p. 257.
[2] *The Economist*, 'Hong Kong: A Survey', 14 November 1964.

support from this hard-headed and conservative-minded group, it is often forced to step warily and to compromise.

The Pacific War and the Japanese occupation did not, then, destroy Hong Kong's pre-war social and economic order; it strengthened it, eliminating some previous conflicts of interests and modifying the position of the British Mandarinate. The latter has lost its 'Peak mentality' and colonial arrogance. It has lost its sense of mission; it is less confident. The local population, especially the businessmen, seem to have acquired greater trust in the Administration. They were impressed by the speed with which the rehabilitation of the economy was achieved, by the establishment of law and order and of a milieu favourable to the acquisition of wealth. The Government honoured its pre-war debts and obligations and compensated its former employees. Its post-occupation record was admirable—it believed in business first. It was forced to this belief by a concatenation of events, including the Japanese occupation, and by Hong Kong's peculiar geographical position.

No group of new leaders has emerged since the war to challenge the privileged, the entrenched and the rich. No trade union, political party or any other association has come forward to effectively challenge the bases of Hong Kong society. Most Chinese seem not to resent these facts, though some, including businessmen, support and speak in favour of Communist China. Hong Kong still has a British Administration, the top echelons of which are almost completely monopolized by Europeans, and some thirty-thousand-odd European expatriates; but it remains a Chinese city in which aspects of Chinese social organization and traditional Chinese values continue to survive. It is a Colony run today—though this is not a result of deliberate Government policy but *faute de mieux*—for a small group of Chinese and European businessmen, experts in the techniques of making money.

VI

A STUDY IN WESTERNIZATION[1]

Joseph Agassi and I. C. Jarvie

Authors' Note: The fundamental thesis of this paper is sufficiently sociologically unorthodox to warrant a preparatory word or two. We hold that there are at least two facets to westernization: ideological and socio-logical. The west is a philosophy, a way of life, as well as a bundle of social institutions, customs and cultural objects. We hold that while the west exports both, it is the ideology which is more important and coherent; that there is more homogeneity in fundamental outlook between the countries of the west than there is in social organization or technology. Indeed we would think that no particular form of social organization or stage of technological development is specially western. Western technology and business practice, however, are adopted at a somewhat faster pace than the ideas and social arrangements which go with them, thus a westerner arriving in Hong Kong and seeing familiar sights like motor-cars and skyscrapers may expect the attitudes and institutions in which these are embedded to be equally familiar. This expectation is mistaken. To con-fute it, we very early bring up, and extensively discuss, situations which someone equipped with a western outlook will find puzzling when he comes to Hong Kong. Situations which reveal the extent of westernization—and of the lack of it.

This paper contains the results of empirical research carried out by the authors. The method we adopted was selective fieldwork; fieldwork, that is, which concentrated on selected problems, not on surveying all aspects of the society. We lived in the society and were in daily contact with its members, some of whom were our informants. Most of our informants were students of the University, whose economic and social backgrounds differ widely, although few come from the very lowest income groups (these groups anyway appear the least westernized). All informants are biassed, of course, and we have always attempted to check what we were told with government officials, anthropologists, and non-university informants.

We proceeded in the normal way, beginning with certain problems, which

---

[1] An excessively compressed summary of this paper was published by the second co-author, under the title 'Face and Façade in Hong Kong', in *New Society*, vol. 3, 25 June 1964, pp. 13–15.

were explored by means of observations made in order to criticize tentative hypothetical solutions to the problems; these solutions were refuted and replaced by other solutions, which were in turn refuted, and so on. Some of these earlier theories are mentioned briefly in section 3. Eventually we were left with a number of hypotheses which we could criticize but not refute, and these we present here.

1 Background

Social change of any kind—including westernization—is piece-meal, haphazard and chaotic, even where attempts are made to organize and plan it. Consequently the student of westernization has to be careful that his work does not reflect too closely this chaos. Possibly our best plan would have been to follow the traditional parcelling-up of society: economics, kinship, politics, religion and culture. This being a short and sketchy study there is not space to deal in detail with all of these, but perhaps a few cursory words on what they were like in Imperial China will be a starting point.

China's economy has always been peasant. Industry was almost unknown, and merchants were very much a despised class, whether they were foreigners or Chinese.[1] The kinship system of China was quite simple. The system was basically patrilineal and the most important groupings seem to have been: the extended family (a father, his sons, their wives, their sons and daughters and possibly the sons' sons' wives) and the lineage, sometimes called the clan.[2] On the whole, the extended family seems to have been the economic unit, the lineages the legal, property and ritual units.[3] Descent, succession and inheritance all went through males. The legal head of the family or lineage was its oldest surviving male member. The Confucian principle of filial piety carried over into the religion, which was mainly ancestor worship, supplemented by elements of Buddhism and belief in spirits and geomancy. About politics it is impossible to generalize. Up to the founding of the Republic in 1911 the system seems to have been very like that in feudal Europe: central control, but much local

[1] For a very good survey of Chinese economic attitudes, both traditional and present-day in Hong Kong, see Dr Marjorie Topley's paper, below.

[2] See Professor Potter's paper, note 1, p. 11, on the different usages.

[3] See Maurice Freedman, 'The Family in China, Past and Present', *Pacific Affairs*, vol. XXXIV, 1961, pp. 323–36.

autonomy in day-to-day affairs. Administration was carried on through a sophisticated bureaucracy. The mandarins, or class of scholar-administrators recruited by public examination, were very highly regarded. Scholars and teachers generally, even those who had failed the examinations, also had high status. Culture, finally, was an upper-class preserve. It required long training and much leisure to compose verse or music, or to paint. All forms of art were ossified many centuries ago and have scarcely developed at all since.

As is well known, the orient was much slower to absorb the influence of the west than was, say, Africa. This was partly because contact came very late in the history to these oriental civilizations; partly because both China and Japan pursued a conscious Closed-Door Policy of isolating their countries from the barbarians, until the Great Powers more or less forced breaches in the insulation; partly because even then, the Great Powers never colonized China and Japan as they did Africa.

Where they did colonize, as in Indo-China, they colonized on top of an ancient and sophisticated culture and social system which absorbed less readily the culture of the westerners than was the case in Africa. And where an attempt was made—in Japan—to take from the west only what they wanted and to keep what they wanted of their own tradition, certain social tensions suggest that what they accept and what they reject is not as much under control as they would hope and like.[1]

We shall argue that something similar is the case in Hong Kong; that although in some respects Hong Kong is westernized, in certain crucial respects it is less westernized than, say, Malaya, where both the indigenous way of life and the westernization have deeper roots. It would no doubt be instructive to compare *in extenso* Hong Kong with Japan and Malaya, which experienced war, defeat, and occupation much more severely than Hong Kong. But this is beyond our present scope.

2 Barriers to communication

Just because Hong Kong is full of Chinese people it would be a mistake to see it as simply a piece of China. This it is not. It is essentially a refugee city; it has been populated over the years

[1] In this matter cf. Arthur Koestler's quite fascinating *The Lotus and the Robot*, London 1960.

mainly by people who have fled from the peasant areas of Kwangtung Province. They are ordinary southern Chinese country people
in most respects, but perhaps in the very act of fleeing they
evidence a willingness to move a little way towards the west and
live under its terms. This unusual and previously essentially temporary population (there used always to be the hope of going
back) did not until 1949 represent a cross-section even of the
Cantonese. Since most refugees fled famine and political upheaval
there were relatively few gentry or intellectuals or artists or even
millionaires among them. So, although Hong Kong was and still
is a Chinese city, it was not a normal Chinese city: its class structure is peculiar and it always was something of a cultural wasteland.

But, to our purpose, it is the lack of intellectuals and the highly
skilled that it is so crucial to stress. The more intelligently aware
refugees were precisely those who would tend to go back as soon
as they knew things had changed. Until World War II, even our
own University was, in its Faculty of Arts, more a finishing school
for young ladies and a teachers' training college of sorts than a
centre of intellectual and cultural activity; in its faculty of medicine
it was a factory turning young well-to-do gentlemen into very
well-off professionals; other faculties hardly existed. It is perhaps
hard for a westerner to imagine a society of nearly one million
inhabitants with no other institutions of education or culture except high schools, one small (so-called) university and nothing else.

The events of 1949–50—that is to say the final success of the
communist revolution—brought of course many millionaires,
gentry, politicians and even a few artists and intellectuals to the
Colony and these latter are to be found scattered among the staffs
of the secondary schools and post-secondary colleges. But
although sociologically the population of Hong Kong is now far
more normally distributed it is still, to a large extent, a cultural
wasteland even though the excuse of this being a temporary,
waiting-to-return-to-the-mainland existence no longer holds.
There are, it is true, vestigial traces of traditional Chinese culture.
A few scholars, a few old-fashioned writers and painters. But one
could hardly claim their arts were alive, developing, exciting. And
as yet those who have adopted western styles have not integrated
them into a coherent synthesis of both traditions. Chinese opera
is a repertory of classics, only altered in details. There are relatively few modern-dress films. For his culture-identification films,

aimed exclusively at the Chinese audience, the Hong Kongite gets Mandarin and Cantonese costume dramas, or turgid melodramas and comedies set in an ambiguous interwar period. One old cultural element does flourish, however, and that is a general philosophy of life which says: 'I am born a Chinese, and there is something inestimably to be valued in this.'[1] Culture lives only in the past, yet to be Chinese-conscious, oddly enough, is not to be an old fuddy-duddy. Even the most far-out teenagers retain their loyalty to Chineseness without much difficulty. Although Chinese social organization is crumbling in the urban areas—there are no longer tight kin groups, collective ancestor worship, filial piety, land to be worked and inherited, marriages to be arranged—there do exist traces of all these items and minimal adherence to them is seen as an assertion of Chineseness.

Traditional aversions, to cheese, to dark skin, to marrying foreigners, all these live on, but very much in the background. Local organizations like Kaifongs (i.e. local traditional communal societies) in the towns will inveigh in the mode of revivalist preachers against immoralities like bars and brothels; meanwhile lineage or clan organizations in the outlying villages will be agitating about how a new reservoir is ruining the *fung shui* (geomantic propitiousness[2]) of their village.

So faced with such mixtures we can come to our first question which is: to what extent is Hong Kong simply a western-type city populated with Chinese faces?

To tackle this problem we will proceed as follows. First we will look at the naivest possible approach, that of the tourist. Then we will gradually broaden and deepen our discussion of his experiences to try to bring out the fundamental conflict which divides west from east in Hong Kong and which impedes

[1] For a remarkable (and frightening) study of this aspect of the Chinese national character and its relation to communism see Robert S. Elegant, *The Centre of the World*, London 1963. Further material is to be found in Dennis Bloodworth's *The Chinese Looking Glass*, New York 1967. But see also James Macdonald, 'China and the "barbarians" ', *New Society*, vol. 10, 31 August 1967, pp. 295–6.

[2] *Fung shui* is a complex of pseudo-scientific beliefs about the 'luck' and prosperity associated with sites for villages, graves, houses, etc. Some description of it can be found in Marjorie Topley, op. cit., pp. 184, 199; Maurice, Freedman, 'A Report on Social Research in the New Territories—1963', op. cit. paras. 47–71, also *Chinese Lineage and Society: Fukien and Kwangtung*, London 1966; and in the papers by Professor Potter and Mr Ng in this volume.

westernization and sets up a tension. We begin with a naive view because in a way sociology must start from it in order to have something to criticize and improve.

3   A superficial starting point

Almost four hundred thousand tourists came to Hong Kong in 1964. It attracted them because it is a very lovely place to look at, because the shopping is diverse and cheap, and because Hong Kong is unique as a city offering all western comforts yet located in the exotic and intriguing orient. Let us put all this, the well-known aspect of Hong Kong, to one side: it can be read about elsewhere.[1] The question is whether Hong Kong is simply a western-type city with a lot of Chinese trimmings thrown in. Is there anything about Hong Kong which the visitor will notice after a few days or a few weeks which will not fit into any neat preconceived picture? Old men with beards and beautiful black-haired girls dressed in slit cheong-sams, Chinese writing on signs and notices everywhere and Chinese temples tucked in various corners—all that is clearly Chinese; miniature skyscrapers, English spoken, and hectic traffic—these are clearly western.

All this is just surface. A tourist at a lesser hotel asks the telephone operator for room service. He is answered in Chinese. 'Is this room service?' is answered with 'Hello'; 'Is this room service?' repeated, is answered with silence and heavy breathing—until the tourist hangs up in exasperation. A tourist goes into a photo-equipment shop and asks if they have a camera Brand X. He is answered 'yes', and shown a Brand Y. He repeats his request. He is again answered with a 'yes' and this time is shown a Brand Z, and so on until he realizes that the answer is either 'no' or 'I don't understand'.

The tourist will get used to this. At first he will explain it to himself in terms of the considerable language barrier. He will discover his error if he stays for more than a few days and meets some local people, European or Chinese, who speak both English and the local dialect perfectly and can enlighten him. If so he will be surprised to find out that they themselves face very similar situations. They go to a shop and ask for such-and-such a product and are shown something else; they ask a question on the telephone and are answered with silence, or even with the telephone

[1] See bibliography in note 1, p. xv, of the Introduction of this volume.

being put down.[1] A businessman or a government officer may say to an employee, 'Go and tell Smith I want to see him.' He will be answered, 'Yes.' The employee will go away and Smith will not arrive. The businessman will then go to the employee's office and say, 'Why hasn't Smith come?' Silence. 'Did you give him my message?' 'Hah?' 'Have you seen Smith yet?' 'Smith. Yes. I'm just going now, he is in room . . .?' If the businessman really knows the place he will catch this cue: the employee doesn't know who Smith is, nor whom to ask about him (except the boss himself, of course, whom he will not ask come what may).

Suppose that you tell a secretary to phone *a*, *b* and *c* and she comes back saying she has phoned *a* and *b* but couldn't find the number of that third firm in the telephone book. You know, then, if you catch the cue, she has forgotten that you said *c* (although she remembers she was to make three calls) but will not come out and say, 'I have forgotten the third name you mentioned.'

Why all this concealment? Why doesn't the shopkeeper say, 'No, we don't stock camera brand X'?[2] Why doesn't room service say, 'I don't understand English' (at least in Chinese)? Why does not the employee say, 'I do not know who Smith is or how I can find him'? Why does the secretary not say, 'I forgot the third name'? Here you have people in situations the westerner is familiar with yet whose reactions are inexplicable to the westerner.

The westerner could understand that in a casual conversation anyone might conceal his ignorance of who Smith is, since the matter is inconsequential; the westerner could understand an employee's concealing such ignorance if it is both culpable and remediable by looking at *Who's Who*. The reaction of our employee is very different: it is not western but Chinese; any attempt to

---

[1] A curious phenomenon is that of wrong-number telephone calls. Sometimes one will pick up the phone and say 'hello' and hear only background noise at the other end. After a while one hangs up. Then the phone rings again and the same pattern is followed. The third time one has one's Chinese maid answer: same pattern. One suggestion has it that criminals phone a number two or three times to make sure they have the right number and thus check whether anyone is in. It seems unlikely they would ring three times or that this casing the joint would happen so often. The only other explanation is that, not hearing the voice they want or expect, the party on the line doesn't speak. Why not, remains a problem. See the letter in the *South China Morning Post* 25.3.66 signed 'Y'.

[2] Of course we must be careful to exclude salesmen who try to persuade you Brand Y is much better than Brand X.

understand it within a western frame of reference will fail because our employee's westernization is a surface, easily cracked.

Our tourist may have left the Colony with an exaggerated sense of the enormity of the language barrier which room service and shopkeepers have not succeeded in overcoming; our businessman may have learned that his difficulties are not a matter of language barrier but of some odd peculiarity of the half-educated Hong Kong people who do room and shop service as well as office work. The westerner who has progressed so far in his knowledge of Hong Kong may now arrive at the second stage of the westerner's reaction, which is to make a fuss in the shop, or the hotel, or—more likely—in his own office. He begins by introducing sharpness into his tone of voice as a prelude to fuss. The reaction is immediate, and identical, be it restaurant, hotel, shop, or one's own office. The restaurant, shop or office goes quiet, and faces go blank. He has met The Inscrutable East. The blank faces surrounding him cannot be called rude or impolite. On the contrary, patient and blank.

The tourist will not encounter The Inscrutable East even if he is looking for it, nor will the more permanent resident, be he businessman or government official—until he (or his associate) makes a fuss. The blank stare which inevitably follows a fuss is not an expression of oriental mysticism as so many westerners still believe: it is a specific Chinese reaction to rudeness. As long as our tourist behaves himself he will not find the mysterious east, especially if he looks for it in a temple or a Buddhist monastery, but as long as he is rude faces round him everywhere will remain blank. What does our tourist or resident do? His pleas aren't understood, his tirade produces a blank face until he's finished, and then everything goes on as before, as though nothing had happened. Perhaps he calls the manager. The manager understands, apologizes, and everything comes out all right. Either he tells you they don't stock what you want, or sees that the food you ordered is brought, etc. Surely the westerner now must revert to his older hypothesis; the trouble must be caused merely by the language barrier!

Often the story ends here. Quite a few residents go around believing that fundamentally the causes of confusion and misunderstanding are linguistic; the trouble is simply that it is difficult to explain to a person you can half-communicate with that he has misunderstood you. The art of living in the east, many old residents feel, is the art of making enough fuss to make it clear what you want and how badly you want it but not too much fuss to be rightly considered totally uncivilized. This view, we think, is very much on the right track but does not go far enough. This can be seen by the fussing westerner who, not pacified, or merely out of curiosity, may demand, even after his request was granted, to know why the staff behaved strangely to begin with. The manager who, we remember, has put things in order, would almost invariably answer by explaining how hard it is to get good staff. But if the westerner persists and asks why doesn't the manager train the staff he's got, presto!—there is one more blank face staring at him. Now it is obvious that the question is not one of language barrier. It is, we suggest, the question of how far a Hong Kong Chinese will go along with his western customer. The employee is rigid, the manager is only a little less so: he may succumb to a little pressure. In face of this, the old hand's technique of sufficient fuss is rather a good one. Why?—A little fuss may force a Chinese to succumb to your demands if giving you what you want may lead to a lesser loss of face than the one incurred by a little more fuss. If you make a big fuss you will be totally ignored. Yet you will also be totally ignored if your demand involves much loss of face—whether you make a fuss, big or small, or not.

It is for this reason that our examples are deceptive: they are in agreement with the 'sufficient fuss' theory which goes only part of the way. For instance, the manager may even be a deceptive case because he too accepts the language of 'never say no', and ignores it when people make scenes; the difference is he has been taught that, with Europeans, certain easily learned responses will better smooth things over than the responses he believes to be right. Things get done when he appears because to call him is to place pressure on the employees to forget their own ideas of how to behave and do what the tourist wants, whatever he wants. The shop *foki* knows what you want better than you do, but if you are more stubborn than he is it is easier for him to do what you say you want, especially if you pressure him with threats about the manager, not because he fears the manager (which indeed he does), but because in this case calling the manager is even worse loss of face than complying with your uncivilized request. In the west to want to see the man higher up is not always a pressure to get your way; in Hong Kong there is no other way to interpret it, simply because calling someone other than the one with whom you do business is an insult to that one, and insult is pressure because insult should always be avoided at all costs.

The fact that in Hong Kong everybody knows better than you what you want is general knowledge. European housewives regularly exchange gossip about their *amahs* (maids) who 'know' how to cook your breakfast even if you contradict them. European teachers keep grumbling about their pupils who know how to please them and will not learn from their teachers what really would please them—especially, of course, not trying to please them . . .

4 Fear of losing face

We believe that all the problems so far raised can be explained in terms of one social institution, familiar to most westerners—face: fear of losing it, and the desire to gain it. We must confess to a certain surprise at finding, on investigation, that this is not a subject to which sinologists have paid much attention. And yet it is a characteristic of Chinese society of such permanence that the remarks of Arthur Smith,[1] written in the last decade of the last century, could as easily have been written yesterday. Indeed apart from Lin Yutang[2] and a slab of linguistic and social ethnography by Hu,[3] we found almost nothing on the subject by scholars—and the little else there is we find both cursory and incidental.

This makes us apprehensive about discussing face, partly because it is an intangible set of attitudes and values, and thus much harder to pin down than structural features; and partly because we have found almost no literature to guide us. Such literature as there is,[4] is hard to use. Miss H. C. Hu distinguishes the two

---

[1] Arthur Smith, *Chinese Characteristics*, New York 1894.

[2] Lin Yutang, *My Country and My People*, New York 1935, see below.

[3] Hu Hsien-Chin, 'The Chinese Concepts of "Face" ', *American Anthropologist*, Vol. 46, 1944, pp. 45–64.

[4] A hunt through C. O. Hucker's *China: A Critical Bibliography*, Tucson 1962, apart from the well-known book by Francis L. K. Hsu, *Americans and Chinese*, London 1953 (which nowhere discusses face), reveals nothing. We consulted Leon Stover, ' "Face": Secondary Verbal Analogues of Interaction in Chinese Culture', a Ph.D. thesis in the library of Columbia University, New York. The excellent bibliography, however, reveals little else in English. In Bloodworth, op. cit., there is a short discussion at pp. 299–306.

words for face, *lien* and *mien*, on the grounds that the former is a social *and* an internalized sanction connected with having a good moral character; the latter, an older concept, is much more social, one involving reputation and having done well in life. Significantly, the author refers to North China (on p. 46) and says *lien* is less used in Central China. Those experts we have consulted in Hong Kong are barely aware of the use of *mien*—which may have something to do with the lack of a sense of community or society in Hong Kong, and the consequent lack of agreed social standards. Suffice it to say that the examples we discuss below correspond to Miss Hu's *lien*, and to her examples of it.

In a vestigial way face exists in our society: e.g. government officials and civil servants are loath to admit mistakes. 'Face-saving' devices are in a politician's tool-kit everywhere. After the Suez crisis and up to this day almost no senior minister in the British Cabinet at the time has had to admit it was a mistake; nor will he. He is a victim of the fear of loss of face and he has ways of avoiding such loss. A decisive difference between east and west in this matter, however, is that in the west we gain status, not face. A lavish wedding reception, a big car, a handsome gift to charity, the friendship of a big shot, a familiarity with western worldly ways, all these and many more can gain a person social assets. In the east these are matters of face, which is status plus something else, like dignity. In the west these would constitute matters of status alone, hardly of dignity. So while in the west 'losing face' (being humiliated) seems to be similar to what it is in the east, 'gaining face', to begin with, and consequently the special syndrome of the institution of face as it is found in Hong Kong, is not the same as in the west. There may be much to do in the west even about gaining face; but the importance attached to face in the east can hardly be imagined in the west, where gaining face is very rarely a total or overriding motive. Our hypothesis is that in Hong Kong it is to a startling extent an overriding motive. And only when one imagines the inflated dimension of gaining face can one start realizing how much more losing face may mean to a poor Hong Kong shop-assistant than to a British Cabinet minister.

Hong Kong Chinese, especially more or less westernized Chinese, try to tell you that face means no more to them than to you. One of our students even insisted to us that there was no Chinese word for such an idea. Despite that student, and his assumed ignorance (even the *Concise Oxford Dictionary of Current English* says this sense of 'face' is a translation from the Chinese), face and especially the avoiding of the loss of it, or helping you (whether you asked or not) to avoid losing it, is a crucial consideration in many social situations in Hong Kong.[1]

Combined with one other factor, namely the traditional view that the Chinese way of doing things is not simply the best, or the right, way of doing things, but the only way of doing things, face explains almost too much. Not only our previous examples are so explicable; not only can it explain why in some cases a little fuss in fact helps whereas in others no degree of fuss will do—we shall exemplify this later on—but it can also explain the depth of the barrier; the great difficulty of explaining to some Chinese that some Europeans in some circumstances do not allow face to be a paramount consideration. But in order to explain all this we must first impress on our western reader that in our own view the crux of the matter lies in the Chinese idea that face is, indeed, above all.

Men are human because they have face to care for—without it they lose human dignity. Now, care for your own face must also involve care for others' face. There is some evidence that Confucius said that to cause another person to lose face is the worst loss of face. This may have been a play on words or a figure of speech; clearly it was not intended to be raised into the canon of behaviour it has become.[2] Confucius said: 'Do not see what is not right, do not hear what is not right, do not speak what is not right, do not touch what is not right.' But especially do not see: how far can politeness and concern for others go? What about the face of foreigners? Two attitudes are possible: first, they do not care about face, *ergo* they are barely human (barbarians, foreign devils, big noses, or what have you); alternatively, you have to care for the foreigner's face because he himself does not know about it. This latter is difficult to do because the westerner causes trouble: however much you try to calm him he may insist on something ghastly like an open investigation of a scandal; he suffers little over other's loss of face. Suppose a teacher does ask a pupil to ask questions, the pupil complies as little as possible because he

---

[1] 'Abstract and intangible, it is yet the most delicate standard by which Chinese social intercourse is regulated.' Lin Yutang, *My Country and My People*, New York 1935, p. 200.

[2] Indeed, in general, it might seem that Confucius might have copied Marx (*'Je ne suis pas Marxiste'*) in disowning much of Confucianism.

might ask a silly one and lose face, or the teacher may not know the answer, and then both will lose face.[1] But, if the teacher insists, the pupil asks a few questions because to disobey would be to cause the teacher to lose face.

There is a considerable lack of communication about face. As we said, the Chinese often deny the existence of face—in order to save face (often yours), of course. When his confidence is gained, he may discuss face with you, but with a resigned feeling that anyhow you will not understand. A local doctor told us that he was sometimes asked by patients for X-ray plates 'to show to friends'. He found out later that this meant the patient wanted to consult another doctor. The doctor didn't mind, but his patient thought that if he knew he was consulting another doctor he would lose face, and that to tell this to him to his face is out-rageously discourteous. A Chinese student who witnessed the authors' conversation about this incident felt vexed and frustrated. He could not consider seriously for one moment that the doctor could expect any patient to say explicitly, 'I want to consult another doctor'; the Chinese in question was a student and a person who had met westerners, as teachers and otherwise, since the age of 11; yet he took it for granted that what the doctor wanted was undoubtedly out of the question: there is a limit to the amount of impoliteness one may undertake to avoid impoliteness to the doctor. In brief, the quantitative approach to impoliteness prevents the discussion of the question of impoliteness: the ques-tion is not 'may I be impolite?' but 'what is the minimum impolite-ness imposed by the situation?'

It has been suggested to us that the whole concern with face is in itself a westernization—an acquisition of semi-western values. We do not think this is so. For one thing classical writers and novelists show us that saving face was a matter of deep concern long before China contacted the west, although fiction takes so much for granted about the social background that one has to look carefully for the evidence. Moreover, face between Chinese is at least as important as face *vis-à-vis* foreigners—not what one would expect if it was an idea taken over from foreigners. Furthermore, face is a minor and rather different social institution in the west.

---

[1] Cf. J. F. Cansdale's discussion especially at pp. 352–3 below.

5   The muffling effect of face

The cause of much misunderstanding, then, between Chinese and westerners in Hong Kong is the westerners' lack of appreciation of the significance of face for the Chinese, as well as the Chinese inability to accept the westerners' relative indifference to face, however tentatively. It is indeed important to note how important for the Chinese their idea of face is, but the story does not end here. The westerner often under-estimates or takes for granted the fact that his own culture allows for a breakaway, for the possible need to transcend its own framework. Moreover, when facing this sort of situation the westerner often views other cultures as entirely rigid. This is a mistake. As E. E. Evans-Pritchard has argued,[1] most cultures allow for flexibility without allowing themselves to be transcended. The believer in magic, to take Evans-Pritchard's example, will feel able to criticize any given magician or oracle, but never magic as a system of thought or of social organization. The same, we suggest, applies to the Chinese system of face. Moreover, the more ingenious and intricate the possibilities offered within a system, it seems, the less likely that that system itself will be transcended. Or perhaps it is the other way around: perhaps the less adequate a system is the more intricate the possibilities within it have to become if that system is to be saved. One way or the other, the Chinese system certainly is both very inadequate[2] and highly elaborated.

So far we have discussed tourists, businessmen and doctors, all in semi-westernized situations and institutions. Let us turn our attention now to situations which are as purely Chinese as can be. We want to bring out a couple of points about Chinese society; that it can often be very devious and that there is an essential lack of impersonalism.[3] In passing, we shall also discuss certain anti-individualistic traits to be discovered in Chinese society, ideology, and character structure.

[1] E. E. Evans-Pritchard, *Witchcraft, Oracles and Magic among the Azande*, London 1937, especially pp. 475–8.

[2] Cf. Lin Yutang: '. . . while it is impossible to define face, it is nevertheless certain that until everybody loses face in this country, China will not become a truly democratic country.' op. cit. p. 203. This harsh contrast accords well with our thesis that face muffles criticism; for democracy is in a sense the institutional encouragement of criticism.

[3] Cf. Marjorie Topley on the lack of a 'fixed price' for consumer goods in her paper below, p. 198.

Take a Chinese family which has a rift between the three generations. The senior members are old-fashioned, monoglot and strict. The youngest generation are pupils of Anglo-Chinese grammar schools, avid readers of English comics and magazines, fans of American films and the Beatles, anxious to be independent and to travel. The middle generation respects their elders but indulges their children. Characteristically, downward communication is easy, but upward communication is inhibited.[1] Grandmother can summon and tick off grandchild. Grandchild, even if he gets a word in edgeways, will not be listened to. Yet grandchild cannot get hold of grandmother and announce, say, his prospective engagement or his wish to emigrate, or, especially his feeling that a previous decision was unjust and the grandmother's conduct open to criticism. We are told that such information can only be communicated by a chain. First a sympathetic more senior member of the family is told, that person passes it on,[2] and so on until the head of the family hears it. At each stage it will of course get toned down for acceptability's sake. Thus grandmother hears of the criticisms of her juniors without losing face in front of the family as she would have done had she listened while the child spoke direct.

Similar problems arise in business and schools; those who are criticized rarely get it straight out from the critic.

Devious this routing of criticism certainly is, and a westerner can be forgiven for immediately wondering: (*a*) whether such attenuated and watered-down complaints will do any good; (*b*) whether there will always be such a chain of communication available when it is needed. The answer to (*a*) is a qualified 'yes'. There is, so to speak, a relative force in the criticism. If all you ever receive are watered-down criticisms, and given that the criticisms to begin with are of differing intensities, then when they arrive all watered-down they can still be of different intensities and, relative to each other, can be more or less severe. However, the stronger the criticism the more it will have to be watered-down

[1] Cf. the analysis of this phenomenon with respect to social class in the second author's yet to be published 'The Idea of Social Class'. See also K. E. Boulding, *The Image*, Ann Arbor 1961, pp. 100–1.

[2] This is not the same as a western mother interceding with her child's father. Western society allows for the child to tell his elders his criticisms and the parent does not necessarily lose face; he has various highly un-Chinese responses available, including the admission of error, of having been beside himself for a while, etc.

and therefore the longer the chain of communication that will be used. Thus there is in reality a careful sort of ironing-out process and it may be that the criticism will sometimes not get through it all. It is not polite to give your criticism of another Chinese direct, that would cause him to lose face, instead you re-route it. But if you re-route it too much it might never reach the person concerned, or he may only know that there is some criticism, not what it is. A Chinese may thus be regularly placed in the position that he knows of a criticism but does not know what it is. What, then, is he to do? There is no question of the direct approach; too much danger of loss of face. The commonest answer seems to be to guess what it is. This guessing game is played in Hong Kong all the time, both in cases of criticism and in others. Whenever there is a situation where a person ought to know what you want he will tend to guess. Thus the grandmother may summon the child and offer to send him to university or to buy him something. This way she might hit the nail on the head, but more probably not. If, for example, a female is shocked by an attempt to marry her off, grandmother is unlikely to alter her values and give up her authority; she may even fail to guess that possibly that is the criticism. In shops when the *foki* mis-hears a request, he guesses, and so you may ask for a bucket and be shown a trumpet because you weren't heard. The shop *foki* having heard 'have you got . . .' but mis-heard 'wireless' may say, 'no, we haven't any', when there are hundreds stacked all over the shop.[1] However, the more westernized reaction to not knowing what is wrong is to enquire, but always deviously. The grandmother may enquire of someone in the middle of the chain of communication. The *foki* pretends to ask a colleague, with the result that another *foki* appears, says 'Yes. Can I help you?', and you have to start all over again.

The answer to (*b*), the availability of chains of communication, is again a qualified 'yes'. Since the Chinese knows that if any difficulties arise they will require such a routing he will prefer to shop and do business in those places with which he has some sort of connection. Now Hong Kong is a large modern society with many isolated people, and many new immigrants with little or no local connections at all. But within these qualifications our state-

---

[1] Only when 'no' is a permissible answer, of course. Thus, looking for an inferior commodity in an appliance shop will often elicit a quick, hushed, shamefaced 'no', as the lowest degree of loss of face.

Victoria
seen from
Kowloon.

A street haircut. On the wall are public health posters
and red notices advertising accommodation.

The Western District. In this old district, the foreground
tenements are subdivided into cubicles, getting 300 to a
building with another 50 in huts on the roof. In the
background, better class accommodation for the middle-income group.

Market. Shopping for fresh food every day
is a Hong Kong habit which leads to solid streets
of hawkers and customers like this one.

ment holds: favour places and businesses with which you have affinal, kin, or friendly contact.

Our explanation for this reliance on chains of communication is this: criticism involves communication. Among respectable Chinese, social life and modes of address are extremely formal and polite, in line with the classical ideals. Communication, however, often requires that one be informal and impolite. Now while informality and impoliteness are to some extent permitted with intimates in respectable Chinese society (and seem relatively unimpaired among the very lowest classes—but these hardly concern us since they are hardly the vanguard of westernization) they are totally out of place with strangers or superiors. Thus relations with strangers or superiors will be less successful than relations with intimates. Thus, if you want success in a matter like criticizing grandmother, intimates, or intimates of intimates, etc. will have to be resorted to—you must choose someone with whom you can communicate. The impersonal institutionalized relationship of *foki* and customer does not override the basic relationship of strangers and therefore those between whom face is most involved. The only people with whom one can properly establish communication are those one knows intimately. In this the society is personalist: in order to communicate with someone you must know him well enough to be able to ignore his social *persona*. Where communication may become necessary one had better see to it that one deals with those one knows, one way or another.

But why will the *foki* lose face just because he doesn't know what you want, why will grandmother lose face if she allows grandchild to criticize her? What is 'face'?[1] Partly it is sheer one-upmanship; partly the avoidance of shame. More respectable than one-upmanship is a core involving knowledge of, and living up to, a code or ideal of behaviour (the *li*). This code is the only dignified way to behave and deviations involve loss of face because they imply either ignorance of, or violation of, the code. There is no room for mistakes; or at least, for mistakes made public. This latter is a curious fact. Chinese don't apparently feel guilty about their mistakes, provided they can conceal them: obeying the code isn't internalized, seeming to obey it is internalized. The Chinese are more concerned with shame (a social

[1] For a brilliant discussion of this question see Lin Yutang, op. cit., pp. 199–203.

phenomenon) than with guilt (a personal feeling).[1] This is not to
say that the Chinese has no fear of making a mistake; but unlike
the westerner who fears both causing damage to the world around
and making a fool of himself, the Chinese seems to fear only the
making a fool of himself. Moreover, in the west the more serious
cases of making a fool of oneself are normally connected with
causing damage; in Chinese society the damage to others comes
in a round-about way: you make a fool of yourself, perhaps by
causing damage to your grandparents, where the damage in question is loss of face, where the loss of face in question results from
a violation or even a seeming violation of the code. . . . Nothing
shows the deviousness of the relation between loss of face and
damage to others as much as the fact that the same criticism may
be given in a face-saving way or otherwise. Thus, grandmother
doesn't lose any face when she hears the criticism indirectly. Were
it said to her face, were it made open that she had made a mistake
or been unjust, then she would definitely lose face. We hope this
gives the reader a glimpse of the intricacy and awkwardness of
certain Chinese mores. One might wonder whether a society can
function within such a heavy framework. We do not know, but
suspect that the answer is no. As a way out, it seems that in certain
circumstances it is possible to ignore the face of those below one,
if one cares to, and without oneself losing face. The criterion for
this seems to be if you consider the persons you are abusing to be
so low that they have no face you are free to go ahead. *Nouveaux
riches* often seem to feel like this about servants, and tradesmen—
whom they abuse freely; many other people also seem to feel it
about coolies.[2]

Thus, the *nouveaux riches*, the Hong Kong new class, simply
make more extensive use of an institutional device already permitted in traditional China, even though it did not conform in
spirit with Confucius' teaching. We may remember that Confucius tried to introduce the personal, even the family, touch into
all social and political situations, and that, like Socrates, he claimed
that damaging others is worse than damaging oneself: causing
others to lose face is a worse loss of face than ordinary loss of

[1] Cf. C. P. Fitzgerald, *The Chinese View of their Place in the World*, London
1964, p. 61.
[2] Lin Yutang quotes the following from the *Book of Rites*, 'Courtesy is
not extended to the commoners, and punishment is not served up to the
lords.' See op. cit., p. 198.

face. The new class observe the mannerisms this idea exhorted, but they limit its application and pervert its spirit.

Again we see how central face is to the Chinese tradition, and how deeply it is connected, not directly with moral codes, but directly with social codes and thus perhaps indirectly with moral codes. It might therefore be expected that Chinese would spend much time studying the code and discussing in detail its application to new situations; orthodox Jews, for instance, would do this as a significant part of their way of life. But this is not the case amongst the Chinese, be they Confucian scholars, traditionally minded, or westernizers. This is another characteristic of Chinese society, its lack of rebellion and critical discussion of its own mores and standards; it is a super-conformist society.[1]

Mr Kvan in his paper[2] touches on some explanations of this in child-rearing practice. He points out the subnormal incidence of left-handedness among Hong Kong Chinese children and at the same time the absence of stammer and of other signs of stress. He interprets this as evidence that Chinese education succeeds in training children in personal harmony and socialization to a greater degree than education does in the west.

This super-conformism would, were the society isolated and left alone, surely entrench itself deeper and deeper, and indeed this is what seems to have happened through the millennia of Chinese recorded history. However, Chinese society in Hong Kong is far from being isolated and left alone and at the same time is far from having given up this intense and conformist upbringing. As might have been expected, a split has arisen in the society over the attitude to be adopted to foreign intrusions into its customs and standards. There are those few who accept the west as completely and as wholeheartedly as they can. These seem to

---

[1] Cf. V. S. Naipaul on India: 'a society which . . . is incapable of assessing itself, which asks no questions because ritual and myth have provided all the answers, a society which has not learned "rebellion" '. 'Indian Autobiographies', *New Statesman*, 29 January 1965, pp. 156–8, especially p. 157. Hsu, op. cit., pp. 362 ff., discusses this interestingly. Every so often a curious outcry goes up about teenage rebellion and increasing juvenile delinquency. This apparently consists in young people smoking, drinking and going to dance halls. Such behaviour is horrifyingly deviate in a society where youth's revolt is firmly crushed by the age of three. The adult reaction creates a curiously out-of-touch atmosphere, rather like the afternoon paper headline 'Sex flourishes in illegal dance halls'. Did they think it was dying out?

[2] Which see, below, especially pp. 338–40.

be mainly the educated teenagers, especially the girls.[1] They are about the only members of the society who seem to be pushing their westernization farther even than would seem sensible. Their social role, however, is in this respect negligible. The greater majority of the society still keeps the west at arms' length, and is highly critical of many of its intrusions. Yet appreciable change is coming about; when so many are cool about it, how can this be? Our answer is that it very often comes about as an unintended consequence of the actions of those who are trying to shore up the traditional social structure. When it comes so sneakingly it may, indeed, shake the foundations of the traditionally successful Chinese super-conformism.

Let us consider an instance where the norms are accepted, the tacit aim is to maintain these norms, yet the net result is a change of these aims. Take arranged marriage. In the classical love story of Liang Shan-Po and Chu Ying-Tai, the girl loses the boy because her father has betrothed her before she has had time to tell him she has someone else she is interested in. She could and, temporarily, does refuse to go through with the ceremony, but her father would lose face thereby, so she gives in. On her way to the wedding she dies at her lover's grave. While she was prepared to violate filial piety and be disobedient, she was not prepared to inflict loss of face.[2]

Now, contrary to widespread western preconception, arranged marriage was not always as brutal and unhappy as in this instance. Indeed, the rationale of arranged marriage is rather humane. First of all it can be said that marriage is more than what goes between two people: it is a contract between two families; it is therefore the business of the two whole families, and thus especially of their heads. Secondly it can also be said that a successful union depends on many factors; including the partners coming from the same background, their being temperamentally suited, and so on. Even these matters, not to say the less personal conditions, are better judged by the mature and experienced than by the young and hot-headed. In the absence of strong aspirations to romantic love,

[1] Why the girls especially? Possibly because of their association of the west with emancipation? Perhaps because, being viewed as inferior, less effort is devoted to their training and retention?

[2] Like a number of Chinese folk-stories this one conceals the harsh philosophy that only death can release lovers from the binding coils of the Chinese social code.

arranged marriage can be made to seem humane, if paternalistic. (After all, this was the case in the west almost universally until a century or so ago.) Most probably the arrangers always sincerely tried to match those whom they thought were personally compatible—and even knew and liked each other—as well as socially and economically compatible, although the latter would tend to count most in any conflict.

Today in Hong Kong there are still arranged and semi-arranged marriages. The tendency is now, though, to go as far as possible towards the western ideal, by letting the match-making submerge and its outcome seem spontaneous. If a university student chooses himself or herself a partner, then the parents will seriously consider the possibility of going along with the match—unless it seems totally unsuitable or involved, e.g. if the prospective partner is a foreigner. If a boy and a girl are at a loose end, the families may engineer the crossing of their paths; and if everything clicks of its own accord, that is success enough. This should be seen for what it is: a terrific compromise with the west. The partners are even allowed to think they have made western-type free choices in order that their families' sense of power in arranging the marriage can be sustained. But this aim of theirs will bring about its own change. One unintended consequence of the actions of such families is that they are destroying the very thing they are trying to sustain. For, since the couple believe they have chosen freely, the likelihood is that when they have children they will let them choose of their own accord, in line with the ideology of free choice they accept. (It could be argued that if the happy couple discovered later in life that their marriage had been partially arranged they might be converted to arranged or semi-arranged marriage. This seems unlikely since their earlier dislike of arranged marriage was most likely due to aspirations to romantic love and this is not something they would be expected to drop so easily.) Unwittingly, then, those parents who compromise with the west too cleverly are contributing to further westernization. Aside from this kind of compromise there are of course means of imposing the new ways on the old, devices available to Hong Kong young people in order to secure the partner they want. The most obvious is the rather drastic method of getting pregnant, traditional the whole world over; its use here is restricted, as it can involve much loss of face if it is too obvious, and extremely successful when applied— for the very same reason. Another device is a Chinese variant on the former: it is simply to be seen together a lot in public. This results in general speculation that you are engaged, and for the family to deny it or to try to prevent the marriage involves them in loss of face. But, of course, if the person being walked out with is 'unsuitable' beyond a certain limit, then stopping the liaison would be less of a loss of face than condoning it.

It is impossible to list all possible modes of loss of face connected with open courting; suffice it to mention the principal reason: courting is trying out, and open courting is open admission of possible failure. Open courtship, hence, is westernization in a very deep sense, in the sense of being able to accept open admission of error, of incompatibility, of the normalcy of rejection; an admission not simply between the couple themselves, but in the eyes of their separate families and neighbours. People say that a few years ago one hardly ever saw courting couples anywhere in Hong Kong. Among university students, 'dating' is still very restricted and awkward; we know of a number of cases of secret dating. More and more, though, couples of all classes, not only students, can be seen going around holding hands and gazing out to sea, semiconsciously doing what they see lovers in American films doing. Sometimes they can even be seen necking a little. Love is being imported: westernization is under way.

Westernization, then, enters both by the front and the back doors. It comes in the front when it is welcomed, especially by the younger generation. Some people still try to push off its frontal intrusions, even when they have no special objections; but it sneaks in at the back door, especially then, because the pushers-off themselves are forced to compromise with it, and the compromise has unintended consequences which undermine the very remnants of the customs which these people are trying to preserve. Arranged marriage is only one case in point. Take also education. Western schools are the best in the Colony, and they are acknowledged to be. The examination results there are the best, English is better taught there, and the pupils from these schools get a better chance to enter university, to go into a profession, or to go abroad for training. Thus both their scholastic value and their cash value is apparent. Tradition-minded Chinese venerate education and thus want their children educated. They also are westernized enough to value high salaries and prestige jobs. Thus they compromise and try desperately to get their children educated at the best schools. Semi-western teaching, reading and speaking English, studying western subjects like modern medicine and British political history, going abroad to the west—all these provide youngsters with a lot more westernization than their families would wish. A face-saving compromise with the west only furthers its intrusion.

6   Face as a standard of behaviour

So much, at the moment, for how the west is affecting Chinese society. We want now to try to explain why the traditional code of behaviour was as it was. Why should the Chinese have a code such that to make a mistake is to violate this code and to lose face? What is so terrible about making mistakes? Why is the code of face as it is? Why should face be more important than settling the issue—with advantages to all the parties concerned? Our guess is that in most situations the social aspects of any transaction are more important than any other aspects. The only exception to this we know of are certain commercial or financial transactions. Traditionally, perhaps, this was not so; but in modern Hong Kong it certainly is, and people are increasingly aware of this fact. Consequently there are increasing numbers of businessmen who may be as purely Chinese as imaginable in family life and in personal behaviour but who, when money is involved, are prepared to be as ruthless as necessary. They will bid at auctions, offer discounts after denying them, allow purchase on trial, and otherwise engage in activities which ordinarily they would evade as they may cause loss of face. Thus, perhaps the answer to our question, why face is more important than happiness, is that usually the social aspect of a transaction is more important than the individual aspect, so that only in such transactions in which this is not the case (e.g. financial ones, or ones between intimates), individual interest may override face. If this be the answer then the following question presses itself most acutely; consider a transaction which is chiefly of individual significance, though with some unintended social aspects; why should the social aspects of even such a transaction have priority over the personal aspects? Our guess, again, is this. The highest value in China is to live properly, which particularly concerns being polite and obeying the rules; and this makes even the social aspect of a personal transaction of supreme importance. In other words, in traditional China being considerate to others is equated with saving others' face, with politeness, and with strict observance of the accepted code. To observe the code is to be human; to forget it is to become barbarian. Ignoring for one moment the question of how adequate the rules are, it still must strike a westerner that the Chinese stress on politeness and consideration for others has simply run mad. Not to hurt others is admirable, but to prefer it to settling issues, to punish yourself for even doing so accidentally, to lie blatantly in order to conceal your having done so, all this seems crazy to the westerner, is crazy by western standards.[1] It is an example of pushing an idea to its incredible conclusion and then getting this conclusion widely accepted, rather than modifying the idea or replacing it by another and thus getting rid of that conclusion.

Why, finally, should such a high value be placed on being polite and obeying the rules? It strikes us as the typical sort of thing a face-to-face society with many conflicts would value above all. Chinese language and manners seem to be ideally suited to a face-to-face society where everyone knows everyone else intimately. When China was like that, no doubt the system worked well. But the ideology has outlived the small-scale, face-to-face society and creates the havoc we have described in the crowded, large-scale, and largely abstract society that is Hong Kong today. Failure to communicate inhibits a large-scale, an abstract society.[2] This raises the further question of why Chinese tolerate this burden of face. We would say that what sustains the institution of face is *conservatism*, since face was workable in the face-to-face society, but is no longer. What, then, keeps conservatism? The answer is obvious: face: it is loss of face even to discuss custom, and how can it be reformed without discussion?[3] Thus face and conservatism maintain each other.

[1] It also seems crazy to Lin Yutang, who tells of a General who made acceptance of his overweight baggage a matter of face. The plane crashed and he lost a leg. 'Anyone who thinks face is good enough to compensate for overweight luggage in an aeroplane ought to lose his leg and be thankful for it.' op. cit., p. 202.

[2] The system may have already been a burden to Imperial China: we do not know. Indicative here is the legend of a bell in the emperor's gate to be struck by anyone with a grievance: it was not long before a rule was made that he who could not sustain his grievance was to be beheaded as a nuisance.

[3] Confucian moralizing and yearning for restoration of the lost Golden Age replace rational discussion of the remedies for present defects. It seems generally true that China has preferred moralizing to criticism and reform. See Lin Yutang's praise of the legalist Hanfeitse and his comment: 'I believe the sooner we stop talking about moral reforms of the people, the sooner

Hong Kong Chinese's stress on face is then at least partly understandable. But surely the Europeans set a different example? On the contrary, the atmosphere of face is so strong that the Hong Kong Government itself is often concerned more with saving its face than with settling issues. Perhaps this is a lesson it has learned from hard and prolonged experience: if you want to get things done you must take account of your own and other people's face; so as an unintended consequence the Government has been Chinesified. The government never admits that it has made a mistake. Yet it is a government of Europeans. It rarely admits that the police so much as laid a finger on a detained person. The police value their face so much that until very recently they ignored all public criticism of any of their activities including the criticism that their attitude of ignoring criticism reflects contempt of the public. All criticism of the Government is distasteful because it involves loss of face to take account of it. Occasionally it is taken account of because there would be too much scandal made by the few non-Chinesified Europeans here. But many another time nothing is done.

Recently the area with parking meters was increased despite fierce criticism and despite the clear fact that the multi-storey car-park for the affected areas was only just beginning to be built. It would have been a loss of face to admit that the co-ordination between the phasing of the parking meter scheme and the planning of the Public Works Department had been poor and postpone the meters.

The Government knows it made a blunder in defending the policy—made in its 'wisdom' as the unfortunate Duke of Devonshire had to describe it in Parliament—of discriminating the pay of married and unmarried women. Whether enough fuss can be made to bring about change is a moot point.

Europeans in Hong Kong have no alternative but to get Chinesified in this way. There is no pressure of liberalism, or a tough press, or the Questions in the House here to make them remember they are not Chinese and are not therefore supposed to care *that* much about face. On the contrary, the moment they forget the consideration of face they meet with those awkward blank

---

shall we be able to give China a clean government.' op. cit., p. 207. A similar point, on the Nationalist Government's failure to deal with the inflation of 1948, is made by Frank H. H. King in 'Flying Money', *South China Morning Post Banking Review*, supplement to the issue of 19 March 1965 at p. 62.

faces and with unfulfilled promises, promises made and reiterated
ad libitum only in order to save your face. Being so much trapped
inside the ideas of face themselves, the longer-term European
residents here can hardly plan the progress of the Colony in such
a way that the importance of face, and the stupidity of worrying
about it when you are ignorant or in need, is taught in the schools
to be a Bad Thing. Yet the 'Old China Hands' are a very influential part of the community. This may be partly because they are
the only permanent European residents and perhaps also because
their long experience of the Chinese is of great help to the tran-
sient. Unfortunately it is not often enough remarked that their
knowledge and experience has been bought partly at the expense
of Chinesification. There again the vicious circle closes.

We don't want to be misunderstood: Hong Kong *is* westernized to a certain extent. Two areas, business and religion, stand
out in this respect. Business has always seemed to be the first bit
of the west that other cultures get hold of. People say Hong Kong
Chinese are very interested in money. We suggest, rather, that they
accept Dr Sun's teaching: take from the west what is useful.[1] The
most immediately useful bit of technique the west offers and, most
important, by far the most easily comprehensible, and least related to face, is the making of money: business. Chinese are good,
if ruthless, pupils of western business.[2] The reason for their ruth-
lessness is rather plain. Business ethics and fair play do not come
gift-wrapped with the mere development of trade and finance. Besides, western business ethics are rather sophisticated and not
easily comprehensible doctrines. Moreover, they clash, among
other things, with Chinese ethical ideals including the idea of face.
Thus business is westernized in all outward respects, but remains
utterly Chinese in its internal organization. In the Chinese business world there is wilfulness and nepotism, exploitation coupled
with paternalism, there is patronage and conspicuous consumption. Yet contrary to the widely heard complaint about the
exclusiveness of the interest in money, we suggest that the success of commerce and business in Hong Kong is due to its greater
simplicity. A society interested in, and active in, business should

[1] 'Chinese learning as the basic structure, western learning for use', Chang
Chih-tung, quoted in Fitzgerald, op. cit., p. 70.
[2] And see also Maurice Freedman's 'The Handling of Money: A Note
on the Background to the Economic Sophistication of Overseas Chinese',
Man, vol. lix, no. 89, 1959, pp. 64–5.

not so widely complain about this characteristic of itself. If most members of a population love money most of them approve of it, and hence will not complain of the love of money or its prevalence, unless they do so as lip-service. In Hong Kong it seems, the complaints are genuine and business is not loved. It is useful to master it, however. Thus it is not so much that Hong Kong is successful in business; rather, business is successful in Hong Kong.

Along with business, Christianity too has had some success: (*a*) as a status symbol (the white man's religion, the rich man's religion, the educated man's religion); (*b*) because Europeans seem to muddle it up with every other aspect of the culture they bring; (*c*) it is thrust forward almost as hard as business, by missionaries, school teachers, and general propaganda including official ceremonies.

In education it might be expected that the British would have succeeded in selling themselves too. True, they have built many schools patterned after English grammar schools. Yet the teaching in most of them and in the vast numbers of uncontrolled 'private' schools, i.e. cheap schools, tends to be Chinese. This means much repetitive parrot and memory learning, examination rat-race, very long hours, no questions asked or answered, and severe, crushing discipline—'character moulding' is the English euphemism.

There is, too, the influence of the mass media. American and British films take up a very large proportion of cinema and TV, far more than do 'Continental' pictures in Britain or the States. One has difficulty in imagining the effects of a parallel situation in Britain, were all the expensive cinemas, and many of the locals, to show mostly Chinese movies. And of course teenage culture, from discs to dances, is entirely western.

One last factor in westernization: of course, the Europeans who go native go native in a European way. We gave one example earlier on: however Chinesified a European is he will never be able to avoid at least a small fuss where a matter of life and death is concerned. And the Chinesified European may be to some extent less objectionable to the Chinese, or, we hope, a little more influential in the process of westernization.

7   Cracks in the surface of westernization

We have argued that fear of loss of face, and the conviction that the Chinese way of doing things is not simply the right way, but the only way that can legitimately be called a human way, are the most important causes making the westernization of Hong Kong slow and difficult to understand. We have further argued that the highly intricate social mechanism of face-saving—which even westerners must accept in order to communicate with Chinese—none the less permits this complex and slow process we call westernization. Yet, as we have stressed, one of the puzzles of Hong Kong is that it is so flexibly westernized on the surface and so stubbornly Chinese underneath.

We now wish to centre on the western surface—and especially the cracks in the surface.

What are the sources of this surface westernization?

In our view, they are the philosophy of Dr Sun Yat-sen.[1] His philosophy has two parts, neither of which was ever articulated as sharply as it will be now, but which nevertheless get across as the main message. The first part is that China is the greatest civilization in the world, and the best, because it is Confucian. It is the historic mission of China to spread its superior philosophy and thus to better the world.[2] However superior Sun Yat-sen

[1] Our account is an interpretation of Dr Sun's major work, *The Three Principles of the People (San Min Chu I)*, and of its influence. Of course, Hu Shih and the May The Fourth movement had a different view about westernization and a lot to say about it as well; their view was, in brief, 'scrap-the-past-and-westernize-fast'; in some respects they had an almost renaissance-like effect; by and large, however, they failed: they seem not to have caught the imagination of a sufficiently wide audience to survive. For the historical background to twentieth century westernization, see B. Schwartz, *In Search of Wealth and Power*, Cambridge, Mass., 1964.

[2] See his intriguing discussion at pp. 18–20 (Part I, lecture III) of the 1953 edition of F. W. Price's translation (China Cultural Service, Taiwan), especially p. 19: 'Heaven's preservation of our four hundred millions of Chinese till now shows that it has not wanted to destroy us. . . . If Heaven does not want to eliminate us, it evidently wants to further the world's progress [*sic*]. If China perishes, she will perish at the hands of the Great Powers; those Powers will thus be obstructing the world's progress.' In the next lecture, after a fantastic imperialist-conspiracy explanation of World War I, Sun gives a diatribe against cosmopolitanism and says, 'Now we want to revive China's lost nationalism and use the strength of our four hundred millions to fight for mankind against injustice, this is our divine mission' (p. 24). He then proves the superiority of Chinese civilization by saying that there was little bloodshed when they had their 1911 Revolution. 'The reason for the small bloodshed then was the Chinese people's love of peace, an outstanding quality of the Chinese Character. The Chinese are really the greatest lovers of peace in the world' (p. 25). Later, in lecture six, all this is attributed to Chinese moral and philosophical superiority.

considered China to be as a culture and a philosophy, he was realistic about its status as a world power. Without power and influence China would never be able to get its message across, to demonstrate how it can be the best-ever world power. Here, according to Sun, is where China can learn from the west. The superior power and influence of the west can be traced to its superior material and social technology. The inventions of science; individualism; democracy; and the planned economy have got the west where it is. The lesson for China is that without these things it cannot fulfil its mission. Thus the second part of his philosophy is that China, the best civilization, should borrow from the west those inferior but vital goods required to make China great politically and economically; political success, however, is not a virtue in itself, but only in that it will allow China to carry out its civilizing mission. Only what is required for this end may be borrowed, so as not to spoil the mission itself. Sun's is a philosophy of superficial westernization: to a strictly definite extent, and for certain definite ends.

Dr Sun (the Father of the Nation) is taught widely in the schools of Hong Kong, sometimes as text, sometimes as garbled version, always as the general ideology in the air. Even those students who have never read him have picked up his ideas. They nearly all have this specific attitude to westernization: we will take from you only what we need, we will not accept anything which goes against the basic precepts of Chinese civilization, like loyalty to family and country, politeness, preservation of 'face', the traditional (Confucian) virtues. The west can give us technique and proficiency; our Chinese identity will remain the same. One of the authors once tried to explain to a Catholic student that Christianity was a form of westernization and might not fit in with Confucianism and a Chinese world mission. He got a blank look, he didn't communicate.

The force of the present thesis may be lost because, unfortunately, many shallow westerners cannot conceive of westernization as anything but the addition of smooth varnish to the local poor-quality commodities. To see how shallow this view is will not be difficult if we try to contrast Hong Kong's superficial westernization with other versions of westernization in other parts of the world. There are a number of general points to be made about westernization in Hong Kong as compared with westernization in, for example, Malaya, or Africa. Let us, again, take a superficial look first. People who arrive here from other colonies are often told, by the old hands; 'this place is different, mind you; we don't push the natives around here, old boy'. This common phenomenon reflects a special attitude on the part of the colonizers towards the Chinese. The 'natives' are not really 'natives' at all, but people like you and I, members of a civilization. If anything will explain why the Europeans should take this view it will be the Chinese own attitude towards themselves. They are convinced, not only that they are *a* civilization, but that they *are* civilization: their philosophy and their manner betrays this and it is a matter of pride that it has always impressed their conquerors. Since the westerners were always regarded as barbarians, and the Chinese looked on themselves as civilized, the British somehow came to accept it. So you have here a clash between a western and an eastern civilization and culture, not a case of civilizing the savages where the western culture and civilization is claimed to be moving in to, so to speak, fill a vacuum. That this has always been the attitude of the colonizers shows through even today in the fact that there is no officially recognized discrimination in the colony.[1]

In the second place, the civilization being colonized here is unique in a number of respects. It is very ancient, pre-dating western civilization a good deal. It is a very strong and deep-rooted civilization, partly because it has a very explicit ideological basis, and because this ideology includes the comforting reassurance that simply having been born Chinese amounts to being inestimably superior to all other forms of life on earth.[2] China is significantly known in Chinese as 'the middle kingdom'; outside of it there are only barbarians. This ideology is overtly racist: to be born Chinese is the greatest privilege; to be born fair-skinned Chinese is to be beautiful as well. On the other hand to be born a European is to be born a foreign devil; to be born a negro is something worse.[3]

Clearly, then, while it is very old, and very strong, China is not one of the world's most enlightened civilizations. Its ideology of

[1] There are traces, of course; the odd exclusively European club; the understanding that it is a disadvantage for a European government officer to marry a Chinese girl. But these are pin-pricks.

[2] Sun quotes the saying 'Gentry of all nations bow before the crown and pearls', op. cit., p. 15.

[3] Social distance tests—ordering nationalities by readiness to enter into different relationships with them—are uncomfortably revealing in Hong Kong.

superiority made its clash with the European colonizers very tense. More so because rules of politeness and deference forbade the overt expression of this tension[1] (except for the Boxer Rebellion, which did not touch Hong Kong). So from the start there has been a tension. However, the west was gentle in Hong Kong[2] and then came Dr Sun with his philosophy of how to handle the west, and everything seemed fine. But the tension still exists. Its roots clearly are partly in the superiority-ideology which lives on among Hong Kong Chinese. It is not easy to say how the ideology is transmitted, because no studies have yet been made of the Chinese family structure in urban Hong Kong, what it has preserved and what it has lost compared with the traditional family. However, our guess is that the family, being a principal medium of education, is the principal medium of transmission. But it should also be remembered that the formal educational system of Hong Kong, while it has certain westernized units, and all schools have some western surface, still to a very large extent relies, and is allowed to rely, on Chinese ways of teaching, which are used by traditionalist teachers who no doubt imbue their lessons with a deal of traditionalist Chinese content too, perhaps more by what is omitted than by what is permitted and encouraged.

The vast majority of Hong Kong residents then, in their social and familial lives, in their ideas and culture, are 100 per cent Chinese. A huge proportion (90·2 per cent)[3] can speak no other language, and the situation of those who can speak but not write

---

[1] The slow-motion quarrel which led to the first Opium War is a case in point. In general the anthropology of quarrelling and disagreement is very interesting in Hong Kong and has yet to be written. Mr Goodstadt mentions in one of his footnotes the curiously public nature of some quarrels, which are openly performed in front of neighbours and third parties, who are invited to take sides. Yet at the same time, on another level, if a boss wants to criticize an employee he gets better results by speaking loudly to a third party so that the person being criticized 'accidentally' overhears, or even by turning away and muttering aloud to himself. Our explanation for this is that once a quarrel has begun face demands that one win it at all costs, but that face is better preserved by not letting the quarrel break out in the first place. This rule makes it even more important to win an open quarrel, so as to be able to blame the vanquished both on the point at issue and for having permitted the difference to leak out.

[2] Chinese customs were taken seriously, Chinese law was permitted to co-exist with British law on some matters, and eminent Chinese were admitted to the highest councils of government.

[3] See K. M. A. Barnett, *The Census and You*, Hong Kong 1962, p. 12.

their own language is still more isolated. A proportion of the children of the Colony (which has not quite enough primary school places and not nearly enough secondary school places—all schools charge fees) go to school for a few years, pick up a smattering of Chinese and less English. A very few lucky ones pick up a lot of both. But the semi-illiteracy is what makes the difference: a Chinese can absorb partial westernization if he can so much as read a newspaper in Chinese; but if not even that, then what hope is there? Even in the fortunate ones we have yet to meet more than the odd person who has achieved an easy-going balance or blend of the east and the west. Mostly the process seems to be an all-or-nothing affair. Those who really make a break-through towards the west go right overboard, leave the Colony and rarely come back. More typical are Hong Kong University students who would, for example, rather discuss their academic problems with each other in Cantonese (albeit with a heavy admixture of English words for which there is no Cantonese equivalent or they do not know it if it exists) although all they have ever been taught and have read in that subject has been entirely in English. Whereas Singapore Chinese students often have English as one of their two or three native languages, the Hong Kong Chinese students seldom—indeed, outside a few happy students in the Department of English, almost never—are completely bilingual.[1]

Another explanation may be that in Malaya they do not all bow to the Hong Kong bible: Dr Sun. Perhaps in going somewhere alien like Malaya Chinese emigrants decided they were going abroad and would expect and be required to make a complete break. Hong Kong people suffer from the illusion that Hong Kong is still the part that it never was of the China that has ceased to exist, or even perhaps of the China that never existed, the mystical essence quite distinct from the territorial reality, and comprising idealized and abbreviated versions of the history, culture, and civilization of traditional China.[2] This pathetic and pathological illusion serves as a focus for the intense Chinese nationalism which is in evidence everywhere in Hong Kong.[3]

---

[1] This curiosity is one of the problems dealt with by Mr Kvan in his paper.

[2] Idealized in what Fitzgerald calls The Golden Age of Tang, see op. cit., pp. 18 ff.

[3] At the moment many virulently anti-communist Hongkongites will praise

Washing. From the dingiest tenements come immaculately groomed people because clothes are washed assiduously.

Balcony. Gossip is the same anywhere in the world

Pavement worship. At a street corner, a woman offers fruit,
chicken, paper money and incense to the hungry ghosts.

Resettlement.
(Li Cheng Uk).
One of the
earlier design
estates in
Kowloon.

Resettlement. (Wong Tai Sin). This enormous estate houses 80,000 people.

Housing Authority (Choi Hung). Taller, more spacious, and more western in looks, these house the better paid workers and clerks.

Bed-space.

Aberdeen mud flats. In excess of 50,000 squatters lived here before clearance in 1967.

Singapore Chinese, not being students of Dr Sun, are able to take to the west much more easily.

That Hong Kong does not take *to* the west, although it does take *from* the west, should by now be clearly enough established. There remains a tension, a lack of attraction to the west, a failure to come to terms with it, which is rather hard to explain. One explanation, already put forward by us, is weak but true: the failure of the Hong Kong educational system to cope with the problem. The system mixes the two elements uneasily, not allowing for the fact that the informal influence of the home is going to unbalance any formal instruction which isn't heavily weighted in favour of the west.

But we have one other explanation to offer, connected with this first one, to be sure, but distinct nevertheless. In brief, we return to our opening point that the west is a complex of ideas as well as a material culture. Not only that, but the west's material culture, is, in complicated ways, tied to its ideas. The simple fact is that you cannot borrow the technology of the west in any serious way unless you understand it; you cannot understand it without studying it; you cannot study it without absorbing some of the ideological atmosphere of the west.[1] You cannot help picking up the attitude to machines, to technology, to the world in general and to life. Thus Dr Sun's philosophical prescriptions carry in them the seed of the downfall of his particular solution to the problem of how shall the west meet the east. What he wants to take from the west won't split off that easily, and what comes in with what is wanted is highly undermining. It is an ideology of freedom, tolerance and responsibility. An ideology of self-reliance, making one's own decisions, being sceptical of authority,

---

[1] We were intrigued to find this view echoed by a Chinese scholar, Mr S. K. Lau of Chung Chi College, in the Chinese University of Hong Kong, in his article 'Whither Chinese Culture?', which is a very interesting discussion of westernization from an ideological standpoint. The author argues that to accept western democracy and science is to accept the whole western ethos from which they emerged. As a result he is critical of Hu Hsih and the May the Fourth reformers. 'Whither Chinese Culture?' by Lao Ssu-Kuang, *Tzu-yu hsueh-jen* (*Scholars and Thinkers*) available mimeographed from the author in a translation by Professor R. P. Kramers.

---

the recent heroic war against the Indian aggressors and pay tribute to Mao who has made it (to parody the *Daily Sketch's* famous Suez headline) GREAT CHINA AGAIN.

being prepared to foster new and daring ideas and schemes. It is also an ideology of practicality and humanity.

These ideas, commonsense enough though they are to us, are not entirely in harmony with Chinese ideas, and the two cannot be reconciled. They cannot be reconciled with concern for oneself and one's family and indifference to strangers; they cannot be reconciled with arranged marriage; they cannot be reconciled with the attitude of trying not to take decisions and responsibility whenever one can quietly transfer it;[1] they cannot be reconciled with the view that old age or higher rank has the prerogative of always being right; they cannot be reconciled with an overriding and obsessive concern with above all not losing face even at the cost of persisting with mistakes.

There are, we suppose, senses in which Hong Kong Chinese can retain their identity and yet westernize. But in no sense can that in Chinese culture which clashes with the foundations of the west be blended with even the superficial west. On such basic issues there is only a yes/no choice. Perhaps the western ideology can be incorporated in Chinese institutions; what cannot be done is to take western institutions within a framework of Chinese ideology. That is to say such behaviour sets up intolerable tensions. This is the prime conclusion of our empirical study.

Our conclusion, then, is inconclusive. This is because Hong Kong people have an inner resourcefulness which is not easy to appreciate without having seen them coping with their immense tensions, and the result of which on general grounds cannot be predicted. However we are rather optimistic: as with Dr Sun and semi-arranged marriage, the original aim to take from the west only what was wanted has an unintended ideological feedback, which in turn alters the fundamental aim.

Hong Kong Chinese have a long road to travel before they can

---

[1] In her paper in this volume and in another, 'Capital, Saving and Credit among Indigenous Rice Farmers and Immigrant Vegetable Farmers in Hong Kong's New Territories', in Raymond Firth and B. S. Yamey (eds), *Capital, Saving and Credit in Peasant Societies*, London 1964, Dr Marjorie Topley comments on the reluctance to employ managers in Chinese-run economic enterprises. The reciprocal dislike of taking responsibility admittedly does not appear in the same manner: were managerial positions with enough prestige and pay advertised, Chinese applicants would be forthcoming, albeit hesitatingly, as they do when the government offers responsible positions; yet accepting a responsible position and managing to accept daily responsibility are not the same, and this should also be taken into account.

obtain a successful blending of west and east. Maybe China's failure to achieve this blend before was a contributory cause of that country being overrun and its culture destroyed by the west's worst-ever export: Marxism. However that may be, the only choice which faces Hong Kong Chinese now, given that neither the mainland nor Generalissimo Chiang Kai-Chek is tolerable, is between two alternatives. The first is the continuing tensions and frustration of being caught between east and west. The second is genuine adaptation to the west on the lines of the Singapore Chinese; taking westernization a bit down nearer the roots, so to speak. That is to say, absorbing a bit more western ideology and a bit less western surface. As we said, we are rather optimistic.[1]

[1] Several friends and colleagues have generously given us their criticisms of this paper, by no means all of which we have been able to accept. In particular it has been suggested that, while our hypotheses make consistent sense, the problems they begin from are problematic. Our very position as probing westerners makes us Taipans, in Dr Topley's sense (see discussion on p. 193 below), shielded from what really goes on among Chinese. We are said to be mistaken in saying that the face-saving-never-say-no attitudes are widespread when no foreigner is present. The character of this criticism is such that extensive research is required to check it. Our paper remains hypotheses checked so far as possible at the moment. It may be possible to take the research further at another time.

PART TWO

THE ROLE OF SAVINGS AND WEALTH AMONG HONG KONG CHINESE

Marjorie Topley, Ph.D. (London)
Sometime lecturer in sociology in Chung Chi College, The Chinese University of Hong Kong, presently lecturer in sociology in United College at that University

THE ROLE OF SAVINGS AND WEALTH AMONG HONG KONG CHINESE

Marjorie Topley

1 Field, methods and sources

(a) The field of enquiry

The sociologist or anthropologist working in Hong Kong is first confronted with the problem of how to define and limit his field of enquiry. Hong Kong society is highly heterogeneous. There are a number of other small-sized ethnic groups besides the Chinese.[1] The latter, who are in the majority,[2] are then divided into groups speaking different dialects and possessing some distinct cultural features. They are also believed to possess temperamental differences by the Chinese themselves. The Cantonese from the neighbouring province of Kwantung predominate and again divide into groups possessing some (generally relatively minor) sub-dialectal differences. Again they are believed to exhibit temperamental differences and minor cultural variations and this belief can affect their social relationships.

Besides the Cantonese are a number of Tiuchew from the Swatow region of Kwantung. They live mainly in the urban area and are among the poorest in the community. There are also numbers of Hakka people: a group whose origin is not clear.[3] Those living in the urban area come either directly from Kwantung or from villages in the New Territories, a largely rural area

[1] Including Portuguese who are descendants of early colonizers of Macau, the nearby Portuguese settlement (they are mainly of mixed Portuguese and Chinese ancestry), Jews who were also established in Macau prior to the foundation of Hong Kong, a number of groups from India and Pakistan, English and other European groups, and Americans. The western groups consist mainly of sojourners.

[2] A housing survey carried out in 1957–8 and covering a stratified wide-scale sample of the population gave the Chinese as 98·64 per cent of the surveyed sector.

[3] They have contradictory traditions pointing to both a northern and a southern origin and today the greatest numbers of them are found in eastern Kwantung. They are also found in Fukien, Kiangshi and Szechuan provinces.

situated on the mainland behind urban Kowloon. Two groups of people live in boat-dwelling communities and engage principally in fishing. They are based on both urban and coastal areas. One is Cantonese-speaking. The other speaks a Min dialect rather similar to Tiuchew. There are numbers of people of other dialect groups, the majority having come to Hong Kong since the war. Cantonese usually class them all as 'northerners' since the majority speak dialects closer to the *kuo-yu* (Mandarin) tongue than is Cantonese. People from the far north are often amused when Shanghainese are included in this category, since their language is incomprehensible to the true *kuo-yu* speaker and in the north they are regarded as 'southerners'. Cantonese is the lingua franca of Hong Kong and has acquired some local characteristics, particularly in vocabulary. Most newcomers acquire a rudimentary knowledge of the dialect after about a year.

Further complexity is provided by the differences between urban and rural social structure. The New Territories were already settled when the British leased the area from China in 1898. Today the people live mainly as they did then, in village communities consisting of Cantonese or Hakka inhabitants or sometimes a mixture of both. Many villages are single surname units consisting of a lineage or part of a lineage tracing descent to a common ancestor. There are some immigrants in the area. Many are refugees from Kwantung and the north and the majority work as vegetable-growers, renting their land from the villagers and living scattered over the fertile valley regions. The social organization, cultural activities and economic basis of life of the villagers, who are in the majority, however, still exhibit a number of 'traditional' features.

In contrast to the rural area the population of Kowloon and urban Victoria situated on the island is almost entirely immigrant. Urban society grew up piecemeal. It is particularly heterogeneous because the people are in different stages of settlement and social and cultural change. People speak of 'Hong Kong families' and 'old Hong Kong' (*lo heung kong*)[1] when referring to long-established members of the community—the former are born in Hong Kong and the latter have lived there for many years—but length of settlement is not always an indication of the degree to which social life has changed. Immigrants have not been uniform in their

[1] Cantonese romanization. All romanizations are in the Mandarin (*kuo-yu*) dialect unless specified.

reaction to change and some long-settled families have clung to traditional ways longer than comparative newcomers. While immigration has affected all Chinese institutions in the Colony to some extent, individual reaction to change depends on a number of factors including type of education received, knowledge of English, contact with westerners and western ideas and changes taking place in China before migration.

The heterogeneity of the urban area places great strain on techniques for a study of the present kind. Yet it is to that area that we need to go for our material since it has been the focal point of economic development. In order to cut down the number of variables I have largely omitted discussion of the Territories except for purposes of comparison at certain points: when it seemed useful to point up differences in attitude and behaviour arising from differences in social organization.[1]

(*b*) *Method*

The size and heterogeneity of the population make the use of normal anthropological methods of research impossible for a study of this kind. The number of variables together with the nature of some of the facts to be determined, the time factor, and assistance available, also made it necessary to rule out the use of questionnaires aimed at obtaining statistically significant results. Limited use was in fact made of questionnaires but they were confined to particular informants from whom data were obtained. These informants were drawn from as wide a cross-section of the population as possible and included persons from various educational and economic levels, both sexes, and various ethnic, and (Chinese) dialect groups. English and non-English-speaking Chinese were interviewed (I should perhaps add that I speak Cantonese reasonably well and read Chinese, and that all interviews with non-English-speaking people were carried out directly in the Cantonese dialect). A number of persons whose jobs are concerned with Chinese economic and social problems were also consulted.

Data from informants were supplemented by my own observations and impressions based on five years' residence in Hong

[1] But see my paper 'Capital, Saving and Credit among Indigenous Rice Farmers and Immigrant Vegetable Farmers in Hong Kong's New Territories' in *Capital, Saving and Credit in Peasant Societies: Studies from Asia, Oceania, The Caribbean and Middle America*, Essays edited by Raymond Firth and B. S. Yamey, London 1964, pp. 157–86.

Kong. Although I was fortunate in having also a number of excellent documentary sources the results are still largely impressionistic. I do not perhaps need to emphasize at length that what I say in this paper is meant to apply to the Hong Kong Chinese generally. Of course exceptions can be found to many of the generalizations I make. It may be that a more detailed study would show that in certain cases the exceptions form a significant number. Nevertheless I should say that I have not met with disagreement concerning the general conclusions from any of the individuals with whom I have discussed the project.

(c) Documentary sources

No field studies using techniques of direct observation have been carried out in the urban area of Hong Kong.[1] However, various surveys mainly of an economic nature have provided useful data. The lack of a recent census—the last was in 1931—has proved a handicap, as it has to several kinds of research in the Colony. The influx of migrants after the war made such a census impracticable and although one is now being conducted, the results will come in too late for inclusion in this paper.

The Hong Kong housing survey carried out by the university in 1957–8 has provided various demographic, social and economic data,[2] and material from a similar survey conducted among residents of an estate in which squatters have been resettled has also been used.[3] A recently published analysis of Hong Kong's economic development has proved useful,[4] as have also various papers produced in connection with a course on industrial relations at the university this year. Use was also made of a report by a committee set up in 1948 to determine the extent to which Chinese law and custom still applied in the Colony.[5] It supplied information on inheritance of land and other properties. In addition, use has been made of a number of miscellaneous government reports and schol-

[1] This is still true of the *urban* area. See Introduction (*Editor*).

[2] Awaiting publication. It covered most of the regular housing of the urban area occupied by 1,265,000 persons in 267,000 households.

[3] Report on the Hong Kong University and the Hong Kong Council of Social Services Resettlement Estates Survey, June–September 1957 (unpublished). For this and note 2 see notes 1 and 2, p. 71 above.

[4] Edward Szczepanik, *The Economic Growth of Hong Kong*, London 1958.

[5] *Chinese Law and Custom in Hong Kong*, Report of a Committee appointed by the Governor in October 1948, Hong Kong 1953.

arly papers produced in the Colony, and a number of works on Chinese in the homeland were consulted.

A particularly valuable source on attitudes and values in regard to economic life have been the local Chinese and English-language newspapers and other periodicals, and the journals of various Chinese associations have given interesting details indicating the role of wealth in status determination.

2   The Hong Kong economy

Hong Kong is in the middle of an industrial revolution. Before the war its economy was based on *entrepôt* trade. As this dwindled after the Japanese occupation more and more people turned to industry and in only fifteen years the Colony has passed through the initial stages of industrialization with which many Asian countries are still struggling and is approaching the status of a mature economy. Hong Kong industry employs one-third of the labour force and some 50 per cent of its people are directly or indirectly dependent on it for their livelihood. A significant proportion of the labour absorbed by new industry is refugee labour coming to the Colony in recent years.

The entrepreneurial *élite* includes an increasing number of Westerners and 'local' Chinese previously devoting themselves to trade. Others were engaged in industry in pre-war years. The more important older industries include rattan ware, ginger preserving and flashlight production. Much capital and entrepreneurial skill, however, has come from China in recent years and Hong Kong has obtained some of the best of the mainland's industrial brains, particularly in textiles which is now the leading industry in Hong Kong. It is largely to new refugee entrepreneurs, particularly from the Shanghai region which was not traditionally a centre for emigration, that we owe leadership in the Colony's industrial development. This in spite of the fact that this group forms such an insignificant proportion of the population numerically. Newcomer entrepreneurs, particularly, are ready to assume new risks, explore new markets and experiment with new products and by their example they encourage others to do the same. Not all of Hong Kong's new entrepreneurs have been industrialists in the homeland. Some have made drastic changes in their mode of livelihood and in coming to Hong Kong, using their savings as capital and applying their skill and imagination to new ventures.

The speed with which the industrial economy has grown up suggests that significant modifications in the traditional outlook to economic pursuits have taken place. Some of the difficulties which industrialization appears to have encountered in pre-Communist China and which have been ascribed to social factors[1] appear to be absent, or of far less importance in Hong Kong.

Many people coming to Hong Kong and who were acquainted with Chinese society in the homeland have remarked on the 'materialist' outlook of the Chinese in the Colony. Although it must be remembered that there are numbers whose extreme poverty makes it necessary for them to devote much time to thinking of ways and means of improving their material lot and meeting their various commitments, the desire for increased wealth is manifest in the behaviour and conversation of people of all economic levels.

Some people, both western and Chinese, try to explain this phenomenon in terms of the southern origins of the majority of the people. The main protagonists of this line of thought are those who have lived in the north of China. One often hears people say: 'In the north, Chinese are more modest and less self-seeking. They are more cultivated.' I have met northerners who still express the traditional point of view that southerners are 'barbarian': not 'real' Chinese. It is amusing to see how westerners who are learning *kuo-yu* and mixing socially with northern people pick up this line of ethnocentrism.

Observers, however, are often guilty of contrasting experience of gentry patterns in China with their experience of contacts with people of more humble origin in Hong Kong. In China it was more likely that a foreigner would mix with members of the gentry classes whereas in the Colony the majority of Chinese are of lower-class origins. The position is not made easier by the writings of various Chinese authors who undertake to explain their people to the west and again tend to represent gentry patterns as those of 'typical' Chinese people.

3   Chinese society and values relating to gain

In looking now at social life in China we must see how far the different Chinese values regarding wealth had meaning in the peasant way of life. The situation most important for us to con-

---

[1] See, for example, Marion J. Levy, Jr, *The Family Revolution in Modern China*, Cambridge, Mass., 1949, especially Chapter 10.

sider is that obtaining in the 'traditional' countryside. The effects of 'modernization' on Chinese organization and values were greater in the towns than in the countryside and it is in rural regions that most Hong Kong people have their origins. Since so many of Hong Kong's industrial leaders come from Shanghai, however, we should also see how the development of this area by westerners may have affected attitudes towards the role of wealth.

I do not think we need to include discussion of the effects of Communist ideology on values in the homeland. People arriving since the Communist era left China mainly because they had either directly rejected the ideology or the way of life which Communist parties had created. There are of course Communists in Hong Kong, but I think it is true to say that their influence on economic attitudes is very limited.

If a major characteristic of western society is the diffusion of economic values through non-economic areas of society as has been suggested,[1] it would seem when we look at China that the reverse process has been at work. Values connected with the family system, class system, the State and closely related education system, and to some extent also religious institutions, have made their influence felt in the economic sector.

The anthropologist Francis Hsu puts great importance on the primary group for an understanding of Chinese economic attitudes and behaviour. In a paper concerned with cultural factors and economic development[2] he describes the Chinese culture pattern as having a basic motif of 'mutual dependence among men' with the relationship between father and sons in the family group at the centre. He then tries to demonstrate how this motif tends to direct the individual away from activities aiming to maximize gain, interpreting sometimes at the cultural, and sometimes the psychological level. Mostly he leans towards psychological explanation. Central to his argument is the assertion that mutual dependence makes for greater personal security than does a system of relationships where this motif is absent. This greater security mitigates the need of individuals to seek security in material

---

[1] See Bert F. Hoselitz and Richard D. Lambert, 'Western societies', in *The Role of Savings and Wealth in Southern Asia and the West*, ed. Lambert and Hoselitz, UNESCO, 1963, pp. 9–43, on p. 11.

[2] 'Cultural Factors', by Francis L. K. Hsu; Chapter IX in: Harold F. Williamson and John A. Buttrick, *Economic Development: Principles and Patterns*, New York 1954, pp. 318–64.

possessions. In contrast, the chief motif of western culture is described as individualism. Because the westerner's 'anchorage among men' is weak, men seek their security in things and try to 'conquer the universe'.

Although mutual dependence as a cultural motif may make for greater personal security as a whole than individualism, Hsu's attempts to demonstrate a direct relationship between general psychological states and general types of economic behaviour do not appear to me to be very satisfactory. They are based purely on cultural observation. The explanations he attempts at this level are sometimes inclined to be far-fetched and fail to explain the particular quality of different types of behaviour.

When Hsu interprets at the level of cultural institutions he appears on firmer ground. Here we can see how the central motif is spun out in a number of institutionalized relationships with mutual dependence among kinsmen as the organizing principle and how they lead to various checks on activity aiming at economic gain.

Even here, however, the explanations are often incomplete. Hsu tries to make his primary group do too much for him and ignores the effects of other institutional arrangements of society which are not directly related to the mutual dependence motif—for example, those of the class structure.

It is the overall cultural arrangements of society that we must examine if we wish to see, for example, how individuals behave when the institutions of the primary group break down. Unfortunately Hsu not only ignores the possibility that not all Chinese were psychologically 'secure', but also the possibility that a weakening in primary group solidarity could be brought about by poverty and other causes, forcing the individual to make his own decisions about his future: that the individual could be put in a position of 'individualism by default' as one sociologist puts it.[1] When describing the organization of family institutions and the personal security which they provide, Hsu very largely gives us the gentry patterns as before.

Now, overseas Chinese family organization is often unstable and the interest in gain of overseas Chinese is considerable. Their 'insecurity' may indeed contribute to this interest but it by no means provides the total answer. The Singapore Malays have unstable marriages but are not economically aggressive. An important factor permitting such interests on the part of the overseas

[1] Levy, op. cit., p. 327.

Chinese is the absence of checks not only from the institutions of the family which are weaker in the Colony, but also from various other institutions which as we shall see are either totally absent or very much modified.

We shall see also that there were circumstances in China in which individuals (including the psychologically secure) could be more interested in gain and more likely to be motivated by gain in their social relationships than was ideally approved. We shall examine these circumstances later. Hsu cites the Chinese maxim: 'Wealth is treasure for the nation. Every family can keep it for only a period of time. It must be kept circulating.' He does so apparently to illustrate the Chinese lack of acquisitiveness. However, it also indicates the possibilities of obtaining a greater share of wealth for one's own family, which in turn could enable socially approved ambitions to be realized. It was for this reason, as we shall see, that the disadvantages of professions carrying low social status were often outweighed by the advantages they offered for quick economic return.

Let us now consider some of the main economic effects of Chinese social institutions.

(a) The family

The Chinese family was a multi-purpose organization possessing a high degree of political independence. It was under the control of a family head, usually the father, and it was his responsibility to see that the male members of the family should stay together at least while he was alive. China's economy was basically agricultural and this enabled a high degree of economic self-sufficiency of family units, which helped to reinforce family solidarity in other spheres. Self-sufficiency was an ideal and goal of the very poor. The peasants who constituted over 80 per cent of the population carried economic self-sufficiency to a high degree.

The ideal that the family should achieve maximum solidarity and recognition that economic self-sufficiency was important to the achieving of this ideal were partly responsible for the desire of peasant families for land. Only with land could they act as a unit. Other reasons for this desire for land will be discussed later.

Since methods of acquiring wealth that were likely to take the individual outside the sphere of family control could disrupt family solidarity or conflict with its system of authority, there was a tendency for work outside or work in which sons could 'better' their elders to be discouraged. Bad communications, relative lack of economic opportunities elsewhere and government policies discouraging migration inside and outside the country tended to preserve the *status quo*.

The gentry families were not economically self-sufficient. Ideals associated with gentry status worked against such self-sufficiency and their consumption and production patterns brought individuals more in contact with the outside world. Even though members of gentry families often had independent sources of wealth they did not usually seek economic independence. The power they exercised in local village and lineage affairs tended to keep them from going far from their homes except in the course of official duties.

The very poor could not always achieve self-sufficiency. In their case members of the family might be forced away in search of work and to take up new occupations. In Kwantung, one-third of peasant families had less than 5 mow of land, nearly half were landless, and nearly 60 per cent of all land cultivated was rented.[1] Exploitation of tenants by landlords and usurers drove people annually from the area. For those with little land, moreover, the Chinese system of equal inheritance among male heirs could lead to fragmentation into uneconomic units, and could drive younger sons away in search of work elsewhere. The maxim 'wealth does not cross three generations' recognizes the effects of this system against wealth accumulation.

In the south, families were often concentrated in villages consisting of a single lineage. This type of organization had certain advantages for individuals forced to leave their homes in search of work. It provided a wide range of kinsmen from whom help could be obtained for the family in their absence, and wealth accruing from property owned communally by the lineage could help finance their journeys to places where economic prospects seemed brighter.

Within the family various tasks were allocated on the basis of age, generation and sex under the general supervision of the family head who also had considerable control over the income and expenditure of members. When the family was economically self-sufficient, productive tasks were distributed according to the above principles. Males were dominant in productive work, women

[1] Levy, op. cit., p. 318.

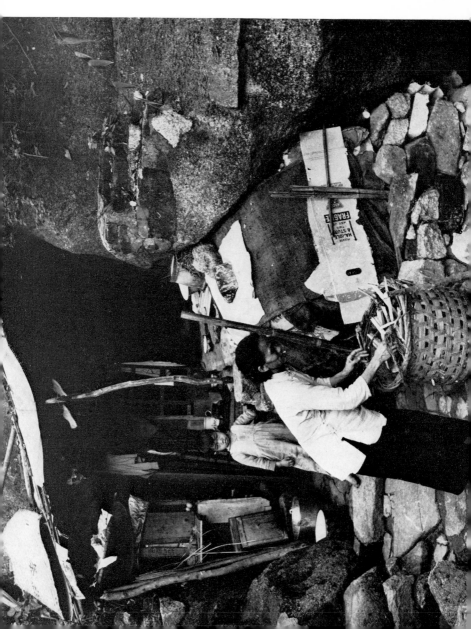

Cave-dweller.

Hillside squatters.

Pavement squatter.

(*Above*) Life on the
pavement (I).

Life on the
pavement (II).

Heroin.

Stone, paper,
scissors. Baby
sleeps peace-
fully through
it all.

engaged primarily in domestic tasks and when they did work out-side, for example at harvest time, their tasks were clearly defined.

A peculiarity of Kwantung economic organization was the role of women in productive roles. Cantonese women worked in agri-cultural pursuits sometimes taking over their tasks from the men-folk who had emigrated. They also worked in silk mills when the silk industry began to develop on a modern basis in the province. These factors help to explain the attitude towards female pro-duction roles in Hong Kong. Again, in the Territories there are numbers of villages from which male emigration to other coun-tries has taken place. There, women have now almost entirely superseded men in agriculture. Even men who do not emigrate look for work outside the agricultural field. While women stay in the villages, the men go to country towns and urban Hong Kong to earn their living. In the urban areas also, there has been little social disapproval of women working and considerable numbers of them are found in industry. In Singapore incidentally, more Cantonese females are found in productive occupations outside their own homes than are females from other dialect groups.

We saw that the Chinese system of inheritance could adversely affect the accumulation of wealth. Another factor working against accumulation and tending to canalize wealth into non-productive uses was the need to spend considerable sums on family commit-ments, particularly birthdays, weddings and funerals. Hsu cites J. L. Buck as showing that many farmers went into debt to meet the cost of such occasions, the average cost of a wedding being about four months' income and of a customary funeral about three months' net family income.[1] The mutual dependence motif is also expressed in a strong obligation to help neighbours and friends as well as kinsmen.

Financial needs arising out of these kinds of commitments led, however, to a lively credit system. While for large sums of money Chinese tended to go to the landlord, pawnbroker and trader, for smaller sums they frequently borrowed and lent among them-selves. Chinese were sometimes capable of high objectivity in their credit relations and of charging large rates of interest. High interest might be paid by neighbours and even kinsmen.[2] Argu-ments about money between kinsmen were also not unknown.

[1] J. L. Buck, *Land Utilization in China*, Chicago 1937, pp. 466 and 468.
[2] See Maurice Freedman, *Lineage Organization in Southeastern China*, London 1958, p. 18.

Arthur Smith, writing in the late nineteenth century, says that interest rates ranged from 24 to 48 per cent per annum.[1] Such high rates were not approved of by the government and in K'ang-hsi's Sacred Edict people are exhorted to be more lenient in their credit relations.[2] Although this impersonal aspect of credit relations appears to conflict with ideals of mutual dependence it finds social approval in the Cantonese maxim: 'friendly feelings have their place but let us be clear in reckoning accounts'.

One result of a constant need for cash was the development of loan associations particularly among the poor. To avoid risks of swindle such associations were usually formed among people with some prior knowledge of each other. Their workings were complex and varied slightly in different areas.[3] The kinds that were popular in Kwantung have been transplanted to Hong Kong. They are also found in Singapore among various dialect groups. Again, to avoid swindle, they usually recruit among those whom the organizer is most inclined to trust: this means, in the overseas urban context, clansmen—people of the same surname, friends, and those of similar homeland origins.

In a note on economic sophistication among overseas Chinese, Dr Freedman draws attention to the importance of the entrepreneurial, managerial and financial skills which such associations taught and their contribution to economic success in Singapore.[4] He points out that success is not due to business training in China because the commercial class played an insignificant role in emigration. Although in Hong Kong a larger proportion of immigrants may be drawn from this class such associations may well perform a similar function for those of peasant background.[5]

Saving for old age undoubtedly played a minor role in China because of the institutionalization of filial piety. However, it could

---

[1] Arthur Smith, *Village Life in China; A Study in Sociology*, New York 1899, p. 210.

[2] See Freedman, op. cit., p. 18.

[3] Various observers have described their organization. See, for example, Arthur Smith, op. cit., pp. 152-60.

[4] Maurice Freedman, 'The Handling of Money: A Note on the Background to the Economic Sophistication of Overseas Chinese', *Man*, vol. LIX, April 1959, Shorter Notes 89, pp. 64-5.

[5] According to information from a Jesuit Father active in setting up Credit Unions on a western model in Hong Kong, traditional type loan associations do not work well in the urban area. Members often do not know each other well and frequent cases of fraud are reported with the head of an association

be important in towns among individuals separated from their families. In some areas religious organizations provided old-age homes which accepted contributions from would-be entrants while they were still young and working.

The importance of the family in China to economic activity can be seen in the application of whole families to the running of economic enterprises in the towns as well as in the countryside; again it can be seen in the extension of the kinship principle to the organization of certain non-family enterprises, particularly those connected with manual crafts. The father–son relationship was often a model for relationships between employer and employee, and master and apprentice. The system of mutual obligations among kinsmen, friends and neighbours gave rise to a system of economic recruitment in which personal considerations were of considerable importance, and this system was carried into modern industrial organization as it developed. Levy, writing about industrialization in China, discusses the harmful effects of such particularism to economic progress at some length.[1]

(b) Class and education

The characteristics of the gentry who formed the highest social class have been summed up as 'owning land but not themselves working it; pursuing a gentlemanly way of life, of which classical scholarship was an important ingredient; forming a "natural" category of leaders in any community in which they lived . . .' The gentry was not only closely identified with scholarship but its members also largely monopolized entrance to the State examinations.

To become one of the gentry class or approximate as closely as possible to gentry ways was the ambition of many Chinese. No alternative way of life was held in such high esteem. A role of the gentleman was to be a leader in his society and teach its social values. His qualifications for this role were mainly knowledge of

[1] Levy, op. cit., p. 18.

making off with the joint savings of members. Since 1963, 13 Credit Unions have been established using various bases for association from residential and parish boundaries to place of work. Total savings since establishment have been HK$90,000 and they have loaned out HK$132,000. The Government is in the process of drafting a Credit Union Ordinance at present which will legalize them [sic].

the classics which formed the 'charter' for many institutions and virtuous qualities which knowledge of the classics was believed to develop.

The role of the gentry in society makes their attitudes towards the worthwhileness of the various forms of economic behaviour important. The emphasis in education on development of personal qualities rather than expertise tended to lead many scholars to disdain technical ability and interest in practical affairs. Smith, writing on village life, describes the unworldliness of village scholars.[1] This in turn tended to inhibit development of the kind of skills necessary for entrepreneurship: those most qualified by intellectual training, wealth and leisure to develop such skills were those who most despised them. Merchants had low status in Chinese society, being reckoned below peasants in the class hierarchy.

On the importance of wealth in the life of the individual, scholars maintained two somewhat conflicting attitudes. On the one hand acquisitiveness was seen as harmful. It affected personal harmony and therefore intellectual efficiency and social poise. Confucius emphasizes that 'A virtuous man makes his principles his worry, not money'. Another proverb points out 'When wealth is unjustly offered to the virtuous man he does not accept; when poverty is unjustly thrust upon him he does not refuse'. Yet another: 'When a basket of rice is offered without ceremony you refuse; when ten thousand bushels are offered in the same way why should you accept?' Although too great a concern with gain was discouraged, it was recognized that without a material competence it was difficult to achieve the personal harmony necessary for the development of qualities of mind. Mencius reasons that without a permanent income the educated man can be of constant mind only with difficulty; the people not at all.[2] The relation of material security to social conduct also is emphasized by Kwan Tzu of the Law and Economy School who points out: 'When the granaries are full you can teach the people manners and restraints; when food and clothing are not wanting you can teach the people notions of honour and disgrace.' In both these sayings recognition is given to the fact that the poor must be expected to have greater concern with matters of material welfare. While

---

[1] Smith, op. cit., pp. 93–7.

[2] See Max Weber, *The Religion of China: Confucianism and Taoism*, translated and edited by Hans H. Gerth, Glencoe, Ill., 1951, p. 160.

both rich and poor were exhorted to be frugal, greater acquisitiveness was more likely to be tolerated from those at the margin of subsistence than it was from individuals who had ample for their daily needs.

The ordinary people fully recognized the economic basis of gentry status. We have this illustrated in one of the rather terse folk-adages in which Cantonese seem to specialize: 'Have money have status; have status have money.' In other words wealth is necessary to achieve high status and once achieved, the economic possessions which are enjoyed bring in still greater wealth.

Trade and commerce provided one of the quickest roads to wealth accumulation even though they carried with them low social status. To check the entry of tradesmen into the gentry class they and their sons were often barred from the public examinations. However, this ban does not appear to have worked efficiently. 'Money reaches the gods' as one proverb has it, and merchants certainly appear to have been able to use their financial position to persuade the authorities to accept their sons for examinations in spite of the exclusion laws.

Trade was seen then as a means to more socially approved ends. Levy discusses the bias of wealthy merchants in China against the training of their sons to take over their commercial functions.[1] Their ambition on retirement was usually to buy land, a symbol of gentry status, and live in the socially approved manner. Thus there was a constant drain away of individuals from commercial pursuits once success was achieved. Chen Ta discussing the return of emigrants from Fukien and Kwantung provinces in the thirties —that is, men who had made their money from commercial pursuits abroad—says that they often made desirable husbands. The gentry were not above forming liaisons with such people by marrying their daughters to them when there was a shortage of prospective sons-in-law of good family in the district.[2]

A further attraction of wealth accumulation and the investment of wealth in land holdings in the south particularly was its role in the improvement of family position in the lineage organization. It allowed a family to exercise greater power in lineage affairs, or to endow its own separate ancestor cult and set up as a

[1] Levy, op. cit., pp. 93-7.
[2] Chen Ta, *Emigrant Communities in South China: A Study of Overseas Migration and its Influence on Standards of Living and Social Change*, London and New York 1939, p. 134.

semi-independent segment. The question of wealth in its relation to both lineage leadership and the segmentary system is fully discussed in a recent work on lineage organization.[1] The power which rich lineages could exercise over neighbouring communities was considerable. Before the arrival of the British in the New Territories the area was dominated by a wealthy group which appears to have had more power over neighbouring communities than did the government in Canton. The basis of its power is said to have been certain economic privileges which it obtained during the Sung dynasty.

(c) *The religious system*

Chinese religion expresses a number of attitudes towards wealth. Let us first consider those of religious organizations possessing well-formulated ideologies. Buddhism, Taoism, and various syncretic systems owing much to the former two in their religious ideas, express two major attitudes towards the importance of wealth. They are related to the two methods open to individuals for achieving spiritual progress: personal cultivation and mutual help.

A concern with personal cultivation is found to a greater or lesser degree in all three kinds of religious system enumerated above. The term which such religions use for personal cultivation is *hsiu-hsing*. It is the same term as that used by the Confucianists who were concerned with developing certain personal qualities. Although the concern of the former is with spiritual ends and the latter with social ends, both recognized the danger of acquisitiveness to the achieving of desired goals. The seeker after spiritual powers and high spiritual status in the next world is urged to rid himself first of the desire for material possessions. Only then is he free to devote himself to the task in hand.

For those unable to follow this path to spiritual achievement, salvationist religions offer an alternative method. This is to build up 'merit' by performance of virtuous acts. Such merit is then seen as 'available' for transfer to all sentient beings and can thus be used for the spiritual progress of all. Whereas the personal cultivation method of progress achieved its greatest popularity perhaps among more intellectual members of society, the mutual-help method was that adopted by the devout of all classes, particularly lay

[1] Maurice Freedman, *Lineage Organization in Southeastern China*, op. cit.

members of the religions. The individual should perform those virtuous acts for which he was most suited by ability and station in life. The rich man was induced to give generously to charity. In this century, as laymen have become more prominent in the Buddhist religion, and with the emphasis in secular life on the value of social welfare activities, charitable works have become a prominent feature of Buddhist activities. A number of religious associations have been formed in China and in overseas communities for the purpose of handling charitable donations. A number of secular Chinese associations are also devoted to this task. The duty of the rich to give to charity was also emphasized by more secular philosophies and was considered a function of the gentleman.

Salvationist religion, then, viewed wealth from two angles. While wealth might prove disadvantageous to those seeking spiritual progress by individual methods, it was an advantage to those seeking such progress by the method of mutual help. The importance of the latter thus mitigated the disapproval which this type of religion might otherwise have expressed for rich members of society.

The need of the poor to devote much of their attention to the material conditions of life is reflected clearly in folk-religion. Its gods specialize in the problems of material welfare and many of its cults are devoted to the achievement of economic success. Even here, however, there is the underlying attitude that concern with economic advancement should be restricted to the achievement of basic material needs.

Religion affected the use of wealth by developing a number of ceremonies for which it was necessary to pay practitioners. They not only included rituals connected with the religion itself and of which the member might avail himself, but also a number of alternative ways of performing rituals required by other institutions of society. Many people would invite Buddhist priests to perform ceremonies as part of the funeral rites of individuals who were not necessarily devout Buddhists during their lives. Taoist priests might also be invited to perform their own type of rituals for the occasion. The more 'orthodox' Buddhist funeral rites are generally more austere and less costly than the type of rituals performed by Taoists. It is interesting to note that in Singapore, where wealth is most important to social success, the more costly type of Taoist ritual is often preferred by Cantonese to the simpler

Buddhist ceremonies. The wealth of the individual is indicated by the employment of great numbers of practitioners and the use of elaborate paraphernalia. Thus both mourner and deceased gain status, the former is also satisfied that he has performed his duty to the deceased, and the latter is more assured of a comfortable time in the other world.

One belief affecting economic values in China is in *fêng-shui* (geomancy). Land and constructions of various kinds are believed to be governed by good and evil influences because of their relationship to certain features of the surrounding terrain. These influences in turn can affect people owning or using these resources. They are not constant, however. The pulling down of a tree or building of a house in the neighbourhood of a particular building or piece of land can be enough to turn a former good influence into an evil one and result in the resource being abandoned.

(d) The State

The relation of the State to economic activity can of course affect the attitude of people towards the worthwhileness of various economic pursuits. Writers on the State in nineteenth-century China have observed that it was not always conducive to economic development. Weber says the rational and calculable administration and law enforcement necessary for industrial development did not exist; that because capital investment in industry is sensitive to 'irrational' rule and dependent on the possibility of calculating steady and rational operation of the State machinery it failed to emerge under the Chinese-type administration.[1] Levy describes how the system of decentralization left the local resident at the mercy of robbers, war-lords and corrupt officials.[2] Vulnerability to unauthorized force placed limits on investment in physical goods and plant and supported the attitude that land was the best form of investment. It is difficult to destroy land.

The relatively greater public security and emphasis on economic development in the early colonies of Singapore and Hong Kong were factors encouraging labour and capital to the area. One of the reasons for the development of Shanghai was that extra-territoriality increased the security of investments. Moreover, western banks afforded a secure form of local investments as an alternative to land.

[1] Weber, op. cit., pp. 100 and 103.   [2] Levy, op. cit., p. 359.

Shanghai has fostered the rise of several important industrial families. Sons in such families remained in industry rather than turning to land-owning and the traditional gentry way of life which their wealth made possible. It is the sons and even sometimes grandsons of the founders of such industrial families who have come down to swell Hong Kong's industrial *élite*.

We would need to know more of the social organization of Shanghai and the surrounding area to fully appreciate the speed with which modern economic development was achieved—Shanghai was thrown open in 1843 and developed from a small unimportant town to an important industrial centre with extraordinary rapidity. The Shanghainese attitude towards the worthwhileness of industrial pursuits must also have been affected to some extent by contact with westerners and western economic attitudes. Another important factor must have been the separation of Shanghai from the Chinese bureaucratic and closely allied gentry structure. Something of the same kinds of modifications must have taken place in Chinese social institutions and values in the city as a result of migration there and of the impact of western institutions, as have taken place in Hong Kong. Before we discuss the effects of migration to Hong Kong, however, let us summarize the main points discussed in this section.

In the homeland certain institutional arrangements and values worked together to discourage a number of activities aimed at maximizing gain. The family system put checks on the means of acquiring greater wealth. It discouraged movement into occupations bringing greater income but placing the individual outside family control. The system of inheritance led to continual division of family fortunes. The idea of mutual dependence was institutionalized in a way which tended to inhibit economic efficiency because it continually introduced personal considerations into economic relationships. The class system allotted a low social status to the tradesman and tended to discourage individuals from entering commerce on a permanent basis. External factors such as poor communications, lack of opportunities elsewhere and sometimes absence of law and order again tended to inhibit emigration into more productive forms of employment.

Acquisitiveness was discouraged by Confucianism and the religious system although it was recognized that at the margin of subsistence a greater interest in material advancement was to be expected. Extremes of poverty could lead to a disruption of family unity and force individuals to act more in accordance with their best economic interests. Folk-religion reflects the greater interest of the peasant in material gain as do also a number of folk-adages. Since the peasant was often denied opportunities for education his knowledge of values contained in the classics was obtained largely by indirect means, through the example of the gentry.

Saving was greatly approved but there was a tendency to disapprove of the use of wealth for mainly productive purposes. More approved uses were directed to fulfilment of social obligations and charitable purposes. Land was an approved form of wealth because it enabled the family to increase its solidarity. External factors also inhibited investment in commodities other than land. Since law and order were often lacking land was attractive because it was relatively indestructible. Large land holdings were associated with the gentry whose status was admired.

Among the factors favouring interest in gain on the other hand was the constant need for cash and goods for fulfilment of social obligations. This encouraged a lively credit system in which the idea of social co-operation was often outweighed by that of maximum gain. Methods for manipulating credit also taught various economic skills. It was recognized that the poor needed to have greater interest in gain than was the ideal. Rich people were not despised if they used their wealth in approved fashion, for example, scholarship and a gentry way of life, and charitable activities. Although trade was despised it was often taken up as a quick route to riches.

4   Society and values relating to gain in Hong Kong

We have already indicated that wealth and maximization of gain are of more importance among Chinese in Hong Kong than in the homeland. Of major importance in determining attitudes to wealth have been the class composition of immigrant society, changes in Hong Kong in Chinese institutions, and replacement of some by those of western character. Contacts with other western institutions and ideas, and with westerners themselves, have also played a part.

The majority of Hong Kong's immigrants came to the Colony to improve themselves economically. Most of them, particularly the Cantonese, had been peasants, small traders or artisans in the homeland. The gentry played a negligible role in migration. In recent years numbers of educated individuals have been coming to Hong Kong. However, they came from an industrial society in which principles of gain played an important part in the ordering of economic relations. The Communist difficulties with the 'capitalist' attitudes of Shanghai are well known. Resistance to Communist ideology appears to have been considerable in the former settlement. People in Hong Kong frequently remark on the apparent absence of effects of Communist doctrines on recent newcomers from the area and the ease with which they fit themselves again into a capitalist-type economy.

Chinese homeland society was also predominantly peasant and working class. However, in Hong Kong many of the Chinese institutional arrangements for checking motives of gain are absent. Not only were few members of the gentry class among the immigrants but within the Colony such a class has failed to develop. There has been, then, an absence of the kind of leader found in traditional society whose function it was to teach the approved anti-materialist values of society. The main reasons why a traditional type gentry class failed to emerge are probably: first, the commercial atmosphere—Hong Kong was created for mainly economic reasons—and the urban residential conditions do not encourage gentry patterns of living; and second, political leadership in the Colony no longer rests on classical education. The importance of traditional qualifications for leadership has also declined in the homeland during this century. Recruitment to the administrative ranks of the Hong Kong Colonial Government is based on western educational qualifications. Hong Kong government is run almost entirely by a civil service and most of the administrative posts in this service are filled by those of expatriate status.

Classical education has declined in importance with the absence of a group to continue its traditions. There has been an increasing desire moreover for the type of education which equips individuals for urban living and occupations and this in effect means either a western or modern Chinese-type education. This is not to say that classical values have no place in Chinese life. Western-type education is regarded as important because it can earn a greater income for the individual. Few are concerned with the moral or intellectual qualities which it might help to develop. The classics are still largely regarded as the main source of virtue. Serious study of classical works, however, has become mostly a hobby for the rich with time on their hands. For the majority the proverb is probably the main source of classical knowledge and its position is to some extent challenged by that of the popular folk-adage which places emphasis on material advancement.

The above factors combine to create a situation in which economic gain is regarded as a major social end. As Chinese themselves sometimes cynically remark: 'Most things are decided in Hong Kong on the basis of whether or not the abacus[1] makes a satisfying click.'

In the absence of traditional methods for acquiring status and leadership they have come to rest largely on wealth and the ability to command wealth. Other qualities of leadership may be important, but without wealth it is difficult to attract the public eye. Government provides for a number of non-salaried positions to which Chinese can aspire and which carry with them considerable power and prestige. At first sight they might appear to compete with position through wealth. In fact, however, they tend to set the final seal of approval on wealth as a means to power. Many individuals singled out for such honours are those enjoying in Chinese organizations positions of leadership which they gained through their command over wealth. At the higher levels of leadership the relationship between wealth and status is more complex, however. The form of wealth can be important and there has until recently been a tendency first, for the older wealth to count for more than new—partly because it carries more guarantee of permanency, and second, for those in traditional Hong Kong economic pursuits to get most of the honours. However, the value to the economy of the new industrialists is increasingly recognised today. This is beginning to be reflected in leadership of Chinese organizations and in the system of government non-salaried appointments. The position is somewhat complicated, however, by the fact that more important Chinese associations have recruited mainly from the Cantonese, whereas many of the new industrialists are of other dialect groups. The question of how the wealthy obtain public recognition will be taken up in more detail in a later section.

In China the terms *kao-chi* and *hsia-chi* (upper and lower levels) were used to refer to class groupings. In Hong Kong they are more often than not used to distinguish rich and poor. The rich do not form a self-conscious class group. Since opportunities

---

[1] A beaded frame for making numerical calculations.

for making and losing money in speculative activities are considerable, the ranks of the rich can change. There is one group, however, who exhibit some degree of class consciousness and are partially defined in terms of wealth. This is the group of 'Hong Kong families'. Their wealth is 'old', being made by their forebears. Their residence in Hong Kong is well established. Family connections by marriage and relationship to founding members is of some importance to this group, although the importance of wealth to their status in the eyes of the community can be seen in the fact that they tend to lose their position of prestige if their wealth does decline. In the past, governmental honours went largely to this group and in fact it would probably be true to say that their 'class consciousness' is largely fostered by the British community in Hong Kong. An important factor in the development of these families was of course the decision made by their forebears to settle permanently in Hong Kong. This was usually a conscious decision and not merely a force of circumstance. The decision to settle might in some cases be connected with the fact that the founders of some of these families were of mixed Chinese and European blood. The family organization they built up, however, was essentially modelled on the Chinese pattern. It is in such families that we see some attempt to build up corporate group organization, to practise ancestor worship in special places reserved for the purpose and to conform with gentry patterns of behaviour as far as urban structure permits. Female descendants and their offspring, however, are often included in group activities, and the soul-tablets of unmarried females are found in their halls. Since such groups have transferred their main allegiances to the Colony, they tend to ignore questions of family origins and status in China and often do not know their village of origin. Family importance dates from immigration and their groupings exist independently of the homeland.

Those Chinese who did not intend to settle had no incentive to build up in Hong Kong a new segment of their lineage of origin or to gather together the representatives of their home lineage into a residential community. The shortage of land to provide a basis for extended settlement, and the lack of means to purchase such land acted as further deterrents. In the New Territories, in contrast, I know of at least one rump lineage of recent immigrant foundation. There the availability of land and the arable basis of society are more conducive to development of this type of organization. The importance of a decision to settle *vis-à-vis* lineage development can again be illustrated from a group in the Territories. The development of this group stems from the action of an individual who decided to retire in the district of Kam Tin of the Territories. He brought down his ancestors' bones for reburial there. Although his sons did not stay permanently in the area, certain property rights in Kam Tin appear to have accrued to the family because of the presence of the ancestral graves. A later descendant succeeding to this property moved in and built up a permanent settlement.[1]

For the greater part of the community genealogical background in China or within Hong Kong is of little importance in the determination of status or class. While some positions have in the past tended to be reserved for members of 'Hong Kong families' it is possible for individuals to obtain considerable status on the basis of their own ability to amass wealth. Since it is also recognized that wealth can pass quickly from one group to another, the humble background of a rich second-generation Hong Kong Chinese is not likely to stand in his way to social success. Opportunities for the accumulation of wealth are further enhanced by government measures: taxation is low, public security is good and there are few legal restrictions to impede the development of business and industry. There are certain difficulties in obtaining capital, however, which will be considered later.

Housing and the structure of occupations have put considerable strain on family organization and helped to weaken some of the restraints on economic activity which were set up by traditional family organization in China. Many households do not include all members of an elementary family. Children who work may live away from home. Fathers often positively encourage their sons to take up new occupations if they can bring in greater income, although the situation may be different when the family owns its own business.

While the economic interests of individuals still come into conflict with obligations towards kinsmen, friends, and, in Hong Kong, people of the same territorial origins, urban conditions provide for a number of situations in which Chinese are dealing with strangers. In dealings with such people Chinese feel free to put their own interest first and usually do so with alacrity. Many

[1] See S. F. Balfour, 'Hong Kong before the British', in: *T'ien Hsia Monthly*, vol. XI, no. 5, April–May 1941, pp. 440–64, especially pp. 445–9.

Chinese have told me that they 'do not like to make friends'. By this they usually mean that they do not want to have their own interests and those of their family thwarted by the economic obligations which such friendships still imply.

Ethics governing impersonal relationships in China were largely the province of religion. While religion had a certain amount of influence on acquisitiveness it is doubtful whether religious ideas in this respect have much influence on the conduct of impersonal business relationships in Hong Kong. In contrast to Singapore, and for reasons we cannot discuss here, Chinese religious organization has not flourished in the Colony and the importance of spending for ritual purposes is not very considerable. One Buddhist attitude which is still of significance, however, is that relating to the importance of charity. There are several devout Buddhist laymen in the business community who give generously to charitable projects. There are non-Buddhists who give equally generously, however. It is not always easy to assess the motive of those who donate to worthy causes. However, we shall see later that there is a tendency for people to give to those organizations which have worked out ways of rewarding their benefactors in terms of prestige.

Chinese contact with Christianity has increased in recent years. As the ban on missionary activities in China has become more stringent, many missionary organizations have settled in the Colony, and there are a bewildering number of sects. The main contact is probably with Christian organized welfare projects. The number of converts is also increasing but I have heard Christian leaders bewail the fact that there is little attempt by Chinese Christians to conduct their business lives in accordance with principles they learn in church. It is pointed out, however, that Christians from the west do not always set a good example of Christian standards of conduct in their commercial relations.

5   Contact with Westerners

The main economic consequence of western contact is probably that it opens up a new range of goods for potential demand and possibilities of a higher standard of living. It may also lead to a greater familiarity and desire to use western-type economic institutions such as banks and the stock exchange. Many Chinese have no direct contacts with westerners, but some of the same results might be obtained through personal observation, particularly of rich Europeans with high status in the community, and through contact with the radio and cinema. Western cultural institutions also try to improve standards of economic efficiency by offering courses to the public on western business techniques.

Although the demand schedule of Chinese may be enriched by western contact, it is not of the same pattern as that of westerners at different levels of income and wealth. Chinese orders of preference are determined by a number of social factors including the role of certain commodities in conferring prestige and helping to make public the wealth of the individual. For this reason, goods made in countries enjoying a high level of prosperity may be preferred to those of others even if they are not of the highest quality available on the market. The demand for different standards of housing is an example of difference between western and Chinese outlook. It would be wrong to assume, as some people do in Hong Kong, that Chinese live in crowded circumstances entirely because they like to. However, there is certainly less demand for space and also privacy than there is generally among westerners. Moderately well-off Chinese often express surprise at the amount of space westerners appear to need and ask why they do not let out part of their accommodation. Chinese often imagine that the westerner with an expensive home must already have the other items of wealth which they themselves would put first on their demand schedule, and are therefore richer than they might be in fact. Although westerners as a group are richer than the Chinese, a comparison of housing standards is by no means a certain indication of difference in overall wealth.

There is one type of individual, however, who is recognized by Chinese as following more closely the western patterns of demand. He is referred to somewhat disrespectfully as the *wōng-mîn kwai-lo*[1] (*wōng-mîn* means 'yellow-faced', that is, 'Chinese'; *kwai-lo* means devil, that is 'westerner'). Such individuals usually have many social contacts with westerners and have often lived abroad where they have obtained their differences in demand pattern. They are sometimes despised by other Chinese because it is believed that like westerners they put their own comfort before social obligations. In fact this may not be so—of either group—and the desire to conform with social requirements and satisfy their new level of preference can put a severe strain on such individuals.

[1] Cantonese romanization.

Rooftop school. Against the Kowloon Hills youngsters go to school on the roof of their resettlement block.

Learning to write. Studies in concentration among rooftop pupils as they strive to master the intricacies of, if the pun be permitted, 'character formation'.

Characters. These must be formed by five-year-olds. Good and bad attempts flank the centre model line.

月光做工花落天空遊山

Tea party.
Student teachers
learn polite
mores!

Social contact with westerners is broadly speaking on two levels. In Hong Kong, unlike in some British colonies and ex-colonies, two social classes of westerners are recognized. Chinese divide westerners into the *taai-paân*[1] (bosses) and *pong-paân* (help-manage). The latter category includes most people who are in uniformed supervisory jobs. The former term has been romanized by westerners in Hong Kong as 'Taipan' and is used commonly in conversation and in the English press to refer to wealthy westerners. The western *pong-paân* is often born in Hong Kong and married to a Chinese wife. He frequently speaks good colloquial Chinese. A number of Portuguese are also of *pong-paân* status. Taipans do not usually speak Chinese; in fact, westerners who speak Chinese will usually be addressed as *pong-paân* when their status is unknown. The Taipan's social contact with Chinese is usually confined to those who speak English—this is not so of many government officials who learn Chinese as part of their job—and are wealthy. Generally speaking, friendships between Taipans and Chinese are likely to be carried on in a western context and open up opportunities for learning western habits of behaviour; those between *pong-paân* and Chinese, on the contrary, are likely to be carried on in a Chinese context and it is probably the *pong-paân* who benefits most from the cultural contact.

6 Concepts of wealth

(a) Major forms of wealth

Most people keep part of their wealth in a non-productive form. Some follow the traditional practice of keeping some wealth in a form storable in the home. Cash may be kept at home, although today the value of bank deposit accounts which provide both an income and greater security is increasingly recognized. Gold bars are still demanded although there is a growing tendency to convert wealth into this form only during emergencies. The demand for gold bars increased, for example, during the Formosa Straits bombardment.

Wealth is put into a number of kinds of durable consumer goods. The object of choice will be determined by such considerations as: (*a*) the prestige they confer; (*b*) their convertibility into cash and ability to retain their original value; (*c*) their use

[1] Cantonese romanization.

and the pleasure they afford. Some goods combine all these characteristics. In buying expensive goods there is a tendency to regard purely pleasurable goods as an extravagance. There is a reluctance to spend more than is absolutely necessary on goods which are only for use. In seeking goods for prestige, the types of goods desired are generally those giving status in the eyes of the Chinese community. They do not necessarily give such status in the eyes of the western community. Even when this fact is recognized, it is usually not regarded as important. Prestige goods are, in a sense, a form of investment because by adding to status and conveying the idea of wealth they inspire confidence in others. They can thus enhance business opportunities. Prestige goods might be purchased when business is bad, for as a Chinese saying emphasizes: 'When business is bad, paint the counter.'

Gold jewellery is prized because it combines all three of the above characteristics. The quality of workmanship may be of minor consideration in purchase, however, because its price is usually lost in resale. Most Chinese, particularly Chinese women, are very familiar with changes in the price of gold and bargaining is confined to the price of workmanship alone. Many women, particularly those of the lower income groups, confine their purchase of gold ornaments to the plainest of items. Heavy gold chains which can be worn round the waist next to the skin are frequently purchased by unattached female servants and are regarded almost entirely as a form of investment. Chinese gold which has a high gold content is preferred because of its value, but its softness makes it impracticable for many forms of jewellery. Chinese always demand a written guarantee from jewellery shops which states the gold content of the item purchased. This will be preserved and brought out in evidence by the owner of the gold if it is offered for resale.

It is not usual for Chinese in either urban or rural areas to keep wealth in the form of food stocks although rice, like gold bars, will be accumulated by certain people during the initial stages of a crisis for personal consumption or possibly for speculative purposes.

We saw that western education is demanded for its income-earning qualities. For this reason parents often regard the education of their children as a form of investment. I have come across many poor Chinese who have denied themselves necessities in order to send their children to school. The investment, however, is for their own future as well as that of their children. A Chinese whose parents have struggled to send him to school is likely to feel strongly his economic obligations towards them. This tends to cause Chinese to use their educational qualifications in the most financially productive way possible. The economic value of daughters is increasing as the demand for female labour, particularly between the ages of 18 and 30, grows. Even Chinese of modest income are beginning to invest in the education of daughters.

Among the durable consumption goods which give prestige to Chinese is a large car. This is as true of traditional individuals as it is of the more westernized. Such cars are frequently decked out with large cushions—seldom in use, antimacassars, dangling dolls and even vases of artificial flowers. We noted that the demand for housing does not usually come as high on the list of preference goods of the Chinese as on that of the westerner. The Chinese home does not provide the same opportunities for prestige as does that of the westerner and in Hong Kong this fact can be of importance. Chinese entertainment for guests is usually in the form of costly and elaborate banquets which need complicated preparation and organization. For this reason, Chinese social life is carried on largely in restaurants. It is not usual for any but the closest friends of Chinese to be invited to the home for entertainment; even when entertaining friends at home the dinner preparations are usually undertaken by caterers. Individuals whom a Chinese wishes to impress with his wealth will therefore rarely see the place in which he lives. Foreigners, who after long acquaintance with Chinese of comfortable income eventually see their homes, are frequently surprised at the poor quality of housing, lack of space and of good quality furniture and fittings. A story told me recently by a friend who was flat-hunting indicates the relative lack of interest in housing *vis-à-vis* other items of wealth. On looking over a new block of flats in which he desired to live, my friend found they were all occupied. The owner himself lived on the top floor. The friend indicated his regret that the owner was unable to accommodate him as he was willing to pay a good rent for a flat in the block. After a moment's consideration, the owner offered his own flat at a rent higher than the others in the block and moved out. He is now living in a wooden shack on the hillside.

As the higher rungs of the economic ladder are reached,

Chinese may begin to build themselves expensive homes. Often they will be more elaborate outside than inside, since the outside can be seen by more people. Some Chinese, particularly the more traditional individuals, may begin to accumulate the kind of goods which in China were associated with members of the gentry class—valuable scrolls, antiques and old Chinese books. The desire to appear a gentleman is often the cause of such purchase, although, of course, many Chinese genuinely enjoy such objects. A desire to appear a gentleman, however, can conflict with the desire to obtain further prestige through wealth and the cost of such items is often emphasized when they are displayed to people. More westernized Chinese, as they advance economically, might order expensive pictures, even statuary, from overseas and have their houses decorated by professional interior decorators. In the early part of the century a very rich Chinese built several houses for himself in Hong Kong which were all designed in Scottish baronial style.

Chinese increasingly use banks for storing valuables, but clearly from the prestige point of view such storage represents a loss. I am told by a member of the banking profession in the Colony, however, that there comes a point in an individual's wealth accumulation at which his desire to show his riches and gain prestige is outweighed by desire that certain people should not know the extent of his fortune. This desire is motivated partly by fear of robbery and kidnapping and partly by the fear of attracting unwelcome attention from the taxation authorities.

Most wealthy Chinese will convert a proportion into producer goods. As in traditional China, land is still a popular form of investment although in the urban area it is not acquired for use in agriculture and seldom for the direct use of a family group. Real-estate, particularly blocks of flats, is a popular form of investment for Chinese of various income levels. Sometimes an attraction of investment in property is that it can be used partly to accommodate relatives towards whom some obligation is felt. They in turn can act as caretakers and help protect the property.

Unattached working women invest in flats and small houses. They rent them out while they are working—this is particularly true of servants in living-in jobs—and live in them in their old age. Many people now save for their old age in Hong Kong. As one Hong Kong psychologist recently observed '... urbanization, industrialization and the increase in social mobility and weakening of the sentiment of filial piety have helped place the aged in a less happy and secure position'.[1] In view of the somewhat uncertain future of Hong Kong—the lease of the New Territories ends in 1997—the attraction of investment in various forms of construction is enhanced. It is reckoned to be possible, even common, to get capital in this kind of investment back in from three to five years.

Investment in plant and machinery is growing in importance. A large proportion of such investment, however, is probably undertaken by entrepreneurs themselves. A committee which sat recently to determine the need or otherwise of an industrial bank in Hong Kong[2] produced some approximate figures on investment in land, buildings and plant and machinery in their report. It stated, however, that its figures were subject to a fairly wide margin of error (see Table I).

For sake of comparison, the figure estimated by the government statistician for all private fixed investment (excluding land) in 1958 was given at HK$400 million. The boom in 1958 in land is no doubt partly connected with the trade recess during that year which affected industrial expansion. There are no unbroken series of figures available for the period to show increases in the number of industrial undertakings resulting from this investment but during 1959 the number of registered factories increased from 4,906 to 5,023.

Table I: Investments (in millions of Hong Kong dollars)*

	1957	*1958*	*1959*
Land	5	14	9
Buildings	11	29	19
Plant and machinery	70	60	85
TOTAL	86	103	113

* The data include only monetized investments. HK$6 = US$1.

One of the biggest drains on capital available for industrial investment is said to be the high price of land. Although the figures given above show the relative importance of plant and machinery as items of wealth over land and buildings, I think it

[1] P. M. Yap, 'Ageing and Mental Health in Hong Kong', paper for the Seminar for International Research on Psychological and Social Aspects of Mental Health in Ageing (University of Michigan).

[2] Appointed by the Governor in January 1959 (report unpublished).

would be wrong to under-estimate the desire for the latter among many small investors not directly concerned with industry. The Industrial Bank Committee was of the opinion that a large amount of investment in industry at risk was through investment of profits earned in other enterprises. Initial investment in real estate appears to be a common way of financing an industrial enterprise in Hong Kong. The normal security for loans for industrial investment is a mortgage on land. Money-lenders and even some banks are ready to grant loans with land as a security at the rate of interest fluctuating from 5 to 6 per cent per annum for the latter and 12 to 18 per cent per annum for the former.

There is a tendency for many Chinese of wealth, particularly those of new wealth, to put it into speculative enterprises. This is largely responsible for the high social mobility in the Colony although the Chinese system of inheritance also does not favour capital accumulation. 'Hong Kong families' have tended to invest in more stable enterprises on the whole and this is largely the reason for the relative age of their wealth.

(b) Wealth and market values

Most forms of wealth enter into the market and their value is determined largely by market calculations. Other factors may, however, sometimes enter into the determination of price. Although the system of fixed prices is growing in all economic sectors there is still bargaining for a considerable number of con-sumer goods. Price discrepancies are due in part to imperfect knowledge of the market but also to the lack of impersonality in many Chinese economic relationships. It is commonly said that two price standards exist in Hong Kong: that for foreigners and that for Chinese living in Hong Kong. Some maintain there is a treble standard: for Chinese, 'local' Europeans—Portuguese of mixed blood and other Eurasians—and westerners; or even a quadruple standard with Americans paying more than English. Such differences are connected with conceptions of the varying levels of wealth among the various groups. Malayan Chinese—distinguished by their Malayanized form of Chinese speech—are believed to be a wealthy group and are charged at the same level as other foreigners in the Colony.

The price of cars on the second-hand market is often influenced by other than market considerations. One type of car fetches a low price because it is believed to resemble a Chinese coffin in shape. European-owned cars fetch more than Chinese-owned because Chinese believe that they are better-cared for, although, in fact, this is not always the case. I am told that proximity to cemeteries can affect the price of land and buildings adversely, although I personally know of no examples in which *fêng-shui* considerations have affected market values in the urban area. In the process of Hong Kong's development, hills have been razed and land extended into the sea. This has considerably altered the terrain but does not appear to have called forth any audible protest from the Chinese. In the New Territories *fêng-shui* is still important. Buildings are sometimes abandoned for *fêng-shui* reasons. One of the reasons for this may be that people do not move around so much as they do in the town. Good *fêng-shui* there can be a valuable item of wealth. The government sometimes pays higher compensation to villagers with good *fêng-shui* when they are being moved to make way for new development. I came across one case of grave-land being sold by villagers to a group of missionaries. A high price was exacted because it was claimed that many ancestors were buried there. Later there was some suspicion as to whether it was in fact a burial plot, at least for human beings. Some of the bones were found to bear strong resemblance to those of the domestic pig.

I am told that at public auctions of land leases, prices might be forced up by Chinese bidders when it is known that the land offered is desired by a European. The reason is that it is believed that if a westerner wants it, he has probably gone to the trouble of having it thoroughly surveyed and it must therefore be worth having.

Communally owned lineage ('clan') land does not usually enter into the market in the Territories and cannot be alienated without the consent of the representatives and elders of the whole group. About one-third of land in the Territories is held in trust for ancestral worship and is not normally sold.[1] It is not totally inalienable although in practice it would become so if a strict interpretation was given to the term 'trust'. Sales have been made when in the general interest of beneficiaries though it is doubtful if this is in accordance with strict custom which is supposed to be adhered to in case of such trusts. Certain tools associated with

[1] See *Chinese Law and Custom in Hong Kong*, op. cit., p. 62. But see my paper 'Capital, Saving and Credit. . .', op. cit., p. 168 f. for further comment.

traditional crafts are not normally bought and sold but as in China are passed on from master to apprentice. This system of training is declining in importance in Hong Kong. There are few religious goods that would not be sold if the price offered were sufficiently attractive. I bought a soul-tablet from a public temple and found out afterwards that it had been placed there for worship in perpetuity.

(c) Services as form of wealth

Most services are evaluated in accordance with market calculations. There are still some, however, which stand outside the operation of the market. They are broadly: (*a*) Services performed by friends and others to whom Chinese feel social obligations and which may be legitimate or illegitimate. (*b*) Illegal services performed between individuals with no prior personal knowledge of each other. They may involve a third person who knows both parties and acts as a go-between. Some people make their living as brokers for illegal deals. Payment may even be made, or an individual might try to make payment, for perfectly legitimate services performed by a government official as part of his normal operations of work. This happens sometimes when an individual imagines that he was being given some priority to which he was not legally entitled. Certain occupations are reckoned to be worth much more than their salary because of their potentiality for earning money on the side. (*c*) Services of a traditional type, for example, those of a doctor practising Chinese medical skills, and those of Chinese religious practitioners.

The first type of service may be paid for by presents other than cash: food, expensive liquor, or even gold ornaments and other valuables according to the importance of the service. Chinese often try to build up an advanced fund of credit by presenting gifts against some future possible need. The time for making such gifts is normally Chinese New Year. It is for this reason that government servants are forbidden to take presents even from Chinese friends or from individuals for whom it appears at the moment that they can render no possible service. The problem of acceptance of gifts is one affecting many westerners with Chinese friends. The second kind of service is more likely to be paid in cash but the methods of payment may be highly involved. It is said that payment for a driving licence obtained illegally is by putting the agreed sum into a cigarette tin which is then passed to the recipient. In such illegal deals the payment may be clearly stated and the more common illegal services may have a fixed price. Payment for the third kind of service is by 'red packet'. The amount to be paid is not—or ideally should not be—fixed and the person rendering the service does not know how much he is getting until he opens the packet. Many traditional practitioners, however, are now pricing their services in accordance with market calculations, although a red packet may still be used to contain the sum agreed upon.

(d) Wealth held by groups

Various kinds of groups own property. Chinese associations which manage charities own schools, hospitals, clinics and welfare centres. Some are particularist groups recruiting according to principles of surname—all Chinese of the same surname are believed to be descended from the same original ancestor although they may come from different lineage groups and their relationship is not traceable; territorial origins; occupation or a combination of such principles. Others, including most of the important charitable organizations are universalist in principle, although they may in fact tend to recruit only from among Cantonese. The value of their holdings is sometimes considerable. One recently raised a total of more than $1 million for charitable purposes. The assets of one group amounted to $1·5 million in 1959 and in the same year it handled income and expenditure totalling $500,000. Nearly all welfare institutions are privately owned although many belong to missionary groups obtaining their major finances from abroad.

In the Territories, certain associations buy land or landed property and use rents for burial of members and to assist members to emigrate to other countries.[1] The government owns a considerable amount of housing, mainly in the form of flats and cottages in which squatters are settled. By the end of 1959 it had built 103 domestic multi-storey resettlement blocks in nine estates and housed 229,956 individuals. Additional housing for refugees and other squatters is owned by voluntary agencies. The Housing Authority—a non-profit-making enterprise—was set up in 1954 to meet the needs of middle-income earners, and many other domestic premises are owned by investment companies.

[1] See *Chinese Law and Custom in Hong Kong*, op. cit., p. 208.

Chinese businesses are largely owned by families and other private companies of which the shareholders are recruited according to particularist principles. One Chinese textile concern with a number of subsidiaries has a spinning mill with a paid-up capital of $5 million subscribed by Shanghainese residents; one of its subsidiaries has a paid up capital of $2 million, another was capitalized at $1·2 million and yet another at $1 million. This latter is one of the few enterprises with a trained managerial staff. Most of the public companies are western-owned concerns.

7 Methods of acquisition of wealth

(a) *Socially disapproved methods of accumulation*

The individual who devotes a large part of his time to wealth accumulation is not regarded with disapproval, particularly if he is prepared to discharge various social obligations and become a public benefactor. There are, however, occupations in which a concern with gain is not considered the appropriate attitude. Certain business methods are also frowned upon, and a few occupations which bring wealth are positively disapproved at least by certain sections of the community. The overall pattern of disapproval is not always identical to that in the west.

Probably most people regard a sense of vocation as necessary for the educator and member of both Christian and Chinese religious priesthoods. The widespread contempt for Buddhist priests in Hong Kong is associated with the great concern they are said to have with financial reward for their services. The attitude that medicine should be a vocation is not so strong as in the west. Doctors practising western medicine are among the richest men in the Colony and many take up medicine for its financial prospects. A number make money out of the dispensing side of their practice and engage in the pharmaceutical business as a side-line. One doctor known as 'Injection Lee' (I have given him a fictitious surname) is said to be worth a million dollars and one informant said it was commonly believed that one year his income tax was greater than the taxes paid by a particular bank. It was dryly remarked by another informant, however, that this might be because of the tendency of this bank to evade its taxes. Although abortion is illegal, there does not appear to be widespread disapproval of doctors who engage in this practice. Similarly there is not much disapproval of those who demand this service.

Chinese do not generally disapprove of businessmen who charge different prices to different types of customer but believe it is up to the customer to get the best price he can. There is a growing feeling, however, that price discrimination in regard to westerners is ruining the tourist industry. I have come across shops that refuse to sell goods to westerners at the same price as they sell to Chinese even when it has been pointed out that the customer is fully aware of the 'Chinese price'. It is not uncommon for goods or services supplied in accordance with prior agreement to be found to be of inferior quality on delivery. Sometimes the salesman was not happy about the agreed price but did not like to pass up business and turn away customers. Many businessmen have a short-range point of view which ultimately can affect their business adversely. One American observer recently remarked that Chinese wish to make $6 tomorrow for $5 spent today and will sacrifice future reputation for immediate gain. This problem will be discussed further in a later section.

Many businessmen hate to admit they cannot provide what is demanded. Shopkeepers will rarely admit that they do not sell a certain item, but will say they have 'just sold out'. They will accept business and then look round for somebody who sells the required item taking a commission for their service as a go-between and helping to raise the price. Inadequate marketing methods are partly to blame for this situation.

The passing off of inferior goods along with products appropriate to the agreed price is widespread in food sales and disapproved of by all customers. Dishonest methods are more likely to be followed when the relationship between customer and salesman is impersonal. It is not, of course, that all businessmen are dishonest with people they do not know. If this were so, Hong Kong could not have reached its present level of prosperity. The concept of business goodwill, however, is still not widely appreciated in all sectors of the commercial and industrial communities.

Copying of products and trademarks which have an established reputation is sometimes engaged in and does not appear to meet with widespread disapproval. The general attitude of indifference may have some basis in historical China where it was not considered unworthy to copy something which was good or admired. A recent correspondence in the press indicates that some people regard the practice of book pirating as entirely honourable, even if illegal, since it makes books available to poor students and their authors and publishers must already have been well compensated financially if they are regarded as worthy of pirating.

Smuggling and those occupations connected with the manufacture, sale and distribution of narcotics are generally regarded with disapproval. However, the grounds for disapproval of the latter are not always connected with the greater good of society at large. Several working-class Chinese expressed the attitude that people engaging in such activities were bad because they ran the risk of being caught and punished and thus bringing calamity on their families.

It is not easy to assess the extent to which bribery is regarded with disapproval in the Colony. Attitudes towards this practice appear to be somewhat mixed. There is fairly widespread disapproval of those who accept bribes and particularly of those who solicit them, but the role of those offering bribes in helping to perpetuate the system is not fully appreciated and there is a tendency to judge such cases on their merits. There is not much disapproval of those who offer bribes in order to obtain speedier performance of legitimate services. Indeed, many Chinese have expressed the opinion that it is difficult for the uninfluential to obtain many types of service without bribery. To report an individual requesting a bribe for providing a speedy service is often thought foolhardy. It causes considerable trouble and does not necessarily aid in obtaining the service desired. There is probably more widespread disapproval of those who offer bribes for illegal services or unfair priorities or who act as 'brokers' in such deals. Even here, however, the attitude is not clear-cut. An anecdote circulating in Hong Kong's business community recently indicates that the power of those able to command illegitimate services by influence and money may sometimes impress more than disgust. This story, which may or may not be true, concerns an architect who designed a structure which fell down. Rather than losing his reputation or even business, it is said, the event gave him considerable face. It was felt that a person who was able to get away with building such a structure must have influence with the department concerned with building permits in Hong Kong, and was therefore a useful man to know.

Gambling was common in traditional China and did not meet with great disapproval. It is very common in Hong Kong and takes many forms. On the other hand, a recent proposal to introduce football pools into the Colony met with strong opposition from certain prominent citizens, including those who are nominated members of the Legislative Council, and had to be abandoned. Letters to the press indicated that there is a growing feeling among Chinese that gambling is a social evil and that there are already adequate opportunities for this practice without resorting to a new and alien form.

There are a number of secret societies devoted largely to making money from 'protection' and promotion of illegitimate forms of business. Although a great many people, particularly among the lower income groups, are forced to join such organizations, the latter are regarded with almost unanimous disapproval.

It is common knowledge in influential circles that certain fortunes have been amassed by methods not entirely 'above board'. The Chinese 'mosquito' press specializing in scandal sometimes puts people in touch with such information. One individual making his money through smuggling is still known as the 'smuggling king' although he has now put his fleet of smuggling vessels to legitimate commercial use and is a respected member of the community. Some people made money during the Japanese occupation—trade with Japan was highly disapproved before the war. It is said that public disapproval of such individuals was weakened because the government took no action against them.

Generally speaking rich people who made money by socially disapproved means can gain status and respect if they are accepted by the influential members of the community. Most people like to associate with the wealthy in Hong Kong and they are likely to be accepted if they later transfer to respectable business and use their money in ways approved by Chinese society. There will usually be people, however, who continue to hold them in contempt behind their backs. Those whose fortunes are based on dubious activities of forebears operating when there was greater legal laxity are not likely to meet with any social disadvantages. I have even heard Chinese boasting about the known or suspected illegal practices of their ancestors.

(b) *Acquisition of wealth and the customary and official law*

Certain aspects of Chinese law and custom of the Ch'ing dynasty still apply in the case of Chinese domiciled in Hong Kong. We have already referred to a Committee set up in 1948 to investigate the problem. The main issues with which it was concerned were: the full extent of application of such law and custom; whether it should, with or without modification, be incorporated by Ordinance into the law of the Colony; or whether it should be superseded by the law applicable to persons to whom Chinese law and custom does not apply or by any other law. In carrying out its task, it approached various groups in the community in order to try to ascertain public opinion on the questions in hand.

Of most relevance to this study is the situation regarding inheritance. As in China, all sons and their male descendants of Chinese domiciled in the Colony divide the estate equally between themselves, the elder son getting the personal and household effects of the deceased and therefore a slightly larger share. Daughters and wives are not entitled to any share, although the former, if unmarried, has a sum normally set aside for marriage expenses, and the latter is entitled to support. The widow can also refuse to consent to division of the estate and so get practical control over the inheritance. She can also be custodian of a deceased husband's share in an estate. Only if the male line becomes extinct and no successor has been appointed can daughters inherit.

In strict custom a father could not by deed or will alter the succession, although he could give verbal or written instructions in matters of detail. In Hong Kong, however, the English doctrine of freedom of alienation appears to have been accepted and acted upon in the urban area. Some Chinese now make wills to determine the distribution of their property and include daughters among their successors. So far this applies mainly to the wealthy group who have more at stake. There appears to be a growing desire in the Chinese community, however, to allow daughters to inherit in cases of intestacy.

In the New Territories individuals are not allowed to will land as they see fit. The committee found a growing desire for change in this respect, although there was still a feeling in the rural community that no changes should be made in the system of inheritance in cases of intestacy. This is no doubt connected with the greater importance of land to social organization in the Territories. Since daughters still normally marry out into other villages —the Chinese practise surname exogamy—their inheritance of land could introduce complications regarding management of their estates. In the town, on the contrary, daughters continue to have close relations with parents after marriage and may live in close proximity to them.

The customary division of property in the homeland tended to work against capital accumulation. One of the arguments of Chinese in Hong Kong against the retention of the Ch'ing dynasty system is that it has already been abandoned in China. The fact that rich people often make wills in Hong Kong might tend to mitigate capital dissipation. The belief that wealth is dissipated in three generations still holds among the wealthy in Hong Kong, but it is interpreted in terms of the attitudes of sons and grandsons towards their inherited wealth. Informants have given examples of rich families which have declined because sons have eaten into their capital in order to live luxuriously, and grandsons 'have not even known how to earn their living'. On the other hand, I am told that when a man dies intestate leaving a family business there is a tendency for male heirs to attempt to stay together and work the enterprise jointly and that some private companies evolve in this manner.

A popular belief among Cantonese is that wealth passes quickly to this group from the Shanghainese. Although Cantonese will usually concede reluctantly that Shanghainese industrial organization tends to be run more efficiently than that of most other Chinese they insist that in a number of small enterprises, particularly those concerned with eating and other entertainment, Shanghainese spend unwisely on expensive décor and staff and are unable to compete with Cantonese in this respect. Cantonese certainly appear to use their capital more cautiously in this kind of business. They claim that Shanghainese often lose heavily in such ventures and have to sell out to the Cantonese.

(c) Credit and borrowing

Chinese borrow to finance business, for their children's education, to fulfil social and ceremonial obligations and for a number of emergencies. There are, however, a number of associations which cater for funeral expenses and which accept periodic payments from those anticipating such commitments.

For smaller sums of money, loan associations exist which are of the kind referred to in discussion of the China background. In addition as in China, people borrow from friends and kinsmen, those of the same surname and territorial origins. They also resort to impersonal sources particularly for large sums of money. In the survey of a resettlement estate conducted in 1957, it was found that 22 per cent of 445 households sharing their income and expenses were in debt to 'relatives', friends, or members of their 'clan' for sums ranging from less than $10 to over $1,000. The largest single group of these debtors (30 per cent) had loans of $201 to $500. The rate of interest charged on loans varied from 1 per cent to over 30 per cent, 16 to 20 per cent being most common. Most loans were for an indefinite period. Forty-two per cent of households had a total expenditure exceeding net income, and 37 per cent of these were in debt to friends, relatives or 'clan' members; 12 per cent were in debt to money-lenders—some to both—and the rest covered the difference from savings and through requests for gifts.

Gifts are sometimes given by parents to sons starting up in business, and money might pass between families on the occasion of marriage of a son or daughter. As marriages in Hong Kong are becoming increasingly individualized—in China they were arranged and sons brought wives in to the parental household—the significance of bride-price is decreasing. Rich families will often give a daughter a sum of money, investment shares, or even a block of flats when she marries and which remain her own property. Bride-price is still important in the New Territories and among boat-dwelling people. A few years ago a group of boat-dwellers tried to fix bride-price for all members of the group.

It is difficult to obtain information on sources of finance to industry. A significant proportion appears to come from such private sources as personal savings of entrepreneurs, friends and relatives. Expansion of established industry is often effected by ploughing back profits but again no precise information is available. The stock market has played a minor role in financing industry. Foreign capital and overseas Chinese capital has been invested in property although it is again difficult to find out how much capital enters with the direct intention of investment in industry. Foreign long-term credits are increasingly available for the purchase of machinery. Banks normally give short-term commercial loans, but medium and even long-term industrial loans are now being given as the importance and profitableness of industry is increasingly recognized. A substantial proportion of bank loans have been outstanding for five years and some have continued for ten or more years. A new type of bank is developing which is orientated to financing local activities rather than foreign commerce, although the main interest so far has been in real estate.

Funds of banks are available from the expanding deposits. The level and stability of deposits are said to justify longer-termed loans than in the past. Outstanding bank loans identified as being for industrial investment totalled $170 million. Sixty-two banks out of 83, including all banks of importance, supplied information to the Industrial Bank Committee although they could not always identify the use to which loans were put.

Total deposits, loans and advances were approximately as shown

Table II: Deposits, loans and advances (in millions of Hong Kong dollars)

	As at 31 December 1957	As at 31 December 1958
Deposits	1,485	1,680
Loans and advances	940	980
Industrial loans and advances	170	205

in Table II. By December 1959 deposits had increased to $2,075 and loans and advances to $1,390. Indications are that significant development in lending policy to industry took place during 1959.[1]

(d) Savings

Most Chinese try to save some of their earnings, sometimes even at the expense of necessary consumption. Some of their savings will be put to use in providing loans to others. Many comparatively poor Chinese are both borrowers and lenders at the same time and their financial interests can be highly involved. Chinese save for many of the reasons that they borrow. I have heard Cantonese express the opinion that Shanghainese tend to spend more on their food requirements than do members of the former group. I have not been able to check the truth or otherwise of this opinion. We have mentioned that Chinese in Hong Kong may save for their old age.

The resettlement survey noted that although the net income of the 455 households sharing income was generally low, 49 per cent managed to save something each month. Of those 69 per cent saved up to $50 a month while 32 per cent saved over this amount.[2] Saving is still a strongly approved activity at all income

[1] In 1967 Deposits were 8,405, Loans and Advances 5,380 (*Editor*).
[2] The largest single group of households (121) were within the income range of $101 to $150 per month. Ninety had less than $100.

levels. Spending for ceremonials, however, is also still approved. An informant who expressed contempt for an acquaintance with an income of $300 a month who spent $50 a month on his own food—excluding rice—also expressed contempt for another who with an income of over $1,000 never gave parties to his friends.

(e) Wealth and status

Most forms of wealth are admired, although there is possibly a tendency to admire most those who have wealth in landed property and those who earn large incomes from professional services. The individual who is rich but has no other claim to high social status will, as I have indicated elsewhere, attempt to use his wealth in a way most likely to catch the public eye and secure him a position of importance. A step in this direction which is most commonly taken is to make one or more large donation to charity through associations which give maximum publicity in return. The main charitable concerns of Chinese are organizations which promote various institutions for public benefit. It has been remarked by informants that it is difficult to keep such organizations from putting into bricks and mortar money which should be put into increasing the efficiency of their organization. In return for money donated for building, such organizations guarantee to place the photographs of donors and inscriptions bearing their names and details of the sum donated in a prominent part of the building. A recent method is to imprint photographs on tiles used in building interiors. One association listed their method for rewarding donors in detail. Under a heading 'Ways of commemorating donors who helped complete phase I construction of an important building', an article appeared in their yearly journal indicating the sections of the building in which donors could have their photographs and names, grading them by the size of the donation. In connection with another charitable project in Hong Kong, a donor of $3,000 was entitled to have a room dedicated to his memory. An architect who had the job of designing a building for charitable purpose described his despair at the number of times alterations had to be made to his plans as the number of individuals desiring a room dedicated to them increased.

When an individual has received sufficient prominence from his gifts he may be invited to be a member of the staff of honorary officials, although he might have to spend additional time and money persuading the board that he is worthy of such honour. A method for selecting officials alleged to exist in respect of one prominent organization might be mentioned. A common method of organizing friendly entertainment in Hong Kong is by the 'birthday' association. It is an informal grouping usually organized spontaneously by individuals fond of wining and dining. For example, one might be formed on the spur of the moment by people who happen to be seated at the same table at a banquet. They will then arrange for a party to be held on the occasion of each member's birthday, the person whose birthday it is abstaining from payment for the occasion. One such association, then, is said to exist among members of a permanent board of directors of a charitable organization in Hong Kong. It is said that it is at their birthday dinners that future appointments to the yearly board of the association in question are made.

Official position will not be taken lightly, for financial obligations do not end at that point. The official will be expected to continue his gifts, to persuade his rich friends to make donations, and when he retires from the board to continue his generosity. As one association has it: 'Each succeeding board not only gives of its best in service to the community welfare but also devises ways and means to overcome financial difficulties met in order to provide ... facilities to the public at large.' To become an official of one large organization, it is said, requires a readiness to donate at least $50,000 a year.

Many associations, certainly all the important ones, have two types of boards of officials: those holding office for one year, and those holding office permanently. It is not uncommon for those elected to the yearly board, however, to be re-elected, particularly if their wealth appears to be stable and they have shown their social contacts to be of value to the association. Many will be content to have stood for office once. They continue to get prestige from having held positions of importance in the past. Chinese inscribe on their visiting cards not only the present positions they hold in such organizations but also those of importance held in the past.

The demand for offices and the desire of associations to get as many wealthy people into their circle as possible has led to the development of many large and cumbersome organizations. One territorial group has a president, 3 vice-presidents, 1 managing director, 2 assistant managing directors, 36 honorary directors,

4 legal advisers, 21 honorary advisers, 45 managers of various charitable sections and other miscellaneous officials. This multiplicity of offices can make for inefficiency in administration. It is partly mitigated, however, by employment of salaried staff for routine work, leaving expansion of finances and decisions regarding their most appropriate use to the honorary officials.

The next step for those seeking further social advancement and power is often to seek membership on a permanent board of directors of a prominent group. Such boards are the policy-forming bodies. Permanent directors because of their length of office ideally should be of unsullied reputation, their wealth should be guaranteed stable, and they should be able to meet with prominent citizens and members of the government in social life with perfect confidence and conduct themselves with refinement. Education and knowledge of the ways of westerners are important. Members of well-known Hong Kong families have been prominent on such boards. Government honours go largely to this type of director, making attainment of such positions even more desirable. The Executive Council which, together with various government departments, helps the Governor to rule the Colony consists of 5 *ex-officio* and 7 nominated members. There is one nominated official member. During the period 1946–60, 16 different members of the Hong Kong community were nominated to office for periods of varying length—that is, some were reappointed several times—and 5 were Chinese. All five are on the permanent board of directors of the most prominent charity organization in Hong Kong. There is a Legislative Council which advises on, and consents to the passing of the Colony's laws. The same 5 *ex-officio* members of the Executive Council serve on this council and in addition there are 4 other official members and 8 unofficial members nominated by the Governor. During the 1946–1960 period, out of 21 nominated members holding office, 9 were Chinese. Six of them are again members of this same charitable group's permanent board of directors. The 15 members of this board are all non-official Justices of the Peace. This is a position which is greatly prized by the Chinese community and brings considerable prestige. It is not a position of great power; the main duties are visiting various welfare institutions and commenting on their efficiency. However, Justices of the Peace thereby have considerable contact with important government officials since visits are made in pairs: one official and one non-official J.P. going

together. There is also an annual Justices of the Peace dinner at
Government House. Examination of the lists of past annual directors of two important associations shows the close relationship
between these posts and J.P. appointments. During the 10 periods
of office covering the years 1951 to 1960, 7 chairmen of one
received badges of honour and 4 were made J.P.s. In the other,
4 obtained badges of honour and 3 were made J.P.s. In the past
the majority of directors and chairmen of prominent associations
were in occupations associated with the traditional Hong Kong
economy: real estate, construction and import and export. Lately,
however, they have included many factory owners and for the first
time one important association has included a Shanghainese member. There is now one Shanghainese J.P. in Hong Kong—J.P.s
have to be British subjects.

Some individuals are members of the boards of various associations recruiting according to different principles. Further, prestige
is obtained by participation in a number of social activities organized by associations throughout the year, particularly those connected with fund-raising campaigns. Prominent members of society
and the government are invited to such functions and association
reports and journals which are distributed to important members
of the public give accounts of these activities and publish photographs of their officials meeting socially prominent citizens and
giving speeches. Members who become J.P.s are fêted by their
associations at lavish banquets which are again given publicity,
and biographical details of officials including a list of their public
achievements and contributions to charity, are published in annual
journals.

Associations then are a major mechanism for turning wealth
into status in Hong Kong. There are other organizations which
give status but do not require their officials to be so wealthy: for
example, technical and cultural associations, and various New
Territory rural committees. Here personal integrity, intelligence
and agreeable personality might count for much more than money
and in the Territories, family and lineage connections might be
important.

Education confers status but we have seen that it is often syn-
onymous with wealth since it is acquired largely for entrance into
the high income occupations. Some educationalists, however,
have prestige because of their former official positions in China,
and the standing of their families on the mainland may command

respect among the more recent immigrants, particularly the intellectual refugees. We have seen that 'Hong Kong families' usually enjoy high status, but this is partly connected with the positions they usually hold in various Chinese organizations. Teachers in Chinese colleges and government schools enjoy considerable status, although those in the numerous small private schools enjoy less on the whole, mainly because their educational qualifications are usually more limited and their salaries are considerably lower. Professional men—doctors and architects, for example—in government service do not perhaps enjoy the same status as those in private practice because their command over income is generally lower. However, there are numbers of positions in government service which are prized partly because they are regarded as 'iron ships' (secure positions) and partly because members of the bureaucracy enjoy prestige in Hong Kong as they did in China.

It is not easy to estimate the extent of some of the largest fortunes in Hong Kong with any exactness. Taxes paid on wealth are not a sure indication because of the possibility of tax evasion. When trying to estimate the fortune of a deceased wealthy man in Hong Kong recently I received widely differing figures from informants. One Chinese estimated 'several tens of millions' while a European businessman was of the opinion that it must be a good deal less than that. He observed, however, that the figure at probate which was in the region of $800,000 was probably less than the real figure, since some of his wealth was undoubtedly handed over in gifts to kinsmen and others during his lifetime. Chinese are fond of discussing the wealth of the socially prominent and the ways it has been amassed. It is very likely that in the telling of stories about prominent men, the extent of their fortunes often becomes exaggerated.

The responsibilities of the wealthy increase with their riches. Not only does the number of kinsmen and friends who reckon they have a claim to financial help grow in size but the amount of help expected also increases. An association to which a man belongs will expect to be given financial assistance from him if he becomes wealthy.

There is little resentment of wealthy people among the poorer sections of the community unless they fail to use their money in approved ways. Men will resent a rich kinsman who does not help them; rich landlords will be resented if they charge rents considered unreasonably high in view of their fortunes. Members of the public will resent those who do not give to charity. In fact Chinese society has few misers. It also probably has few rich men who give money without any desire for prestige in return. Few give their money anonymously, although there are some important exceptions, of course.

While there is more desire on the part of the majority of people to attain similar wealth and status to the rich than to see them lose their position, there are certain people who disapprove of the financial basis of power in the community. They believe that if greater use were made of election processes, this would help bring forward individuals, whose qualifications for leadership were superior, to help the government in running the Colony. Others argue that in the immigrant society of Hong Kong, which includes numbers of people who do not think of the Colony as their permanent home, it is the wealthy who stand out as having the greatest stake in the community. While maximization of gain continues to be the guide to action of the majority, a poor man in a position of power, it is said, is more likely to be tempted to use such position to improve his fortunes at the expense of the community's interest. We cannot, however, discuss further the validity of such arguments here.

Perhaps if the role of taxation in providing social services was better understood there would be more desire to see the rich pay out more of their income in this form. Most uneducated people do not understand the function of taxation and imagine taxes are used as they were in traditional China—to increase the fortunes of government servants. There is some resentment of the fact, which is regrettably true, that westerners can usually get certain services with a speed which without bribery is not possible for the majority of Chinese.

8   Distribution of wealth

(a) *Social class*

We have seen that status and power rest mainly on wealth from almost any source, and wealth and position can change from generation to generation. Conditions therefore have not been favourable to the emergence of social classes: stable groups consisting of individuals who are marked off from others by a combination of such factors as wealth, occupation, ways of dress, education, speech, antecedents and nature of their possessions.

We suggested, however, that a possible minor exception to this rule is found in the existence of the 'Hong Kong family' group who define themselves by characteristics in addition to wealth. Besides the importance of ancestry and length of residence to their self-consciousness there is also education. There is a tendency to send sons to British universities. Occupations tend to be in the professions and in traditional pre-war economic pursuits. Due to the overall importance of wealth in the community, however, their position of superiority is by no means unchallengeable. Such families tend to lose positions as they lose wealth even though they continue to gain respect from the western community. The future may see their position of leadership usurped more and more by the industrial *nouveau riche* as the latter obtain more positions in the Chinese associational network.

A general characteristic of the 'families' regarding material possession is that they tend to place less emphasis on the importance of conspicuous consumption and prestige goods than do the majority of Chinese. This is no doubt due to their more secure status position. We saw that their money tends to be in more secure forms of investment, whereas the desire of the majority of Chinese for maximum gain tends to lead to a strong attraction for speculative enterprise. The desire for different goods, however, is affected by many factors. There may be a difference between traditional and westernized individuals and we saw that Chinese term as 'yellow-faced devils' those individuals who are closest to westerners in their patterns of preference. Differences exist again between individuals in the urban and rural areas.

(b) Urban and rural differences

The bulk of the rich live in the urban areas and rural society offers far less opportunities for amassing wealth than does that of the industrial urban area. There are rich country-folk who make money out of rents from their land, but many of them live in the town area. The better-off villager is more likely to spend money on a house for his family than is the town-dweller because his residence and position in his family is more secure. Travelling through the Territories one can see the modern structures of the richer villagers standing up in their reinforced concrete splendour above the level of the traditional one-storey houses of the others. The villager spends more on ceremonial consumption than his opposite number in the town because his stronger and more traditional family organization makes such expenditure more important. When investing in production goods he will turn first to agricultural land for the use of his family as would the rich peasant in traditional China. He might also, however, invest in a shop in the local market town and put a kinsman in charge of business activities.

Country families with members working overseas tend to be richer than their neighbours and much of the money earned by the emigrant will be sent home for use of his family: for housing, education and land purchase.

Due to changes in government, the gentry class has declined in the country as it has in the towns. Some of the traditional prestige symbols found in poor New Territory villages—certain roof designs permitted only to those the emperor wished to honour, and wooden banners listing government honours obtained by ancestors—suggests that such villages once contained members of gentry status. This is borne out by examination of lineage records. Today, even in rural society, wealth may be of considerable importance to status. However, there are indications that the relationship between the two is not as clear-cut as in the urban area. I recently heard of a case in which a letter from a father working in England reversed the decision made by a village wife to send their daughter out to work. He argued that 'everybody' knew he provided enough for the family's needs. They would 'lose face' because the neighbours would scorn them for putting extra money before the reputation of their daughter. Working in the city would ruin her marriage chances in her home area; the family would no longer be able to vouch for her virginity, and she would also forget the agricultural skills demanded of wives in village life (particularly in emigrant villages as we saw). In the urban area, neighbourhood opinion may play little role in determining conduct, and those living close by may be completely unknown.

(c) Traditional individuals and wealth

The extent to which a traditional outlook and way of life will affect an individual's economic position will depend on where the traditional emphasis lies. A Chinese may be very traditional in etiquette, dress and other material habits but have a non-traditional attitude towards the importance of gain. He may conduct his business with a degree of impersonality not possible in traditional society. On the other hand a man holding strongly to traditional social values might be less efficient in wealth accumulation. He might, for example, spend more on ceremonial, save in non-productive forms—in jewellery and gold bars—and leave cash idle. He might run his business in accordance with principles not making for maximum profit and invest only with enterprises where he has personal knowledge of the organizers. However, he might also be less inclined to speculative types of investment and therefore run less risk of losing his money in risky projects.

There is no correlation between degree of traditionalism and level of income. Certain occupations tend to attract traditional individuals, for example, those connected with making and selling of gold and jade jewellery, Chinese medical practice, the selling of herbal medicines, and running of tea-houses. Some of these demand, of course, traditional type knowledge and attitudes but can also be highly profitable. Traditional individuals are also found, however, in various kinds of 'modern' occupations.

(d) The western community and wealth

We observed that westerners as a group are richer than the Chinese although some of the latter are among the richer members of the community of Hong Kong. The level of incomes for westerners tends to be higher than that of the Chinese and their standard of living is also higher. The levels of income at which Chinese and westerners consider people to be poor, comfortably off, or rich usually diverge widely even among Chinese and westerners of the same education and occupation. This difference in attitude is of course linked with differences in opinion as to what constitutes a minimum wage and living standard, and different expectations of what income is possible for people of the same qualifications in the two groups. Generally speaking, a Chinese can command a lower income for a particular job than can a westerner. This is particularly noticeable in managerial work. Chinese tend to be reluctant to pay well for managerial staff.

The way in which westerners hold their wealth is partly conditioned by attitudes towards their length of residence. Few westerners own their own housing. The majority of western-run business firms and other enterprises house their expatriate staff free or at a nominal rent. Those who are able to save will usually hold part of their money in their home country and in investments in enterprises abroad. When investing locally they tend to put their money in western-run public companies. Government servants are forbidden to invest on the local stock exchange.[1] An increasing number of westerners, however, are coming to Hong Kong to start industries, a big attraction being the cheapness of labour. A shortage of various kinds of industrial labour is beginning to be felt in Hong Kong and competition for workers is starting to force the price up.

9   Uses of wealth and income

(a) Roles in the family regulating use of wealth

Decisions regarding allocation of wealth between different uses usually rest with the father. Here his contribution to family income, which is usually the most significant, backs up his traditional position in this respect. Sometimes there is an adult son who is able to command a greater income than his father and who wishes to make his own plans for allocating his income. Such plans can conflict with those of his father, although such conflict is usually resolved in favour of the latter.

A man controlling a family business in which his sons work will have greater control over the use to which income is put. His sons —and daughters—may not receive a regular wage but be given pocket-money which varies in amount with business prosperity. This is most likely when the business is a small shop or restaurant. The influence of family heads over their children's income may be weakened when housing conditions and transport problems force the latter to live and work away from home. However, we saw above an example of an emigrant father continuing to exercise control over the economic decisions for his family. It may be that such control is stronger in the rural areas where there is greater family solidarity.

(b) Decisions concerning the use of wealth

The question of what factors can influence decisions on the use of wealth and income between consumption, saving or investment,

[1] In fact forbidden unless prior permission has been obtained from the Colonial Secretary. The position of government servants and local investment has been taken up in various General Orders. In 1965 more liberal

has been taken up in various parts of this paper. Factors of importance are immediate and anticipated family needs, the needs of relatives in the homeland, feelings about the future security of Hong Kong, degree of permanency of residence, ambitions for status and power and familiarity and trust in banking institutions and knowledge of the market. Generally speaking townsmen are more adventurous in new types of investment than are rural dwellers. For example, although vegetable production can bring in high profits the village dweller clings to rice production which is something he understands. Most vegetable farmers are immigrants from areas where vegetable production formed a traditional occupation and they are often experts in this field. The greatest experts are reckoned to be immigrants from the district of Kwantung.[1]

(c) Acquisition and use of wealth under industrialization

There is a tendency for Chinese investors in all fields to look for the maximum gain in the shortest period. A reluctance of certain people, who are not themselves entrepreneurs, to invest in industry is due partly to the fact that profits may be slow in coming. Many Chinese still prefer to invest in non-industrial property and trade because of the relatively quicker return of capital and profits.

When investing in industry, the overwhelming desire of investors is to look for quick profits by whatever means present themselves as attractive in the short run rather than to look for opportunities for starting long-term investment. The financing of industries which offer quick profits may be purely speculative and undertaken by financiers who might otherwise be in the property market and have no real intention of long-term support of the industry. During a boom there may be considerable speculation, although banks tend to discourage this by raising interest rates to those wishing to borrow for such purpose. In the late forties a boom in the film industry led to formation of a number of companies. The bad quality of films, small investment and hope for quick returns with good profits led most companies to go out of business by 1950. Today only four companies which have their

[1] See also 'Capital, Saving and Credit . . .', op. cit., at various pages.

arrangements were made: local investments have to be reported to the Government after they have been made but prior permission is no longer necessary.

own studios exist, with 30 others using the facilities and even actors of these four.

Entrepreneurs in Hong Kong industry still largely supply their own capital from personal savings and by investment elsewhere. Some supply their own labour, at least in the early days of production. The next step is usually to establish a partnership, and the final step, a private company. Many newly created industrial enterprises are family concerns. The bigger concerns, some owning subsidiary companies, are nearly all Shanghainese, many having brought down their capital and technicians from Shanghai. There are few public industrial companies and little industrial activity on the local stock exchange.

One of the weaknesses of Chinese industry is a common failure to recognize and face the problems of expansion. Most Chinese hate to employ managerial staff—this is true also in farming enterprises run by immigrants in the Territories—and often the man in charge next to the owner is only a foreman. Many neglect the training of workers. They also fail to make long-term calculations and assess the most efficient methods of allocating costs. It is difficult to get information, but it appears that generally speaking Shanghainese industrialists tend to be more advanced in such matters. They make some attempt to train workers within the industry and send technical and managerial staff on courses abroad. One Shanghainese factory spends about $780,000 yearly on welfare services which include free medical services and tuition in English. It was largely as a result of differences in the running and organization of Shanghainese and Cantonese factories that they were until recently classified separately by the Government Labour Department.

One factor inhibiting industrialists from training workers is fear of competition. The view is that the trained worker, particularly the worker who is taught the various manufacturing processes, will break away and set up a rival concern. One factory brings its technical experts in from abroad for this reason and many employ kinsmen as managers to prevent business secrets leaking out. As in the early days of western industrialization, the role of more efficient marketing methods and sales promotion techniques in affording an industry advantages over its competitors is not widely recognized in Hong Kong.

Particularism in recruitment is still found in certain enterprises. It is common in the retail trade and in concerns where subcontractors are involved, for example in the construction industry. One advantageous effect is said to be that it tends to mitigate industrial disputes since a foreman will be held responsible for the good conduct and efficiency of the people he produces. With a growing shortage of industrial labour the role of particularism in recruitment, however, appears to be diminishing in importance in Hong Kong.

Industrialists, generally, appear to fail to appreciate the gain in efficiency from better working conditions and higher wages, but Shanghainese large-scale concerns do seem to demand greater efficiency from their staff and recognize that to obtain such efficiency might mean a greater financial outlay in wages and machinery. A Shanghainese industrialist interviewed recently by an economic journal in Hong Kong is reported as saying: 'Machinery and techniques are never too new, and investment is never too much.' He has established a technical department in his factory to increase production and improve quality. Some of the older industries are now suffering from miserliness in wage policy and are losing workers to the newer textile concerns. For the past six years a handful of leading manufacturers in the flash-light industry have been trying to persuade their fellow industrialists to form a trade association to introduce consistency, improve production techniques and raise wages, but nothing has been achieved so far.

Industrialists are now protesting that they are short of finance, particularly the smaller concerns. Failure of many entrepreneurs to give sufficient details of their venture, of the people running it, and the market in which they expect to sell products no doubt inhibits many investors. Although banks now play a considerable role in financing industry they are reluctant to finance individuals who have not proved their productive efficiency, managerial skill and knowledge of raw material prices and trends. The commonly known sources of finance to medium and small factories are the Chinese banks and private financiers. Commercial banks supply a limited amount. It seems, however, that many industrialists have to turn to 'black-market' sources: 'hot' money which moves around in time with economic and political changes in surrounding areas and for which interest rates up to 30 per cent a month are charged.[1] It appears, however that there is beginning

[1] Report of the Industrial Bank Committee. It appears that it is these sources which industrialists were unwilling to reveal to the committee.

to be greater confidence among local financiers in the future of local industry and an increasing interest of American capital in local enterprises.

Many difficulties in the acquisition of wealth for industry then are connected with the deleterious results of a desire for quick and greatest possible profits. The feeling of the Industrial Bank Committee appeared to be that industry does not need a new source of capital in the form of a special bank but it does need to increase its efficiency and think out its organization and intentions carefully with a long-term view in order that more of the available wealth will be canalized in its direction.

Some of the conditions which fostered Hong Kong's industrial expansion bear strong comparison with those fostering England's industrial revolution. The local entrepreneur accumulated capital from trade and commerce in the pre-war trading years; and industrialization is to a large extent based on trade as it was in England of the eighteenth century. One might even stretch a parallel and say that the labour which helped to build Hong Kong's industry came also as a result of land-reform in the countryside—of mainland China. There are also the same sort of inequalities of income and *laissez-faire* capitalism as fostered British industrialization.

In Hong Kong neither trade unions nor government enforce the socially acceptable minimum of wages. Until recently the influx of people from China has tended to extend the perfectly elastic stretch of the labour supply curve and lower the socially acceptable minimum to the level prevailing on the mainland. Entrepreneurs are primarily interested in profitable export markets with the result that they want to preserve a low level of wages to ensure their competitive position abroad. They tend to neglect the home market and the possibility of higher internal demand following from higher level of wages.[1] Several observers have remarked on the resemblance in social conditions resulting from the two industrial expansions: of England and Hong Kong. We must remember of course that it has taken the west a long time to reach its present attitude towards both the justice and economic value of better working and living conditions. There

[1] This problem is discussed by Dr Szczepanik in a paper entitled 'A Rational Wages Policy for Hong Kong' read at the course in Industrial Relations for Top Management held at the University of Hong Kong, 7 to 11 March 1960.

are signs that at least the second of these values is becoming more widely realized and that some of Hong Kong's community leaders are also beginning to concern themselves with the first. Perhaps as the population becomes more stable and Hong Kong becomes a community in the real sense of the word this former value will become more widely acclaimed.[1]

Concluding Note, 1967

This analysis was first published in 1963 and it is now 1967. I have not made any radical attempts to bring the text up-to-date although I have appended a few additional notes mainly dealing with revisions of detail.

Very recently, however, and I write in October 1967, a desire has been expressed in Hong Kong by various responsible persons to see the Colony's economic boat rocked about a bit and set on a new course: to subject it to fresh winds and not worry so much as in the past about the delicacy of its structure. This changing attitude can I think be linked with certain events taking place in the last few years and a brief comment on them is in order here.

In April 1966 rioting by young people took place in Kowloon (see chapter 14, below). It was triggered off by a hunger strike conducted by a young man in protest against an extremely small fares increase on a cross harbour ferry (this ferry is used by considerable numbers of workers in getting to and from their place of work each day). The young man was subsequently arrested. The attitude of some of the rioters towards the hunger striker is of some interest. At the Commission of Inquiry into the disturbances witnesses stated that they 'followed' the youth because they felt he was not out for personal gain—to better his own lot. His motives were unselfish. There seemed, that is, to be some indication that young people today are capable of being inspired by a leader who is not wealthy but expresses community virtues.

[1] Since completing the manuscript I have had opportunity to read Robert M. Marsh, *The Mandarins: The Circulation of Elites in China, 1600–1900*, Glencoe, Ill., 1961, and Albert Feuerwerker, *China's Early Industrialization: Shen Hsuan-Huai (1844–1916) and Mandarin Enterprise*, Cambridge, Mass., 1958. Prior knowledge of the contents of these works might have led me to either amplify or modify certain passages, although it would not have affected my general analysis of the China background.

This hunger striker interestingly enough bridges the gap between East and West in a certain sense. He claimed to be an incarnate messiah (a common claim of traditional reformist leaders in pre-modern China) but he was western educated and had scholarly interests of a western kind (one being a desire to translate T. S. Eliot's *Four Quartets* into Chinese while in prison).

Investigations into the possible causes of the rioting considered the economic conditions prior to the outbreak. It was noted in the *Report of Commission of Inquiry* (Hong Kong, 1967) that earnings from exports and tourism continued to expand and bank deposits in general continued to increase; that the increase in the average cost of living had been approximately 2 per cent per annum over the past eight years which had been 'more than compensated' by an average increase of 8 per cent per annum in wage rates in the manufacturing industries where records are kept. No statistics were available to show wage rates or earnings in other jobs, and those relating to manufacturing reflect only approximately 55 per cent of all industries. But, the Commission noted, it appeared many wage earners had been able to improve their position and standard of living (but then uprisings occur as a rule when conditions are improving rather than not).

The Inquiry also considered the possible effects of a bank crisis in 1965 in which there were runs on certain banks. The strength of the banking system was said to be little affected by the runs, and total deposits at the end of February were only 2 per cent below January 1st; but the runs did affect a large number of people, both depositors who incurred direct loss through banks being able to meet only a percentage of their deposits—there were 114,000 accounts in one of the failing banks—and those who queued up outside other banks to withdraw money owing to loss of confidence. An anxiety about certain aspects of the banking system and the publicity given to rumours was demonstrated again in April and November of that year when runs on other banks were only averted by swift government action and strong support from major banks.

The crisis revealed that certain banks had tended to maintain insufficient liquidity—too many of their investments were long-term. Many Hong Kong banks are family concerns and some have grown out of money-changing establishments with perhaps less sophisticated knowledge of banking than others. Many learnt a bitter lesson. Stricter lending practices than before this crisis have resulted, however. This has led to a tightening of credit in many spheres.

I think it true to say that the 1966 riots left many people— including some of the social scientists and social workers giving evidence at the Inquiry—feeling that there was some economic and social discontent in the Colony. Also that there seemed to be now a generation of young people emerging who identify themselves more with Hong Kong and its economic and social future than did their parents. This generation is more interested in Hong Kong and more apt to protest at situations which their parents might tacitly accept. The material and other aspirations of this generation have probably been rising with the betterment of conditions but with visible results not keeping pace. Material aspirations themselves may have been affected by the rapid expansion of tourism referred to and increased opportunities for seeing comparatively wealthy people. In 1966 there were 505,733 tourists visiting Hong Kong with 458,238 of these from Europe or the U.S.A. (figures from the Hong Kong Tourist Association).

This year Hong Kong has seen disturbances of a different nature and cause—relating to political events here and on the mainland. I cannot here go into the complex political factors involved although it is clear that the majority of demonstrations were of a different kind than in the 1966 riots. Nevertheless the original dispute triggering the situation was economic—between factory management and workers. The cost of living has also seen a rise as a result of the disturbances generally. Support of the people for the government and police in this new situation has been remarkable but there is a growing feeling that something must be done to justify this support: in labour reform, local govern- ment and better housing to give some examples. A Housing Board was in fact appointed by the Governor in 1965 with the assessing of housing needs for people of different income levels as one of its important tasks. Clearly this is a very complex task and much more quantitative as well as qualitative information is needed. The need in fact for more social surveys and other types of investigations is increasingly realized by Government and other institutions relating to the people of Hong Kong. At present an urban families study is underway; a study of the needs of Hong Kong industry for higher level manpower has just been completed (not yet available for comment); new re- search units have been formed at the two universities in the

Colony, and smaller units exist in individual colleges which might be expected to add to our knowledge of economic and other problems.

In 1966 the economist's view was that there was nothing in the situation which would have led one to expect a riot but the Commission itself felt that worries about the general economic situation and uncertainty as to the future, together with 'psychological fears' of inflation arising were a source of public concern and created an atmosphere in which demonstrations could find support. Hong Kong today may well be on the brink of social and economic change. How much change there will be remains to be seen. But many people feel that we will never have quite the same society again.

PART THREE

SPECIFIC SOCIO-ECONOMIC PROBLEMS OF HONG KONG

E. F. Szczepanik, Ph.D. (London)
Formerly senior lecturer in economics at the University of Hong Kong, is now with the Economic Analysis Division, FAO, Rome

Judith Agassi, Ph.D. (London)
On the research staff of the Massachusetts Institute of Technology

L. F. Goodstadt, M.A.(Econ.) (Manchester), Dip. Agric. Econ. (Oxon.)
Sometime lecturer in economics in the University of Hong Kong, now assistant editor of the 'Far Eastern Economic Review'

Michael G. Whisson, Ph.D. (Cantab.)
Formerly director of the Drug Addiction Research Unit of the Discharged Prisoners Aid Society of Hong Kong, presently at the School of African Studies, Cape Town University

Portia Ho, M.A.(HK)
Formerly tutor in philosophy in the University of Hong Kong

E. Kvan, Cand. Theol. (Copenhagen)
Senior lecturer in psychology in the University of Hong Kong

J. S. Cansdale *is a pseudonym*

I. C. Jarvie, Ph.D. (London)
Associate professor of philosophy in York University, Toronto

VII

PROBLEMS OF MACRO-ECONOMIC
PROGRAMMING IN HONG KONG[1]

E. F. Szczepanik

In rapidly industrializing Hong Kong there is a wide range of economic and social problems on the solution of which the welfare of all of us and our children depends. In this paper I intend to examine some of these problems and the methods used to solve them.

In the first part, I shall concentrate on the balance between economic and social development. The second part will deal with the main problems of industry, the growth of which determines the pace of both economic and social progress. In the concluding part, I shall raise some basic institutional problems in our community life.

I A balanced economic and social development

(a) *Economic progress*

Measuring the economic progress of Hong Kong is not an easy task. Using the traditional yardstick, we can point out, as the Chairman of the Hong Kong General Chamber of Commerce did recently, that the aggregate value of our external trade (exports plus imports) has grown from HK$9·3 billion in 1951 to HK$9·8 billion in 1960.[2] Thus it took us ten years to achieve this 5 per cent increase for, meanwhile, there was a heavy depression with its bottom in 1954 and a mild recession in 1957–8.

Net business profits assessed for tax purposes increased from about HK$640 million in 1951–2 to approximately HK$680

---

[1] *Editorial note.* This contribution is the Presidential address read before the Hong Kong Economic Association on 28 April 1961. Some of the statistical data have been up-dated by the editor of this volume in the footnotes to provide a more recent perspective which broadly shows a much sharper upward economic trend in the early sixties than in the stormy fifties, as the author rightly envisaged in his paper.

[2] HK$17·6 billion in 1966. (*Editor*)

million in 1958–9—an increase of only 6·5 per cent—again with a very low volume of profits in 1952–6. The growth in the number of factories and industrial workers and the high level of building activity are often regarded as most obvious signs of increasing prosperity. The number of workers in registered and recorded factories increased from some 95,000 in almost 2,000 establishments in 1951 to 232,000 in over 5,200 establishments in 1960.[1] Real capital formation increased from HK$160 million in 1951–2 to about HK$775 million in 1959–60. However, a comparison of these last figures with business profits clearly shows that this high capital formation could not have been financed entirely from internal sources: a very large proportion of capital came from abroad, which means that this money was not available for other purposes.

None of these figures says anything about the standard of living. A very small improvement in the total value of trade, a relatively slow rise in the level of business profits and a high increase in capital formation appear to indicate that with the population growing from some 2 million in 1951 to 3 million in 1960 there could have been practically no increase in *per capita* consumption.

An accurate proof of this contention could be given only with the aid of social accounts which the government has never as yet attempted to produce. According to my private estimate, the *per capita* consumption at 1952–3 constant prices *fell* from HK$1,600 in 1950–1 to about HK$1,400 in 1958–9. This drop by some 14 per cent could have been partly compensated by a probably very substantial increase in the national income during the last two years. However, even on the most optimistic assumption we could only suggest that the 'pay-off' period, following the profound economic and social change of the past decade, is only just beginning.

(a) Social progress

An account of social progress is much more difficult than an economic balance-sheet. The absorption of a huge mass of refugees is undoubtedly a most remarkable achievement. Almost full employment in an economy receiving immigrants, with the natural rate of population growth exceeding 3 per cent *p.a.*, can

---

[1] 635,300 workers in over 10,413 establishments in 1966. (*Editor*)

hardly be found in any other country. Credit is due, first of all, to the population as a whole for patiently bearing the hardships without manifestation of 'social tensions'; secondly, to the entrepreneurs for providing employment opportunities; thirdly, to the Government for supplying the necessary minimum of social services; fourthly, to numerous social organizations for alleviating the hardships and thus mitigating the tensions. From these four factors, I should like to choose only one, viz. Government social expenditure, for a cursory examination as it is here that some tools of economic analysis can be applied.

During the past six or seven years roughly one-fifth of the government's expenditure has been for social services. With the total government expenditure now approaching HK$1,250 million,[1] the actual sum of social expenditures can be estimated at HK$200 million. Assuming that the national income of Hong Kong is now in the region of HK$5,000 million, some 4 per cent of it seems to be spent on social services by the government alone. This includes education, health and all kinds of urban services, such as public housing and resettlement, sanitation, recreation, etc. Making allowance for social services provided by voluntary public organizations, the total may reach HK$250 million, about 5 per cent of the national income and roughly HK$70 per head a year. The proportion is not small, the absolute amount—not high.

With this expenditure pattern, Hong Kong has increased its school population from some 170,000 in 1951 to about 570,000 in 1960.[2] This is a very impressive record but it should be remembered that probably at least 150,000 children between the age of 5 and 15 are not yet in schools. The number of hospital beds was only 4,337 in 1951; it now exceeds 8,000[3] but this is only 1·77 beds to each thousand of the population. The number of persons resettled rose from some 150,000 in 1955 to 360,000 in 1960,[4] but the October 1960 government survey showed that around 600,000 persons still needed resettlement.

Even these few figures show the enormous volume of social services which still have to be provided to eliminate squalor, illiteracy and inadequate medical attention. It should be clear that with the present rate of spending on social services, there is a very slow improvement, if any at all. What could be done therefore?

[1] Approaching HK$1,900 million in 1967. (*Editor*)
[2] 983,000 in 1966. (*Editor*)   [3] 13,300 in 1966. (*Editor*)
[4] 903,000 in 1966. (*Editor*)

(c) *Balancing of social and economic progress*

Looking at the structure of government expenditure, we notice that apart from some 20 per cent spent on social services, almost 30 per cent is spent on civil administration, nearly 45 per cent on economic services and about 5 per cent on defence. Could this structure be changed?

Leaving defence expenditures unchanged, a small shift can be visualized by preventing civil administration expenses (including maintenance of law and order) from growing and by replacing the expatriate staff by local staff. A major shift, however, would result only from a reduction of expenses on economic services, i.e. on agriculture, fisheries, industry, commerce, transport, communications, etc. Any decision of this kind would be very dangerous from the economic point of view. But it is possible to maintain the present high rate of economic expenditures and change only the methods of financing. Greater reliance on internal and external loans might release a substantial part of current government revenue for social services. Loans for economic purposes would probably appeal much more strongly to would-be-lenders, both at home and abroad, than loans for social purposes which, therefore, have to be financed chiefly from current revenue.

In connection with this, it might perhaps be useful to disperse the popular fear of the burden of public debt. An internal public debt is no burden whatever, if its redistributive effects are neglected. The interest on this debt is repaid by the community to the same community. There is no burden on future generations for it is always posterity paying to posterity and usually it is the same John or Peter who pays taxes and who also gets them back in the form of interest on government bonds held by him. As to the repayment of capital, the need does not arise at all for the government can always issue new loans to repay the old loans.

An external debt is, of course, a real burden. But it should be remembered that if an external loan is used for an increase of the country's productive capital, it results in such a rise of national income that there is usually more than enough to repay interest. (This argument does not apply, of course, to city halls, public monuments, churches, graveyards, etc.) Moreover, foreign lenders often do not require repayment and are satisfied with the income from interest. There is always a possibility of converting an external loan into an internal loan. Finally, there are such things as debt moratoria and even a flat refusal to pay. Although I am far from recommending this last course of action, it may be worth mentioning that, unlike a private person, no government can be put into prison even if it does not pay its debts.

Apart from public debt, an opportunity for improving the balance between social and economic expenditures may be formed by a rise in taxation and other forms of government revenue. There is not much scope for the increase in the standard rates of taxation in Hong Kong but a steeper progression is feasible. Taxation of income originating outside the Colony and not taxed elsewhere deserves consideration. Taxation of distributed business profits requires attention. Some indirect taxes on such items as alcohol, tobacco and even motor-cars can be further increased. New taxes on such items as fire-crackers, mahjong sets, playing cards, transistor radios, etc. could be introduced. The recently proposed public lottery deserves strong support and I do not see any moral objections to it in spite of some holy smoke which has already been raised around the project. A lottery merely redistributes the national income and, being a perfect game of chance, it cannot cause any unfavourable redistribution from the social point of view. (The community remains on the same 'social indifference curve'.) Simultaneously, a lottery may provide a fairly easy form of equitable general taxation without involving any waste of human time and energy as with horse races or gambling in Macau.

An important field of social services, so far entirely neglected in Hong Kong, could be covered by the introduction of a national insurance scheme to provide relief in case of sickness, death and even unemployment. Such a scheme, with a very modest 1 per cent contribution from employees, 2 per cent from employers and 2 per cent of the standard wage from the government, has been recently initiated in Indonesia, a country much poorer than Hong Kong.

A device which would increase the volume of social services without involving any cost to the community is voluntary work. Although there are many devoted voluntary social workers in Hong Kong, I believe that we are only scratching the surface or rather 'licking the cream' of our society. I think that there is a large unutilized potential of voluntary service among the women in Hong Kong. Educational and health services in particular could be provided by many women who have time enough for mahjong, bridge, fashion shows, cocktail parties or just sheer boredom. The problem is simply that of organization or 'mobilization', to use a more aggressive term, and perhaps greater specialization not on a religious but on a service basis. In view of the limitations imposed on public funds by a relatively low level of national income, the scope for voluntary charitable work in Hong Kong is enormous.

(d) The interaction between economic and social development

The desirability of improving the volume and quality of social services in any community is usually motivated by their beneficial effect on the productivity of the population, apart from social welfare being good in itself. However, any increase in social services ultimately competes with the provision of material goods and economic services. The long-run solution, therefore, must be sought in a rise in national income to such an extent as to allow for a comfortable margin of social expenditures.

Our population is growing rapidly. Admitting that we shall probably never stop the flow of refugees from Mainland China, we should reckon with a 4–5 per cent annual growth of the population, and try to achieve the corresponding increase in national income. In order to ensure some material and cultural improvement, a further increase of 2–3 per cent should be aimed at. Hong Kong's national income, therefore, should grow at the rate of about 7 per cent a year. Starting with a hypothetical level of HK$5,000 million in 1960–1, we should aim at an increase of HK$350 million this year, HK$375 million next year and so on. To obtain such a steady rise, we must have a steady increase in real capital and the volume of annual investment should depend on its productivity. The more productive is the capital, the less of it is required. Investment in social and economic 'infrastructure' (schools, hospitals, resettlement blocks, roads, piers, reclamations, water reservoirs, etc.) has a very low productivity or, in different words, a very high capital–output ratio. This ratio is much lower in light manufacturing industry but no industry can grow without simultaneous development of the infrastructure.

Studies in other countries, never yet undertaken in Hong Kong, estimate the average incremental capital–output ratio at between 3 and 4. On this basis, our desirable annual rate of investment may be placed between HK$1,000 million and 1,400 million. For 1959–60 the actual investment has been estimated at HK$775 million. It may be now reaching HK$800–900 million. All these figures are quoted here only for the sake of illustration. However, if they are not far from the truth, we seem to be constantly short of the rate of investment which would ensure an optimum rate of economic growth.

It is here where, I believe, serious attention should be paid by the government. An analysis, even in very approximate terms, of the past and projected growth path of the economy should be attempted. From this, conclusions should be drawn for the shaping of a sound economic policy, especially with respect to compensating government investment, if the private sector does not invest enough, and with respect to the guidance of aggregate investment to the fields promising the best prospects for the future.

Having said so much about the government, I hasten to add that in the free enterprise economy of Hong Kong the primary responsibility for ensuring an optimal rate of investment and income growth rests with the private sector, especially with its industry, to which I am now turning my attention.

II A balanced growth of industry

(e) *The structure of Hong Kong industry*

In all the developing economies which recognize the principle of free enterprise, industrialization implies a heavy reliance on small-scale units. This is chiefly due to scarcity of capital and managerial limitations, apart from various social factors. Hong Kong industry is also essentially small-scale industry. The average number of workers in registered and recorded factories in 1960 amounted to only 44. Moreover, as a large number of establishments employing less than 15 workers is not recorded at all and thus unknown, one can guess that the average size of Hong Kong factories is probably as low as in Taiwan (8 workers) and almost certainly lower than in Japan (26 workers).

The main weakness of smale-scale industry consists in a low capital–labour ratio which is manifested in a low degree of mechanization and thus low productivity of labour and low wages. Small size, although not necessarily a low rate, of profit is usually quoted as the reason for the emergence of a vicious circle because there is not enough to plough back in order to improve the capital–labour ratio. I believe, however, that in the Hong Kong situation this is a secondary, financial problem and I will examine it later. The primary reason for the unsatisfactory technological state of small enterprises is conservatism or resistance to change on the part of the owners.

Improvements in small industries are not easily obtained by mere advice and guidance from experts. Progress must come from the entrepreneurs themselves. They must be convinced of the economic advantages of modernization, take the initiative, and apply their ingenuity. One of the ways to achieve this objective is to concentrate public assistance initially on selected enterprises or groups of industries which hold the best promise of success with quick results. Once some of these small industry owners have been successful as a result of adopting improved equipment or techniques, their friends, relatives or neighbours in the same trades are likely to follow their example.

The enthusiasm and interest of the owners of small industries in technological advancement can also be aroused by means other than financial incentives. In Japan, for example, the government has been conducting various contests including one for the selection of model workshops or factories and for the grant of annual awards to those enterprises which have shown the greatest improvement since the initial survey was conducted. In Hong Kong the only popular 'industrial' contest is the annual Miss Exhibition competition. But at the annual Agricultural Show awards are given to farmers for real, productive effort.

Governments and other public bodies cannot try to modernize simultaneously all types of small industries in the country because the financial and personnel resources are usually inadequate. What is required, therefore, is a concentration on some selected industries. For this purpose, some assessment of development prospects of various industries is necessary. This can be obtained through interviews with small industrialists, combined with simple sampling surveys and market studies. All this will probably be undertaken by The Economist Intelligence Unit which has been recently entrusted with this task by the Federation of Hong Kong Industries. The way in which the results of this investigation will be utilized is not yet clear. I believe that it should call for the establishment of an Industrial Extension Service in Hong Kong.

(f) *Industrial extension service*

An Industrial Extension Service advising and assisting small industrialists in the application of modern technology and management methods is one of the most important devices for the improvement of small industries in many Asian countries. It is often said that not the lack of know-how but the lack of the necessary 'carriers' to transmit such know-how hampers technological innovation in small enterprises. In the field of agriculture, improved production in many countries of the world has been made possible through the work of agricultural extension services. Some of the principles and techniques developed in this field have been applied to small industries with equal effectiveness.

As in the case of agricultural extension services, there are three basic approaches in applying the extension principles to small industries:

(i) The individual approach, in which extension workers maintain personal contact with the owner-managers and render advice and assistance on the spot.
(ii) The group approach through demonstration and pilot plants or group training programmes.
(iii) The mass approach through meetings, exhibitions, publications, and other mass media.

In practice all three methods can be employed in combination. However, experience shows that the individual approach has proved most effective. It enables the extension workers to devise specific measures suited to the needs of a particular enterprise. On the technical side, for example, personal attention can be given to the removal of any defects in the existing production equipment and process, the addition of new machines or processes, the introduction of new items of manufacture, and better utilization of raw materials and fuels.

Short of the individual approach, the group approach through demonstration and pilot plant may be useful in cases where there is a concentration of the same type of small industries in one locality, as is often the case in Hong Kong.

Finally, the use of the mass approach can help in arousing public interest and, sometimes, in changing the attitude and outlook of small industrialists.

Japan and India are the two countries in Asia where a Small

Industry Extension Service on a comparatively large scale has been introduced. In Japan, a Small Industry Advisory Service was established in 1948. An interesting feature of this service is that it sends 'diagnosis' teams to individual enterprises. These teams are composed of business management, production and engineering experts who conduct a thorough investigation of all aspects of the enterprises visited, and recommend specific measures for their improvement. These services are provided free of charge either by the central or prefectural governments. There are now some 680 consultation centres throughout the country. In addition, the Smaller Enterprise Agency is subsidizing some 590 centres operated by the prefectural governments.

To put Hong Kong in a comparable (and thus competitive) position some 40 Small Industry Advisory Centres would be necessary. This might cost a lot of money and the argument will probably be advanced against any such scheme that it would serve only a section of the economy. To this it may be replied that a similar extension service has been in operation in Hong Kong's agriculture for many years and an even more advanced (and fairly expensive) form of research service has been functioning to benefit the local fishing industry since 1952. Moreover, agriculture and fishery provide probably only about 5 per cent of the Colony's national income, while the manufacturing industry contributes at least one-quarter. On this basis, the money spent on Small Industry Extension Services in Hong Kong should be roughly five times as much as on agriculture and fisheries. In fact, we are spending on all the services provided by the Commerce and Industry Department only some HK$8·3 million a year,[1] while the combined cost of the Departments of Agriculture, Forestry, Fisheries and Co-operative Development is about HK$7·1 million (figures based on 1960–1 estimates).[2]

(g) Financial problems of small industries

Technological improvement in small industries ultimately depends on availability of finance. Most Asian countries have made a considerable effort to aid small industries to finance their activities. Special institutions have been set up in many countries to make loans to small enterprises. Measures have also been taken

---

[1] HK$21·6 million in 1967. (*Editor*)
[2] HK$12·1 million in 1967. (*Editor*)

to encourage the regular banking system to give more attention to small manufacturers.

In Hong Kong a bankers' committee in 1960 rejected the proposal to set up a special industrial financing institution. The present system was found adequate as no evidence was made available to the committee that the industry lacks finance. At the same time, the bankers' report confirmed that the rate of interest of 10 to 14 per cent *p.a.* is not uncommon and that 'there are loans by the smaller banks or by private individuals at very high rates against little or no security or for enterprises involving a very high degree of risk'. The bankers admitted that these last rates 'vary between very wide limits' and that they 'have no precise information on the subject'.

I do not claim to have 'precise information' either but I believe that most of our industrialists can offer 'little or no security' and that it is precisely their enterprises which involve 'a very high degree of risk'. As the bankers' committee decided against an industrial bank, there is considerable scope for expanding commercial bank credit to small enterprises. To this end, a credit insurance or guarantee system needs to be evolved. In Japan, for example, the development of such a system which provides insurance or a government guarantee to financial institutions against possible non-payment of small industry loans has greatly helped the expansion of commercial credit facilities for these industries.

In the administration of a financial assistance programme for small industries, decentralization is imperative for the sake of efficiency and effectiveness. Banks servicing these industries should set up branch offices or agencies in all important small industry centres. Fortunately, this development is now taking place in Hong Kong.

The effectiveness of the credit system has in many cases been limited by the rigidity of conventional methods and approaches. There is thus a need to relax the security requirements in respect of small industry loans. Above all, there should be a re-orientation of the attitude of the staff dealing with such loan programmes.

There are cases where, on account of lack of clear direction or established criteria for evaluating project priorities, the examination of loan applications from small industries has become an extremely slow process. This is particularly so in cases where the staff has not been trained for this kind of work. While no written rules or operational manual can replace the personal judgement of an experienced staff, the establishment of a set of clear-cut 'eligibility criteria' for various forms of small industry loans would permit more orderly and speedy handling of loan requests and ensure that investments are channelled to the most desirable industries.

In this connection, it may be noted that the government of South Korea has adopted a 'value points' system for evaluating the priority of small industry loan applications. Under this system, each loan application for the supply of equipment and machinery is evaluated in terms of the industry's 'essentiality' to the national economy, i.e. of export potential, utilization of indigenous materials, import savings, and employment creation, as well as technical and management soundness and financial status. Under this rating system, the total 'value points' for the most desired project would be 400; the priority of each loan application is then determined in the order of the 'value points' calculated.

It is increasingly recognized that, to be effective, credit assistance to small industries needs to be combined with technical and managerial advice. From this point of view, the hire purchase scheme presents several special advantages. It permits a certain degree of control and orientation of investment and it guarantees the loans by providing for re-possession of the equipment by the financing institution in case of default by the entrepreneur. In addition, it may be used as a convenient means of promoting standardization of machinery, encouraging the domestic manufacture of equipment and improving the services of machinery importers and dealers.

The operation of a successful hire purchase scheme requires a small number of technical staff who would be able to assist the small industries concerned in all matters connected with the selection, installation and maintenance of the equipment and machinery. In India, hire purchase financing has been greatly facilitated by the assistance of the Small Industries Service Institutes which provide all the necessary technical advisory services and, in fact, help the lending agency in examining the loan applications. A similar institutional arrangement in Hong Kong would be a natural complement to the developing system of hire purchase finance.

(b) Organizational problems of industry

The immediate effect of the increase in the degree of mechanization in a small enterprise is the creation of a series of management problems. With improved equipment and machines, the volume of production generally goes up. Hence, additional working capital as well as markets will have to be found; an adequate supply of raw materials must be ensured; and, in some cases, a change in the division of work among employees and in the wage system may be needed. In addition, increasing attention will have to be given to the problem of maintenance and repair. To deal with these problems efficiently, the manager can no longer rely simply on his memory or on rule-of-thumb methods to keep track of all the transactions in his business. Some record keeping, including a simple cost accounting system, may be needed in order to enable him to assess the performance of the business and to reach decisions on a more intelligent basis.

Benefits from modernization will depend largely on the ability of the manager to cope with these abrupt changes in management functions. Most owner-managers of small industries were originally skilled workers, foremen, sometimes graduates of technical schools; some came from non-industrial occupations such as commerce. The changes in management functions brought about by mechanization are often beyond their ability. Thus there appears to be need for a major effort on the part of the public authorities to promote appropriate management training schemes for small industries.

This conclusion is now gaining a wide recognition in Hong Kong. However, no practical solution has yet been found. Neither the Labour Department's courses, nor the University's extramural courses or Harvard professors sponsored by the Jaycees have touched the typical, small, Chinese industrialist in Hong Kong. It appears that the solution could be found only by the establishment of a Small Industries Service Institute which would operate through its Extension Service as mentioned earlier in this paper. A complementary means could be seen in strengthening the existing industrial associations, all of which are extremely weak and practically neglected. Some fostering of small industry co-operative societies could also be envisaged as an obvious task for the government's Co-operative Development Department which, up to now, has been almost exclusively concerned with farmers' and fishermen's societies. For this purpose, flatted factories working under the same roof may well be conceived of as a convenient organizational basis.

Without attempting to sum up the various ideas and proposals mentioned in the second part of this paper, it should be clear that the whole complex of our small industry problems requires a well-conceived, co-ordinated and almost all-embracing programme of action. I believe that nothing short of a separate Department of Industry would be adequate. Shifting responsibility on to an essentially voluntary body, the Federation of Hong Kong Industries, deprived of funds and personnel, is simply a method of avoiding an enormous challenge. To meet this challenge properly, large funds and qualified personnel are obviously necessary. I have no doubt that the expanding economy of Hong Kong can find both.

III   A balanced institutional growth

When discussing the problems of the community's welfare, economists distinguish actual, feasible and potential welfare. A movement from actual to potential welfare implies a shift of the current efficiency locus (determining the actual welfare) by means of a feasible change in the institutional framework of the economy.

To define what is a feasible institutional change in Hong Kong is essentially a political problem. Opinions on this subject differ widely: from a complacent endorsement of the paternalistic system of colonial government to wild dreams of an independent city-state. It is not my purpose to discuss these various possibilities. However, having said so much about our economic and social problems, I should be failing in my duty if I did not end on one modest institutional proposal of a general nature.

I believe, as I have said on several occasions, that Hong Kong is now entering a phase of organizational change which is an inevitable consequence of our social and economic development. The range of problems facing us now is so enormous that we simply must have new organizational means of formulating public opinion on the basic issues of our economy. For this purpose I have suggested the possibility of establishing a Hong Kong

Economic Council. I called it a 'talking shop' and I think that in spite of a fast-growing number of various emporia in our tourists' paradise, there is time to have one arcade for such a talking shop. Its functions, importance and status in the community would grow in time. If properly organized, without too much of a reformistic spirit and evangelistic fervour, without any constitutional changes, a Hong Kong Economic Council could serve a useful purpose in finding out what the community really wants and how these wants should be satisfied: more schools or more houses; more hospitals or more repair-shops; more recreation parks or more ship-breaking yards; City Hall or an industrial extension service, etc. All these are decisions which have to be taken by a handful of our 'obedient' and able civil servants who often must be appalled by the responsibility placed upon them. They seek a way out by forming advisory boards, *ad hoc* committees, by sponsoring associations and federations. What I am proposing, therefore, is only to take one rather bolder step along the same road, by establishing a forum where advice on all the major economic problems could be given in the light of a carefully considered balance of opinions with the welfare of the whole community in mind.

VIII
HOUSING THE NEEDY
Judith Agassi

The extent of Hong Kong's housing problem is formidable indeed. On the basis of the 1961 census it has been estimated that out of the population of approximately 3,133,000 about 1,000,000 are unsatisfactorily housed, about 511,000 in squatter huts and other wooden structures, 140,000 in bed-spaces, 69,000 in verandas and cocklofts, 56,000 on rooftops, 50,000 in shops, garages and staircases, 26,000 in boats, 20,000 on the streets, 12,000 in basements, and 10,000 in stalls and caves.[1]

By far the most spectacular housing effort in Hong Kong is that of the Government Resettlement Department. The origin of resettlement was in the days of the previous mass influx of refugees from China, when squatters flooded the central areas of Kowloon and Victoria. This mass squatting not only caused enormous fire hazards, but also made impossible any development of not yet built-up land. Government therefore decided to provide with cheap accommodation all those whose structures were being demolished for development purposes. As most of these squatters were then of the lowest income groups—penniless refugees, unskilled or unemployed—the principle was accepted of the lowest possible rent to cover capital expenditure over a considerable time—forty years in the case of the big blocks. In the first period of the emergency, government built huts, but in 1953, when 50,000 squatters were made homeless overnight by a disastrous fire, the new Resettlement Department decided to exploit the scarce land more fully and began to build the by now familiar six-storey blocks. These are solid concrete, built to last. In the beginning of the scheme there existed a plan to improve the accommodation in these blocks by removing partitions between pairs of 'units', thus providing small self-contained flats for families. Today, when there are nearly half a million people living in these blocks, such a change seems near-impossible as it would require the building of new accommodation for a quarter of a million already 'resettled' people.

[1] Speech by Mr A. de O. Sales to Annual Public Meeting of the Hong Kong Housing Authority, 1962.

What does resettlement offer? Ninety-eight per cent of re-settlement tenants live in standard units of 120 square feet, i.e. 24 square feet per adult (children counting as half adults). Walls, ceilings, and floors are bare concrete, windows have wooden shutters, and the one door leads out on to the public balcony which serves as a general thoroughfare for the whole floor. Inside each unit there is one concrete bench, where kerosene stoves for cooking are placed. As each room houses at least five people, often not only members of the same family, cubicles and bed-spaces are partitioned off—vertically and horizontally—obstruct-ing the small flow of air between window and door. Much family life overspills over to the public balcony and the stairs. Worse still many tenants in these blocks are employed in home industries —producing mainly plastic flowers and rattan articles at home.

The resettlement blocks are enormous concentrations of people: one floor houses up to five hundred people, some blocks up to three thousand; each estate has thus the population of a medium-size town. Each floor in a block contains one and only one sanitation unit with taps but no basins and with separate latrines for males and females.

The large positive aspects of resettlement should not be over-looked: the standard rent of HK$15 per unit is very low, and makes even small incomes go a longer way. All estates provide space for rooftop primary school classes, children's clubs and playgrounds, as well as clinics and other welfare offices. But the drawbacks are large too: the extremely high concentration and proximity of such a mass of people is detrimental to their health, especially in view of the high incidence of active TB in Hong Kong.

The chief of one of the largest voluntary welfare organizations in the Colony goes so far as to say that life in many of the squatter huts seems to him to be healthier than in the resettlement blocks; and this in spite of the absence of sanitation and running water in squatter areas. One certainly gets the impression that the re-settlement kind of barracks-accommodation is detrimental to self-respect and that it weakens the urge for self-improvement of its tenants. The cleanliness of public spaces and the surroundings of the blocks deteriorates rapidly. And it is no longer true that resettlement tenants are all from the lowest income groups[1] and that therefore their standards of cleanliness and housing should be

[1] See Mr Goodstadt's paper.

expected to be low. Many people living in squatter huts at present and in recent years, are not the original occupiers; they are tenants paying considerable rents to the original squatters. People earning regular wages as semi-skilled and skilled workers often choose to live in squatter huts for want of any other accommodation near their place of work. Many families who have been living in resettlement estates for years now have incomes above $400 a month.

Even greater anomalies are to be found in the choice of candidates for resettlement: for, not only squatter huts have to be demolished for the purpose of public development schemes, but sometimes also ordinary houses, and some of their tenants—who also qualify for resettlement—definitely belong to middle-class income groups. The Resettlement Department has tried to cater for these people by providing better-standard end-bay rooms and some self-contained flats, with rents of up to $65 per month. But these house only 2 per cent of the resettlement population and cannot satisfy the existing need. It is obvious that by now a good number of resettlement tenants earn enough to pay considerably higher rents and that they should be encouraged to aim at higher standards of housing.

In spite of the huge building effort of the Resettlement Department, the squatter problem is far from being solved. The number of squatters seems to grow even more rapidly than they are resettled. There are now about 600,000 people classified as squatters in the urban areas and many more in the New Territories. Government plans to step up its building programme in order to catch up with the situation; it now plans to resettle as many as 100,000 in one year. The new blocks have a slightly more pleasing design from the outside, but they will be even taller, and still without lifts, of course. They will have central corridors, and it has been mentioned that some units will have private balconies. But, regrettably, there are no plans for increasing the basic living space, and, apparently there is no intention of improving washing and toilet amenities. In consequence, the density and lack of privacy will remain the same. At the end of the programme, in five years' time, one million Hong Kong citizens will be living in these enormous rabbit-warrens and will go on living in them perhaps for decades to come.

A new Government venture which meets most of these criticisms is the Low Cost Housing Project; this is also being designed and built by the Public Works Department, but these new estates are not being built exclusively for squatters, and they are going to be managed not by the Resettlement Department but by the Housing Authority. Their first tenants are about to move into the first completed block in the near future. I shall describe the Low Cost Housing scheme in greater detail later on.

Outside Government there are two large non-profit housing bodies, the Housing Authority and the Housing Society. The former, a statutory body founded in 1954, is the larger by far. It has housed approximately 38,500 people up till now. It was founded in order to provide suitable accommodation to the $300–900 income group. It works on the assumption that for economic health a family should not spend more than one-fifth of its income on rent. Vacancies are advertised. Applications are examined and the applicants are interviewed by trained staff. This is a lengthy and expensive process, but it is essential for ascertaining that those families in the greatest need of housing will occupy the flats appropriate to their size and income. The great majority of the Housing Authority's flats have been allocated to the $400–600 income group. The Authority found it difficult to build flats at rents of under $65. Most flats are for families of five or more. There are however a good number of flats for smaller families in two existing estates and more are under construction. Only in the So Uk estate has the Authority succeeded in economizing to such an extent that a considerable number of flats could be supplied for rents of under $70. One of the economy measures was having no lifts: these blocks are no more than eight floors high, and the higher floors contain the cheaper flats.

Most of the Housing Authority blocks are very high, have good lift services and safe playing areas are provided on several floors. The basic principle of the Housing Authority is to provide a minimum living-space of 35 square feet per person, with the size of the living space and the rent varying according to the number of the occupants. Each flat has its own toilet with a tap where a shower can be attached by the tenants, and a small kitchen with concrete shelves and a sink. Most flats also have small balconies where clothes are dried and flower-pots kept. Although tenants of nearly all the flats have to install double-decker bunks for children, and all have to curtain off a bed-space for the parents, the great majority of flats look well-kept and cherished.

Further evidence for that is the fact that rents, which are

collected monthly, are promptly paid throughout. All public spaces, corridors, staircases and courtyards, are cleaned by contractors and are kept in very good condition. The estates have shops which are let out at free market rents as an extra source of income so as to help keep the domestic rents low. The amount of social amenities, such as schools and clinics, varies from estate to estate; some could do with much more, especially nursery schools. An especially good idea seems to me the party-rooms at the Ma Tau Wei estate, where families can celebrate and use catering facilities.

The demand for the Authority's flats is very high and many applicants have to be disappointed. There exists in Hong Kong a very great number of skilled workers, white-collar workers and other lower-middle-class people who are in desperate need of decent accommodation at a rent they can afford. The Authority's building work, even its dearest blocks in the North Point Estate— at an average rent of \$22·25 per person—are a great bargain compared to accommodation provided by private builders. The Authority has succeeded in reducing building costs from \$25·76 per person in the first stage of their work to \$12·11 per person.

The Government's assistance to the Authority consists in the allocation of Crown land building sites at half the auction price, which is claimed to be one-third of its actual market value. Up to now the Authority has been allocated 65·7 acres and has paid Government \$19½ million. Government originally financed the Authority by lending it funds from the Colony's Development Fund, the first \$45 million at 3½ per cent interest, the remaining \$111 million at 5 per cent interest. So far the Authority has paid Government \$9½ million in interest.

Government did not require repayment of capital, so that the capital repayment element of rental income could be available for further development. Up to June 1960 Government increased this loan fund periodically, but then it informed the Authority that it would use any available funds for its own resettlement and low cost housing projects in order to cater for the under \$300 income group for which both the Housing Authority and the Housing Society had provided very little. Up to the Authority's 1962 public meeting, information about Government's further financial policy towards the Authority was rather vague. Though some members of the Board hoped that Government would provide further loans, they could not quote any definite promises. If no further loans are forthcoming, after the completion of the estates now under construction, the Authority will be able to house only 4,000 people a year—instead of housing 25,000, as it had envisaged. It is to be hoped that Government will find the additional funds to keep the Housing Authority working to capacity.

The Housing Society is a smaller body, incorporated in 1961, which works under similar conditions as the Housing Authority; it also is allocated cheaper sites and Government loans, but its connections with Government are looser and it receives interest-free loans from some large private firms who aim at obtaining accommodation for their employees. Up to the beginning of 1962 it had housed nearly 31,000 people in eight estates, and flats for nearly 16,000 additional persons were under construction. Many of the Society's principles and methods are very similar to those of the Authority. Applications are also dealt with carefully and the principle of one-fifth of the income on rent is observed. Thirty-five square feet per person are provided, as well as kitchen and toilet and in the majority of flats, a balcony. The high blocks have lifts, and public spaces are very clean and tidy. The Society also has a staff of trained housing attendants who collect the rents and supervise the efficient functioning of the estates. Here too there are no arrears in rents.

In both organizations tenants have to sign an undertaking not to take in lodgers, but are permitted to give shelter to a near relative. To avoid overcrowding when the young families are growing, exchange with larger flats is aimed at. In the Society's estates one finds the same picture of house-proud families managing well in—for European standards—extremely cramped conditions. The Housing Society has made a greater effort to cater for the under $400 income group. 57·8 per cent of the total accommodation owned by the Society can be let to families with incomes of up to $350. This includes 28·04 per cent of the total units which can be let to families with incomes up to $300. The lowest income which can be considered for a self-contained flat has been found to be $260. This has been made possible by somewhat lowering construction standards in one estate which accommodates many factory workers, in doing without balconies in another—and providing on each floor a drying room instead. To help single men and women the Society maintains at one estate dormitories, and this kind of accommodation is also in great demand. In order to tackle the problem of housing families with incomes of \$160–300, the Society built two blocks with communal facilities in the Kai Tak area, and is planning another one in Aberdeen. These blocks assign one toilet to each two families. Both have keys and share the responsibility for keeping it clean. The largest families, those of eight or nine persons, have a toilet to themselves. As no sinks are provided in the rooms—only a concrete bench—a large communal kitchen with taps, basins, individual food lockers, and space for cooking is provided on each floor. Actually the women prefer to do the cooking itself on kerosene stoves in their rooms and the estate managers have encouraged them to build closets around the cooking bench. But it would be wrong to say that the communal kitchens are not used. They are used for storing food and especially for washing, cleaning and preparing the food and for washing dishes. A rota of housewives is prepared regularly for cleaning the kitchen and this seems to work very well. Next to the kitchen a space for washing clothes is provided and this is used extensively.

The Society charges \$37 for a 'flat' of this kind for four people—the rent rising gradually to \$77 for one for nine people. The two 'communal facilities blocks' house 4,485 persons in 824 flats. They are exclusively occupied by workers' families, largely the same 'low income group' people that live in resettlement blocks. But these blocks—though teeming with children—are tidy and clean and the general atmosphere is cheerful. The Society is justified in pointing out that 'whilst communal facilities for families must always be deplored, the superiority of this block over the resettlement types cannot be denied. The tenants appear to recognize this and develop an estate pride and responsibility.'[1]

More decent housing for the under \$400 income group—no doubt the largest group of Hong Kong's population—is urgently needed. The Housing Society's experience in this field is very important: it has definitely established that it is economically feasible to provide self-contained accommodation for smaller families earning as little as \$260 p.m., and decent accommodation with communal facilities for families earning from \$160–300 p.m.

It certainly seems that Government when planning the new Low Cost Housing Estates has learned from the Society's experience. Government is planning to house 20,000 persons a year

[1] The Hong Kong Housing Society, *Annual Report*, 1961, p. 9.

in these new blocks. They are built on the central corridor plan; the basic space is 35 square feet per person—as in the Housing Authority and the Housing Society's estates. The first seven-storey block has recently been completed and a second twelve-storey block is under construction. The ground floor of one block is going to house a nursery school and a children's play centre. The first block provides units for smaller families only— i.e. for four and five persons. Each two families share one toilet, the cleaning of which will be their responsibility. The original plan to provide communal kitchens (like in the communal facilities blocks of the Housing Society) has been abandoned. Instead it was decided to fit out the small individual balconies with simple kitchen facilities. A concrete bench with raised sides runs the width of the balcony and running water and drainage are provided. Experience will show whether the tenants prefer this private access to running water in spite of the very cramped conditions—to the more spacious, though communal, facilities provided by the Housing Society.

These new blocks will be allocated to families with incomes below $400. As the Resettlement Department does not possess the necessary staff for satisfactorily selecting the tenants the task of management has been handed to the Housing Authority, which possesses both the staff and the experience.

It seems to me that it would be wiser in the long run to build more of this kind of low cost housing and less of the resettlement type. All squatters and resettlement tenants who belong to the appropriate income range should gradually be given the chance to choose this better-standard type of housing. Low cost housing provides citizens with the minimum of space which is essential for their health and the education of their children, and gives them just enough privacy in order to preserve their dignity and self-respect. This kind of housing certainly is more costly, the necessary screening and interviewing of applicants is a lengthy process; also, to make these densely populated estates a success they need continuous and expert management. But this extra investment of money and effort certainly will pay off in the long run.

Unfortunately there are in Hong Kong also many families of the lowest paid workers who earn less than $160 p.m., those without a breadwinner in regular employment, and those handicapped by widowhood or sickness; many of them, whether they technically qualify for resettlement or not, are in urgent need of housing; they will still need the cheapest safe accommodation that can be constructed to provide them with shelter—i.e. the resettlement type.

Besides these important large-scale housing schemes there exist in Hong Kong several smaller housing bodies. The Hong Kong Settlers Housing Corporation is building an estate which will accommodate 8,000 people. Three of the largest employers in the Colony, The Hong Kong and Yaumati Ferry Co., the Hong Kong Telephone Co. Ltd, and the Taikoo Dockyard and Engineering Co. Ltd, have built hundreds of small self-contained units for their employees. Important building work on a smaller scale is done by voluntary welfare organizations. A few fishermen's 'Better Living Societies' have been given assistance by Government and by voluntary bodies in providing their members with decent housing on land. The Church World Service has built many stone cottages for the resettlement of refugees. The Lutheran World Service constructs small housing blocks for refugees, and especially refugee fishermen in several of the islands (the Resettlement Department forms the building sites); this organization also does a very valuable job of welfare housing for problem families: ex-TB-patients with a rural background are provided with simple houses as well as with sufficient land, equipment and funds to become self-supporting as small farmers.

In conclusion—non-profit-making housing will be needed in Hong Kong for years to come, to provide housing for those most unsatisfactorily housed, to cater for the growing population, and gradually to raise the general standards of housing. It seems to me unwise to invest so much in the resettlement block-type of accommodation—not even in order to free the much-needed land for development as quickly as possible. The health and the morale of the human beings who are being 'resettled' is much more precious in the long run. The Housing Authority and even more the Housing Society have shown that many of the under $400 income group can be housed decently at a price which they can afford. Government's Low Cost Housing Project should be warmly welcomed.

The valuable supply of self-contained small flats for skilled workers, clerical workers and other lower-middle-class families that the two established housing societies have contributed should certainly not be curtailed and more employers should be encouraged to house their employees.

Co-operative housing societies should be encouraged and financially helped; they could contribute much to solve the housing problem of many middle-class families. The help of voluntary welfare organizations with the housing of special groups and problem families is greatly to be appreciated.

IX

URBAN HOUSING IN HONG KONG, 1945-63
L. F. Goodstadt

1 Introduction

The rapid growth of cities has become a major problem of life in Asia. The urban populations of this region have risen so fast since the war that it has been impossible in most cities to provide sufficient services and amenities to maintain decent living conditions. Hong Kong has shared this experience but it provides a special example of urban growth. The rate of increase has been very high. The population of the Colony has multiplied almost six times since 1945. The urban area[1] has a density of more than 200,000 to the square mile.[2] Hong Kong is a special case, too, because it has almost no natural resources, has received almost no foreign aid, lives by exporting and, through post-war industrialization, has achieved one of the highest records of economic progress amongst the 'non-advanced' countries of the world. This is the background to my essay.

This study has two aims. The first is to isolate the economic factors which have a bearing on the housing situation. The second is to uncover the social implications of the Colony's housing problems. I have tried to treat the economic and the social questions separately in order to simplify the analysis. But this treatment is not altogether satisfactory, and the distinction is rather an artificial one since the two are very much bound up with one another.

It is not easy to present an adequate review of a city's housing problems in a single essay. The subject is vast because housing affects the entire life of an urban community. It has not been possible to discuss many topics as deeply as they deserve nor to make the analysis as rigorous and consistent as it should be.

---

[1] Used in this study to mean Hong Kong, Kowloon and New Kowloon.

[2] Delhi, usually considered an extreme example of population growth and densities, has an average density of only 136,000 to the square mile. *Report of the Asian Seminar on Urban Community Development*, ECAFE Nineteenth Session, 5-18 March 1963, Manila, Philippines (ECAFE/87, 1963), p. 13. Here may be found other examples of Asian urban growth.

Furthermore I have only space to treat those issues which I consider of most importance. This study is not continued beyond 1963 because both government policy and the private housing industry have radically altered since that date.

To many citizens of Hong Kong, some of the facts I present and the conclusions I draw will be hard to swallow. Hong Kong cherishes many illusions about itself but on no subject has there been so much talk and so few facts as on the housing situation. Yet on such complex and crucial problems as housing, it is essential to have an accurate and systematic review of the facts before there can be any planned programmes of improvement.

2 Sources of information

Information on social and economic developments in the Colony is extremely scanty.[1] Most printed sources are referred to in the footnotes. Most of the statistics available are subject to large degrees of error. In the main, they can only be used as indicators of general trends. In employing them, I have tried not to make them bear more weight than they can carry.

Information on the real-estate sector was obtained in a series of interviews carried out in the summer of 1963. Some data and a great deal of background information has been gathered from a sample survey of records in the Land Office. In addition, the advertisements for housing in a leading Chinese newspaper were surveyed.[2] I have been fortunate in obtaining the assistance of a large number of civil servants, social workers and businessmen whose work brings them into close contact with Hong Kong's housing problems. I might add that two years spent living with monoglot Chinese families gave me some first-hand experience of the conditions I shall be describing.

3 Hong Kong Chinese attitudes to housing

Dr Majorie Topley has pointed out that Chinese demand schedules —for housing in particular—differ considerably from those of the

---

[1] Eileen L. Younghusband, *Training for Social Work in Hong Kong. A Report Prepared for the Government of Hong Kong* (1960), p. 12; *Report of the 1963 Working Party on Government Policies and Practices With Regard to Squatters, Resettlement, and Government Low Cost Housing* (Mimeo), p. 1.

[2] *Wah Kiu Yat Po*, the leading Chinese daily in this field.

westerner.[1] Chinese, in Hong Kong at least, do not seem to attach a very high priority to living in accommodation of a standard that westerners would consider as essential for health and comfort. Savings, clothes, jewellery, the outward signs of wealth and status rank higher than good housing once a Chinese has found a place in which to cook, sleep and keep his possessions.[2] It is quite an old custom in the Colony for people to cut down on their living space whenever they feel the need to save money.[3] Of course, to some extent, these attitudes to housing merely reflect the general problem of finding decent accommodation in Hong Kong, as the Census Commissioner has pointed out:[4]

> In so far as economic success can be measured by employment status, it would appear that while the successful man prefers to live in a whole house or in a self-contained flat, he is willing to accept sub-standard housing if need be. This willingness is perhaps the true measure of the housing famine.

The Chinese man spends a large part of his day outside his home. His hours of work are long. He tends to eat at work, at cooked-food stalls or in restaurants. Many sleep on their employer's premises. The Chinese place less value on privacy than westerners, and they do not seem to resent living under the curious scrutiny of neighbours and relatives of every degree.[5] Space for active children inside the home is not the problem it would be in other communities. Active games are not encouraged: the 'good' child spends its time studying quietly or helping its parents. Even where land is relatively plentiful, as it is in the rural New Territories, villages and houses seem hardly spacious by western standards.

[1] See above, pp. 192-5.

[2] It is a constant surprise to see impeccably turned-out people emerging from the meanest slums. Significantly, in a survey of 1957, when housing conditions were worse than today, 61·2 per cent of the sample were 'satisfied' with their present accommodation, and only 41·8 per cent indicated a willingness to move from their present homes. W. F. Maunder and E. F. Szczepanik, *University of Hong Kong, Hong Kong Housing Survey, 1957* (mimeo), part II, Tables H57A, H58A.

[3] *See Report of the Housing Commission, 1935,* Hong Kong 1936, Appendix II, p. 265.

[4] K. M. A. Barnett, *Hong Kong Report on the 1961 Census,* vol. III, p. cxiv.

[5] Quarrelling—often frighteningly frank to the westerner—is often done publicly with neighbours invited to take sides. Neighbours play an important role in mediating.

If the Hong Kong citizen compares housing in the Colony with that of China—a very obvious comparison to make since half Hong Kong's population was born in China—he will discover that conditions are not much better in the People's Republic. Under the 'First Five Year Plan', the housing position of Mainland cities declined sharply.

> Between 1949 and 1956, per-capita housing space had declined from 6·6 square metres to 5·1 in Peiping, from 4·06 to 3·06 in Wuhan, and from 5·7 to 2·97 in Shanghai. For 1957, the average housing space per capita in 175 cities was 3·5 square metres, varying from 4·9 in small cities to 2·2 in big cities.[1]

This is not very different from the situation in Hong Kong.

Although none of these facts provides an adequate excuse for poor housing standards, they do tend to minimize the stresses which inferior accommodation can cause. While poor housing is a serious problem in any community, cultural factors in Hong Kong seem to make inadequate housing a less serious problem for the Colony than it would be in a western country.

4   The supply of private housing

The supply of public housing is assumed to be an arbitrary quantity governed by official policy and largely without influence on the private sector. The supply of private housing is a more complicated matter. Theoretically, it is determined by the amount of capital the Colony's entrepreneurs are prepared to invest in building homes. This investment depends in turn on the profits developers expect to get from house construction compared with expected profits from non-domestic buildings or from investing in other sectors of the economy. The profits from housing projects have proved to be as high as those of any sector of Hong Kong's economy. In practice, many entrepreneurs are kept out of housing construction by the need for specialized knowledge and large amounts of capital in most housing development projects.

Other factors also affect the amount of housing constructed. The first is the speed with which buildings are completed. This

[1] Choh-Ming Li, *Economic Development of Communist China. An Appraisal of the First Five Years of Industrialization*, Berkeley and Los Angeles 1959, p. 215.

depends on the capital equipment of the construction industry, the number of skilled workers available,[1] the weather and so on. As far as speed of building is concerned, Hong Kong's construction industry seems relatively efficient.

Another factor of major importance is the amount of land available for building. In urban Hong Kong, the supply of land is severely restricted.[2] The provision of more building land depends on the creation of new sites through reclaiming from the sea or the levelling of hills. There is a fairly large reserve of land in the rural New Territories, most of which, for a variety of reasons, has not been considered suitable for development for non-agricultural uses. One large new town, Tsuen Wan (population 1961: 82,322), has grown up in the New Territories,[3] and Government has plans for two more similar developments.

In this situation, the answer to the land shortage is the more intensive development of the existing stock of building land. Before 1955, it was not practicable to redevelop existing urban sites because premises built before the war could not be torn down without risky and expensive legal proceedings.[4] In 1955,

Table III:[5] Number of tenement floors 'excluded'

Year	Tenement floors excluded
1956–7	998
1957–8	975
1958–9	1,390
1959–60	1,128
1960–1	1,483
1961–2	2,268
1962–3	7,244

[1] There are serious bottle-necks here: a shortage of scaffolding erectors, for example. There is a shortage of architects too. It has been estimated that the ratio of executive architectural staff in Hong Kong to the volume of construction is only half that of the United Kingdom.

[2] So severe is the shortage that 'the present Public Works Department programme for resettlement estates adjacent to the urban areas will come to an end by 1969 or 1970'. *1963 Working Party Report*, op. cit., p. 10.

[3] For details of this town's growth, see David C. Y. Lai and D. J. Dwyer, 'Tsuen Wan: A New Industrial Town in Hong Kong', *The Geographical Review*, vol. LIV, no. 2, April 1964, pp. 152–69.

[4] *Hong Kong Annual Report* (hereafter *HKAR*), *1957*, pp. 12, 27.

[5] These figures are derived from *Tenancy Inquiry Bureaux Monthly Reports* (mimeo, unpublished).

the procedure was simplified, and the number of sites redeveloped has increased rapidly. This is brought out in Table III which shows the number of tenement floors 'excluded', that is, the number for which permission to demolish and redevelop was given. (The ordinary tenement house has three or four floors.)

Until 1956, intensity of site development was limited by severe legal restrictions on building heights. Nevertheless, the average height in storeys of new buildings increased from 3·15 in 1951 to 4·75 in 1955.[1] With the easing of restrictions on height in 1956, it became possible to build multi-storey blocks of apartments.

For the years before 1957, it is not easy to get an accurate picture of the supply of housing. What we know is that in 1938 the urban population had sufficient housing to meet the legal requirement of 35 square feet of living space per person. A fifth of the tenement floors and almost all the European-style housing was made uninhabitable by the war.[2] By 1946, therefore, the city had accommodation designed to house some 640,000 persons.[3] By the end of 1946, the Colony's population had already risen to 1,600,000, and by 1950 it was 2,360,000. Of these, some 80–85 per cent would have been dwelling in the city.

From 1945 to 1956–7, new housing had been provided for about 150,000 people but almost half of this housing was for the higher income groups.[4] By 1957, the total accommodation was sufficient at pre-war densities for 790,000.[5] But the population had now reached 2,677,000. By 1957, then, there was an extreme shortage of housing. The increase in population had far out-distanced the supply of housing. This grave deficit is what created the housing problems of the Colony. Any steps taken today to solve the problems are, in effect, attempting to undo a situation which developed in the first twelve post-war years.

[1] *HKAR, 1957,* diagram facing p. 188.
[2] *Final Report of the Building Reconstruction Advisory Committee* (1946), pp. 5–13.
[3] Calculated from the data given *HKAR, 1956,* p. 144; *HKAR, 1957,* pp. 8, 186.
[4] This is possibly an under-estimate. At present densities, the figure would be much bigger. The estimate is based on 'Land and Housing', *HKAR,* especially *HKAR, 1958,* p. 159, and *HKAR, 1959,* p. 172.
[5] This calculation assumes that all housing was proportionately as over-crowded as tenements. It is based on figures given in 'Land and Housing', *HKAR, 1956* and *1957.*

After 1957, the situation changed. This is set out in Table IV.[1] This table indicates the relationship of supply to the increasing population. It assumes that the entire urban population would be looking for private housing.[2] (This was not the case, as will

Table IV: Rise in housing and urban population, 1958–63

Year	Annual increase in accommodation (persons) (1)	Annual increase in urban population (2)	Column (1) minus column (2)
1958	141,121	110,900	30,221
1959	122,474	97,280	25,194
1960	221,349	81,700	139,649
1961	154,131	182,700	−25,569
1962	49,003	258,000	−208,997
1963	53,838	99,770	−45,932
Total	741,916	830,350	−88,434

be shown later. Legally, however, almost all the increase in population should have been privately accommodated because the erection of temporary structures—not classed here as housing —was supposed to be prevented in this period.) What Table IV does reflect quite accurately is how near the supply of private housing came to meeting the needs of the increasing population.

Table IV shows that 1958–60 housing was being supplied faster than the population was rising. The housing situation was improving, and supply was beginning to make good part of the deficit that had developed 1945–57. After 1960, further increases in the population and a sharp fall in the number of persons provided with new housing caused the situation to deteriorate. The gains of the previous three years were wiped out and, by the end of the six-year period, the population had increased by 88,434

[1] Tables IV, V and VI are calculated thus: urban population is estimated from 'Population', *HKAR* for the relevant years; net changes in the supply of housing are based on 'Land and Housing', *HKAR* and the appendices thereto. 'Land and Housing' gives only changes in 'Units of accommodation'. These are converted to 'Numbers of persons' by multiplying 'Units' by factors to be found in *Housing Forecast*, Public Works Department, August 1962 (mimeo, unpublished), Appendix F. I first published these tables in 'The Housing Gap', *Far Eastern Economic Review* (hereafter *FEER*), vol. XLIV, no. 7, 14 May 1964, pp. 353–6.

[2] Private housing is taken to mean all property on which rates are levied. For later years, some housing provided by Government is classed as private because rates are paid on it. This does not affect the argument.

persons more than there were new homes for. Compared, however, to the twelve-year period before 1958, the position by 1963 was only slightly worse. The amount of new housing was within almost 10 per cent of the amount needed to contain the rising population.

Although the total increase in accommodation 1958–63 is quite impressive, I should point out that this figure is calculated on the basis of 1962 housing densities. If, instead, we calculate the total increase in terms of pre-war density standards, the picture is less impressive. By pre-war standards, this new accommodation would have been sufficient, not for 741,916, but for only some 520,000.

Table IV shows that there are two sides from which to tackle the housing problem. The first is the rising population. The housing situation could be controlled and, possibly, improved if population increases could be held at reasonable levels—chiefly through cutting off illegal immigration. On the other side is the question of ensuring that there is no fall-off in the net amounts of new housing provided each year. The fall-off 1961–3 is extremely puzzling when we consider that the value of new housing completed in 1963 (by cost of piling and construction) was 11 per cent higher than in 1960, yet the increase in the number of persons housed was 76 per cent lower than in 1960.[1]

Part of the answer is provided by Table III which showed a very sudden spurt of buildings scheduled for demolition 1961–3. But the type of housing that was being built was also changing, and this had important consequences. Table V sets out these changes.

Table V: Net annual changes in supply of housing (by number of units)

Year	Houses	Large flats	Small flats	Tenements	Low cost housing
1958	−76	472	1,924	6,377	2,516
1959	−26	630	2,041	5,104	1,293
1960	−366	−1,782	2,049	12,183	1,911
1961	−7	825	2,537	5,681	5,394
1962	2	970	1,892	−731	6,692
1963	218	2,871	3,591	−1,280	4,650

Developers were concentrating on flats both large and small after 1960. This is important because the average tenement holds

[1] *Nigel Ruscoe's Annual Hong Kong Register, 1964* (Hong Kong: FEER), Table XXVIII, p. 69.

roughly three times as many people as live in a large flat and two and a quarter times as many as the average small flat holds. This combined with the number of buildings demolished, reduced the amount of new housing provided.

The effects of changes in the type of housing provided are even more clearly brought out in Table VI. This table shows the annual net changes in the number of people housed in different types of accommodation. It demonstrates clearly that the key to the amount of new housing in any year is the net increase in the number of new tenements built.

Table VI: Net changes in the supply of housing (by number of persons)

Year	Houses	Large flats	Small flats	Tenements	Low cost housing
1958	−608	2,832	15,392	108,409	15,096
1959	−160	3,780	24,328	86,768	7,758
1960	−2,928	10,692	16,392	207,111	11,466
1961	−56	4,950	20,296	96,577	32,364
1962	16	5,820	15,136	−12,121	40,152
1963	1,744	17,226	28,728	−21,760	27,900

The decline in the number of people accommodated in new tenements 1961–3 has not been fully made up by the increase in the numbers housed in other types of accommodation.

Because of the restrictions on redevelopment in the first post-war decade, the supply of housing deteriorated sharply. With the boom in redevelopment after 1956, the supply improved very greatly. This has had a noticeable effect in slowing down the rent spiral as we shall see. It is obvious, however, that the supply of new housing will have to be increased even more if the Colony's housing problems are to be solved and the homes of its citizens improved.

5   Demand for private housing

Demand for private housing is composed of several elements. Basically, almost everyone who lives in the Colony must be provided with a home in some sort of structure. This fact is what sets the level of potential demand. But not everyone is housed by the private sector. Some are housed by Government, some in low cost housing, some in makeshift shanties. These people are not looking for private housing. Very rarely do they move back into private accommodation. Thus, they do not directly influence demand for private housing.

Here, therefore, our first task is to work out the numbers who require accommodation in permanent structures which are privately owned: that is, the number actually in the market for private housing. We can estimate this number by subtracting from the urban population those housed by Government in one way or another together with the number of squatters.[1] This is done in Table VII.[2]

Table VII: Number of persons in the market for private housing

Year	Total in Government-financed housing plus squatters	Urban population left to be housed by private sector
1956	552,000	1,598,000
1958	626,000	1,787,000
1960	956,000	1,636,000
1963	1,308,000	1,825,000

What does this table demonstrate? Firstly, it measures those who have become the responsibility of Government. (Squatters will eventually be provided with public housing.) Secondly, it measures the numbers who are, potentially, buying (or renting) private accommodation. The increase 1958–63 in those in the private market was only 38,000. The amount of additional private housing supplied in this period was sufficient, we have seen, for 741,916 persons (Table IV above). Overall then the pressure of demand on the private market is smaller than it was in the years before 1958.

But this pressure has slackened simply because the number of squatters rose by almost 250,000 and the numbers in Government-financed housing by 466,000 in 1958–63. The pressure could not have slackened if some 700,000 had not left the market for private housing. The excess of increased supply over increases in demand in the six-year period has had beneficial effects on both rents and overcrowding. But these benefits have to be paid for

[1] For the definition of 'squatter', see *Review of Policies for Squatter Control, Resettlement and Government Low-Cost Housing, 1964*, Appendix II, p. 20.

[2] This table is based on the same sources as Table IV (see p. 263, note 1, above). However, the two tables are measuring quite different things. Table IV estimates the adequacy of new housing related to the rising population. Table VII demonstrates how people have reacted to the housing shortage by leaving the market.

by the community through the spending of increasing amounts of public funds on housing.

The demand for private housing can be further divided into two elements. Firstly, there are those who already have a place to live, which they either own or rent. Secondly, there are those who are looking for a place to live. It is this second element which is the more important as far as the determination of market prices is concerned. We can explain the working of the two elements in the following way. Those who have somewhere to live are the basic pressure on the market which, together with the supply of housing in the past, has established the current level of prices. Those looking for somewhere to live (either as new entrants to the market or people wanting to change house) are an additional pressure on the market which sets the new level of prices for the future.[1] In the discussion of rents (below), I show that those who do not change house do face rent increases but these are much lower than the increased rents that are paid by those who move from one flat to another.

Those who have bought flats since 1956 have tended to be permanently satisfied in their demand for housing. Once a person has bought one flat, he rarely sells it or buys another. Less than 5 per cent of the flats I have examined have been sold more than once over a period of six years. A slightly higher proportion were bought by persons who already owned a flat. On the whole, those who buy a flat leave the market for private housing.

Information on the number of people moving house is not very detailed. In 1955-7, households were changing their accommodation at the rate of 10 per cent per annum.[2] The 1963-4 Survey[3] showed that 83 per cent of households renting private accommodation in 1963-4 had not changed house since 1959. This means that households were moving at less than 4 per cent per annum in the four-and-a-half-year period. This is a considerable reduction on the previous figure and reflects the improved position of supply in relation to demand for private housing. Turnover of tenancies is highest, it appears, when housing is in very short supply, and rents are rising rapidly.

[1] Here I have ignored the effects on prices of people leaving the market because the numbers in the market did increase 1958-63.

[2] W. F. Maunder and E. F. Szczepanik, *Housing Survey, 1957*, op. cit., part II, Table H40A.

[3] This refers throughout the text to a large random sample of households and their expenditure made in 1963-4 which is, as yet, unpublished.

We do have reasonably accurate figures for one group of people who change house: those evicted for redevelopment. Their numbers are given in Table VIII. Not all of those evicted remain in the market for private accommodation—16 per cent or more become squatters.[1] This indicates that the pressure on prices from people moving house would have increased sharply from 1961.

When we turn to the demand for private housing for purchase, we find a perplexing situation. With the high rents that new flats can command and increases in the general level of rents (discussed below), we might imagine that there would be no shortage of

Table VIII:[2] Numbers evicted for redevelopment

1956	17,764
1957	18,053
1958	35,020
1959	20,304
1960	26,694
1961	40,824
1962	130,392
1963	162,860

buyers, both those seeking profitable investments and those seeking to escape from rising rents. In practice, new flats are not easy to sell. There have been frequent reports in the press since 1956 of the difficulties that developers encounter in finding purchasers. This partly because of poor advertising and salesmanship.[3] But the difficulties have a deeper cause.

With the huge increase in urban population unmatched by a similar rise in the stock of houses, a 'sellers' market' for housing should exist in the Colony. The Colony ought to be very competitive in buying up new apartments. In fact, this has not been the case.[4] Developers have been forced to offer increasingly easier hire purchase terms to persuade the public to buy. But even this measure has not been over-successful. In buildings where pay-

[1] *1963 Working Party*, op. cit., p. 7.

[2] Based on *Quarterly Reports of the Tenancy Inquiry Bureaux, 1956–63* (mimeo, unpublished).

[3] *FEER*, vol. XLIII, no. 1, 2 January 1964, p. 37.

[4] On this imbalance of supply and demand—which should not be exaggerated, however—see *Hong Kong Annual Departmental Report by the Commissioner of Rating and Valuation for the Financial Year 1962–63*, p. 25.

ments can be spread over five years, the majority of buyers prefer to complete their payments in under two years.[1]

These facts suggest that developers have not yet succeeded in exploiting properly the potential mass market for flats. Those who buy flats are the fortunate minority who have managed to accumulate enough savings to make large down payments on flats and to pay heavy instalments over a short period.[2] Such large savings are not possible for most people who are spending on average a seventh of their incomes on accommodation.[3] With interest rates of 1·2 per cent per month or more on hire purchase terms, they cannot afford to pay on the longer-term hire purchase arrangements. The difficulties of finding purchasers ought to keep prices of new flats down. As we shall see, restricted competition amongst developers offsets the relatively small size of the market.

We now have to consider changes in the level of 'effective demand': that is, the aggregate amount of money that is spent on private housing. Changes in effective demand are related to changing income levels. Over the last eight years, incomes have risen quite sharply in Hong Kong. In 1957 average monthly household income was $480.[4] The 1963–4 Survey showed that the average household expenditure is now $650 a month. There is practically no unemployment in Hong Kong today. Indeed, in many industries there is a serious shortage of skilled workers. This situation has caused a rise in the level of wage rates as the Labour Department's *Index of Industrial Wage Changes* shows:

Year	1959	1960	1961	1962	1963	1964
Weighted average	100	121	126	131	137	156

These wage rises represent a real increase in the standard of living, for there has been little inflation in Hong Kong as the *Retail Food Price Index* indicates.[5]

End of year	1959	1960	1961	1962	1963
Index	100	98·4	100·8	100·8	105·5

[1] Survey of Land Office records. Some developers tell me that very few people even request the longer terms that are offered.

[2] People prefer not to pay for a flat until the building is actually completed even where they could afford to do so.

[3] *1963–4* Survey.

[4] W. F. Maunder and E. F. Szczepanik, *Housing Survey, 1957*, op. cit., part II, Table H24A.

[5] Base = 1947. This seems to me to be the only component of the *Retail*

Thus it has been possible for the average household to pay an increasing proportion of its income on accommodation. But it is worth noting that rents and wages have not risen proportionately to one another. The rise in wages 1959–64 of 55 per cent has been matched by an increase of only 16·4 per cent in rents.[1] Between 1948 and 1955, the proportion of household expenditure spent on accommodation rose from 9 per cent to only 9·4 per cent.[2] By 1963–4, some 14 per cent of household expenditure was on rents.[3]

There has thus been a significant increase in the amount of money which the average citizen could spend on housing. It is here that a certain danger lies. When people have more money and can afford improvements in their living standards, it may become intolerable for them to put up with housing standards which do not improve. The contrast will be even more sharply marked the more standards rise in every other sphere of their lives.

6   The price of accommodation

Now that demand and supply have been reviewed, we can examine the prices that are paid for housing. Once again, housing built with official funds need not concern us for its prices are set arbitrarily. Once again, to discover the causes of the situation today, we have to go back to the beginning of the post-war period. In 1950, Hong Kong's population was 2,360,000. This population was composed of two elements: permanent residents of the Colony; and those who had fled from post-war China in the wake of civil war and political upheaval. This latter group had high hopes of returning to China once the political situation had calmed down. In the meantime, they, together with the rest of the Colony, were enjoying a post-war boom. The 'temporary' inhabitants had not come to Hong Kong empty-handed. The

[1] 1963–4 Survey.
[2] Edward F. Szczepanik, *The Cost of Living in Hong Kong*, Hong Kong 1956, p. 6.
[3] 1963–4 Survey.

Price Index which has any meaning today. The food figures are calculated from 'Retail Price Indices', *Special supplement, no. 4 to Hong Kong Government Gazette, 1960–64.*

rich had brought their fortunes; the ordinary people had carried down jewellery, foreign exchange and Hong Kong bank-notes.[1]

These temporary residents had to pay dearly for their housing and so did Hong Kong residents who rented flats. Men with property to sell and principal tenants took full advantage of the situation. If we examine 'key money', for example, we find that it was extremely high. It was usually equal to around six months' rent in the more expensive buildings and equal to over a year's rent for cheaper flats.[2] With the complete inability of Hong Kong to house its population in 1950, and the influx of refugee wealth, and an economic boom, there was every reason for housing to be expensive.

Since 1950, rents and prices have continued to rise. People buying flats in the period 1950–62 have faced large increases of price. Advertisements in *Wah Kiu Yat Po* provide the following data on newly built flats offered for sale in 1958 and 1962 as well

Year	Average price
1950	$6,134
1958	$17,765
1962	$28,351

as the average price of flats in 1950.[3] (The increase of almost 200 per cent 1950–8 was due to the fact that the property being sold through the newspaper in 1950 had been built pre-war.) The increase between 1958 and 1962 suggests the reason why anyone who rented a flat in a new building in this period could expect to pay a substantially higher rent than people in less-recently completed buildings—his landlord had paid a bigger price to buy the new flat than that paid by the owner of older apartments.

Rents too have increased. The Government Statistician reckoned, on the basis of a limited sample taken from government employees living in private housing, that rents rose 80 per

[1] For how large the sums involved were likely to have been, see Wong Po-Shang, *The Influx of Chinese Capital into Hong Kong since 1937*, Hong Kong: Kai Ming Press 1958; Chang Kia-Ngau, *The Inflationary Spiral: The Experience in China, 1939–50*, Massachusetts Institute of Technology 1958, pp. 274, 304, 320–1.

[2] I have discussed the 1950 situation in more detail in 'Rents Revisited', *FEER*, vol. XLI, no. 4, 25 July 1963, pp. 261–2.

[3] The figures for 1958 and 1962 refer to the cheapest flat offered for sale in each advertised new building. I originally published these data in 'New Rents for Old', *FEER*, vol. XLII, no. 1, 3 October 1963, pp. 40–1.

cent 1947–59. This meant an annual increase over the twelve years of 6·7 per cent.[1] The Commissioner of Rating and Valuation made a survey of rent changes 1958–62 which indicated that in these years average rents were rising at 2–3 per cent annually.[2] The 1963–4 Survey discovered a rise of 16·4 per cent since 1959 in the amounts that households paid in rent—an annual increase of 3·6 per cent. Why rents rose faster 1959–63/4 than 1958–62 can be explained by the fact that there were more people moving house from 1961 (see Table VIII above) which increased the pressure on the market from the demand side.

This is borne out by Table IX:[3]

Table IX: Changes in rents paid by households

Have not changed house since 1959		*Have changed house since 1959*	
Age of building	*Percentage increases 1959–63/4*	*Age of building*	*Percentage increases 1959–63/4*
Pre-war	2·6	Pre-war	16·6
Post-war	9·0	Post-war	48·3

This table provides statistical support for what I have argued previously: that the pressure on prices is exerted not by those who are already settled in accommodation but by those who are seeking new homes. Table IX also indicates how much higher is the price of tenancies in post-war buildings. This, as we shall see, is partly due to rent controls and partly to the higher selling price of new flats. As more and more people move to post-war buildings, we can expect the average rents paid by the urban population to continue to increase. This may sound paradoxical—increased supply making for higher prices—but it is understandable if we remember that old and new buildings are not identical. Apart from anything else, the costs of building flats today are higher than before the war, so prices and rents must be higher.

It is interesting that the increased supply of housing and the slower growth of the numbers seeking private accommodation 1958–63 should have such an effect on rent levels. The reduction of the annual rate of increase from 7 per cent to between 2–3 per cent and 3–6 per cent illustrates how quickly rents react to changes in supply and demand.

[1] *Hong Kong Salaries Commission Report, 1959*, Appendix D, p. 112.
[2] *Rental Study by Commissioner of Rating and Valuation, 1962*, p. 11.
[3] 1963–4 Survey.

Unfortunately we do not have the data which would allow us to compare changes in rents per square foot. Clearly, if people today are paying higher rents for smaller houses than they were four years ago, their real rents have risen much more than my figures indicate. In view of what I have said about the very small rise in those needing private housing in recent years (see Table VII above) and the increased supply, people are probably not occupying less space today than six years ago, although the average size of units of accommodation has certainly decreased.[1] It is reasonably safe to assume, therefore, that rents per square foot would have risen by the same amount as household rents.

So far I have implied that rents and prices are set by the unhindered operations of supply and demand. This is not the case. Rent controls, discussed later, affect the market and so do certain peculiarities of the market itself. In Hong Kong, although the urban area is relatively small in size, few like to move away from their present neighbourhoods. People prefer not to buy flats, even as investments, at any distance from their present homes.

In general, people are not well informed as to where there are vacant premises to let. Usually, vacancies are advertised by word of mouth, by caretakers (in the larger buildings) and on 'red papers' posted outside the building or, in some districts, on a special wall. Flats to let are not commonly advertised in the Chinese press.[2] Similarly, the rent that the individual pays depends on a personal bargain struck after haggling with the landlord. The amount of variation in rents caused by haggling is, I feel, quite large. Sometimes the advantage goes to the tenant but, naturally, sometimes it goes to the landlord.

The market for new flats for sale is even less 'perfect'.[3] Competition amongst property developers is very much restricted.[4] A close examination of these restrictions and 'monopolistic'[5]

---

[1] *Annual Departmental Report by the Commissioner of Rating and Valuation for the Financial Year 1961–62*, p. 13. But the number of persons per unit has fallen.

[2] They were quite common in *Wah Kiu Yat Po* in 1950, but by 1958 they had become very few and far between.

[3] In the economist's sense of the word.

[4] For a fuller analysis of restricted competition, see my 'Competition in Development', *FEER*, vol. XLII, no. 2, 10 October 1963, pp. 117–19; ' "Competition"—by Agreement', *FEER*, vol. XLII, no. 3, 17 October 1963, pp. 161–4.

[5] Again, in the economist's sense of the word.

tendencies makes it difficult to avoid concluding that greater competition would have damped down considerably the increasing amounts paid for housing in Hong Kong. It is hard to put up with poor housing conditions; harder still to pay rising prices and rents for inferior accommodation. But hardest of all is to know that a significant part of the rising costs of the community's homes is due to a lack of competition amongst those supplying the Colony's housing.

7 Rent controls

Government actions have played their part in the story of rising rents. It is popularly believed that Government has forced up the price of flats by its policy of selling Crown Land for the highest price it can get. It is true that by insisting on a full economic price for its land, Government has done nothing to minimize the effects of rising property values on the cost of housing. Government's policy can be defended on the grounds that land values reflect the profits that developers obtain from their sites. Secondly, the price received by Government is public revenue spent on the community as a whole. Thirdly, if Government sold land at artificially low prices, the profits of the private developer would increase.[1]

Government has attempted to keep the level of rents down by direct action. Pre-war domestic premises have been subject to rent controls since the end of the war.[2] Post-war buildings were left uncontrolled until 1962. The principal reason for the failure to apply rent controls to post-war buildings was the fear that the flow of new buildings would diminish if the returns of developers were curtailed or the profitability of property owning were impaired.[3] In fact, the controls on post-war property introduced

---

[1] This is true because if the developer is acting rationally, he charges the highest price the market will pay. The market does not suddenly find itself unable to pay this price just because Government lowers land prices. Therefore, the price paid to the developer would be unchanged. But his costs would be lower if land prices were reduced. His profits would, in consequence, be higher.

[2] For the background to rent controls, see *Rent Control: Report of a Committee Appointed by Governor in February 1953*, pp. 6–12.

[3] *HKAR, 1957*, p. 11; *Proposals for Rent Increase Controls and Security of Tenure for Certain Classes of Domestic Premises in Hong Kong*, Hong Kong 1962, pp. 15–16.

1962–3 demonstrate that it would have been possible earlier to devise controls which would not have frightened off property developers. In a survey I made of developers, July–August 1963, I discovered that they were unconcerned by the new controls. Up till now, controls in post-war property seem to have achieved their object—though I have personal knowledge of several cases where the controls have been ignored. In the future, the pressure to ignore the rent controls in these premises is likely to produce widespread breaches of the law.

Government efforts to peg rents in pre-war property have largely failed. Obviously since breaches of the rent control ordinances are illegal, the amount of information available is scanty.[1] Table IX showed that rents in pre-war (presumably, controlled) property have been rising since 1957—in spite of the law. One official (but unpublished) comment in 1961 on the situation is worth quoting:

> Many sub-tenants are paying much the same as they would do in new buildings. De-control or an increase in permitted rents might mean little to these tenants as they are already paying rack rents and would have to pay little if any more for similar 'spaces' in new buildings.[2]

It has been estimated that 80–85 per cent of sub-tenants in old buildings are paying more than the legally permitted rents to their principals.

There is some evidence to show that it is the principal tenants and not the landlords who have benefited from illegal rent increases. Rent control was modified in 1953 to allow a limited increase in rents. Before this could take place, official forms had to be completed. By 31 March 1954, 32,700 landlords had applied for these forms, but only 467 principal tenants had applied for the forms which would permit them to pass a proportion of their increased rents on to their sub-tenants. Landlords were increasing rents on a wide scale and, one imagines, principal tenants were passing on the increases on just as wide a scale. This evidence suggests that landlords were observing the law before 1953 and were prepared to go on doing so. Principal tenants, on the other

---

[1] Details of the workings of the rent controls for which no references are given were obtained from the Secretariat for Chinese Affairs.

[2] This clearly applies only to a portion of tenant population. Most pay lower rents.

hand, were not. *The Interim Report of the Reform Club's Committee on Low Cost Housing, Slum Clearance and Development 1955* presented a survey which showed that in some areas sub-tenants were paying 220 per cent more in rent than the law allowed, while the land-lords were receiving only the legal rent. There is no reason to think that the position of sub-tenants in controlled property has improved since 1955.

That the landlord receives only the permitted rent, which has remained fixed since 1953, has important consequences. Firstly, the only way in which he can increase his income from the pro-perty is to redevelop. Thus rent controls on old property have encouraged rebuilding. Secondly, the landlord has no incentive to spend anything on repairs. Thirdly, Government revenue is reduced—an important point in a low-tax economy like Hong Kong. Property rates are based on the annual (legal) letting value of premises. By freezing rents on such a large amount of property, Government froze part of its own income.

Although the rent controls have not prevented increased rents in pre-war property, they have helped to keep these rents at substantially lower levels than those in new buildings. The Reform Club Report, previously referred to, stated that rents in new buildings were 100 per cent higher than in old ones. The 1963–4 Survey supports this finding.

Table X: Monthly rent per household

	1959	*1963–4*
Built pre-war	$47.96	$49.84
Built post-war	$110.5	$132.3

Table X shows the considerable financial saving that is obtained by living in pre-war property—in spite of illegal rent increases. This financial advantage increases over time. The Reform Club found that rents in pre-war property were, in 1955, 50 per cent of those in post-war buildings. Table X shows that they were only 43 per cent in 1959 and had fallen to 38 per cent of rents in post-war property by 1963–4. These lower rents are what induce some 20 per cent of those evicted for redevelopment to find their way to other pre-war buildings. But the amount of rent-controlled property is diminishing as Table XI shows. Thus, the number who can benefit from these controls is declining. Redevelopment, up to 1962, was, in effect, a form of decontrol.

Table XI: Percentage of rated units of accommodation subject to rent controls

	Hong Kong	Kowloon	New Kowloon
1957	66	54	55
1959	57	40	45
1961	47	34	33
1962	44	20	25

Hong Kong's Government is not really in favour of controlling rents. It tried on two occasions to permit controlled rents to rise, but was prevented by public opposition.[1] The whole question is politically so delicate that, I understand, Government prefers not to make suggestions for positive action on the subject. It prefers the unofficial members of the Legislative Council to take the initiative. But Government has little choice but to retain controls and was under strong compulsion to extend their coverage in 1962. If controls were lifted, rents would certainly rise and continue to rise in the future. Already, some 16 per cent or more of those moved out of old property prefer to become squatters rather than pay the higher rents they would face on going to another flat.[2] If rents were allowed to rise freely, we could expect a further serious increase in the number of squatters. Thus controls have been retained and extended to limit the numbers of squatters for whom Government would otherwise be responsible.

It is worth discussing the reasons for the failure of legislation to provide full protection for tenants. Legislation of this kind depends for its enforcement on the willingness of tenants to seek their own legal remedies. This the Chinese are reluctant to do. In 1953–61, less than eight thousand tenants sought the assistance of the Tenancy Tribunals. The courts themselves have been unwilling to impose heavy penalties for breaches of the laws protecting tenants from rent increases.

Those tenants who have taken their problems to the Tenancy Inquiry Bureaux have often been persecuted in revenge by their principal tenants—an easy matter in the congested conditions under which they live. Plenty of publicity was given to the Land-lord and Tenant (Amendment) Ordinance, 1953, but it was misunderstood by many of those it affected. Public misinformation on the citizen's rights is common in Hong Kong. Though the public now has, through the Public Enquiry Service, better access to reliable information on the legal protection to which

[1] *HKAR, 1957*, pp. 12–13. [2] *1963 Working Party Report*, op. cit., p. 7.

tenants are entitled, the majority of tenants still seem to be ignorant of their rights, and it is doubtful whether they would enforce them even if they did. It seems unlikely, therefore, that legislation could ever be really effective in controlling the Colony's rents over a longish period of years.

8   Squatters

A squatter is one who lives in a structure, usually makeshift, in a place where the law does not permit him to dwell.[1] The number of squatters determines the amount of housing that Government must provide in order to solve the squatter problem. Any increase in the number of squatters reduces the number who must be housed in private buildings. The squatters, therefore, transfer part of the burden of providing accommodation from the private to the public sector.

It is a mistake to think of squatters (or former squatters who have been resettled) as markedly distinct, either economically or socially, from the rest of the community. The 1961 Census collected data[2] for 'Special Divisions' which allows squatters and resettled people to be compared with the rest of the urban population. In almost every respect—unemployment, number of immigrants, women in employment, to mention but a few characteristics—the squatter and the settler exhibit the same social and economic characteristics as the Colony in general.

There are only three major points of difference. Of the squatter and the resettled population, a lower percentage are employers than in the urban population as a whole. Secondly, it contains a higher proportion of children under 20 years of age. Thirdly, it contains fewer of the more recent immigrants and more of those who came to the Colony before 1956. (Apparently, the more recently a man has arrived in Hong Kong, the more he relies on conventional accommodation.)[3]

As far as we can tell, squatters, from the earliest days of squatter colonies, have tended to be a general cross-section of the urban population.[4] They have, it seems, been distinguishable from the

[1] Though pre-1959 structures are tolerated by Government. *Review of Policies, 1964*, op. cit., p. 20.

[2] But it did not publish these tables.

[3] Though this is not true, apparently, of the 1962 influx of immigrants.

[4] D. C. Bray, *Survey of Squatters, 1951–52* (mimeo, unpublished) seems to support this conclusion.

rest of Hong Kong only by the kind of homes in which they live. In the middle of the post-war period, a university survey of resettled squatters found that they were neither the very rich nor the very poor. They formed a middle economic group.[1] This pattern was confirmed by the 1961 Census.

It seems to me that the squatter hut ought to be regarded as no more than another form of accommodation in a city where housing standards are low. I find it difficult to see that, on balance, the person who lives in a wooden shack is very much worse off than the occupant of the expensive overcrowded dwelling unit so typical of private housing.[2] It is true that squatter areas are difficult of access, subject to natural disasters, lack many basic amenities, and, by their nature, are fire hazards. But against these defects must be weighed the lower costs, the greater freedom, privacy and access to fresh air that exist in most squatter settlements.

Over the years, the *Hong Kong Annual Reports* have shown that, in spite of all Government's efforts, the number of squatters has continued to grow. In 1956, there were about 300,000 squatters. By 1963, there were 534,000 squatters still to be resettled. Natural increase might account for some 90,000 of this rise. The rest have come to the squatter colonies from other sorts of housing. Why do people become squatters? The large proportion of children in the squatter population suggests that many squatters have larger than average families. Accommodation for the large family is difficult to find. A second cause is the difficulty of renting space in the diminishing number of pre-war buildings, in which rents are lower. Thirdly, there is the powerful attraction of the chance of being resettled.

In general, therefore, squatters seem to be people who have no choice but to live in a flimsy shack. They have failed to find conventional accommodation at prices they feel they can afford to pay. It may not be easy to understand why, for instance, since 1958, the number of squatters has risen by 232,000 (even though some 376,000 squatters were resettled 1958–63) while at the same

---

[1] Though they have fewer wage-earners, C. S. Hui, W. F. Maunder and J. Tsao, *Hong Kong's Resettled Squatters. The Final Report on the 1957 Sample Survey of Resettlement Estates* (typescript, unpublished), pp. 44, 87–8.

[2] *1963 Working Party Report*, op. cit., p. 8. HKAR, *1954* states that the average squatter family had 80 sq. ft (p. 3). The average family in a tenement had only 64 sq. ft according to HKAR, *1953*, p. 104.

time the housing situation had not been getting seriously worse. Here, the problem is not so much the quantity of housing available as the difficulty of finding vacant premises to rent.

A man evicted at short notice may not have time to scour the district to find somewhere to live. Yet his family must be housed immediately; so he becomes a squatter. People work long hours in Hong Kong and do not enjoy regular week-end holidays. People do not have the leisure to hunt down a home. When faced with the prospect of taking time off work (and thus losing money) to look for a place to live, or, alternatively, of becoming a squatter, the latter may seem a reasonable choice. Even those with leisure may experience considerable difficulty in finding a suitable place to move to.

If the general standards of housing were better, there would be less inducement for people to become squatters. When the difference between conditions in conventional housing and those of squatter huts is so small, it is no wonder that people are willing to flee from high rents to wooden shacks. I am only surprised that the number of squatters is not increasing at a faster rate.

9 Housing conditions

The 1961 population of the urban area was 2,582,901. Of these, some 567,939 persons lived in housing built of temporary material or in accommodation not designed for domestic use. This means that one in five of the urban population was not provided with permanent domestic accommodation of any kind. These 567,939 persons contained 124,772 households. Although living in these unsatisfactory conditions, almost exactly half the households (62,160)[1] were paying rent for the space in which they lived. This, in itself, is a telling comment on the housing situation.

Undesirable as the housing standards of one-fifth of the population are, conditions for most of the others in the city are not much better. The physical condition of resettlement housing is relatively high, because Government is both developer and landlord and keeps the buildings in good repair. Conditions are less happy in private buildings. Much pre-war property is lacking in sanitary facilities and other basic amenities. With rent controls, there has been little incentive for landlords to make repairs or improvements in old buildings.

[1] *1961 Census Report*, op. cit., vol. II, Tables 002–013, pp. 3–9.

In 1957, while 95 per cent of all buildings had government mains and were connected to a government sewer for waste water, 50 per cent of the tenement floors had only a tap, and only 30 per cent had a bath.[1] With redevelopment, the standard of amenities ought to be improving. But the sites redeveloped are not necessarily the worst slums but those which offer the highest profits. In the new buildings developers rarely do more than meet the minimum legal requirements, and these they will ignore if they can. The post-war blocks are rapidly becoming slums because of poor building standards, a disinclination amongst landlords to pay for maintenance, and because buildings are used by more people than they were designed for. (A profit-conscious developer will build flats as if they would be used by, say, four people, knowing full well they will be lived in by twice this number.) An official statement on conditions in post-war buildings is very blunt:

> The people in these buildings may well present a more serious health hazard, and bring up their children mentally, socially, and physically more handicapped or stunted than if they had been in controlled or even uncontrolled squatter shacks on the hillsides.[2]

I could not adequately describe the filth, the infestation, the lack of light and fresh air that is typical of most buildings, pre-war or post-war. When a flat contains two or three times as many as it was meant to be used by, even the ordinary daily routines, cooking or washing for example, become major problems. With rooms partitioned into cubicles, many occupants have neither light nor ventilation. When we add to these conditions the fact that, by overseas standards, much building work is shoddy and property is rarely repaired, it can be imagined how conditions steadily deteriorate.

In very few buildings is life physically comfortable. There is a constant struggle to maintain the high Chinese standards of personal hygiene and cleanliness in cooking, to keep cool in the hot humid summers, and even to obtain a little quiet for children to do their homework. On top of all this, many domestic units are used for industrial and commercial purposes as well as for living.[3]

---

[1] *Final Report of the Special Committee on Housing, 1956–58* (mimeo), p. 8.

[2] *1963 Working Party Report*, op. cit., pp. 7–8.

[3] The situation cannot have greatly improved since 1957 when only 66 per

One must wonder again why more people have not become squatters. It is indeed fortunate for the Colony that however bad housing conditions are, life in most other respects has a great deal to offer Hong Kong's citizens.

10   Population and housing densities

In 1931–61, the density of population on Hong Kong Island rose 144 per cent; in Kowloon and New Kowloon it rose 496·2 per cent.[1] In 1961, there were on Hong Kong Island, 54 persons to the acre; in Kowloon, 306 to the acre; in New Kowloon, 112 to the acre.[2] These figures are somewhat misleading. Hong Kong Island is sparsely populated over most of its area. The bare steep hills included in the land area of the urban boundaries reduce densities on paper while doing nothing to reduce them in reality. Some 80 per cent of the Colony's three and three-quarter million inhabitants live in only 12 square miles of the total land surface of 400 square miles.

Densities are not uniform throughout the urban area. There are 14 'black spots'—Census Divisions with populations in excess of 1,800 to the acre.[3] (They contain about 200,000 people.) Until 1962, legally there was nothing to prevent the erection of a twenty-storey building, raising the density of population on its site from 2,000 to 10,000 to the acre.[4] Redevelopment always means higher densities because it involves more intensive use of the ground area. Densities will get higher for as long as redevelopment continues. With the urban land shortage, increased densities through new buildings seem unavoidable.

It is more difficult to generalize about housing densities. There is a great deal of unevenness in the square footage of living space per person. There are some well-known 'black spots'.[5] An unofficial survey of the four worst districts in 1956 gave an overall average of 15 square feet per adult. In the worst of the four, there

[1] *1961 Census Report*, op. cit., vol. II, p. lxii.
[2] ibid., vol. II, Table 019, p. 11.   [3] ibid.   [4] *HKAR, 1963*, p. 36.
[5] For early post-war examples, see R. H. Hughes, 'Hong Kong: An Urban Study', *The Geographical Journal*, vol. CXVII, part I, March 1951, p. 11.

cent of tenements and 74·6 per cent of non-tenements were used purely for residence. W. F. Maunder and E. F. Szczepanik, *Housing Survey, 1957*, op. cit., part I, Table S20A.

were only 12 square feet per adult.[1] In 1963, it was not unknown for 60 or 70 persons to be living in a three-room flat.[2]

Fortunately, we do have a benchmark to help us. In 1957, the average number of square feet per person was 30.[3] Twenty-nine per cent of households had a habitable area of 50–90 square feet; 32 per cent had a habitable area of less than 50 square feet.[4] These figures tell their own tale of overcrowding.

The legal minimum area per adult was, until 1960, 35 square feet.[5] It was, in fact, impossible to enforce this minimum after 1937.[6] The average number of persons per unit of accommodation jumped from 9·9 in 1936 to 17·4 in 1939 with the pre-war refugee influx. By 1947, it had reached 21·7. Thanks to the numbers who had been resettled, the figure had dropped by 1956 to 19·6 per unit.[7] Not surprisingly, Hong Kong's housing standards were declared to be as low as, if not lower than, those of any Colonial Territory in 1957.[8] Since 1957, the overall position seems to have improved. By 1963, the average number of persons per unit of accommodation had dropped to 16·83.[9]

Although there has been an improvement in the general position, overcrowding in pre-war buildings has become worse. I have already discussed the reasons for this. We should now look at the results. The serious consequences of this overcrowding seem to have first become apparent in 1960. In late 1960, I am informed, Tenancy Inquiry Bureaux officers discovered, for the first time, numbers of double- and triple-tier bunks in passage-ways, verandahs and cocklofts in Kowloon. I understand, too,

---

[1] *HKAR, 1956*, p. 144.   [2] *1963 Working Party Report*, op. cit., p. 8.

[3] W. F. Maunder and E. F. Szczepanik, *Housing Survey, 1957*, op. cit., part I, Table S16A.

[4] ibid., part II, Table H50A.

[5] There now appears to be no legal minimum.

[6] *Memorandum for the Special Committee on Housing. The Housing Situation, June 1957: and its Probable Future Development under Existing Conditions* (mimeo, unpublished), 1 October 1957.

[7] ibid., Appendix D.

[8] *Memorandum for the Special Committee on Housing: Housing Standards* (mimeo, unpublished), 8 October 1957.

[9] Calculated from the urban population, less the number resettled, divided by the total number of units of accommodation. (This is how Government calculated the figures for previous years.) This is not a very good measure. It exaggerates overcrowding for 1956 and 1963 and ignores differences in the size of units. With the data available, I have been unable to devise a better measure.

that the census enumerators found large numbers of households (estimated at anything between 5,000 and 50,000) sharing bed-spaces on a shift system. Since this was previously unknown to the Tenancy Inquiry Bureaux, it is probable that this was a very recent innovation in 1961. These developments in 1960–1 indicate the seriousness of overcrowding in old buildings.

We do have a fairly accurate picture of overcrowding in the resettlement blocks. These multi-storey blocks were planned from the beginning to allow only 24 square feet per adult. The Resettlement Department admitted that: 'The building on a large scale of permanent sub-standard cubicle accommodation [i.e. the multi-storey blocks] would in the long run prove an embarrassment rather than an asset to the community.' It was also admitted that: 'The density, ventilation and amenities of these blocks are not satisfactory.'[1] Government justified its low standards on the grounds that to provide the legal minimum of 35 square feet per adult would have increased costs by a third and required more land.[2]

Government's principal miscalculation was of the rents former squatters could afford. Had Government set more realistic rents, it could have provided more space for its tenants.[3] Resettlement estate tenants could have afforded more than $14 a month for 120 square feet. As I have suggested, it is extremely doubtful whether squatters have been the poorest class in the Colony. Even in 1952, the Chairman of the Urban Council believed that squatters could find $35 a month for public housing.[4] In 1957, occupants of ordinary domestic space were paying a rent 6·5 times higher than that of similar accommodation in resettlement estates[5] —though there was no great difference between their average incomes. And the gap between what settlers and the rest of the community pay for housing has widened because resettlement rents have remained fixed while other rents have risen. By setting the standard resettlement rent too low, the community has obtained public housing of a lower standard than necessary.

[1] *HKAR*, 1954, p. 4.

[2] *Resettlement Department Annual Report (RDAR), 1954–55*, p. 46.

[3] Though this would have slowed down the programme. But is there any point in building permanent structures which are sub-standard? Is this not a case of building today the slums of tomorrow?

[4] D. C. Bray, *Survey of Squatters*, op. cit.

[5] C. S. Hui, W. F. Maunder and J. Tsao, *Hong Kong's Resettled Squatters*, op. cit., p. 93.

In 1959, for health reasons, Government recommended lowering resettlement densities to allow 35 square feet per adult. This proved impossible to carry into effect, and today the area per person is often officially reduced by a third as residents' families increase in size.[1] Resettlement accommodation, while not as overcrowded as the worst private buildings, is at least as overcrowded as private housing as a whole.

Not surprisingly, the most popular accommodation in Hong Kong is that for which the Housing Authority is responsible. This is designed to give tenants a minimum of 35 square feet per adult, private cooking and sanitary facilities and a balcony. The rents charged are in line with those in private housing.[2] If all housing in the Colony were of this standard—minimal though it is by comparison with the west—the housing problems of Hong Kong would be a lot nearer solution. As things are, it seems impossible in the foreseeable future to provide 35 square feet for every adult in the Colony.

11   The social implications of the urban housing problem

We can make a number of generalizations about effects of inferior, overcrowded accommodation. The cramped space in which most families live restricts the activities of their members. What can a man do in even 35 square feet? The poor conditions make the home very unattractive, and it is a place in which members of the family spend as little time as possible—especially in the summer. This leads, for example, to children wandering unsupervised in the streets where they have plenty of opportunity to observe such undesirable activities as drug-taking.[3] Again, the city is so crowded that there are only 236·09 acres of public parks, playgrounds, rest gardens etc. in the urban area.[4] Under the town planning standards adopted after the war, there should be at least 783·25 acres.[5] The difficulties of finding accommodation makes

[1] *1963 Working Party Report,* op. cit., p. 9.

[2] This housing is described by J. T. Fraser, *Annual Report of the Hong Kong Housing Authority for the Period 1st April 1962 to 31st March 1962.*

[3] This is made more serious by the fact that most children only go to half-day school sessions.

[4] G. M. Tingle, *Annual Departmental Report of the Chairman, Urban Council and Director of Urban Services for the Financial Year 1962–63,* p. 69.

[5] These standards are laid down in Sir Patrick Abercrombie, *Hong Kong Preliminary Planning Report,* Hong Kong 1948, p. 7.

it hard for people to live as close to their blood relatives and clansmen as they might wish. On the other hand, this difficulty of finding any homes at all in post-war Hong Kong seems to have prevented the development of 'villages' in the urban community. People are mixed together regardless of their origins. Apart from a few exceptions (Shanghainese in North Point and Chui Chow in Kwun Tong), there are no linguistic or dialect concentrations. This mixing up of the community seems to be useful in preventing the urban area from breaking up into self-contained (and, possibly, hostile) groups of people each located in a particular district.

Table XII:[1] Tuberculosis, infant and neo-natal mortality rates

Year	Tuberculosis Death rate per 100,000	Percentage of total deaths	Infant mortality Rate per 1,000 births	Neo-natal mortality Rate per 1,000 births
1953	130·6	11·16	73·6	25·8
1958	83·8	11·2	54·3	23·4
1963	49·05	8·9	32·9	18·9

We can be sure that the lack of amenities and the gross over-crowding do not promote the welfare of Hong Kong. But it is very difficult to find indicators which will permit the accurate measurement of the ill-effects that one imagines must follow from bad housing. A 1962 ECAFE Seminar listed the major consequences of urbanization in Asia: health hazards; inadequate housing; weak educational system; lack of opportunity for advancement; crime and anti-social behaviour; lack of recreational facilities; the need to develop home economics extension and training for family life.[2]

Hong Kong certainly suffers from inadequate housing and lack of recreational facilities. But the rest of this list would not apply to Hong Kong in 1963. If we take two criteria—health and crime—we find that Hong Kong's squalid housing is like a benign tumour—unpleasant but not fatal. Despite the housing problems we have described, health standards have risen and 'Serious Crime' has diminished. Table XII shows a dramatic improvement in the tuberculosis and infant mortality rates. The importance of this

[1] *HKAR, 1963*, Appendix VII, pp. 453–5.
[2] W. W. Yung, *Report of Attendance at the ECAFE Seminar on Urban Development Held in Singapore from 10 to 20 December 1962*, W.H.O. WPR/ER/1, 21 January 1963, p. 4.

table is not that it proves that housing has no effects on health. Health standards would improve a lot more if housing were better. The table shows that even when housing was getting worse (1953–8), these death rates fell. The fall is undoubtedly due to better medical services and a higher standard of living. But Table XII does suggest that the effects of poor housing are very much offset by rising standards in other areas of life. The crime figures tell exactly the same story and help to demonstrate that the evil consequences of inadequate housing can be minimized through rising economic prosperity and an efficient government machine.

Table XIII: Serious crimes reported to the police (per 1,000 of the population)

1953	1958	1963
9·07	6·03	3·82

(Source: *Hong Kong Annual Reports*)

Adverse effects of inadequate housing have shown themselves in two fields. The first is the effects on society of large numbers living in squatter colonies largely unpoliced and unregulated by Government. Here racketeers flourish, and there is a real danger of open disaffection[1]—especially when Government tries to introduce some control in them. There is a grave political danger that these squatter colonies might become a law unto themselves as one well-known area (Rennies Mill) was until 1961. Improvement of conditions in squatter areas requires Government intervention. But this intervention is resented.

The second field is resettlement. The social consequences of resettling people in multi-storey blocks have not been altogether favourable. The settlers have gained a great deal financially. Their fixed low rents give them an advantage over the rest of the community. As wages rise, resettlement rents form a smaller and smaller proportion of incomes. In addition, the resettlement estates have been provided with a wide range of welfare facilities which are not so generally enjoyed by the rest of the community. There are cheap schools ($6 a month per child), free or low-cost clinics (50¢–$2), milk bars, school meals, libraries and community and social centres. The cost of living is thus much lower in the estates than it is for the average Hong Kong resident.

[1] *1963 Working Party Report*, op. cit., p. 13.

The significance of the superior financial position of resettled people can be demonstrated in two ways. Analysis of data in the Department of Anatomy, University of Hong Kong, suggests that, on average, children in resettlement schools are as tall and as heavy as children classified as belonging to the 'high' socio-economic group in the Colony.[1] This would support the contention that settlers enjoy higher standards of living than the community at large.

The second indication of the greater wealth of resettlement estates is the amount of private property tenants have begun to buy as investments. This practice was almost unknown until a year or so ago. With their savings, these Government tenants are becoming private landlords.[2] Settlers owning $150,000 to $200,000 worth of property are not uncommon. Well-informed sources say that money is flowing from resettlement estates into private property at the rate of several millions a month. These people are not buying homes for themselves. They are seeking profitable outlets for their obviously considerable savings.

Although the financial position of settlers has improved, their new environment seems to have created certain social problems.[3] I should emphasize, however, that these problems do not make people any less eager for resettlement accommodation. The ordinary person probably does not realize that there are any drawbacks to life in multi-storey blocks. There are, however, indications that social tensions are increased in moving to resettlement estates. While settlers are, in general, as law-abiding as the rest of the community, the rate of common assaults is significantly higher amongst them than in other parts of the city.[4] Similarly, the proportion of family disputes is almost twice as high in estates as in the rest of the urban community.[5]

Those familiar with the estates tell me that adolescents show

[1] I should emphasize that this is my own conclusion from the data for which the Department of Anatomy is not responsible.

[2] *FEER*, vol. XLV, no. 5, 30 July 1964, p. 217.

[3] These are similar to those found in England among slum dwellers who have been rehoused. See, for example, Michael Young and Peter Wilmott, 'Families on the Move', *Family and Kinship in East London*, London 1962, part 2.

[4] This conclusion is based on my own analysis of unpublished police statistics. I should emphasize that the police are not responsible for this conclusion.

[5] *Secretariat for Chinese Affairs, Quarterly Reports* (mimeo, unpublished).

marked 'teddy-boy' tendencies. I understand, too, that there are
proportionately more juveniles on probation from resettlement
estates than the rest of the Colony. The Resettlement Department's *Annual Reports* have laid stress on the need to teach tenants
of multi-storey blocks basic hygiene, proper disposal of rubbish
and so on. (Indeed, the estates seem to be dirtier than squatter
areas.) All in all, there is strong evidence that on the estates there
has been a weakening of social values and controls and a rise in
social tensions.[1]

Why is this? It is hard to give a definite answer. Possibly,
because of the unpleasantness which accompanies the process of
resettlement.[2] Possibly, too, people find it difficult to adjust, to
the change from the independent life of the squatter to the
regulated life of the estates. In Hong Kong, most people have
little contact with Government. In squatter areas, the contact is
even less. On the estates, however, there is much closer contact
with officialdom than in the rest of the community. Rents have to
be paid promptly. There are strict rules governing tenancies.
Resettlement Department officers are stationed on the estates to
enforce these rules. Businesses have to be registered and must
conform with the various ordinances and rules that apply to them.
The police patrol the estates. In short, the settler is brought into
contact with the host of official regulations necessary for the
efficient administration of large concentrations of people. This
contact is something which, in most cases, is outside the experience of the former squatters.[3]

Other factors which may be a source of strain include the fact
that the squatter has no control over whom his neighbours will
be nor to which estate he will be sent. The fact that estates are on
the fringe of the urban area (at some distance from cinemas, big
restaurants and shops, tea-houses and other forms of amusement)
may, perhaps, create a feeling of isolation from the rest of the
community. The situation has not been helped by the way in

[1] This has been remarked on to me by a number of professional social
workers. It was, perhaps, no accident that the 1956 riots began in an estate.
[2] The degree of unpleasantness involved can be gathered from *1963
Working Party Report*, op. cit., p. 18.
[3] People who have spent several years under the Communist régime in
China seem to adapt best to life on the estates, I am told by officers working
in the estates. They take official regulation for granted and appear to understand the necessity for rules and regulations. They also have a clearer idea
of what they are entitled to receive from officials.

which estates have been planned. Unlike new towns in the United Kingdom,[1] the estates have not been designed to meet any wider needs of their inhabitants than that of providing accommodation for large numbers and the most basic amenities.

A factor of greater significance than those set out above is the lack of privacy and the high densities of multi-storey blocks. There are some 2,000 people living in a seven-storey block. Access to each family's room is by a corridor running the length of each floor. In summer, the windows and doors of the rooms have to remain open because of the heat. Sanitary facilities are shared by each floor. This amounts to communal living. There is as little protection from the curiosity of neighbours as in tenement cubicles. But whereas Hong Kong Chinese seem to be able to tolerate communal life with 20 other people living on one floor or in one flat, communal life involving 200 is more than they can comfortably bear.[2] Interestingly, Government has remarked: 'The essential need is to restore to these deprived lives something of the dignity and pride which privacy affords and communal living, for all its advantages, denies.'[3]

It is significant that the fortunate few who have been resettled in single-storey cottages do not appear to suffer from the problems commonly found in the estates. Since the major difference between cottage areas and resettlement estates is one of densities and communal living, I think it is safe to assume that much of the estates' social tensions is caused by the numbers of people who live on them and the lack of privacy.

It may seem that I have devoted overmuch space to resettlement estates. However, I feel justified in discussing them at length. Already one-sixth of the Colony's population is living in them. Space for another 900,000 adults is planned 1964–70 and a technical planning target of additional resettlement accommodation for 1,900,000 in 1964–74 has already been set. The estates are too important for their problems to be ignored by the rest of Hong Kong.[4]

---

[1] Estates are in fact similar in size, at least, to new towns, ranging from 10,000 to 64,000 inhabitants. *RDAR, 1962–63*, Appendix I, p. 29.

[2] The problem of privacy will largely disappear in the new-style blocks now being constructed. See ibid., p. 13. But the problem remains of what to do to remedy matters in existing blocks.

[3] *HKAR, 1956*, p. 29.

[4] *Review of Policies 1964*, op. cit., p. 10.

12 Home ownership

In western countries, people are encouraged in a number of ways to own their own homes. There are felt to be social advantages in home ownership. It gives a man a stake and roots in his community—an important point in an immigrant community like Hong Kong. It provides his family with security. Even if the bread-winner becomes unemployed, falls sick or dies, his family is certain of a roof over its head. In Hong Kong, there has been no way in which a man could buy his house except through his own unaided efforts,[1] unlike western countries.

There were in 1961 581,077 urban households.[2] Of these 14·21 per cent owned their own homes.[3] When we look at the major groups of home owners by type of accommodation, the significance of the number of home owners is considerably reduced. Of the 82,576 home-owning households, 16,877 owned a whole flat and 13,627 a room or cubicle in permanent domestic buildings. But 30,962 owned a wooden house or shack. Thus, 37·5 per cent of house owners were, in fact, squatters occupying illegal structures which will eventually be torn down and their owners made tenants in resettlement estates.

Widely spread ownership of housing is not an unmixed blessing in Hong Kong. Since the war, buildings have got larger and taller. They are divided into large numbers of small units which are sold off singly. This has created multi-ownership of buildings on a vast scale as is shown in Table XIV:[4]

Table XIV: Increase of multi-ownership of buildings, 1948–62

Year	Number of new buildings	Number of shares
1948	1	5
1953	40	246
1958	670	9,955
1962	260	9,749

(Note: the number of shares is approximately equal to the number of owners.)

---

[1] This has already changed with the assistance of the Commonwealth Development Corporation.

[2] All data on home ownership is from *1961 Census Report*, op. cit., vol. II, Tables 012–013, pp. 3–9.

[3] This does not contradict what I said earlier about few people buying more than one flat. Each flat, though owned by only one person, is usually shared by several households.

[4] *Report of the Working Party on Sub-divided Buildings, 1962*, Appendix I, p. 125; *HKAR, 1963*, p. 62.

Multi-ownership has created many problems.[1] Amongst the legal ones are the question of public liability; the rights to sue and negotiate; how to enforce the provisions of Crown Leases for the proper use and upkeep of the building. There are numerous social problems as well. Such common facilities as corridors and stairways are usually filthy, and the building fabric is not properly maintained because of the difficulty of the large numbers of owners in a single building co-operating to manage their property.

Multi-ownership has another disadvantage. If ownership of property were concentrated in a few hands, it would be easier for Government to exert pressure on landlords to keep buildings in a decent state and in good repair. As it is, with so much division of ownership of property, it would be almost impossible to police whatever measures Government might introduce for the welfare of the inhabitants of these large buildings. The disadvantages of multi-ownership are so numerous that, until they are overcome, it seems that more will be lost than gained by increases in the numbers owning the Colony's accommodation.

13 Women and property

Traditionally, among the Chinese, the right to own land belonged to men.[2] In the past, Hong Kong appears to have followed this custom. A woman's savings were used not to buy land and property but to buy gold and jewellery; or they were loaned out at interest; or, very often, simply hoarded. This has now changed. Table XV indicates the importance of women as purchasers of accommodation.

Table XV:[3] Sales of new flats in new buildings, 1956–63

Number of sales in sample	Number of purchases made by:					Total purchases involving women
	one married woman	one spinster	one widow	jointly with a man or men	by more than one woman	
691	235	36	20	49	34	376

Over half the sales of new flats 1956–63 were transactions which involved women. Very few of the purchases were made in

---

[1] *Report on Sub-divided Buildings,* op. cit., pp. 1–6, gives a good description of these problems.

[2] Maurice Freedman, *Lineage Organization in Southeastern China,* London 1958, pp. 11–16.

[3] Survey of Land Office Records.

partnership with men. Thirty-four per cent of all purchases were made by married women acting by themselves. These women appear to be of every standard of education—from the illiterate to those writing educated hands. There is no correlation between the price of flats or their locality and the number of women buyers. Indeed, I have found only one building in this period in which less than half the flats were sold to women. Supplementary evidence does not support the opinion that any great proportion of these flats are only nominally owned by women; that in reality they belong to men (husbands, brothers and so on). All the evidence suggests that most of the flats bought by women genuinely belong to them. The Land Office records further indicate that female ownership of property until 1956 was not very important.[1]

Property-owning by women is a significant change. In the first place, it cuts across the traditional order of things. More important, it gives a woman security in a way not conferred by jewellery or hoarded bank-notes—or even by money-lending. A woman cannot be deprived of a flat she owns. It cannot be mortgaged or transferred without her consent. A husband can always take away money or jewellery by force or stealth if necessary. Thirdly, a woman owning a flat is less economically dependent on the men in her family. She can use her property either to obtain income or to live in.

It is not difficult to see why women should have taken to buying flats. There is a general movement in Asia to grant women a more equal position with men.[2] In China, the Communists have radically altered the economic and social status of women.[3] In Hong Kong itself, the literacy rate of women under 24 years is very close to their male contemporaries',[4] which indicates a growing equality of opportunity. The number of women owning property

[1] All but one of these flats are in buildings that have replaced property exclusively owned by men. Redevelopment has caused a substantial transfer of property-owning from men to women.

[2] Philip M. Hauser (ed.), *Urbanization in Asia and the East*, Calcutta 1957, p. 40.

[3] C. K. Yang, *The Chinese Family in the Communist Revolution*, Massachusetts Institute of Technology 1959, pp. 141–9.

[4] *1961 Census Report*, op. cit., vol. II, Table 159, p. 69. Even in the rural and conservative New Territories there has been a great change in this field. The female literacy rate jumped from 4·14 per cent to 44·61 per cent 1931–61. ibid., vol. II, Table 158, p. 69.

is so large because renting out flats is very like money-lending (a traditional female practice) but with better security. It is a simple business in which little technical knowledge is required. Buying flats to rent out is an attractive investment because of the continual rises in rents. In addition, landlords enjoy a superior social status in Chinese society. Unlike Singapore Chinese,[1] Hong Kong men do not seem to resent the development of economic independence amongst women—at least, not that independence created by property-ownership. At the lowest reckoning, property-owning by women marks an important extension of the economic activities of Chinese women in Hong Kong. Because this development has occurred in a society which traditionally has not made provision for female-property owning on a large scale, it could call for some painful adjustment in the relationship between men and women.

14   Housing and the Hong Kong economy

The housing shortage has fed a long-term boom in the construction industry. In 1950/1–1962/3, $2,588,000,000 of private building work has been completed. Of this $1,629,000,000 (63 per cent) represented domestic accommodation.[2] The building and construction industry employed 58,209 in 1961. Its relative importance as a source of employment can be judged from Table XVI:

Table XVI:[3] Working population by selected industries, 1961

Industry	Numbers employed	Percentage of working population
Textiles	195,702	16·42
Retail and wholesale trade	88,196	7·40
Building	58,209	4·89
Food manufacturing	57,196	4·80

The numbers employed in building are equal to almost a third of those engaged in textiles—the Colony's biggest export industry. Demand for housing has helped to develop a major industry and has contributed substantially to the creation of employment.

[1] Maurice Freedman, *Chinese Family and Marriage in Singapore*, London 1957, pp. 42–3, 56–7.
[2] *Rating and Valuation Annual Report, 1962–63*, op. cit., Table X, p. 44.
[3] *1961 Census Report*, op. cit., vol. III, Table 237, p. 25.

If we examine the broader relationship between housing and the economy, we find there are many costs created by the housing shortage. If Hong Kong were adequately supplied with accommodation, both the public and the private sector would have larger sums for investment in other fields more directly productive of economic growth. There would be, for instance, more to spend on roads and education, more for new plant and capital equipment. With better housing conditions, there might be an improvement in the productivity of the labour force.

Table XVII: Visible trade deficit, 1959–63 ($ HK millions)

1959	1,800
1960	1,920
1961	2,040
1962	2,270
1963	2,421

(Source: *Hong Kong Annual Reports*)

On the other hand, it is widely held that the boom in property (housing in particular) has been of great advantage in at least one respect: attracting investments from overseas. This is an important matter because of the large and increasing deficit in the visible balance of trade which is set out in Table XVII. Some $6,500,000,000 of overseas capital is estimated to have been invested in Hong Kong, 1945–62. Of this, some $5,000,000,000 was from Overseas Chinese.[1] Not less than half the Overseas Chinese investment would have been in property (mainly housing).

The profits arising from property investment are felt to stimulate local savings and encourage people to invest rather than to hoard. The property industry helps the accumulation of capital, for the profits made by developers appear to be reinvested in Hong Kong, not only in other property but also in manufacturing industries and commercial enterprises.[2] Rising rents have probably held down demand for consumption goods, thus checking imports and encouraging exports.

This discussion of the economic benefits which have followed from the housing boom is not altogether satisfactory. Would

[1] Hu Lan-shih, 'Overseas Chinese Capital in Hong Kong', *Economic Bulletin*, 19 August 1963.
[2] Developers usually have a wide range of business interests. Property is often regarded as a profitable side-line.

Overseas Chinese have sent money to the Colony in smaller quantities had there been no boom? They sent money to the Colony not simply because of its profitable investment opportunities, rather, however, because Hong Kong is the natural refuge of Chinese 'scare' money in politically troubled and often anti-Chinese South East Asia. Similarly, Chinese believe strongly in saving as much of their income as possible, so perhaps the effects of the housing boom on savings and consumption are not very important. Even the employment given by the building industry may not be as significant as first appears because the Colony has suffered from a shortage of workers and has had low unemployment rates in recent years.

All one can safely say about the favourable influence of the housing boom on the economy is that its effect is marginal. The shortage of housing and the rising prices it has commanded have reinforced certain favourable factors which already existed—savings, overseas investment in the Colony, etc. Since these factors are amongst those most necessary for economic progress, it is just as well that the housing situation has helped to strengthen them.

15   Conclusions

Urban housing in Hong Kong is a serious problem. Its ill-effects have been mitigated to a considerable degree by rising prosperity and Government's efforts. While there has been an improvement in the private sector since 1957, much of the improvement has been achieved only at the cost of increasing numbers of people who become squatters. Serious criticisms can be made of the type of housing in which Government has resettled squatters, but steps have been taken to improve the design of future multi-storey blocks. A host of charges can be levelled at Hong Kong's housing, but in criticizing, we should not lose sight of the efforts being made by the private and public sectors. New permanent domestic accommodation was provided for an additional 1,118,000 persons, 1958-63. This is an impressive achievement by any standards. It should be remembered, too, that Hong Kong is a small economy dependent for its survival on the uncertain business of selling goods to foreign countries.

The basic problem in tackling the housing situation is one of balancing competing demands for capital. Should Government and private investors increase the flow of capital to housing at the expense of the rest of the economy? How far can this be done with safety? But there is no doubt as to which has priority. Unless the economic prosperity of the Colony is secured, it will be impossible to make any progress in tackling the housing situation.

On the one hand, there is the need to see the housing problem against the background of the Colony as a whole. But, on the other hand, no community, not even Hong Kong, should be satisfied until all its citizens can take for granted the right to decent homes. Hong Kong has not arrived at this happy position but she has made a valiant attack on her housing problems. The success that has been achieved is all the more remarkable because Hong Kong began with few natural advantages. It is also a tribute to Hong Kong that the Colony has accepted a large degree of public responsibility for the solution of the housing shortage without discriminating against the post-war immigrants who originally created the problem. In Hong Kong, housing may be bad. But at least all share in the same chance of improvement.[1]

In the four years since 1963, the bottom has dropped out of the market for private accommodation and rents have fallen very widely. In part, this is the result of the cumulative effects of the resettlement programme which has absorbed a great proportion of housing demand (the millionth tenant entered resettlement accommodation in October 1967). But more important, it is due to a decline in the elasticity of demand for housing in recent years.[2] Government is now tackling the problem of improving the standards of public housing (densities in particular) and is moving towards a slum clearance policy.[3] On the social implications of overcrowding in resettlement estates, it is significant

---

[1] The research for this paper was financed through a Commonwealth Scholarship awarded by the Government of Hong Kong.

[2] The unpublished data sheets used for the *Household Expenditure Survey, 1963/64* and the *Consumer Price Index*, Hong Kong 1965, show that the expenditure elasticity of demand for housing is not only less than 1 but declined significantly between 1958 and 1963/4. (This survey is the one referred to earlier in the text as the 1963/4 Survey.) I have not yet published the results of my analysis of these data but I made use of them in presenting evidence to the Commission of Inquiry into the Kowloon Disturbances, 1966 (Morning Session, 8 August 1966).

[3] See *Report of the Housing Board for the Period 1.4.65 to 31.3.66* and *Report of the Working Party on Slum Clearance and the effects on Urban Redevelopment etc.*

that the serious Kowloon riots of 1966 and the communist inspired disturbances of 1967 both recruited young demonstrators in the initial stages from Kowloon resettlement blocks. It is only fair to add that the 'teddy boy' element soon lost intreest in the 1967 disturbances when the communists showed the full extent of their political virulence.

X

SOME SOCIOLOGICAL ASPECTS OF THE ILLEGAL USE OF NARCOTICS IN HONG KONG[1]

Michael G. Whisson

1 Introduction

Opium has been used for its euphoric and medicinal effects for many centuries in China.[2] With the expansion of trade between Britain, India and China in the eighteenth century, however, the extent of smoking increased until it became a matter of imperial concern, both on account of its evil social effects and its cost in foreign exchange. In 1800, Emperor Kiaking forbade the importation and growth of opium, but this edict had no effect and the illicit trade continued to grow. In 1860, after the second 'Opium War', the importation was legalized, and remained legal until 1917.[3]

With the establishment of the League of Nations, international co-operation was instituted to reduce the traffic, and Hong Kong attempted to phase out the use of opium in the colony. This had been first attempted following the International Opium Conference at Shanghai in 1909, but had proved ineffective. The importation of opium became a government monopoly, exercised through a private company from 1909 to 1940, when the monopoly was terminated and all imports of opium and its derivatives, other than for medicinal purposes, became illegal.[4] While the phasing out of opium had seemed excellent in theory, in practice smuggling replaced importation by the monopoly, and Hong Kong, a customs-free port, was almost powerless to stop it.

In China, despite edicts and sporadic attempts to reduce opium

---

[1] The research upon which this paper is based was made under the auspices of the Hong Kong Discharged Prisoners' Aid Society, to whom acknowledgement should be made.

[2] *The War against Opium* (Tientsin Press Ltd 1922) records that opium was recognized as a cure for dysentery in the tenth century. An anti-opium edict, issued by Emperor Yung Cheng in 1729, was aimed at smoking, not at the medicinal use of the drug.

[3] Evan Luard, *Britain and China*, London 1962, p. 25.

[4] G. B. Endacott and A. Hinton, *Fragrant Harbour*, London 1962, p. 82.

smoking, no real progress was made until the Communists gained complete control of the country in 1949. From then on, Hong Kong and Macau became the refuge of those who wanted opium, as well as of those who had fled for economic and political reasons.

Some of the refugees from the north of China brought with them the art of making heroin from opium or morphine, and as police pressure on the opium divans increased, forcing them further from the centres of Hong Kong and Kowloon, many addicts changed from using opium to the cheaper and more convenient heroin. This was scarcely recognized as being widespread until about 1955. Until 1958, when the walled city of Kowloon was brought into the orbit of vigorous police activity, there remained a place in the heart of the colony where drugs were freely bought and sold, a place which could form the base for more wide-ranging trafficking in the colony. It is against this background of tolerated vice that one must see, at least in part, the place of narcotic drugs in Hong Kong today.

The attitude of the Chinese towards opium varied considerably from place to place and from social class to social class in pre-revolution China. In Kwangtung, where opium was plentiful, there were smokers in every class of society. Among the wealthy the habit was approved and a rich father would encourage his son to take opium. Among the sophisticated urban businessmen and the landlords, the appearance of the opium pipe was as indispensable to the conclusion of a business deal or a good meal as liquor in the west. It was also considered the least of the vices which might ruin a wealthy family. Excessive indulgence in sexual adventures, drinking or gambling was felt to be far more destructive of individual health and family fortunes than the regular use of opium; and opium, it was argued, calmed the passions and excesses of youth—so reducing the temptations of other vices. But while this was the attitude of the wealthy families, the common people, particularly those in the rural areas, were less impressed by the social niceties.

Petty tradesmen, craftsmen and peasants were more aware of the dangers of opium, and the addicts who had lost their property and their capacity to earn an honest living, through over-indulgence in the drug, were the objects of suspicion and scorn. A young man might try a little in the divans when he visited the towns, but he would no more boast of it within the family than he would boast of his visits to the brothels after smoking. A family would lose face among its peers in the village if one of its sons was a known addict, and there was no controlled institutional framework within which any but the old men might take modest amounts with approval. Those who used opium were considered to be deviants, and tended to drift into the urban delinquent strata of society, assisting in divans, gambling houses and similar businesses.

The pre-revolutionary Chinese situation was parallel in some respects to that found in eighteenth-century English society, where 'cordial for the vapours'[1] was admissible for the ladies, while gin was abhorred by the middle classes as the scourge of the indigent poor and criminal elements. In the setting of Chinese high society, whether it was legal or not, opium had its proper place. Social pressures controlled its use, the individual users remaining within their normal social group. Outside that class, the individual would tend to be forced out of his family group into the company of other addicts.

The enormous expansion in the use of opium, due to British promotion of the trade, was followed in the 1930s by the introduction of large quantities of heroin by the Japanese and by northern Chinese learning the art of manufacturing heroin. These events have been used to foster the myth that the evils of opiates stem from the foreigners. In addition to being a sop to the pride of the Cantonese, this myth could well be a minor factor encouraging Cantonese apathy in dealing with what they consider to be an evil in their society. Since the foreigner brought the drugs in, and the foreigner controls the port through the colonial government, then it is really for the foreigner to stop the traffic and the addiction, just as China has done.

Over the past ten years or so, Government efforts to suppress the traffic have been developed, enlarged and made more efficient. Police and Preventive Service techniques have been improved, and their efforts have been reflected, in part, by the steady increase in the price of heroin, together with an increase in adulteration of the drug. Despite these efforts, the volume of heroin and morphine seized in a year has yet to reach 8 per cent of the minimum estimated needs of the colony's addicts.[2]

[1] R. C. Sheridan, *The Rivals*.

[2] Total seizures of heroin and morphine have not exceeded 280 kg. in a year. Addicts in custody and undergoing voluntary treatment claim to have

The slow implementation of the laws relating to opiates, at a time when there was not only a large number of drug users, but also a large number of refugees, some of whom might well have come in order to maintain their supply of drugs after the Chinese Communist government suppressed the traffic, has had the effect of making a most profitable legitimate trade into a far more lucrative illegal trade. The rewards for the successful trafficker are very great, and he is dealing in a commodity for which the elasticity of demand is very low. His turnover is limited only by the capacity of many of his customers to obtain cash, although the popular image of the addict spending every cent of his income on heroin is not always wholly accurate. The profits from the traffic are available for investment in other forms of crime and corruption, or in legitimate business enterprise.

2   The process of supply

For there to be 50,000 heroin users in Hong Kong (and this is a low estimate based largely on the numbers that are caught) two preconditions must be met. First, there must be a ready source of supply which offers a reasonable profit to the trafficker. Second, there must be a predisposition within the society towards the use of narcotic drugs.

The poppies from which illegal opium, morphine and heroin are derived are grown mainly in a mountainous and largely ungoverned area where Laos, Burma, Thailand and Yunnan Province of China meet.[1] Without an agreement between these four states to make a concerted attack upon these fields, their destruction in one state would be practically pointless, militarily difficult and politically inadvisable, since none would want a dissatisfied peasantry on the borders with their ideological opponents.

From the hills the morphine or opium is carried to the ports of South East Asia from where it is shipped to Hong Kong and

[1] *United Nations Bulletin of Narcotics:* October–December 1964.

---

smoked an average of about 200 mg. per day, which would amount to 3,650 kg. *p.a.*—all of which would be imported as morphine or heroin. The quantity of seizures is recorded in the Annual Reports of the Commissioner of Police (Hong Kong Government Printer). This assumed only 50,000 heroin addicts. In addition to these there are at least 30,000 opium addicts according to unofficial estimates, whose demand for raw opium is not included in the above calculation.

to other parts of the world. For many years Hong Kong was said to be the major centre of distribution for much of the world, having an almost free port, minimal customs inspections, a free currency and a large home market. It is now believed locally that these advantages have been outweighed by the relative efficiency of the Preventive Service and the police, and that Hong Kong is no longer the great *entrepôt*.[1] Despite the efforts to prevent them from entering the port, the importation of opiates is still a simple business limited only by the shortages in the growing areas and the imaginations of the smugglers as they think of new ways to bring in their cargo when the old ways are discovered.[2] It is not difficult to conceal four tons in the twenty-five million tons of shipping that passes through Hong Kong in a year.[3]

If seizures are a fair guide to actual imports, then most of the drugs, in value if not in bulk, are brought in in the form of compressed morphine blocks. These have to be processed by a simple technique to make heroin, which is the most popular drug of addiction in the colony.[4] 'Factories'—which may be in private bathrooms—have been found all over the Colony and in Macau, although knowledge of their whereabouts is one of the better guarded secrets. It seems probable that the various sections of the trade—importation, processing and selling—are independently organized and that there is little vertical integration. Each man would tend to know only one or two men, from whom he buys, and to whom he sells. Those who finance the importing and the manufacturing are believed to keep well away from handling the drugs, and hence keep themselves well insulated from the police. Such a structure within the industry eliminates the mythical tycoon, the archetypal Dr No, who controls a vast network, although at each stage there are fortunes to be made. It also makes the task of penetrating the traffic much more difficult for the police, as the traffickers genuinely do not know very much about the business beyond their own specific functions. The result is to

[1] The Press release from the International Seminar on Narcotics Traffic, Paris (November 1964) observes that the main route of entry for narcotics into the U.S.A. is by the 'Eastern Route', i.e. that which enters the U.S.A. through its east coast ports from France, Turkey and the Middle East.

[2] One seizure made by the Police and Preventive Service in 1964 was of blocks of morphine concealed inside sealed tins of coffee.

[3] Annual report of the Department of Commerce and Industry.

[4] See note 2, p. 301, above.

produce something approaching perfect competition within the trade, the chief imperfection in the market stemming from the fact of illegality.

Distribution of the drugs, which are broken down into packets containing about 50 mg. of pure heroin, together with adulterants to make a total of about 80 mg., is carried out by a number of syndicates which buy in bulk and usually distribute through a number of addicted sellers, who permanently man sites known to the addicts in the area. The selling points are readily discovered by the police and are frequently raided. The sellers are arrested, but more are not difficult to recruit from the addict population. A selling point may well reopen for business within half an hour of a raid, having moved to a new location, but leaving another employee of the syndicate behind to direct known customers. Only by observing a selling point, whether mobile or stationary, for a considerable length of time, can the police have much expectation of being able to identify a syndicate and arrest its leaders with a good chance of securing a conviction.

Syndicate organizers, and those involved in the earlier stages of the industry, are very rarely addicts themselves, but addicts are usually employed in the hazardous tasks of selling to the public, carrying small quantities of drugs and money to and from the sellers, and watching for police. These men know little that they can disclose under pressure of withdrawal while being interrogated by the police. When they appear in court on charges of possessing or selling dangerous drugs, their poor physical condition and obvious addiction can make them objects of pity rather than anger to the bench.

Some peddlers, operating on a smaller scale, buy directly from the larger syndicates, middlemen or manufacturers, and provide a home delivery service for more prosperous addicts, who are thus free from almost all risk of detection. The men who actually carry the drugs to the clients are, as far as is known, usually addicts. A similar service is available for tourists who can arrange connections through bars in the tourist areas.

Through the segmented organization described above, heroin of a wide range of quality can be provided to the public with various degrees of security from detection (depending upon the ability and willingness of the customer to pay) with a minimum possibility of any one man or syndicate knowing very much about the industry as a whole. Competition exists between the various selling syndicates through minor variations in the quantity of heroin in a pack, in delivery service, availability at all hours, and in price reductions for bulk purchases. Discounts on bulk purchases enable some addicts to finance their own habits by breaking bulk and selling to their friends, thus drawing in more customers for the trade.

3 The demand for narcotics

The process of supply can be seen simply as a clandestine economic activity with a fairly high degree of risk, producing a correspondingly high profit. In simple terms, the demand for heroin can be seen as being for a commodity which has a very low elasticity of demand in a market which has a built-in tendency to expand. Most addicts spend nearly all their legitimate earnings and beggings on drugs, their consumption varying from day to day as their income varies. Many, particularly among the older men, control their consumption, while others resort to various forms of crime in order to boost their incomes and their consumption of drugs. Since, in order to maintain the effectiveness of the drugs, the quantity consumed must be slowly increased, pressure is placed upon the addict to increase his income by all possible means. The expansion of demand is limited by the probable excess of deaths among old addicts over new users at present,[1] and by the tendency among otherwise law-abiding addicts for their incomes to fall as a result of their addiction when they become unable to hold a steady job.

Three major groups of factors may be seen as predisposing the population of Hong Kong to a high incidence of addiction. First there are the historical and cultural factors which have led to a large number of former opium users being concentrated in Hong Kong. Second, there are the factors which may be subsumed under the rag-bag category of social disorganization or *anomie*.[2] Third, there is the snowball effect—the tendency of addicts to increase their own security of supply by spreading the habit to others.

Since the law was not rigorously enforced for many years after

[1] This is a guess based upon known addicts, i.e. those arrested and convicted on drug charges, and those undergoing voluntary treatment.

[2] *Vide* E. Durkheim, *Suicide*, trans. John A. Spaulding and George Simpson (Glencoe, Ill., 1951), pp. 241 ff.

opium became illegal, divans flourished and a business organization developed to keep them supplied. The existing addict population was reinforced by refugees from China after 1949, creating a large body of opium smokers, and a few heroin users, in the colony. While most would have recognized that opium smoking was actually illegal in Hong Kong, as indeed it had been in China for many years, they would not have considered indulgence in their habit any more blameworthy than that of the motorist who drinks a little, and no more likely to be detected for some time. As police pressure on the divans increased, most smokers changed to the cleaner, cheaper and more convenient heroin, unaware of its far greater potency. For several years, and probably even up to the present, the solid core of the heroin-using population is made up of men who first smoked opium when it was fairly readily obtainable.

It is never sound science to generalize about the psychological characteristics of a people, although it is a most popular recreation among those who have had a passing contact with foreigners. There is, however, in Chinese thought, some emphasis upon the importance of tranquillity in the face of adversity. This can be seen in part as a reaction to natural catastrophes, dense populations and distant administrations. Opium and its derivatives possess the power to relax the smoker, enabling him to put aside the problems which might otherwise disturb him. The positive function of opium within Chinese society may be seen therefore, as a means whereby a cultural value was enhanced by the leaders of society as a social class, and as a means whereby the individual could be relieved of feelings of inadequacy in the face of his innumerable compatriots and his remote rulers.

The social disorganization has stemmed largely from the flood of refugees which has helped to increase the population from about 1·6 million at the end of the war to about 4 million in 1965. Most of the refugees came from the rural or semi-rural areas of Kwangtung, where they had been living in villages made up of one or two clans, which exercised a considerable measure of social control over their members—guarding their morals, arranging their marriages, and providing them with their subsistence through the family farm. The institution of the extended patrilineal family was supported by inherited land as the main capital resource, by the ideological and religious values placed upon filial piety and obedience, and by the physical proximity of the kin group. The Sino-Japanese war, followed by the Communist revolution, the redistribution of land and the flood of refugees, has shattered the integrity and often the existence of the extended family. In some cases individuals have lost touch with all but their own immediate family of orientation, and the impact of resettlement housing, distributed according to bureaucratic estimates of need, has been to limit the capacity of families to regroup within a small area. For the individual this has meant the sudden removal of the most important part of his system of social control, although links of sentiment, often expressed in generous giving and lending, remain within quite large groups. We observed earlier that it was the case in China that opium used in its proper context was approved, but that outside that context it became a vice and the symbol of moral deterioration. For all but a very few wealthy and well-established families, the proper social context has ceased to exist, and that most fragile of institutions, the simple family, lacks the strength to control its deviants in many cases. With heroin easily available and its properties well known and attractive, the deviant can readily express himself in addiction.

The sudden transition from rural to urban living has also made demands upon the working habits of the immigrants, particularly the older men. Many find these new demands a strain. Large manufacturing units, needing regular hours of work and a steady effort throughout the long working day, contrast sharply with the equally strenuous, but less ordered working of the farm, small store or workshop. Many have sought to pursue handicrafts, but in the face of competition from the mass-produced articles, these have tended to become relatively less profitable. Others, lacking skills, have drifted into petty trade as hawkers, or into casual occupations, where the short-term rewards are often far in excess of what they could have earned in industry.[1] Despite the oft-repeated cry from the factories that they are in need of more workers, large numbers of men have been unable or unwilling to make the transition from the rural to the modern industrial environment, and prefer casual occupations. These jobs often demand that a man should work intensively for a period, then be idle for some time. The custom tailors who work through the night to complete an order in twenty-four hours, the dock

[1] Based upon conversations with addicts and hawkers, together with figures from the Annual Reports of the Labour Department (Hong Kong Govt.).

coolies, the rickshaw men and the construction workers hired on a daily basis, are all men upon whom great physical demands may be made for a short period, but who may then find themselves with time on their hands. Such workers, by virtue of their general lack of education in the uses of leisure in an urban environment, their working habits and their inability to adjust to industrial discipline are addiction prone. Heroin gives them the additional energy at those periods when they most need it to sustain a long effort, and provides them with a relaxing and initially inexpensive habit when they are not actually working. For those who have lost their identification with their extended family and have found no other social group to which they can adhere, the fellowship of the 'followers of the way' (*Tao yau*) provides them with an identity and a loyalty which is physically and psychically binding. Similarly, those who, while occupied in factory work, or in some other regular occupation, take heroin, tend to drift out of regular employment into casual occupations where they can be paid on a daily basis and take time off when they need to do so. Casual work thus tends to lead to addiction, and addiction to casual work.

In a rural community, and in any society where handicraft industries are the rule, the individual can expect to become his own boss at some stage—the patriarchal system of the villages made such a position almost inevitable. The Cantonese are frequently categorized by foreigners as men dedicated to becoming their own employers, and hence unwilling to lose themselves in large-scale business. But Hong Kong is slowly eliminating those who would employ themselves by making their efforts uneconomic. Many men therefore, particularly the poorer and less skilled, can look forward to a life of labour, with no security in old age unless they have children able and willing to care for them. This situation contrasts sharply with the declining years of their own grandparents in the country, which were softened by care and respect. Those who have children can invest in them, and hope that the investment will give a return when they need it, but those who lack children have nothing to save for. The poorer workers have no future—and few have much faith in an existence after the present one. For such men, heroin, if available, provides a fairly cheap way of enjoying the present and of forgetting the future. It can be seen as a rational response to an accurate appraisal of their lives and future. Whilst they might affirm that they desire a long life, and fear an early grave as a result of their habit, death is no more a deterrent to them than it is to the tobacco smoker.

It may be argued that the conditions described above as pre-disposing sections of the community to high addiction rates are present in any rapidly industrializing country where large numbers of rural folk have been drawn into the towns. This is true, and a cursory glance at Britain or at the urban centres of Africa[1] during comparable periods of their development reveals that the available drugs for escapism, alcohol or cannabis, have indeed been considerably used, although they lack the addictive potential of heroin. It should also be noted that few countries, if any, have matched Hong Kong for its sustained rate of population growth and industrial development since 1948, nor for the effective separation between the workers and their rural homelands.

In addition to the social disorganization that has stemmed from the transition from the rural to the urban industrial situation, heroin-taking may also be related to the sheer density of population in parts of Hong Kong, and to the speed of change within the colony. When people are housed, five in a room, in fifteen-storey blocks of rooms, giving population densities of up to 10,000 per acre, then considerable friction is almost inevitable. Foreigners will occasionally affirm that the Chinese do not object to what would be considered gross overcrowding in the west, and indeed there is far less friction than an observer from the west would expect. In part this flows from the cultural heritage, with its emphasis upon tranquillity. It represents a remarkable capacity to adapt to difficult conditions, but it demands that the family in its room should shut its eyes to much that goes on outside, and that it should be uncomplaining. Under such conditions, the heroin addicts are certainly preferable as neighbours to the drunkards, or to those who drown their boredom in noisy music. For the man who finds the proximity of his fellows a strain, heroin provides a quiet and unobjectionable escape—and the roofs and lavatories of the resettlement blocks are often the retreat of men escaping through heroin from the pressures of population around them.

In the five years up to 1964, industrial wages (as recorded by the Labour Department)[2] rose by about 50 per cent, and the real

[1] See, for example, Philip Mayer, *Townsmen or Tribesmen*, London 1963, Ch. 6 *passim*.
[2] Labour Department press release December 1964.

income of most men working in Hong Kong also appears to have risen very rapidly. This has been accompanied, however, by very wide differences in wage rates for jobs which could be done by the same people. Such variations are generally a reflection of nepotism and ignorance of opportunities, which limit entry into many jobs, together with the difficulty of travelling far to one's place of work. One effect of this had been to produce a situation very similar to that described by Durkheim[1] as *anomie* —change so rapid as to make rational adjustment almost impossible. Under such conditions, he observed—at the crests and troughs of the trade cycle in the nineteenth century—suicides tended to increase. Heroin-taking can be seen, socially, as being a less final means of escape from the world during a period when that world appears to be defying the economic moral law of effort and reward being closely related. Drug-taking can also be seen as a means of adjusting expenditure to a rapid rise in income for those not familiar with means of saving. It should be made clear here that we do not refer to the absolute level of wages as having risen so high that the recipients do not know what to do with them, but to the rate of expansion.

Some support for the thesis discussed above is provided by the experience of Macau, which had a similar influx of addicts from China after the revolution, but where a different pattern of urban living pertains. When the government took stern measures to repress addiction in Macau, these were largely effective, and gained some popular support in a territory which has expanded and developed far more slowly than Hong Kong. Whilst the proportion of the adult males in Hong Kong addicted is variously estimated at between 5 per cent and 15 per cent, the estimate in Macau varies between under 1 per cent to 4 per cent[2] and drugs are, by common consent of administration and addicts, very difficult to get.

Further support for this emphasis is suggested by the relatively small number of known female addicts. While the men have tended to have their social roles greatly changed, and their individual significance reduced, the role of the women as the bearers

[1] E. Durkheim, op. cit.
[2] Responsible estimates of male addicts in Hong Kong vary between 50,000 and 150,000 in a population of about 1 million adult men. Estimates in Macau vary between 500 (official) and 3,000 in a population of about 75,000 adult men.

and protectors of children has not changed. At the same time, they have improved their relative status through their ability to support themselves and their families. The dominance of their familial role has remained, while the men have tended to become unnumbered labourers where once they were independent farmers or craftsmen.[1]

In the context of the consequences of social disorganization, it is pertinent to consider the crucial relationship between the rulers and the ruled, since this is involved in the respect of the people for the law, and its executive arm. This is important in any discussion of heroin, since it is illegal, and offenders against the Dangerous Drugs Ordinance supply 60 per cent of prison entrants each year. We have seen that there are reasons why there should be many addicts in Hong Kong, but there are also reasons why the people do not make efforts to eliminate addiction by reporting illegal acts to the police, even if the police had the resources available to pick up all known addicts in possession of their drugs.[2] But in addition to mere apathy, which we have seen can stem from the crowded living conditions, the society of Hong Kong, at all levels, makes the execution of the law much more difficult by allegations of corruption against the police, particularly those who deal with the drug traffickers. Very rarely is evidence brought forward to support the allegations and there is some evidence suggesting that there are sections of the force which can mount operations involving many police over a period of months without any leakage of information to the criminals being observed. It is obviously in the interests of the drug traffickers to foster the popular distrust of the police, but many of the more vociferous and influential police baiters are almost certainly innocent of involvement in illegal narcotics. The baiters are, however, rarely able to avoid all contact involving friction with the police. The proliferation of the motor-car, and the

[1] Women addicts are very few compared with the men, at least as far as is known. About 700 women are sent to prison each year, compared with over 10,000 men. In a sample of 96 interviewed, 44 had records of prostitution and drug offences, 29 drug offences alone, 12 prostitution offences alone, and 11 other offences. The majority of known women addicts therefore were women who were not conforming to a normal marital role.

[2] Addiction *per se* is not an offence in Hong Kong. In order for a conviction to be secured, the police must prove that the suspect was either carrying drugs, or was in the act of smoking when arrested.

consequent number of traffic offenders, whether caught or not, combined with the increasing responsibility for good order in society which has come to rest upon the police with the decline of extended family authority, has placed most people at some time on the wrong side of the law, and of its officers. The ordinary middle-class citizen, once aligned with the police against the law-breakers, now finds himself aligned with other lawbreakers against the police—sometimes in no more than vague protest against the encroachment of a bureaucracy that he is not yet fully ready to accept. He is therefore more ready to listen to criticisms of the police and to pass them on to others, and less willing to identify himself with the forces of law and order by giving sworn statements or appearing in court. This process is an almost inevitable concomitant of urbanization, particularly on the scale of Hong Kong. It is true in London, and probably in most other big cities. Among the working classes in Hong Kong, the objections to giving information to the police about narcotics are generally phrased in more specific, but rarely verifiable, terms. It is said that there is a fear of reprisal from the drug rings if information is given, that some of the police are in league with some of the traffickers, that the attitude of the police towards informers is one of suspicion and contempt, and that the cost of going to court to give evidence is more than the working man can afford.

In addition to the consequences of urbanization, there is the factor of Chinese culture. Despite over a century of British administration, Hong Kong remains a Chinese city. The Chinese have not been prepared to modify traditional attitudes towards foreigners merely because British imperialism has become benign, but instead they have maintained their feelings of superiority over the western way of life. The police, regardless of their nationality, are the executive arm of a colonial government. The British police are working for their own government and are relatively rarely accused of corruption. The Chinese police are, in a sense, cultural traitors, and are frequently accused. The population at large, on the whole, tolerates the colonial status as being the best possible for them at present, but will do little positive to assist in maintaining the colonial power. Hence there is the oft-berated apathy among the vast majority of the Chinese—an apathy which has often been argued to be a part of their way of life. This argument is false, as can be seen from the performance of China in most fields over the past fifteen years, during which time tremendous social responsibility has been developed.[1]

We have observed, in considering the demand for drugs, how the development of Hong Kong has tended to increase the number of the addiction-prone, whilst discouraging the people from supporting what efforts have been made by government against addiction. This lack of popular support has probably been a factor discouraging government from making significant efforts to reduce addiction, other than through the work of the police and the prisons.

In addition to creating a large number of addiction-prone people, Hong Kong, through its former opium smokers, has a core of men who have been addicted or habituated to opiates for over fifteen years. Addicts, particularly when faced by repressive laws[2] and virtually no escape from their habit, tend to try to spread the habit to as many others as possible. There are many good reasons for this. If a large number of men are addicted, then the social stigma attached to addiction tends to be lessened, and the sanctions exacted by society tend to be smaller for those caught. Thus, no peddler, no matter how large his business (and one syndicate caught in 1964 was estimated to have a turnover of a million Hong Kong dollars a year), has been sentenced to more than ten years imprisonment, while sentences of forty years and more have been given in the U.S.A. The ordinary addict, caught with a single day's supply, can expect a sentence of six months or less, where his counterpart in America might get ten times that length of sentence.[3] Also, an addict who makes another man addicted helps to increase the total demand for the drug, thus

[1] N.B. The period 1950–1965, prior to the 'Cultural Revolution'.

[2] A full discussion of the differences between the permissive English system with its emphasis upon the medical problem of addiction, and the American approach with its emphasis upon the law enforcement problem of drug use may be found in Edwin M. Schur's *Narcotic Addiction in Britain and America*, London 1963.

[3] 25 men, selected at random from those arrested in Hong Kong in October and November 1964, had accumulated a total of 132 convictions on drug charges. Of these, 38 were fined, bound over, or were given sentences of one month or under (whether they opted for a fine or a short sentence was not always recorded); 61 were between one and six months; only 5 were over one year. Since 1957, the average length of sentence for narcotics offences in U.S. district courts has been over 70 months (U.S. Treasury Dept., Bureau of Narcotics, *Traffic in Opium and other dangerous drugs for the year ending Dec. 31, 1963*).

ensuring his own supply. A peddler would not be prepared to risk carrying drugs to one man, but if that man can find a dozen friends, then the trade becomes profitable. When the addict is short of money, as most eventually are, another factor operates. In addition to increasing the security of his own source of supply, by increasing the total demand for the drug, he may be able to act as a middleman himself, financing his own habit by selling to others. Since addicts are generally fairly sympathetic to each other whilst actually on the drug, an addict with a number of addicted friends can usually share a smoke if he is unable to afford to buy for himself. The 'followers of the way' are also good companions in adversity. The addict is despised by the majority in Hong Kong society and is a social leper. His own ego suffers a great deal from the rejection of his former friends and relatives, even when they continue to help him financially. His ego can be boosted by a further consumption of drugs, which both relieve the feelings of inferiority, and express a defiance of the respectable society which has rejected and hurt him. By increasing the numbers addicted, the individual addict gains a security from knowing that others are as weak as he is, and gains revenge upon the society which has hurt him.

4   The creation of an addict

The reputation of heroin as a destroyer of bodies, minds and families should, it might be imagined, reduce the infectious nature of addiction; but the actual short-term effects of the drug are probably equally important, since many may be tempted to try a small amount, believing that they will not get addicted. Friends who have tried the drug, whether addicted or not, may well affirm that this is so.

A small quantity of heroin, whether inhaled or injected, produces a feeling of slight dizziness, followed by increased strength and well-being. The user feels strong and is indeed able to work harder and longer than before. He feels more confident in dealing with any situation which may present itself. If he copulates, he takes longer to achieve orgasm, which may please both himself and his partner if he has previously been nervous and over-hasty. If he has any pains, they are deadened. If he wants to sleep, he will sleep well and deeply after the initial euphoria has declined a little. If he feels hungry, then his hunger is assuaged. After such an experience, the experimenter will probably feel none of the withdrawal symptoms so graphically described in medical textbooks and popular American literature. He will probably be tempted to try the drug again, particularly if he is feeling depressed, or sick, or if his friends suggest it. As with cigarette smoking, the second experience tends to be happier than the first. After several smokes, the experimenter may well find himself suffering from feelings akin to those of an alcoholic hangover. A fresh dose of the drug will remove such a feeling, but it will return, more sharply than before. If he is aware of the effects of addiction—as most are in Hong Kong—and appreciates the social stigma attached to the habit, he may then panic. Afraid, or ashamed, to tell his family or friends, he tends to turn to those who will understand—those who are already 'followers of the way'. Hopeless themselves when away from the drug, but able to function fairly effectively when under its influence, their doctrine tends to be one of acceptance of their situation—the way is very easy, until the addict is jolted so hard by poverty, disease, the distress of his family or the pursuit of the law that he seeks what now seems, temporarily perhaps, the slightly easier path of withdrawal. Unless well protected during withdrawal, he usually prefers not to complete the painful process, and stops the pains with more heroin. Afterwards, he may well be in a poor physical condition, and as his habit has made him unaccustomed to tolerate what would be, for others, normal discomforts, he tends to relapse. He blames his friends, his physical weakness or anything else apart from his own desire for the drug for his return to the way. Even after complete withdrawal and a return to full health, the simple way out of worries, responsibilities and pain is still open to him, and he knows that heroin can resolve those difficulties—if he takes only a little and does not get addicted again. He will believe, perhaps, that he cannot be caught twice, and that he can control his habit a second time—but he is wrong. For some, relapse into drug-taking after a period of voluntary or compulsory abstinence is deliberate—a rational renunciation of all problems save one—that of supplying his habit. While addicted, the addict is able to explain all his problems, all his inadequacies, in terms of his habit. He may assert, and believe, that if he was not addicted, then he would be fully able to cope with all that society could put before him. The self-image is reassuring for him—but it is false, as he discovers very soon after he has ceased to be addicted. The former addict not only has to deal with a backlog of neglected duties and debts, he has to deal with his own inadequacies which drove him to become addicted in the first place. He has to face the stigma of having been addicted, and the world is unwilling to trust him. Such burdens can be set aside by a return to the habit—and most men prefer to take this course on several occasions before they finally die or succeed in keeping off drugs.

5 Conclusion

In this paper we have sought to describe some of the principal historical, cultural, social and individual factors which have contributed to the high rate of addiction in Hong Kong today. As with most social phenomena, narcotic addiction cannot be tied to a single social or psychological cause—just as heroin affects the body and brain in a variety of ways, so a variety of factors combine to encourage its use. The sociology of addiction can be likened in some respects to that of venereal disease, in that it is generally contracted through some pleasurable and socially disapproved act, and is transmitted from person to person. In seeking to combat addiction, it may well be that the methods used by governments to deal with venereal disease would be more suitable than those at present practised. However, the social fact of addiction, stemming from the structure of Hong Kong society, will not be eliminated without some revolutionary changes in that structure.

XI

THE STRUGGLE FOR AIR
Portia Ho

The problem of tuberculosis is only one aspect of Hong Kong's whole medical problem, but it is the most serious aspect. Despite the concentrated efforts made to tackle this problem, it remains intractable owing to the magnitude of the other problems, social and economic, with which it is inextricably involved.

Hong Kong has been ranked among those places suffering most acutely from the rapid infection of TB; some statistics even classify the colony as having the world's highest rate of infection. Although the mortality rate of the disease has apparently been decreasing in recent years, as a result of the BCG vaccination campaign and the practice of ambulatory chemotherapeutic treatment, the rate of infection remains more or less constant. An average of 250 cases of TB are still being notified weekly. Apart from the unknown number of unnotified and undiscovered cases, an average of between 12,000 and 13,000 cases of TB is recorded every year. The factor most favouring the spread of this disease—overcrowding—is every moment gaining ground.

A cursory glance at the growing population figures is enough to conjure up an appalling prospect. It seems as if nothing but a drastic 'crash' programme, as has already been suggested by a few eminent personalities—notably the Hon. Dhun Ruttonjee, one of the most active and effective enemies of the disease—can hope in the long run to cope with the seriousness of this situation. Not even the authorities would deny that the anti-TB campaign has been inadequate. But before anyone starts throwing stones, the many difficulties and frustrations should first be realized in full.

It is estimated that about 2 per cent of the adult population in Hong Kong is in need of medical treatment for TB, with a smaller percentage of active TB occurring under the age of 15. This is but an approximate conjecture, as no thorough survey of the whole population has been made. It is possible that there is a much greater number of TB sufferers walking about in the streets than is known. Even so, the approximation of 2 per cent is obviously very serious when it is remembered that the sickness rate amongst normal adults in Hong Kong is only about 3 per cent, according to various surveys in industrial institutions. A higher incidence of TB is recorded amongst drug addicts, who number anything between 50,000 and 150,000. Within this group, the percentage rises to some 9 per cent. Not only are drug addicts physically more susceptible to TB and potentially more drug-resistant but, as Dr Moodie observed,[1] a number of them were initially TB sufferers and only became addicted to opium derivatives afterwards, to relieve their coughing. Ironically, such drugs only aggravate their disease. The mortality rate of TB remains the highest compared with other prevalent infectious diseases. In 1963, for example, of the 12·8 per cent of patients who died of infectious diseases, 8·9 per cent were tuberculars. Out of the total number of consumptive patients, 1,762 died.

The majority of these patients are poor and cannot possibly afford unsubsidized medical treatment. It is estimated that about 50 per cent of the present population are economically dependent upon the government clinics for out-patient treatment, and a minimum of 80 per cent for in-patient treatment. This situation is further aggravated by the fact that there have always been many more men TB patients than women, a universally observed phenomenon of TB of which no satisfactory explanation has yet been found. In 1963, there were 8,975 registered men patients and only 3,995 women patients. This means that many of the poorer families will be plunged into acute financial hardship once their bread-winners are unable to work as a result of contracting TB. TB is a lengthy and tedious disease which, in some cases, may even be chronic, and in general offers little hope of a rapid recovery. For a considerable time, the dependents of these patients will probably have to look elsewhere for financial support.

Generally speaking, the hope of a rapid recovery from TB has been particularly reduced in Hong Kong by several factors, the greatest of which appears to be the housing problem. The colony has an average density of 8,000 people per square mile, and in its more thickly populated areas, the average density is 3,000 people per acre, which is said to be ten times higher than the densest slum areas in the U.K. According to the 1961 census, Kowloon has a gross density of 200,000 per square mile. The same census pointed out that nearly 900,000 local inhabitants were living in

[1] 'Tuberculosis in Hong Kong', Sept. 1963, by Dr A. S. Moodie, until recently the Senior Specialist in the Government Tuberculosis Service.

accommodation which then appeared to be 'gravely inadequate'. This figure included those living in squatter huts, bed-spaces, rooftops, shops, garages, corridors and staircases, verandahs and cocklofts, basements, stores and caves, boats and hulks and perhaps an additional number of pavement-sleepers. It should be remembered that this figure already excluded the enormous number of people living in the resettlement estates, which are themselves centres of overcrowding. The thirty-three resettlement blocks in Wong Tai Sin, for instance, house over 81,500 people.

But mere figures do not tell much. It has to be realized what it really means when 'home' for a family of eight means no more than a single bed-space, sandwiched between two others, one above and one below; or when one bed-space has to be shared by three families in rota every twenty-four hours; or when one has to live in the midst of rubbish heaps and permanent stench in the squatter areas; or in a flat where sunlight and fresh air are unknown and which is in danger of collapsing beneath the weight of some twenty families of under-nourished, sallow-faced tenants. All, of course, quite shocking unless you yourself live in such conditions.

In addition to such intolerable living conditions, which inevitably accelerate the rate of TB infection and prevent its effective cure, there prevails in the community, generally speaking, a certain amount of ignorance and prejudice which leads to an exaggerated belief that to be infected with TB is a personal disgrace and tragedy. There are some people who habitually condemn this much-dreaded disease in the same way that they condemn leprosy. They tend to run away from it, and above all, to hide it when they contract it themselves. This is true even of people of higher social status, probably because TB is regarded by many as exclusively the poor man's sickness; the symbol of strenuous living, poor housing, malnutrition and starvation. One serious result of this is that people usually do not voluntarily go to a district clinic to be X-rayed unless it becomes absolutely necessary. This often means that they come too late, and that the problem of curing them has already become so much more complicated.

The psychological burden which a predominantly ignorant and superstitious society like Hong Kong thrusts upon its TB victims sometimes makes it immeasurably difficult for the helpless TB patient to face his illness. He is likely to live in unrelieved anxiety and fears. Ironically enough, his greatest and most immediate problem is not how to get well but how to escape from the fate of being a social outcast. The threat of isolation is so insufferable for him that he will try every means to battle against it, even at cost to his own health and the health of those around him. Many patients have found it necessary, for example, to go on working and over-straining themselves for fear of losing their jobs. Again, in order to secure for themselves sympathy, friendship and affection they dare not let the secret be known even to those closest to them. They have reasons for their fears: they are so surrounded by ignorance that if they risk letting the truth be known they will probably find themselves at the mercy of harmful opinions. When they themselves are equally ignorant it becomes worse. One TB patient, for example, had a very difficult time making up his mind because, not knowing anything about TB himself, he had been told by some friends that it is chronic and incurable and by others that it can easily be cured by a daily walk along the sea-shore.

The spread of TB in the society of Hong Kong can perhaps also be related to a number of habits, prevalent in this colony, which pay little attention to the question of hygiene. What can be said to be very harmful is the habit of eating together and sharing the same dishes with chopsticks: eating with separate dishes is a sophistication which few Chinese families care for. Again, some Chinese families—and the poorer ones in particular—in their desperate attempts to save money, try to manage on a meagre diet consisting of little more than salted fish and dried vegetables: which more or less must weaken their constitutions and bodily resistance. But perhaps the most detrimental habit, and one with a decided effect in accelerating the infection rate of TB in Hong Kong, is the widespread habit of spitting—not at all an uncommon sight, wherever one goes. Despite the law passed, early in 1933,[1] against spitting, the habit remains uncontrollable. The law itself is so weakly enforced that it seems as if it has been totally forgotten. As a rule one finds public places, especially those frequented by the poor and ignorant (the majority of the population) strewn with sputum. Unfortunately not even patients

---

[1] 'Any person who without lawful authority or excuse . . . in or into a public place or vehicle or ferry or any building to which the public have access, spit, except into a receptacle or channel for sewage, sullage, or waste water shall be liable to a fine of $500 or imprisonment for 3 months.' *Law Book*, vol. V, ed. 1950, Chapter 225, Section 3, p. 307.

coughing and waiting in the public clinics care to abstain from intermittent spitting, and it is by no means a novelty to see policemen themselves spitting. The heavy construction work going on everywhere, thickening the air with clouds of sand and dust, inevitably makes breathing difficult for all and must be taken as causing more spitting than otherwise would be necessary.

For those receiving ambulatory chemotherapeutic treatment, no complete recovery can as yet be guaranteed, as it can be under other circumstances. There have always been cases where the patients only get worse because circumstances, as well as the patients themselves, do not co-operate. A great difficulty arises in the question of regular attendances: not many patients can afford waiting in the public clinics all day long whilst they are supposed to be doing something else and, as a result, some of them go there as seldom and as irregularly as possible. For the sake of convenience, some patients seek help, despite its being uneconomic, from private doctors who consume what little fortunes they have but do not always succeed in helping them to get well. Thus there are patients who find themselves drifting from one private doctor to another until, almost penniless, they find their way to a government chest clinic—and then only to be told that they are already so seriously ill that they have to enter hospital. Some cases have proved themselves physically resistant to the effects of the first-line standard drugs, but there is also the percentage of disobedient patients who do not follow instructions. Some patients do not hesitate, the moment they seem to be getting better, to throw their drugs away. But on top of this, there is the psychological factor in TB which must not be overlooked: the difficulty for anyone of trying to overcome chronic depression and worries. For this reason, indeed, attempted suicide cases among TB patients occasionally try again.

What, apart from the preventive measure of vaccination, is being done to tackle the problem of TB? In brief, there exist in Hong Kong at present less than two thousand beds for full-time in-patient treatment, only four full-time Chest Clinics and a small number of charity organizations.

The beds are provided by Government Hospitals, by Government-assisted Hospitals or by Private Hospitals. In 1962 there were altogether 1,748 beds, representing a ratio of 0·5 per 1,000 of the mid-year population. In 1963, the total rose to 1,820, the ratio thus only rising to 0·51. Obviously this fell far short of the standard of 0·7 per 1,000 endorsed in the Heaf/Fox Report.[1] The greatest number of beds are available in the Government-assisted Hospitals, most of which are run by the Anti-Tuberculosis Association. In 1962 there were 1,480 of these beds and by 1963 they totalled 1,596. The number of private beds has remained static at 110, and the number of Government beds decreased from 148 in 1962 to 114 in 1963. The fees for these beds vary a great deal. If a patient is paying for everything himself it would probably cost him his fortune, as is shown in the accompanying table.

	$
Specialist consultation fee	50–100
Hospital daily maintenance fee	45
Minor X-ray investigation	50
Major X-ray investigation	180
Course of radiotherapy (25 treatments)	2,000
Minor operation fee	200 $\}$ + 20%
Major operation fee	1,500 $\}$ for anaesthesia

(Quoted from *Development of Medical Service in Hong Kong*, p. 10.)

Poorer patients, however, may receive free treatment or at least treatment subsidized by the Government. If a patient is lucky enough, he can even enter the Grantham Hospital, which is reputed to be the best of its kind, at no cost to himself. This self-supporting hospital was founded in 1957 by the Anti-Tuberculosis Association as a new addition to its other hospitals—the Ruttonjee Sanatorium, the Freni Memorial Convalescent Home and the Haven of Hope Sanitorium. The Grantham Hospital used to charge $18 per day for a bed, but now that the general living standard in Hong Kong has risen, the fee has been increased to $20. The Government is helping to maintain 576 of these beds, which makes it possible for a considerable number of patients to enjoy free or subsidized treatment. The hospital has an excellent site in the rural outskirts of Hong Kong, its eight-storeyed building soaring above a vast expanse of green fields—a pleasantly isolated haven for TB sufferers who, apart from the privilege of having the service of some fifteen doctors (including some first-

[1] Professor Heaf and Dr Fox are the two TB experts invited by the HK Government to study the problem of TB in HK. The Heaf/Fox Report, however, has not yet been published and further details about it still remain 'confidential'.

class specialists), an efficient staff of about four hundred, spacious and airy wards, and a pleasant, quiet atmosphere, have also a church and a cinema. This is in very sharp contrast to one of the poorer hospitals, miserably huddled in a slum area, with appallingly crammed wards and an oppressive sense of hopelessness and death.

Out-patient treatment is available in the Government Chest Clinics, which altogether are staffed by over forty doctors and nurses. The most recent statistics illustrate the heavy attendance at the existing four Chest Clinics.

Clinics	*No. of attendances in July '64*	*in August '64*
Wanchai Clinic	16,382	16,357
Sai Ying Pun Clinic	12,051	10,260
Kowloon Clinic	30,752	28,280
Shek Kip Mei Clinic	21,504	18,928

* The two public holidays in July explained the greater no. of attendances

To make sure that those patients receiving ambulatory chemotherapeutic treatment are well taken care of, regular home-visits are being made by a number of social workers under the supervision of the Senior Tuberculosis Almoner. There are now fifty-one tuberculosis social workers, each responsible for the Tuberculars residing within a defined area. At present, each worker has to visit regularly 1,000–2,000 homes, at a minimum average of seven visits per day. A sum of $300,000 is set aside by the Hong Kong Government every year to finance some of the poorer families. Each family is entitled to receive a maximum grant of 75 per cent of its bread-winner's former incomes.

Late in 1960, the Lutheran World Service, sponsored by the U.S. Government, started in the Colony a very important 'pilot project' of rehabilitation to help the post-Tuberculosis patients by re-integrating them into a normal and healthy pattern of life—physically, economically, and psychologically. It was begun as a result of the discovery that a service of this kind did not yet exist in Hong Kong. The project first makes sure that the patient has been discharged from hospital with a certificate of recovery, that he is now non-infectious and that he is physically fit for a certain degree of work. Having evaluated the degree of work-tolerance of each patient, it then rehabilitates him according to his needs. If the patient is physically unfit to resume his former trade, he will be taught a new profession, commensurate with his physical condition. The project also makes sure that the patient will be re-employed according to the best of his qualifications. He will be helped to start a small business if it suits him. Poorly housed post-tuberculosis patients and their families will be properly re-housed, with furniture if necessary, in a place no longer detrimental to their health. Big farming families will sometimes be resettled in the rural districts with a small-holding to work on. With its principle of not helping any patient for more than six months, the 'pilot project' of the LWF/WS is now handling an average of 20 cases every month. From June 1961 to August 1964 the total number of successful cases amounted to 330. This project of rehabilitation has been organized on a small scale with the hope that its temporary responsibilities will soon be assumed by a large-scale local agency. At present, it continues to function energetically and with increasing success.

Plans are still being made by the authorities to improve existing conditions, especially under the instructions of the Heaf/Fox Report. It is hoped that, in addition to the 'existing or proposed' 2,256 beds of 1963, there will be at least 1,250 additional beds by 1972. A further three to five Chest Clinics, to be built between 1967 and 1972, are also being considered. But plans mean nothing if they cannot efficiently be realized. An enormous sum of money will be required. Is this capital obtainable, and even if it is, can it be guaranteed to be well used?

The most important question now is how to carry out plans in the most economic way. How shall the largest number of reasonably good beds be provided, with the smallest amount of money and within the shortest possible time? By 'reasonably good beds', is not necessarily meant luxurious beds, certainly not the camp beds which should not exist at all, nor the decrepit beds in some hospitals which, sooner or later, must be replaced by better ones. Moreover, when Tuberculosis beds are under consideration, it should be remembered that, with the situation as it is at present, a rapid turn-over of beds is not possible because, in general, only the most seriously ill obtain in-patient treatment. It is vital therefore that a better bedding system be devised to accelerate the present rate.

There seems no better answer to these questions than the 'policy of progressive patient care', suggested by the Hon. Dhun Ruttonjee, Vice-Chairman of the Hong Kong Anti-Tuberculosis

Association. By this policy he means that different grades of beds should be available to all patients so that they can be transferred from one type of bed to another, not according to what they can afford, but according to their physical condition. It is hoped that under this system, no patient will have to be confined to the same expensive bed in a luxurious hospital for an indefinite length of time. Mr Ruttonjee envisages three kinds of general hospital bed, furnished differently for the different stages of illness: the Acute General Beds, the Subsidiary General Beds and the Cheap Elementary General Beds for the convalescent and the chronic. These beds are classified according to their facilities: the Acute General Beds, being fully furnished for emergencies, are the most expensive at $50–60 a day: a less fully furnished variety will be available at between $20 and $25 a day. Similarly, the Subsidiary General Beds, for less seriously ill patients needing less medical care, should be available, according to Mr Ruttonjee, at a cost of $12–16 a day, while the Elementary General Beds, being the cheapest, should be available at a daily cost of $5–6. This has been planned by Mr Ruttonjee, as he explained in his 1964 Budget Speech on 16 March, 'to provide a more adequate hospital service at a cost which the Colony can afford'.

These practical suggestions, applicable to 'general' beds as well as to TB beds, deserve to be seriously considered. It is particularly of importance that a hospital should be built as soon as possible and with all possible means, for the chronic TB patients who, unwanted in most hospitals, have scarcely anywhere to go[1] apart from being sent home. It should be remembered that sending these patients back to a healthy society without adequate isolation and medical care is extremely dangerous and is hardly perhaps the best way of solving Hong Kong's community health problem.

The staffing problem also demands much attention. There have been many complaints made about the staff shortage, especially amongst the nursing staff. Miss Sheila Iu, matron of the Grantham Hospital, emphasizes the difficulty, not of training the nurses, but of recruiting them. 'There is still this aversion to contact with patients known to be suffering from TB,' she explains, 'which not only exists among the potential staff, but is prevalent also among

[1] The only institution closest to being a chronic hospital, run by a local charity organization, is poorly equipped and appallingly overcrowded, and conditions there are so miserable that it can hardly be said that all the patients are treated as human beings.

their relatives and friends.' Miss Iu further draws attention to the importance of developing the staff's ethical qualities: 'Your staff have to be very patient, tolerant and understanding,' she says, 'especially when they are looking after long-term TB sufferers, who have to stay in hospital for months and perhaps even for years.' This humanitarian standpoint is supported by Mr Ruttonjee: 'We should teach our staff that patients should be treated as human beings and not treated as some of them are in some of the hospitals.'

More positive steps need to be taken to substantiate the doctor's catchword that 'Tuberculosis should be seen and not heard'. As early discovery of the disease always helps to simplify the cure, a comprehensive project of case-finding, which at present remains in the tentatively planned and controversial stages, should be carried out, as far as it is possible, unhesitatingly and without fear of the inevitable difficulties. In the long run, an annual survey of the whole population seems to be the only tactic which promises a permanent victory in the Colony's war against TB. The popular excuse, 'You cannot force people to come out', is valueless now that some countries have succeeded in making this compulsory. Since such a general survey cannot be carried out immediately, as a preliminary step the most overcrowded districts should be examined. At the same time, much more should be done to clear the still prevalent clouds of ignorance and superstition which surround the problem of TB. The responsibility must not be left alone to the Anti-Tuberculosis Association which, within its limitations, can do but very little.[1] The anti-TB campaign in Hong Kong can perhaps be much more successful if the Government, in addition to taking the leading role itself, gives fuller and more generous support to all such efforts.

It should be remembered, however, that fundamentally the problem of Tuberculosis in Hong Kong is by no means a medical problem *per se*. It would indeed be unfair thus to simplify the problem and so shift all the responsibilities on to the medical authorities, the doctors and the nurses, some of whom, within their spheres, have laboured hard without the appreciation and encouragement they deserve. A permanent solution to the problem depends upon effecting an improvement in the entire social framework of the Colony.

[1] The Association occasionally distributes leaflets and shows films, but only on a very small scale.

XII

PROBLEMS OF BILINGUAL MILIEU IN HONG KONG: STRAIN OF THE TWO-LANGUAGE SYSTEM

E. Kvan

Schools are insufficient in Hong Kong and a number of children will probably never enter a proper school. Secondary schools are few, at least good ones; only between 5 to 10 per cent of the children in primary schools get places in government or government-aided secondary schools and the possibilities for getting through to University are minimal in most other schools. The school fees in the middle schools are from $300 to $500 per year with about 30 per cent free places. The cost of a University education is around $4,000–5,000 per annum, with probably about 15 per cent free places through scholarships and bursaries; actually more than one-third of the undergraduates are in receipt of grants—but not full grants.

There are two universities, one Chinese (the Chinese University of Hong Kong), the other English (the University of Hong Kong). It is the latter I shall concentrate on since it is bilingualism that interests me. The University of Hong Kong is a residential one and the courses are all on the English pattern. The Faculties are Arts, Medicine, Science and Engineering. The official medium of instruction in this University is English and more than 90 per cent of the Undergraduates have passed through the Anglo-Chinese branch of a secondary school, where English is used as a medium of instruction from Form I.

The examinations are mainly written, as is customary in English universities, and external examiners from other British universities are appointed in all departments, visiting their particular department once in three years, while in the other two the papers are set and assessed in correspondence with the teachers of the University.

Finally it is essential to mention that a recently graduated young man can earn about $1,400 per month if he begins as a teacher or between $1,500 and $2,000 if he is a medical man—3–5 times the average family income. A graduate is regarded as a family life insurance policy and an enormous pressure is often resting on the shoulders of those who, through very hard work, innate abilities and a great deal of luck have succeeded in surviving the rat-race of primary and secondary schools and finally in getting access to the University through the Matriculation Examination. We can say that these undergraduates live in a bilingual milieu. By far the greater majority use their second language, English, in auditoria and examination rooms, but in their daily lives together with their family and friends they speak one or more of the Chinese dialects.

Without attempting to explain what I mean in any detail, but from my general knowledge over several years of the University undergraduates and of other groups of young Chinese people I have known, I should say that the courses in the University cause great difficulties to the students.

The following reports on observations will give an impression of some of the difficulties. First I attempted to form an impression of the reading speed of the undergraduates in English; this figure was quite unknown to other members of the University staff, even if they had a very clear feeling of the students' understanding of the written or spoken word. Without going into detail with regard to the methods employed I shall here only say that I am fully aware of the difficulties involved in the comparison of reading speed in various people. I do not think they invalidate my results. Let me quote a part of the instructions: 'Read as fast as you can read this kind of material—read as you would read "background material"; do not read it as if it was a textbook to be learned by heart but in such a way that you can answer a couple of general questions afterwards.' The text was of the same degree of difficulty as University material in general and the questions were multiple-choice or sentences to be corrected to get the same meaning as the text just read (without reading the text again); these questions were given at the rate of one question to about 100 words. The importance of reading with different speeds was stressed and the dependence of speed on the relative difficulty of the text and the circumstances and purpose of reading it underlined. Again without attempting a defence of the indefensible—a comparison of reading speeds—I shall only quote some results; they have been confirmed again and again. Amongst the first-year students about 50 per cent read at a speed of less than 150 words per minute, 75 per cent under 175. This corresponds to a speed of one page in an average book in 2 or 3 minutes, or about 15–20 hours for an ordinary novel or biography, 15–20 hours of solid, steady work. And it must be remembered that rates of 80–100 words per minute are not rare, even in good students. In the U.S.A. such speeds are quoted for children of 12–13 years of age. And American children are regarded as slower than English children—again far behind Scottish children, educated as these are with a 'fearful efficiency'. In the end, it turned out that these reading speeds are similar to those quoted for English University students reading French, *their* second language. Perhaps the best expression of my results would be a quotation from Guerney's summary of his observations: 'The upshot would seem to be that the average pupil after studying French for four or five years cannot be considered an efficient reader capable of dealing with ordinary French texts for information or pleasure.'[1] In this quotation read: 'English' for 'French' and '8–10 years' for '4 or 5' —and then remember that these same Hong Kong students are able to take examinations in this very language of English. This gives the paradox.

Let me add at this point that as a result of these and similar observations I attempted to try to increase the reading speed without decreasing the degree of comprehension. My results seem to indicate that this is possible in the course of 12–13 practice sessions, but it is of course impossible to say how permanent and extensive such an improvement would be. During these practice sessions I had the opportunity to observe the reading habits of a great number of students and to ask them questions about it. The results are set out in detail elsewhere but are well summarized in the following anecdote. During the course the readers were supplied with various practice material, amongst others an ample supply of copies of *The Listener*; in these copies I had chosen a number of lectures, mainly from the Third Programme, on a variety of general subjects which I supposed were of interest to a University group, very often directly concerning University life and studies. These lectures were more difficult than the text of the tests used in each session but of the same degree of difficulty as very much of the material normally encountered in University studies. As usual the participants were instructed to read the text as fast as they could read this kind of material for the purpose of writing a very short and very general description of the tenor of

---

[1] D. Guerney, *An Experimental Enquiry into the Value of Silent Reading*, Leeds 1931; quoted in Ll. Wynn Jones, *An Introduction to Theory and Practice of Psychology*, London 1934.

the text. But the students neither could nor would choose their own copies of the journal and of the lectures—stating that they had no particular interests; the only exceptions to this were the very best and fastest readers. For the great majority reading is a heavy task demanding the overcoming of a great internal resistance.

Or we can express it in another way, as the results of another investigation which I undertook after the results of the first investigation had shown that the reading speed is the same, or less, than the average reading speed in English children under 14. The test used in the second investigation was Schonell's Comprehension Test B.[1] This test includes a speed factor, as it is most often given with a time limitation. (I have tried to give it without such a limitation, without much change in the results.) Originally this test was thought too easy for University students as it has been standardized only for children up to 14 years of age—and given to University teachers with English as their mother-tongue it presented no difficulties whatsoever and was completed correctly in about one-third of the stipulated time, 15 minutes. But given to the undergraduates it proved that the results of the first investigation were not accidental. The test differentiated successfully between the participants; only very few were able to answer all questions correctly within 15 minutes; out of a representative group of 50 only 3 answered all questions—and only one correctly in all cases. Compared with English children, using the English standards, the average reading age was 11·9–12·0, while in another investigation 75 per cent had a reading age of under 13·3. When the test was given to a total of seven streams of secondary classes in two schools and later to several other streams in both secondary and primary schools it showed clear and consistent progress from class to class for all the percentiles. The results gave much information about very many interesting details with regard to teaching methods and the personality of the teachers. It is of importance to observe that a reading age of about 12–13 years is the same as the reading age Schonell found as the average for the whole of the British population. Whatever the tests used, whatever the circumstances, the results have always been the same in 'naive' subjects: whether difficult pieces from Bacon or of poetry, whether an easy piece from a newspaper or a short story, whether there are many questions or few in the comprehension

[1] F. Schonell, *Backwardness in Basic Subjects*, London 1949.

test, whether the questions are presented together with the text or after the text, all the texts were read with the same speed, often with catastrophic results for the comprehension—or for the rate of reading—without stopping or looking right or left. This is the general rule—confirmed by the few exceptions, the competent readers.

I think these results are significant. Supported by Werner and Kaplan's investigations of children's understanding of words and their meanings it seems possible to maintain that at about the age of 12–13 a radical change takes place in the use of English in the British-American children who have English as their mother-tongue, and who go on to be competent readers.[1] There is a re-structuring, if you like, of the vocabulary and a change in the understanding of the character of the sentence structure; together they make it possible to move with much greater freedom from situation to situation—abstract thought and ideas become a possibility, a new instrument is formed which is the foundation for the rapid development of the reading habit in those for whom reading becomes a vice— as it ought to be at least for a time.

English is only one of the languages employed by Hong Kong students. Chinese is the other. Here we must mention a complication. In a way we all live not only in bilingual surroundings but in multilingual ones. It is purely conventional to say that a cultured man who knows only his own mother-tongue is mono-lingual. In Hong Kong this is also the case, to an even higher degree. The predominant spoken language is Cantonese, a dialect, so-called, spoken by about 50 million people without too great variations. But Cantonese is not used as a medium for writing; many expressions have no 'correct' characters. Some newspapers print short stories in Cantonese but apart from that only the Bible and *Pilgrim's Progress* are available in Cantonese. In the primary schools the children learn to use a form of the North Chinese dialect (Kuoyu), now the official language for the whole of China, both for letter writing and the writing of essays. Books and news-papers are written in one of several forms of that language, some-where between the classical and the spoken language. In addition the bigger children are taught classical literary language. Simplify-ing a very complex situation in a very brutal manner we could maintain that the students have at least two Chinese 'languages', a

[1] H. Werner and E. Kaplan, *The Acquisition of Word Meanings*, Monographs of the Society for Research in Child Development, 1950, vol. 15.

spoken and a written language, with several possibilities for choice within each with regard to style, etc.—many more than the possibilities for choice given in the English language. It is obviously very difficult to compare the results of reading tests using Chinese material—much more so than with English material where we found it impossible. But some tests have been given and here are the results.

The English text used for the testing described above was of general University standard (whatever that means); I therefore chose a general introduction to Chinese history written especially for University students as the text for the Chinese tests. The text is written by one of the teachers of the University for the use of first-year students and is by other experienced Chinese teachers described as typical.

The test has been given to numerous groups—again with rather uniform results. In one group of 118 freshmen the average speed was 300 characters per minute, varying from 100 to 580. The average score on the comprehension test was about the same as in the English tests—perhaps a little higher. This speed was much higher than the average rate obtained by using English material—being three times the maximum in English. This rate of reading reveals quite a different kind of competence in reading, and will result in the reader covering much more ground with much greater certainty. But there is another figure which must not be forgotten: out of this group of 118—and of many similar groups—there were only 62 who would attempt to read the Chinese text at all. Many regarded themselves as so bad in Chinese that they would not even attempt the text and that in spite of the fact that they have all read Chinese for the Matriculation examination. And this is not just guessing, the students themselves stated this reason for their refusal to read.

This makes the comparison between the two language tests more difficult still but this matters only very little in view of the fact that I cannot see how it is possible to compare texts in English with texts in Chinese. Woodworth[1] maintains that the speed of reading is the same in the two languages, because even if Chinese readers can read more characters per minute than they can read words (in English) they need to use more characters to express an idea than we use words in English. Woodworth quotes the example of 'Psychology', in Chinese '*Hsin Lieh sheuh*'; one

[1] Robert S. Woodworth, *Experimental Psychology*, 1st ed. London 1938.

word but three characters. However, it is quite unreasonable to compare the individual parts of a modern compound, such as this, with English words. On the other hand Miller maintains in *Language and Communication* that Chinese has the lowest redundancy of all written languages. Comparing e.g. Greek, English and Chinese, Miller informs us that to express the same text, Greek uses 37,000 syllables, English 29,000 and Chinese 17,000 only. But then *he* seems to have committed the error of having identified each character with a syllable in the alphabetical languages. You cannot compare the information from the character, in all its complexity, with the fragmentary information from the visual representation of a sound complex. But let us return to this problem again later. Suffice it here to say that it does not seem possible at the present juncture to compare the information obtained from the two languages because we have no reliable instrument with which to measure. And we shall therefore not be able to say anything about a person's degree of bilingualism by comparing the results of his efforts in reading the two.

Following a suggestion by Saer, I have tried to establish a situation where it would be directly possible to compare the strength, as it were, of the two languages in the individual.[1] The task is verbally to produce the first association coming to mind upon seeing a visually presented word in Chinese or English. The reaction time is registered electricallʌ and the response itself is noted. The words are 50 words in both languages—the one set being the equivalent of the other; all the words should be present in the vocabulary of a 3-year-old. The presentation is randomized both with regard to language used and to particular words. From the investigations made so far it appears that it should be possible to place all the bilingual readers of the two languages on a continuum between monolingual Chinese and monolingual English individuals. But not only the relative reaction times are of interest; also the number of translations among the answers, of replies using the same or the other language and of course the nature of the answers when they are true associations, are very revealing.

In yet another attempt to penetrate further into the results of the bilingual education I obtained two sets of essays, on the same subject but in the two languages, from a group of students who had

---

[1] H. Saer, *Experimental Inquiry into the Education of Bilingual People*. New Educational Fellowship, Education in a changing Commonwealth, London 1931.

just completed their annual examination in their respective groups. Of the 100 participants some had come up through the Anglo-Chinese System, others through the Chinese, i.e. using English and Chinese as the medium of instruction, respectively. I asked several competent judges to assess the (anonymous) essays with regard to maturity and as far as possible disregarding the linguistic expression of detail. It seems clear that the students who had used Chinese as a medium of instruction but had studied English as a subject, were showing greater originality of thought and greater maturity in general than those who had used English as a medium and had Chinese as a subject only. This was very obvious in the English essays, in spite of the limitations on the English of the second group, and my Chinese judges said it was even more obvious in the Chinese essays. This result corresponds closely with the impressions of experienced educators that the pupils in the Chinese-medium classes are more responsive, more interested in their surroundings both in and outside of the school.

A possible explanation of this difference seems to be the change of language in Form I of the secondary school when the pupils are about 12–13 years old. If we assume that the possibility of 'being able to convey' is one of the most characteristic human traits—to establish a relationship with the persons around us rather than to convey 'information'—then it does seem more than likely that this sudden reduction of the possibilities for expression would cause a neurosis fully as severe as the one we find in children backward in reading and writing for reasons which can be counteracted by special training. I think the picture will be complete if I just add that one is not likely anywhere in the world to find 'better pupils' than those in the Anglo-Chinese schools—better with regard to discipline, obedience, and ability to work steadily through well-prepared material.

To the difficulties created by the change of language in the school must be added the peculiar difficulties springing from the many languages which are involved: for the Matriculation examination these pupils work mainly with texts in the classical language written in the classical period which is as different from the modern spoken language as Latin is from French or Italian, or Chaucer is from modern English. It would therefore appear that their language used for the description of the phenomena of everyday life, including scientific phenomena, does not develop on a par with their interests and general academic progress. Here we must remember that the characters in and by themselves give only very vague instruction with regard to how they should be pronounced and only little information with regard to their special meaning in this particular context. Unless a character has been learned in a formal learning situation it requires great expenditure of energy for the individual to acquire this character—leading to a high degree of compartmentalization between the common and the specialized vocabularies, with a rather small number of characters being allotted to the first group.

This means in practice that the spoken language of these pupils stagnates at the level of the 12–13-years-old, the age at which they last used it as their only real medium of instruction and expression. What this means for the possibilities of expressing and controlling the emotional forces released at about the same time as the language change will require much further study.

Furthermore, at this stage a new conflict develops—the conflict between the Chinese traditional approach to scholastic work and the less traditional western approach. The immediate conflict is undoubtedly made much less acute by the fact that most of the teachers are themselves trained in the Chinese traditional way and tend to transfer this method from the Chinese literary studies to the whole curriculum.

The ultimate conflict, however, is increased rather than decreased by this approach. So far as our students go it can with advantage be summarized in the following anecdote: a couple of years ago all Faculties and Departments were at one in their report on the Matriculation examination: 'The candidates rely by far too much on learning by heart instead of working in an independent and original way with the questions'—all except the Department of Chinese which wrote: 'it is clear that the candidates have not memorized a sufficient amount of material'.

But before we attempt to draw conclusions with regard to the difficulties involved in the two systems of education, the Vernacular and the Anglo-Chinese, it will be necessary to consider the instruction provided in the primary school—and even before. Here an inspection of two samples of Chinese handwriting would be useful to illustrate my point. (Plate 23)—Before the division takes place at age 12–13 the two groups have been in the primary school for 6 years and very many in the kindergarten before that. At all stages, when the child leaves the kindergarten (at 5–6 years of age), the primary school, the secondary (Middle) school, even the University, the Chinese language uses the expression: *bi yeh* (graduated)—and at all stages the child will receive diplomas and certificates. This is characteristic. The formal instruction begins as soon as the child enters kindergarten, most frequently at about the age of 3, counting age in the western fashion. The kindergarten lasts for two years and even if there are many activities (which is far from the case in the majority of kindergartens) the most important activity is the instruction in reading and writing. When the children sit for 'the entrance examination' (*sic*) to the primary school, most of them can read, write and take dictation in about 100 to 160 characters. Some are very complex, 20 or more individual strokes are necessary to construct them, to write them. Compare them with the school maturity tests common in the west, e.g. the test published by Charlotte Buehler.[1] The test demands that the 5-year-old shall be able to *copy* a circle—'the test has been successfully completed if the two ends of the circle meet!' —or note in the same test the table and chair (in profile) which the child should be able to copy to the extent of making them basically recognizable. Compare such a test with the details of the Chinese characters which the child in the Hong Kong kindergarten *must* learn by heart and be able to *reproduce*—not just copy or recognize—at the same age of 5 (see plate 23). This result is obtained only by daily practice during the years from 3 to 5, both in school and at home. They practise at least a half-hour daily in the kindergarten—and in Primary I at least one hour must be spent at home practising handwriting. Further it must be remembered that the pencil (or soon the brush) must be very carefully controlled in a way much more elaborate than the way it must be controlled in the writing of English letters. Learning to write has always been regarded as much more than just learning to form the characters. It is at the same time an instruction in the ability to control one's temper, and to develop personal harmony.

Looking around for ways and means first to express and then assess the results of this very strictly formal instruction—a system which is so much older than anything found outside China— I noticed that among the more than 2,000 schoolchildren and the several hundred University students whom I tested with the

[1] Charlotte Buehler and B. Hetzer, *Testing Children's Development*, New York 1935.

reading tests hardly any were left-handed, writing or playing.[1] This contrasts very markedly with the position in England. Assuming that the generally accepted views on the subject are meaningful, it seems likely that many children must have been forced to change from left to right hand and the absence of stammer and similar symptoms of particular stress would then be an expression of the general uniformity of this society and of the force wherewith the individual personality is formed and socialized.

When we consider the effect of the early formal training we must not stop at writing but go further back into the developmental history of the children. As little as the teachers will allow the children to do so, as little will mothers permit the children to use the 'sinister' hand for eating purposes. It is indeed probable that the table manners are the primary influence, the writing habits the secondary.

There is no doubt that the adult pattern for table manners is inculcated at a much earlier age than in north-western Europe. The tools are simpler, two chopsticks, a bowl and a short, well-shaped spoon in chinaware. The eating habits seem universal without regard to social or economic standing and are of so ancient an origin, at least 2,000 years, that nothing in the table manners of Europe can be regarded as comparable. Also the European habits are more complicated, dependent as they are on the type of the meal, the time of day, the circumstances under which we eat, while the bowl and the sticks are equally useful and equally acceptable under all circumstances, and at all ages. But a person eating with his left hand is not acceptable at the Chinese family table; it would immediately interfere with the neighbours' use of his chopsticks as the family sits around a relatively small table sharing the food from the common dishes in the middle of the table. (On two occasions I have had occasion to observe participants eating with the left hand, in one case a foreigner, in the other a Chinese, and the interference of the chopsticks was both persistent and severe.)

[1] An experimental survey of some three hundred children indicates that inherent left-handedness occurs as often in the Chinese population as in a western European one. The most revealing test appears to be the picking up of pea-sized oily steel balls with the help of a pair of chopsticks in tl : left hand. The use of left hand, as we shall see, is never taught (or perm itted) but the ability to use it is a result of transfer only.

Considering both lines of thought and observation we come to the conclusion that the formal education of the child in Chinese society begins earlier, is much more uniform and more restrictive than the equivalent training in the west.

There is a further detail of the Chinese education which seems of immediate interest when we consider the effects of early training on the development of personality, a detail which at least to some will appear indicative of the possibility of difficulties during the development of not only our students but of all children trained in a similar way. These difficulties are different from our difficulties in western Europe to such a degree that a westerner can see this difference and ask about its importance in a way which habit so often prevents us from seeing and asking in our own culture, with regard to our own development. The point is that a very great number of children of all classes, and probably nearly all, from birth and until about the age of 2 (western reckoning) is in fairly uninterrupted contact with an older person. Neonates apparently most commonly sleep with the mother or a person taking complete care of the child, an *amah* or a relative, and the day they usually spend on the arm of the mother (or mother-figure) or more often tied in a cloth to the back of the 'caretaker'. To the observer the babies often appear to be in a very uncomfortable position on the back of the other person; it is far from always that the head is being supported and young children of 6 or 7 can be seen playing happily around, with a baby tied to their back, baby deep in sleep and the head rolling around in the most appalling manner. But that the children are happy is quite obvious from the way in which they revert to the back of older persons whenever they later in life, as even quite big children of 4 or more, need comfort in a stressful situation. Even foreign children who have had a Chinese nurse behave quite clearly in this way; nothing else will comfort them as quickly and as thoroughly. It seems very reasonable that many Cantonese people seem to think that special aversions or difficulties go back to about the age of 2 when, their old nurse tells them, 'they were so terribly naughty'. It is tempting to see the process of being put down from the back—and perhaps even more seeing the younger brother or sister taking one's place on the back—as a situation fraught with the danger of a 'birth-traumatic' experience at the age of 2. This same general aspect of early permissiveness and later strictness appears also in the toilet training of the children. There seems to be no great interest in training the children to very early cleanliness: in the summer the young child is allowed to run around without trousers and in the winter many will still wear the wonderful contraption which appears to be normal trousers when the child is standing up but opens up automatically at the rear when the wearer squats. It then becomes easier to teach the child a fairly simple act: to squat at the appropriate time, without regard for clothing and other European difficulties; also in the choice of place the child is allowed a much greater variety, indeed the number of permitted places seem much greater than the number of prohibited ones.

In general the training of children produces a child which finds it easy to adapt itself to the world of the adults, and which from the age of 2 is expected to develop as fast as possible. A permissible over-generalization seems to be that the parents treat a child of $2\frac{1}{2}$ as parents in western Europe would treat a grown child. The relationship is not ostentatiously intimate, but there is a mutual respect and feeling of belonging, as it were. The child is not sent to bed in the evening or out of the room if there are guests. (If, indeed, the family have several rooms and separate sleeping quarters; according to one housing survey less than 10 per cent of all families living in substantial houses or flats possessed a room in which no one slept regularly.) The events of the world of the adults are also the events of the child's world. Indeed, after 2 there is no special child's world. Often the children get tired and lie down to sleep wherever they are, whenever they feel like it— and it seems more often than not to be on the hard boards of the floor just under a strong electric bulb without a shade and next to a wireless receiving set playing at full strength, with other children or the adults producing as much noise as is humanly or mechanically possible. This withdrawing into oneself, the exclusion of all that impinges on the senses, seems characteristic for both the young and the old—both in the literal and in the derived meaning of the words. The connection with the students' way of working or living seems obvious. Later in life the students will often work—and work successfully—under circumstances like the ones outlined here. Experimentally it will probably be possible to investigate this ability for withdrawal and selective attention to a small part of the surroundings only; it could of course be yet another result of the early training in the sense that it limits the choice of overt behaviour and imposes sanctions, permitting no other choice—but it seems to build on selectivity with regard to the amount perceived which is superior to and different from ours. Much recent work on bi-aural input for example would seem highly relevant here and experiments should be made to assess individual and cultural differences in this field, perhaps yielding yet another measure of a dimension of the personality produced under these circumstances.

Bringing together the earlier considerations about reading ability with these later considerations, mainly about childhood training and education, it would be reasonable to investigate whether possibly the special kind of behaviour called linguistic behaviour is structured as differently in the two cultures as so many other parts of the general behaviour seem to be. Or whether we can speak about common human traits in this field, using the words in their loosest possible meaning, common traits stronger than all differences. It would not be possible to go into details at this point, partly because I am not competent to do so, and partly because I do not think the description of the Chinese language is as yet at such a stage that it would be easy to give a general description of, e.g. the function which sentence-structure exercises in Chinese. But I do think it would be possible at the present stage to undertake psychological investigations of this question; investigations which perhaps would show us one of the reasons why so many of our undergraduates apparently work at the level of a child of 12–13 as far as the reading of English goes. Not, of course, because I think that the Chinese language as such is at the level of a 12–13-year-old; Chinese is in many aspects the most highly developed and most sophisticated of all languages, but because for example the relationship between the individual word and the sentence is different in English and in Chinese, or because the structure of the sentence plays quite a different role in the two languages, both factors therefore interfering with the Chinese readers' understanding of words and sentences in English.

The structure of the Chinese language is quite different in many aspects from English. The dichotomies which are so important for the function of our language are often non-existent in Chinese— but on the other hand the absolute dichotomy between the spoken and the written languages has no parallel in English. We are here not so much concerned with the spoken language—even if a thorough psychological study of the relationship between the two and of the effect of using two so different sound systems as the

Cantonese and the English undoubtedly must be undertaken within the scope of this general line of investigation. Indeed the tools for such an investigation are being created by philologists at the moment. In some ways the spoken language can be said to be one of the relatively simple languages, using fewer sounds in fewer combinations than many other languages—but the written language is very complicated. Instead of the alphabet the Chinese language uses no less than 214 radicals and a very great number of signals for the possible sounds, in order to describe the phenomenal world. In many ways there is a great similarity between learning to write an English word and learning to write a character—according to the Chinese themselves there are only five different strokes in all characters ever written—but it is impossible to produce a collection of all the characters under less than 214 different headings (instead of the 26 of the English alphabet); it is not a linguistic arrangement as in Western dictionaries. The simple characters are often of greater importance in describing the world in so far as they contain a certain picture-value, not present in our (written) words, while in another way they are even more dependent on the sentence and the whole of the context than our words. I think there is here a question which demands investigation—and perhaps the tools are ready in the method described by Werner and Kaplan. The relevance of their investigations, mentioned above, can perhaps be judged from the following summary; at about the age of 12 they find that the children in reading no longer experience the words as embedded in the sentence, neither is the structure of the sentence dependent on the words in such a way that the surroundings of a word and the word itself influences each other in each case, but it appears that the sentence structure is now fixed and the general meaning of a word is also fixed, independent of the sentence as it were. This is of course a great over-simplification and operates with a dichotomy between form and content normally not acceptable to Werner. But it appears to me that the Chinese written word in the commonly used written languages is best described as the centre in a cluster of meanings and only the total situation, which stretches far beyond the single sentence in many or most cases, will tell us the meaning the author had in mind when he wrote it. If this is correct, the basic approach to reading in the two languages would be very different and the habits acquired by learning the one would be entirely useless in coping with the other. In other words the teaching of English as a second language would have to begin at quite a different point from where it begins now.

The connection between language and culture has been discussed very often since the day of Goethe and Helmholtz and many linguists, in modern times headed by Sapir and Whorf, have maintained that the different linguistic structures and approaches in the different languages influence our perception to such an extent that the phenomenal world of the speakers of different languages are quite different and incommunicable to speakers of other languages. However that may be, I think we can all agree that language is a most important tool for the socialization of the individual. It is undoubtedly true that the language often depicts an older social reality, as when 'royal' in a republic is used to describe the best—'a royal meal'. But it seems to me permissible to say that there appears to be a high degree of agreement between the role of the word in a sentence and the position of the individual in our present-day society in Hong Kong. Perhaps this agreement could be used experimentally in such a way that the results of a linguistic investigation would be of great importance for an understanding of the way in which the individual experiences the world around him.

As an example of what I have in mind I shall quote the following case: the connection between the structure of languages and language behaviour is described in the following way by Miller:

> Language A words convey little information—there is little uncertainty as to what responses should follow from the use of such words. Then language A speaking subjects may be allowed more freedom in their responding (e.g. in a free association test) because of the certainty of stimulus response relationship.
>
> Language B words convey much more information and language B speaking persons tend to congregate on similar responses for the purpose of cutting down on the information available and thereby increase the information communicated.[1]

Miller's examples are French and English, respectively, but from general observations it would seem plausible to say that the difference between English and Chinese is a much better example —but in saying this a whole research programme is already given.

[1] George A. Miller, *Language and Communication*, New York 1951.

Is it possible here to find an explanation of the language behaviour of the Chinese and of the immense fear of originality in
studies? Is it possible in such images to see mirrored the relationship between the members of society? Is the preponderant interest
in 'correct behaviour', '*li*' both in classical and in very recent times,
the desire for conformity, created by great social uncertainties and
by the ever-present pressure from the family and society itself in
the structure of the written, as indeed of the spoken word? Does
the individual learn to understand his dependence on all others
by learning the language—is the need for staying in one's position
within the family, within society, within the party, continually
brought home to the individual by the use of a language where
position is so important and the properties of the individual
word relatively non-significant? Do such considerations lead us
directly to the experimental techniques of Else Frenkel Bruns-
wik who in her studies on personality through perception comes
very close to describing a personality type common among bi-
linguals: 'exaggerated verbal emphasis upon certain ideals of
conduct and related expressions of protestation'—and would our
conclusion be the same when she continues 'indicating shortcomings rather than strength with respect to the traits in question
in the subjects concerned, in other words: self deception?'[1]

Perhaps these indications have given a feeling for the difficulties
our students are up against—and of the difficulties we meet when
we attempt to describe and to discover cause and effect. I should
like to express the hope that we should be able to overcome some
of our methodological difficulties, in the same way as the students
do overcome so many of their difficulties—not because we are
particularly ingenious but because the rich and fascinating culture
which is the Chinese cannot but open the eyes even of 'western
barbarians'.

[1] Else Frenkel-Brunswik, *Personality Theory and Perception* in R. R. Blake
and G. V. Ramsey: *Perception—An Approach to Personality*, New York 1951.

XIII
CULTURAL PROBLEMS OF CHINESE
STUDENTS IN A WESTERN-TYPE
UNIVERSITY
J. S. Cansdale

The problems I wish to discuss, or perhaps I should say to present impressionistically, concern the difficulties which I believe Chinese students experience in studying in a western-type university and attempting to benefit by such an education. The foreigner ('western person' in Chinese) coming to teach in Hong Kong University is first aware of these as his own problems: his students cling to the authority of the printed word, are unwilling to discuss academic problems, and seem to be afflicted by an overpowering lack of curiosity which may cripple their studies. As the teacher comes to know his students, he begins to see that his problems are also, and primarily, theirs. I would state as the central problem that the most intelligent and lively students are very much aware of their dilemma: they do not know what kind of people they are. Those with less insight, the average students, try to solve this by attempting, consciously or unconsciously, to assume the role, or rather the series of disconnected roles, which the teacher seems to expect them to play. The most articulate may come to terms with this dilemma of the choice of roles by making conscious decisions; some deliberately accept the western intellectual standards they are offered. Unfortunately for the community, these are often the most anxious to leave Hong Kong altogether and make their lives in the west which has so much to offer them. I want to pose the question: how does this quest, deliberate or blind, for his identity affect the Hong Kong student?

Before advancing my observations I wish to enter two caveats. The first is that I am not a professional anthropologist or sociologist. Secondly, any insights I may claim have been gained by personal acquaintance with students and graduates as friends: so that I am careful to avoid violating any confidences and to deal with problems so widespread as to avoid presenting them as those of any one individual. I am very much indebted to those of my friends who are themselves Hong Kong University graduates; to them I owe both corrections of crude errors and positive suggestions. The errors and the rash speculations in this paper are my own.

The University of Hong Kong is a British-type university, and I shall employ British terminology because education in Hong Kong is based on the British pattern, and American terms are not always exact equivalents. The medium of instruction is English, in which the students attain a high degree of proficiency. Some students come from Malaysia: most of these are Chinese. The great majority of students are local. Of these, a few are Indian, Pakistani or local Portuguese, a very few are European or American or Australian, but most of them are Chinese. Less than half of the students live in Halls of Residence; most of the rest live at home, and have to adjust themselves as best they can to the rival often conflicting, demands, of their student life and their duty as sons or daughters of a Chinese family. The Chinese name for the University is a traditional one meaning 'the Hall of the Great Learning'; but in fact the newer words for primary and secondary school—'small learning' and 'middle learning'—encourage the idea of the University as an extended type of school rather than as a new intellectual venture. It is merely another stage in the period of tutelage, not a door into intellectual and social freedom.

A child born in Hong Kong inherits a complex, perhaps a chaotic, culture. Hong Kong is a sophisticated urban community. Most citizens pay lip-service, and often much more than lip-service, to the classical culture of China, which called itself the Middle Kingdom but was open to foreign influences, and was deeply conservative but not rigidly inflexible. The British administration has imposed certain unfamiliar concepts of law and justice: thus the presentation of gifts to officials has become bribery, the ancient duty of looking after members of your family has become nepotism, and so on. In the midst of widespread poverty there is a high standard of material comfort and a great deal of ostentation in the display of such status-symbols as big cars and expensive wrist-watches. Institutionalized racial discrimination exists only in a few strongholds of colonial, or of Chinese conservatism, and in everyday life racial tensions are often imperceptible. There are, however, some undesirable consequences of living under a foreign administration. It seems to heighten a traditional Chinese fear, that of self-commitment; students often seem afraid of expressing any opinion in case it should prove unacceptable to the government. I think this is an economic rather than a political point. The government is one of the chief employers of graduates, especially arts graduates; it is made up of westerners, who often seem to be incalculable; and it therefore behoves the undergraduate to be careful. I am not, of course, stating a fact about government policy; I am expressing a very widespread student opinion. I know that individual students, like their counterparts all over the world, are very much concerned about the major problems of the world—the threat of nuclear weapons, the means of population control and so on; but they have caught the atmosphere of caution which prevails everywhere, and hesitate to commit themselves publicly.

However, probably the most immediate and important effect of the British administration is that the key to the best jobs and the most influential positions is a command of fluent English. Until the inauguration, in the autumn of 1963, of the Chinese University of Hong Kong, any student who looked forward to taking a degree had to accept the fact that he must study and be taught in a foreign language, probably to the detriment of his own Chinese language and culture. A further complication of his problems is that native Hong Kong people speak the Cantonese dialect of Chinese as their mother-tongue. This dialect is so different from the standard National Language (*Kuoyu*) as almost to constitute a separate language, and the idioms of written Chinese have to be learned: the child will not write as he speaks. Thus, unless he abandons Chinese altogether, he has a heavy burden of language instruction in his own tongue before he even begins to contemplate learning English. The pre-eminence given to English greatly complicates an already complicated language problem.

We in the west have an impression, gleaned mostly from novels of the Ming and Ch'ing Dynasties, of the great Chinese family, several generations and the families of several wives all surrounded by one great wall. This was always an upper-class institution; and only the merest traces of it still exist here and there in Hong Kong. It was never a reality for the peasants and workers who make up the great majority of the people of China. Nevertheless, the modern child learns certain attitudes which stem from the great family. His relations with parents, grandparents, and older and younger siblings are more rigidly defined than they are in the west. I have the impression that this life is wonderful for babies and satisfactory for children, but that it imposes a severe strain on adolescents, specially those who go to Anglo-Chinese schools and are introduced to a world alien to their grandparents and possibly to their parents too.

The Hong Kong child learns also, from his wider environment if not from his home, to set a high value on material possessions —an aspect of Hong Kong life which is often the object of scornful comment from refugees from the north. At the same time the child may attend a mission school and come under the influence of Christianity which presents him with a very different ethic. If he has any interest in the aesthetic culture of China he discovers that he is inheriting something sterile, static and derivative. 'Chinese painting', as it is taught in afternoon classes to leisured women, or as it appears on hand-painted Christmas cards, is a thin and depressing trickle of copies of copies of copies. There is a sad paucity of original writing in Chinese—in which the tradition discourages originality anyway. Music, save for folk-music and theatre music, was never one of China's great arts. As for entertainment, films made in Hong Kong tend to be either shadows of western 'musicals' or watered-down, glamorized versions of traditional Chinese stories filmed in an idiom which it is not unfair to describe as 'epic'. The beautiful stylized techniques of classical acting are reduced to commonplaceness, and the effect is one of effete vulgarity. The one vital theatre in Hong Kong is the Cantonese popular drama, often called 'opera' because of the preponderance of singing in it. Very few students will admit to an interest in this lively, raucous drama, with its crude stage effects, interminable stories of suffering women and, I am told, obscene dialogue (my Cantonese is not equal to assessing this). Most students dismiss it as 'vulgar'. It certainly is vulgar in the good old sense of belonging to the people; whether it is less desirable than the type of film I have described is a matter of opinion.

Culturally, then, the Hong Kong child inherits a piecemeal hodge-podge of western music, entertainment and visual art; he has no framework into which to fit his pleasures. Furthermore, there is a noticeable listlessness about the urban pleasures of Hong Kong. In the rural hinterland, among the peasant farmers and the water people, people work hard and, on their festival days, play hard. City people are contemptuous of the naive village festival; if they have any pretentions to status or wealth they cultivate the lacklustre and expensive. The urban middle-class family, from which most of the students come, do not maintain their traditional tastes; they tend to retain only certain disjointed but powerful ideas, especially those connected with family relationships, and to turn to the west for all their material needs, including entertainment.

If the child attends an Anglo-Chinese school he learns an ideal kind of western liberal individualism; he is taught that he must think for himself, that this is not only a duty but—more bewilderingly—a pleasure. This is the ideal; but in fact the child may drift into attitudes which are inexplicable to him but which seem to please the people who teach him. If he comes into contact at this time with Christianity he learns that it claims to be exclusive —a claim which is not made by any of the traditional faiths of China with which he may or may not be familiar. He may well become highly intolerant, thus coming into conflict with a non-Christian home in which there will either be no religion at all, or the ethical conservatism of Confucianism, or the relaxed rituals of Mahayana Buddhism. He may even begin to speculate anxiously on the eternal destiny of his non-Christian parents. Again, to take another alien idea, he learns from his school and perhaps from his reading that in the west youth is highly valued: youth he is told, is forward-looking and progressive, idealistic and eager to assert its energies. This must conflict with the teaching he has imbibed from the family, in which the young are expected to obey and reverence the elders for no other reason than that they *are* elders. The Chinese child, who is probably submissive by training, finds himself cast in the unfamiliar role of idealistic, energetic, western-type of adolescent.

At adolescence, too, comes another problem for the child who aims at a high standard of English, that passport to security and status. As soon as he enters an Anglo-Chinese secondary school, at the age of 11-plus, he begins to be taught in English, and from henceforth the best of his energies must be devoted to cultivating his English. Many teachers hold that this switch is made at the worst possible time. They argue that just as the child is reaching the time when he would normally begin to consume any kind of reading-matter he could get his hands on, when his intellectual appetites are voracious and not very selective, and his curiosity is becoming thoroughly aroused, his mother-tongue is forced into a secondary place in his education.[1] Because his English is not yet

[1] See Mr Kvan's paper.

adequate to the demands of his curiosity, he is forced back into reading simple material which does not engage his interest, and gradually he loses his appetite for books. At the same time, he may feel he has only a precarious hold on English, which may encourage him to depend on rote-learning rather than on reasoning, to the further blunting of his curiosity. We must remember too that the traditional methods of teaching children to read Chinese encourage habits of rote-learning. One has only to go past a Chinese primary school to hear the small voices upraised in chanting the reading-book in chorus; and the scholar could, and perhaps still can, repeat the classics by heart.

An important factor in encouraging rote-learning—to which the Chinese student is already predisposed—and in discouraging the independent thought to which education pays at least lip-service, is the pressure of examinations. All teachers deplore this pressure which makes nonsense of their professional training and ideals. I was once remonstrating with a second-year university student who did not appear to be doing any work at all; he replied that it was the first year since he was 5 years old that he had not had to face a vital examination in May—there being no second-year examination in his course. He described the whole weary ladder for me. There is keen competition to get into a Government or Government-aided primary school. It is so intense that often a child is not allowed a second chance; if he fails his end-of-year examination he may not get permission to repeat the year; if he is not given permission he must leave, and his chances of getting into a good secondary school are thereby much diminished if not annihilated. Thus at any time from the age of 6 onward a child may be marked, perhaps for life, with the consciousness of being a failure. For the rich there are private schools some of which are not too demanding in their intellectual requirements; but for the rest, failure in a Government or aided school means failure for life. It is not surprising that some students stagger into the University at 18 with all interest and pleasure in studying choked. What is surprising is that any interest at all survives.

Furthermore, with the exception of a few places in secondary technical schools—which are regarded as very much inferior in the predominantly literary culture of the Chinese—post-primary education means the British grammar-school type of education. Into this mould all children who pass from primary to secondary school are crammed. Here—to the continuous chagrin and frustration of the teachers—children assimilate an idea of education which means the cramming-in and regurgitation of facts. This is exacerbated by the facts being in a foreign language. In romantic dreams, the Chinese scholar is an elegant, cultured gentleman; in Hong Kong actuality he is a fact-crammed grammar-school child. Only the clever minority cut through the facts to the life of the subject.

There is another feature of western school life which bewilders the sixth-former in an Anglo-Chinese school. I had not noticed this for myself and I am indebted to a friend, herself a product of the system, for this point. The Chinese image of the scholar does not include the kind of sociability which appears to be essential to the western image of an educated man. The Chinese see scholars as, in Milton's phrase, 'pens and heads sitting by their studious lamps': the sixth-former finds that he is expected to attend what are oddly called 'social functions'. He finds these 'functions' bewildering and unpleasing. He believes that people in the west play party games by way of relaxation. In his heart he knows that a scholar is dignified, cultured and rather elderly. He plays games because he feels this is what is expected of him.

Children at school are further worn down by the fact that parents, who often do not understand the child's school milieu, think that education is instruction, and that the more instruction he has the better. Thus you may find that children even of primary school age may have additional coaching every day. Play is a criminal waste of time. A fourth-form student of 15 told me how her evening is laid out. On returning from school she has a cup of tea and then practises the piano until the family evening meal at six. Almost certainly she practises her 'piano' for the competitive Music Festival; almost certainly she does not play for mental refreshment, or for fun. After supper on four evenings of the week, a private tutor comes to give her an hour's tuition; at about nine o'clock she starts her homework, which probably takes her the best part of two hours. At about eleven she goes to bed. I am afraid this may be typical. The gifted child stands it, though with deprivation of all the normal interests of an adolescent: the under-average child finds it a terrible strain. Too often I have seen the eyes of a weak student filling with uncontrollable tears, and heard the pathetic avowal 'I *will* work harder', when I am sure that he, or she, is simply not suited to the academic education which is the only secondary education in Hong Kong.

This, then, is a rough indication of the university student's background. What are some of its effects?

Firstly, it must never be forgotten that there are many people, not necessarily contented people of course, who can find this living in divided and distinguished worlds positively stimulating, or who are at least capable of formulating their problems consciously. To watch them opening out and discovering themselves is the teacher's greatest reward. Because they can consciously set about the solution of their problems they will not figure largely in this discussion: but we must never forget that they are there.

But for the rest, the majority, the teacher's chief problem is that intellectual curiosity has been killed in them. I have already suggested one cause, rooted in their childhood—the stifling, at the age of 11, of the demand for new interests which the student cannot satisfy in English, the language of his education, and which therefore die for lack of sustenance. 'Study' is equated with desiccating rote-learning. Recently a medical student told me innocently, 'Students in the Faculty of Arts don't have to work they only have to think'. I would not suggest that the malady is peculiar to medical students. Indeed, it may be even more deeply rooted in the Chinese tradition of liberal studies. Here the elders are the repository of truth; so that it is unthinkable that a teacher should ever utter a challenging half-truth in order to start a discussion among his students. A teacher asks, 'Can you see anything wrong with what I have just said?' and after a long pause the acknowledged leader of the class rises and says, 'Honourable professor would not tell students anything wrong'. The anecdote was reported to me from Japan, which shows that the malady is not a local one, but it might well have come from Hong Kong. Students are seeking a small capsule labelled TRUTH which can be swallowed and assimilated. This is not peculiar to the East, of course, but it is sanctioned by the powerful tradition of respect for the elders and their wisdom. This is more powerful than the superimposed western idea of thinking for oneself. Perhaps the students feel insecure, and so cling to authority; or perhaps they feel that diffidence towards the wisdom of the elders is a proper attitude. John Bunyan, with his compassionate insight, has a character named Diffidence—but she is the wife of Despair.

This deadness, incuriosity, diffidence, whatever it is, makes it hard for students to ask questions or for teachers to elicit them. A student who asks a question may 'lose face' by appearing ignorant, or he may be thought to make the teacher 'lose face' by the implied criticism of the lucidity of his exposition. Or—ghastly abyss of possibility—the teacher may not know the answer. I remember a very angry young graduate who had been doing her period of practical teaching for the Diploma in Education. In the staff common room an older teacher had taken her on one side and said 'Now, my dear, you are young, and I should like to give you some advice'. The first piece of advice was 'Never let a child ask a question, in case you don't know the answer'. The student was angry and horrified that any teacher should talk like that—a tribute at least to her own vitality and, let us hope, to the education she had had in the University.

But it may be unhappily true that the student does not ask questions because he does not want to; he resents being asked to think or to read outside the prescribed syllabus. To the average student there are three kinds of books: text-books, reference books and story books. There are students, of course, who will go into the University Bookstore and buy a paperback just to see what is in it; there are students who follow their own interests, often with small encouragement from their friends who are apt to clap on to them such nicknames as 'Bookworm' or 'High Seriousness'. But they are not the norm. A student, an unusually good one, intelligent and hard-working, once asked me to suggest what she might give to a friend as a present. I suggested a book. 'Oh no,' was the reply, 'you don't give books as presents.'

Again, the invitation to students to make a synthesis of their studies usually meets with little response. Suggested comparisons between English and Chinese lyric poetry never succeed in striking a spark. Perhaps the question is phrased badly. Perhaps the student is ignorant of Chinese literature and does not want to confess his ignorance to a westerner. Or perhaps the approach to Chinese studies is so different that the student cannot or does not wish to make a bridge between the two diverse disciplines. There may be a great gulf between his Chinese culture and his superimposed western culture. For example: in writing his weekly essay a student may well begin by expressing his own ideas and thoughts, expounding them at some length and concluding with a quotation from an established critic—as much as to say 'I am right because Professor X says so'. An English student of equivalent intelligence will begin his essay with the quotation from Professor X, analyse and assess it as fit for acceptance or rejection. For the Chinese student the authority clinches the argument. How much more must this be so when the language of discussion is Chinese and the authority of the elders therefore more pressing.

The weak student, of course, will simply copy uncritically the printed word. 'Why do you write at the beginning of your second paragraph "In conclusion we may state . . ." when your essay goes on for another six pages?' The face is blank. I re-word my question until the meaning is clear. The student replies, 'That's what it said in the book.'

The impact of alien ideas on the student often does not have the effect of sharpening his critical faculty. On the contrary, students arrive in the University docile and obedient, prepared to accept the eccentric ideas and attitudes of the British but not necessarily prepared either to understand or to evaluate them. Even the Christian religion, which of all western ideas makes the strongest appeal to students, is kept apart from life. I have often noticed that Christian students do not put their Bible and prayer book and devotional works into the bookcase with their books; they seem to have nothing to do with the intellectual life of every day.

One of the worst consequences of living in divided and distinguished worlds is that the Hong Kong student often displays an almost frightening ability to adapt himself, physically, mentally, and morally, to the pattern which he thinks his education is imposing on him. He tries to assume the role of A Student, rather than to get pleasure and intellectual satisfaction out of his studies. Of course, first-year undergraduates everywhere feel that they are entering on a new stage of life, but the Chinese student in Hong Kong has, for reasons I have suggested, to assume the role far more deliberately, and he clings to any indication of what that role should be. In one of the women's halls of residence I have noticed that the most well-thumbed periodical in the common room is a magazine called *Seventeen*. Most of the girls enter the university nearer 19 than 18 but *Seventeen* gives them an idea of what a young girl in the 'emancipated' western context ought to be like. It is a lifeline.

Intellectually, again, students adapt themselves to what they suppose westerners want. An extreme, though not untypical, example may be found in an English composition paper set for sixth-formers. The first part of this paper consisted of an essay on the influence of the cinema. One candidate in particular expatiated on the appalling influence of the cinema on the morals of the young. You would never have supposed that the author was young himself. Every conceivable crime was to be traced to the influence of the cinema. However, the second part of the paper invited the candidate to write a letter to a friend in hospital to cheer him up, and the same candidate wrote: '. . . David and I went to the movies last night. It was a wizard movie. It was a murder movie and the detective had done it.' Clearly, the candidate had a vague idea that high moral sentiments are approved by teachers; and of course it must be added that the tradition of essay-writing in Chinese education encourages this sententiousness. No doubt his second part, more lively if less elegant, represented something more like his real feelings. Where there is this painful desire to please it is unlikely that there will be much honesty or independent thought. It is, of course, unfair to see this student as deliberately dishonest; he only wants to know what is expected of him. He has no desire to 'express himself'—a desire, indeed, alien to his traditional culture, so that he does not understand why his western teachers demand this of him, and in his essays keeps to unexceptionable platitudes.

Once in the University, the undergraduate feels that Being A Student compels him to take part in the strictly forbidden ritual of 'ragging' the freshmen. The authorities have forbidden this, but occasional outbreaks occur, in spite of the heavy punishment meted out to offenders. The ritual humiliation of the freshmen is utterly alien to Chinese society which is based on the idea of 'face', of holding up your head and not being ashamed before any man; and thus even apparently harmless demands (like making the freshmen lie on the floor) are made with a nastiness and a bitterness which is not found in western universities in which ragging is customary. I very much doubt whether anyone really enjoys it; but they believe it is something that students do. When I say freshmen in my university were never ragged the students look astonished and ask how I ever got to know anybody. I point out that I got to know the people whose interests I shared—poets, or hockey-players, or bell-ringers, or Methodists, or musicians, or Socialists, or whatever the interest, however cranky, might be—and not those who had got together for no other purpose than to make me look a fool. This reply is regarded as very eccentric indeed. 'You see,' they explain kindly, 'after the freshmen have been ragged they feel they belong to our group.' My reply that if people had set out to humiliate me I would not want to belong to their nasty group is regarded as almost indecent; it is so blatant a violation of the way in which they are told students behave.

In his book *Fragrant Harbour* Mr R. D. Ommanney describes the childish games played at parties by Hong Kong undergraduates and says that they seem to enjoy them. I would not altogether agree with this; from talking to students I find that many are bored by them but feel—perhaps from their schooldays—that they are the games students ought to play. It is true that if dancing is suggested, as a pastime more suited to their age-group, the suggestion is often defeated by members of a powerful extreme Protestant group which not only forbids its members to dance but forbids them to be present when other people dance. Many students would like to dismantle this whole edifice of protracted childishness; they simply do not know how to set about it.

There is, I suggest, a good reason why they are unable to find the end of the string which will pull the whole building down. Their student life is not, I think, coherent or complete. Students have to try to resolve the tension between the values of home and the apparent values of their education, and they do this after a fashion by treating the latter as a series of disconnected and sometimes contradictory roles. Their life in the University thus means the assumption of one *persona* after another; the role of A Student is fragmented. This speculation first came into my mind when I was passing a notice-board in the Main Building of the University. The newly formed Softball Club had posted a notice inviting students to softball lessons at the University Sports Centre. The Sports Centre is not fifteen minutes' walk from the Main Building, but the notice said 'Meet at 4 p.m. at the Main Building. Transportation provided.' Here there seem to be two people—the Sporting Student who plays softball, and the Ladylike Student (of either sex) who does not walk up the road but is conducted properly in a wheeled vehicle. Life is only explicable in terms of roles. I was once carrying several large books to the university so I put them in a rucksack as obviously the most convenient means of carrying them. I was met on the steps by a student who asked affably: 'Are you going on a picnic?' As it was nine o'clock on a Monday morning in the middle of term this would have been improbable; but it was clearly less improbable than the idea that a person could be carrying a rucksack and *not* going on a picnic.

I will advance another, fairly harmless, example which may illustrate the tyranny of middle-class city *mores* rather than those of the Student's role. One of the most popular forms of recreation in this colony of many islands is the launch picnic. On such an occasion many of the women students—not all, of course—arrive at the pier in ordinary street clothes. It seems that they cannot cross the road, or walk across the pier, in picnic clothes. As soon as the launch casts off they change into slacks or shorts; when the destination is reached they change again into swimsuits. On the way home the process goes into reverse. As the students seem to enjoy this sequence of roles one need not complain. It is when they do not appear to enjoy the role that it becomes burdensome. The childish party games, or the lugubrious Annual Balls—at which students behave with depressing formality and little appearance of energy or enjoyment—are institutions which enable the student to assume yet another *persona*.

The most serious complaint against this role-playing is often made by the more lively and adult students; it is a complaint against the highly restrictive and stultifying conventions laid down to govern the social relations between men and women students. Some typical complaints are: that a girl cannot sit next to a boy in a lecture without being thought 'forward'; that there is never any really vital or serious talk between men and women students (or, as they call themselves, 'boys' and 'girls'); that students can never 'go Dutch', however short of money the boy may be; and that there is a continuous flow of insipid sexual badinage between men and women, making real friendship all but impossible. There are established pairs among students who are known to be 'going steady'; on a very rough estimate I would say that more of these student love-affairs end in marriage than is the case in an English university, but it is hard to see how, in the ordinary framework of rigid formality, they ever begin. In spite of the fact that most Chinese families are fairly large, so that siblings of the opposite sex are the rule rather than the exception, the sexes seem wide apart, and the role of A Co-Ed is beyond the ambition of most of the girls. To this dismal generalization there are, of course, exceptions. Men and women work together in tutorials, share the work of editing student periodicals, sit on the Union Council together; but the atmosphere of priggish formality is more widespread than it should be. The most stable and emotionally satisfying group seems to be the group of 'classmates', coming up from the same schools and sticking together throughout the University.

Moving, then, from one role to another, the student sooner or later comes to realize that he has no central core of personality. Again and again, the intelligent and the sensitive and the receptive —far more than the submissive and the torpid—cry out, often articulately and deliberately: 'I don't know who I am.' Some typical phrases are: 'I'm Chinese but I have no country', 'I'm not a real Chinese, I'm just a "Local Foreign Devil"' (using a very uncomplimentary phrase), 'I'm Portuguese but I can't speak Portuguese and I don't even *want* to.' To such a student the west, with its liberalism and its intellectual excitement, is very engaging. The last thing he wishes to do is to retreat into his traditional culture. This restlessness, this sense that something very import-ant in life is passing him by, may be the tragedy—I do not con-sider the word too strong—of the Hong Kong Chinese student. However, if he has normal resilience and enterprise he will go on until he finds some activity which is especially valuable to him, which does not simply offer yet another role. Examples of such activities come to mind. Work-camps, for example, in which students perform such services as laying a concrete path to serve a village or a squatter settlement, are becoming very popular. There is no traditional sanction for such activity—indeed, there are powerful traditional divisions between those who work with their hands and those who do not. In the cosy bourgeois world of the Hong Kong middle-class woman, her role is to assist in the organization of charity balls and bridge drives. There are, then, few conventions to restrict the young man or woman student who voluntarily puts on an unglamorous shirt and shorts and spends the week-end mixing concrete and exchanging badinage with slightly bewildered, very much amused, and decidedly friendly village people. On another level, a student may find the answer to his search for himself in advanced academic work, solving problems for himself, discovering the pleasures of academic debate. A Ph.D. is not just another *persona*.

It is often said that the students from Malaysia are more lively and energetic, and more prepared to commit themselves, than the local boys and girls. There may well be reasons why they are intrinsically livelier, connected with their greater involvement in politics and more immediate patriotism, but there is one reason which is not often given but which I think contributes to their more relaxed attitudes: they are so far from home that they are less oppressed by the great problem which besets the Hong Kong student: the tension between being a student and being a son or daughter—particularly a daughter. The family still controls its younger members fairly rigorously, and a student member of a family must take a position of deference and humility within the family, when his education is urging him to be positive and to think and speak for himself. Wherever family duties conflict with his obligations as a student, it is the latter which must give way. I know, for example, of a student who had to take a lengthy bus ride to pay her respects to the head of the family every day over a fairly long period. The fact that this entailed missing lectures and classes appeared to mean nothing to the elders, and the student would have been unfilial if she had remonstrated. Parents often seem to the western observer to be exacting and selfish, and this is sometimes felt by students themselves, although they feel family demands to be paramount even if they seem unjust. This does not prevent many students, especially girls, from expressing the relief they feel in the freer life of a hall of residence. For some students, the first night in the hall is the first time they have ever slept outside their own home; but they adjust themselves very rapidly.

A final point must be added for completeness. Many of the people who teach in the University are non-Chinese, and of this group the majority are British. The childish desire to please the inscrutable Occidental often extends into undergraduate life and generates, inevitably, an underside of resentment against the foreigner. The student may feel that the European teacher is trying to re-make him rather than helping him to find himself. The academic staff, therefore, easily become *they*, to be if necessary outwitted and hoodwinked rather than to be trusted and made friends with. There are of course many exceptions to and modifications of this attitude—the life of a European teacher would be intolerable if there were not—but the attitude does from time to time become apparent. Perhaps the student whose dominant attitude is one of mistrust is the man who still wants, like his nineteenth-century forebears, to assimilate western technology and be left with his own way of life; or perhaps his adolescent curiosity has been so effectively killed in him that he is no longer aware of wanting anything. There remains, however, the student who values the liberalism of the west, not merely its technology, and who tries to enter into its ways of thought. It is he who is most painfully aware of the problems of his own identity; but it is probably also he who has most to gain by enduring and trying to understand the clash of values in his environment.

XIV
A POSTSCRIPT ON RIOTS AND THE
FUTURE OF HONG KONG
I. C. Jarvie

Since the Introduction to this volume was written in the spring
of 1966, Hong Kong has seen two riots in quick succession—
April 1966 and May–August 1967. This recurrence, after ten years,
of the violence feared and planned for by government and police,
raises questions both about the internal stability of the Colony,
and about China's attitude towards it. At the risk of the word
'transition' in *Hong Kong: A Society in Transition* taking on a quite
unwanted irony, the following reflections are offered and dated
in case events do outrun them.

Internal stability

The fact that despite overcrowding, low wages, water shortage,
and lack of political outlets, post-war Hong Kong had suffered
no serious disturbances apart from the riot of 1956 was a point
of pride and of puzzlement for the Colony. The 1966 riot, which
grew out of protests against ferry fare increases, certainly
corrected any over-confidence. Most of its participants were
young people, at least judging by the photographs and arrest
records, and, despite widespread public disapproval of disorder,
sizeable numbers were at times involved. It is very significant
that the 1966 riots broke out over a domestic Hong Kong issue
—this should make us take it very seriously indeed. By contrast
both the 1956 and 1967 riots related to outside political matters:
1956 was a riot of nationalists; 1967 a riot of communists.

The 1966 riot appears to have begun because the Star Ferry
Company's application for governmental permission to raise
fares seemed about to be granted. A handful of young people—
some perhaps even mentally disturbed[1]—were sufficiently moved
by what they conceived to be the hardship this would lead to,
that they initiated small-scale demonstrations. In particular, one

[1] So Sau Chung went into a mental hospital in 1967, and Lo Kei committed suicide.

young man, So Sau Chung, began a 'hunger strike' on the con-course to the ferry pier itself. He attracted a great deal of attention among the commuting crowds, in the press, and, especially, amongst young people. Although he was arrested for obstruction on the second day, it was not long before his 'supporters' were marching in the streets (which is forbidden in Hong Kong with-out police permission) and the police were having to quell riots. Exactly where the transition occurred between the genuine pro-test and out-and-out riot is difficult to determine because riot developed sporadically.

The problem the riot raises is, 'Is Hong Kong prone to riot?' After the riot of 1966 the Hong Kong Government set up a commission of enquiry. Its members were the Chief Justice, the retired Vice-Chancellor of the University of Hong Kong, a senior social worker, and a lawyer. The first two were Europeans, the last two Chinese. After more than a month of public hearings and a good deal of deliberation they produced a *Report*[1] which rehearsed in great detail a narrative of the riot and which con-cluded that the explanation of the riot was not that Hong Kong was riot-prone, but that the Star Ferry Company and the govern-ment had been remiss in their communications with the public. If only people had known why the ferry company was requesting an increase, and that this would be considered by the government in the light of all the factors, including hardship,[2] riot need not have occurred.

The Commission's report has to be looked at in the context of speculation surrounding the riot. The public hearings proved something of a sensation in the Colony because a great many charges and counter-charges were aired. For example, the theory was put abroad that the communists had incited the riot and that they had been paying money to the rioters. Another theory put abroad was that elements in the police had incited the riot by bribing rioters—all in order to embarrass certain liberals in the Colony. Yet a third theory put abroad was that an elected member of the Urban Council had herself engineered the riots in order to discredit the police, and so on. The Commission therefore had a

[1] *Kowloon Disturbances 1966 Report of Commission of Inquiry*, Hong Kong 1967.

[2] In fact the government's review machinery (the Transport Advisory Committee) only recommended to the government an increase in the first-class fare the previous month (March).

very difficult job in that it had both to deal with the rumours and to try to find out whether the riot was caused by anything in particular. The final theory it advanced incorporated but did not altogether accept a certain amount of sociological argumentation given by myself and others which suggested that a much deeper problem in the social structure was exposed by the riots than simply a lack of communication between the people and the company and the government.

My thesis was that Hong Kong was riot-prone because it had developed an acute generation gap. My argument was roughly as follows. Hong Kong's population consists largely of immigrants from the countryside of Kwangtung province—a somewhat backward and socially rather conservative area. These peasant peoples have come to Hong Kong and adapted themselves to the conditions of a fast-moving port and industrial city. And they have raised children in an environment where parental values really do not mean very much and where the educational system doesn't allow parental values to mean very much. These young adults raised entirely in Hong Kong are now beginning to make their mark on its society. They are young people who have no personal memories of bad times in China, who have been brought up in attenuated and dispersed families, in overcrowded tenements, who know only urban and industrial surroundings, who have been educated in heavily westernized schools, and exposed to a wealth of western cultural influence. Hong Kong is to them a home, not a haven of refuge, and they judge it by different standards than their refugee parents. Especially do they match it to the worlds portrayed on TV, in comics, movies and advertisements. They are experiencing a revolution of rising expectations; they expect more than their parents and are thus more frustrated than their parents. Stability and lack of disaster are not for them enough.

For young people who have no money and little education, but only hope and ideals, Hong Kong society offers very little in the way of encouragement and hope that things will get much better in their lifetime or that of their children. In the public hearings when the Commission had as witnesses the young people who had been arrested in the course of the riots the gap between the lives they led and their ideals was very striking.

It is very easy and seems to have been a tendency among officials to dismiss these young people as ill-educated, semi-criminal, rather inarticulate and shiftless socially marginal people.

Some of them certainly were. But there was quite a bunch who were perfectly ordinary schoolchildren and young workers. The very fact that they were caught up in what might be called the first political demonstration in connection with domestic issues in Hong Kong since World War II is indicative of something or other. There is even something encouraging about it, granted the form it took was unfortunate. Not unnaturally, neither the government nor the *Report* mentioned or commended this growth of political consciousness.

Both my own theory of the riots and that propounded in the *Report* have serious weaknesses. Mine because it does not explain why the generation-gap precipitated riot just when it did. In defence I could only say that when the situation is riot-prone all that is needed is a trigger. For my theory I would claim that at least it has the sociological touch: this in essence is what the *Report* lacks. Several things are wrong with the theory of the *Report*, and they all flow from its lack of sociological perspective. How lack of communication leads to riot is not explained. Why broadcasts, loudspeakers and leaflets failed to remedy the lack of communication is not explained, unless it be by the 'momentum' of the riot once started. Why poor people should riot over an increase in first-class fares is also not explained, unless that is put down to lack of communication and rumours about the effects on the cost of living, including other ferry companies' fares. Most serious of all, the *Report* is not sociologically objective: it simply assumes the rioters were misinformed; it never contemplates the possibility that the government is misinformed. If only the rioters had known the facts they would not have rioted, we are asked to believe. That the rioters are in a certain situation and that they view and experience the world from this situation quite correctly is not even suggested. If only they knew that the government was sincerely concerned for them and benevolent all would be well. Such a view applied to the U.S. riots in Watts, Newark and Detroit leads to absurdities. 'It's all a big misunderstanding, you see.' Real social conditions, and people's discontent with those conditions to the exclusion of any vested interests they may have, these are what enable riots to occur.[1]

Though both theories have their weaknesses, there is some

[1] For an excellent example of how to analyse riots see Daniel P. Moynihan's 'Riots: Where the Liberals Went Wrong', *Boston Globe*, 6 August 1967, pp. A-5 ff.

coming together over the recommendations that they make. Communication gap or generation gap, we all agree that much more needs to be done by the government and the educational system to foster a sense of Hong Kong identity, a sense of belonging to a valued community. More education, better housing, and attempts to encourage character-building rather than shiftless modes of activity are all uncontroversial enough. In fact the Commission endorsed all the more sensible proposals for making strenuous efforts to improve conditions, as well as to explain how much better conditions are than they were and how much has and is being done.

To sum up the 1966 riot, then: if it reveals a gap between aspirations and realities, then this is being ignored in official circles and presumably nothing will be done about it. Government ambivalence may be indicated by the way they combine a bland front with careful training of the police for riot duty. In 1956 complacency was apparent in the officially acknowledged confusion and incompetence of the police.[1] No doubt complacency has been thoroughly wafted away by now.

Attitude of China

In the 1967 riots we see a completely different situation. One factor is, however, constant. Namely that, once a riot starts in Hong Kong, the city has considerable hoodlum elements with no particular political connections which are prepared to go into the streets to riot and throw stones, bottles and acid to bait the police. This may be the case in any large city (cf. the U.S.A.), but it seems to be more true of Hong Kong than had hitherto been thought to be the case. Apart from this basic similarity of personnel the 1967 riot was different because it was a political riot. Indeed it was *the* political riot always feared in Hong Kong—the riot instigated by communists. Hong Kong had always tolerated the communists. China is Hong Kong's major source of food. The Banks and emporia of communist China are dotted throughout the colony. They have their newspapers and schools, their party organization (albeit a clandestine one), they negotiate with the British at Canton District level with a certain amount of amicability. Up to 1967 it seemed as though Hong Kong got along pretty well with its large neighbour.

[1] See *Report on the Disturbances in Kowloon and Tsuen Wan*, Hong Kong 1956.

The 1967 riot appears to have started in the following way. There was a strike, which became a lock-out, and when blackleg trucks tried to cross the picket lines there was a clash. Fighting broke out, the police were called, and the fighting spread to become rioting, with the communist newspapers issuing the clarion call to the faithful to back the workers. These riots were the most prolonged and violent of the three, with menacing crowds having to be shot at, with attacks with knives, hooks, Molotov cocktails and so on. Moreover they spread from their point of origin in Kowloon over to the Island itself, which neither of the previous two riots did.

For nearly the first seven weeks of disorder the police did not call out the troops, although the British airlifted an extra 2,000 in. They were called in first to take over border patrol after a shooting incident there (see below), and then they were used to cover and back police as they raided communist headquarters.

What is the explanation of these riots? China, as mentioned in the Introduction to this volume, gains economically very considerably from Hong Kong. It also gets rid of some of its undesirable elements to Hong Kong. My own view is that the 1967 riots were not instigated in any way by Peking. They were a blunder by the local party. Once the police intervened in a communist labour dispute the communists felt compelled to give support. The original dispute was itself quite quickly settled. But by that time workers and communists had clashed with the police, been beaten, arrested and gaoled. This also dragged Peking in: what could she do when her own people called for support? In her turn, however, Peking over-escalated: she protested to the British, demanding release of the convicted rioters, punishment of the police for their 'sanguinary atrocities', apologies to the rioters, and the handing-over of the governor for trial by the masses. In the fantasy-world of Peking these may have been seriously meant. Certainly in January 1967 Macau had succumbed to demands almost as humiliating. More likely, though, the Chinese, like poker players, were raising the ante in order to gain the maximum effect from a compromise. However, it transpired that the British authorities, although their position was strategically hopeless, were in no mood to compromise. Everyone knew, of course, that Peking could take Hong Kong with a telephone call: in 1941 Hong Kong had fallen to the Japanese in seventeen days. Both the British and the Chinese know it is indefensible when the attacker holds the mainland. Moreover, there is every reason to think that both sides not only know this, but they each know that the other side knows it. British talk of defending the Colony and Chinese talk of liberating it are both just that: talk. So why should Peking initiate any serious move on the Colony in this haphazard way? One explanation of how the blunder came about attributes it to the fervour the mysterious great proletarian cultural revolution generated in the party stalwarts in Canton. One clear result of the cultural revolution is that political soundness is to be established by demonstrating ardour for the thoughts of Chairman Mao. Canton appears to have been a bit backward in cultural revolutionary fervour, but had been regaining ground in the months before the Hong Kong riots. In backing the Hong Kong workers there was a god-given opportunity to display revolutionary spirit and to oppose the ogres of British colonialism and American imperialism.

In this perspective the Hong Kong riots take on the appearance of yet another cultural revolution project that got out of hand. Peking presumably did not object to a bit of confrontation, but would have no reason to welcome ill-thought-out attempts to liberate Hong Kong right away.[1] The cycle in China proper of protest and demonstration being encouraged, then getting out of hand, being criticized and finally the army being brought in to cool everyone off seems to have happened in Hong Kong. Peking's initially bellicose support of the rioters tapered off very considerably, and when a mob charged across the border and besieged the Hong Kong border police, and the Chinese border guards fired across the border, first the British brought in the Ghurkas, then the Chinese brought in the People's Liberation Army. Their role has been to bring discipline to the border by discouraging incidents, and calming down those that begin.

Of course it is still possible that Peking is concealing its aims. It seems more plausible to think that Peking is struggling in a terribly confused and charged situation which changes from day to day to act in what it conceives to be its self-interest, avoiding

---

[1] This interpretation is confirmed by reports of statements by the defector Wu She-tung, formerly general manager of the China Publishing Company in Hong Kong. See the Associated Press report out of Taipei, 9 August 1967, partially summarized in the *New York Times* of 10 August 1967, p. 2.

the alienation of grass-roots support for struggle and the cultural revolution. So what of Hong Kong's long-term prospects?

The glib assumption that because Hong Kong is economically valuable to China it can count on continuing must be dropped; it was mistaken before, it is manifestly mistaken now. Yet the Hong Kong Government is in a strong tactical position. It is not going to resist Peking physically if a take-over is what they seriously want. At the same time, so long as it rules, it is not going to be a client of Peking: rioters will not be allowed to run in the streets in the name of Mao Tse-tung or anyone else. Moreover it has the backing, so long as it successfully holds firm, of the majority of the adult population, who did not flee China for nothing. It can therefore be expected that stringent measures against the rioters will be pressed home, and that perhaps the indulgent attitude towards communists and their activities will be modified.

So neither the internal position nor the external usefulness of Hong Kong have changed. Only one new factor has to be allowed for. The cultural revolution makes it absolutely clear, if it was not so already, that in China ideology is supreme, and where ideology and economic considerations clash one can by no means rely on economics carrying the greater weight. Economic considerations can and will be overridden where they conflict with ideology. The most striking case of this is of course the closing of the entire school system for a year. The resulting economic consequences to a developing nation in terms of the loss on investment and the loss of long-term gains is almost incalculable. The loss of production too from the mammoth demonstrations staged throughout the year when schools and factories were closed is also incalculable. Given these facts about China it would seem clear that Hong Kong's economic value is no longer convincing solely as a reason to expect its continued existence. Should Hong Kong become a centre of ideological conflict, it seems pretty clear that those in Peking will settle it on ideological grounds. That Peking will try to keep ideology out of it in economic self-interest may be attested by its survival in 1967. If at the nadir of the cultural revolution, with sporadic pitched battles breaking out in China, and chaos or even civil war in the air, Hong Kong was preserved, there is hope that when things are more stable in China Hong Kong will be 'safer' too.

It would be appropriate to end this postscript with a plea for

Hong Kong and a hope for it. The plea is to encourage study of this society which is both fascinating and under-studied and which for the moment still can be studied. The hope is that this fascinating enclave in Chinese society, this incredible relic, will survive in some form or other, and will go on being a place which is completely absorbing and exciting both to live in and to study.

12 August 1967

INDEX OF NAMES

INDEX OF SUBJECTS

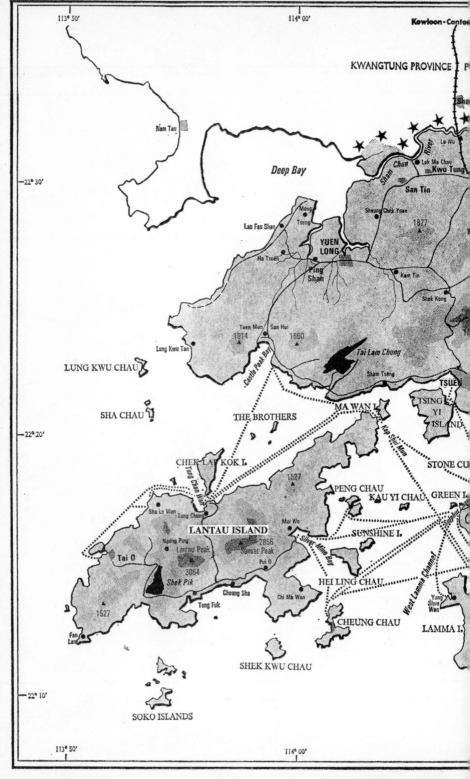

HONG KONG an